Golfing in
Washington

The _Complete_ guide to Washington's golf facilities

Fourteenth Edition
by
Daniel MacMillan

Published by:

MAC Productions

Golf Guides Since 1986

Waiver on Accuracy
We have gone to great lengths to provide the golfer with an up-to-date, accurate and comprehensive guide to golfing facilities in the state of Washington; nevertheless, we all slice it out of bounds from time to time. Each course reserves the right to change their prices and policies at any time and we will not be held liable for any inaccuracies presented in this book.

Library of Congress Cataloging-in-Publication Data
MacMillan, Daniel E. ; Golfing in Washington;
The complete guide to Washington's Golf facilities (fourteenth edition)
1. Golf course guide-Washington State
2. Travel-golf related in Washington State

Printed in Canada

Cover photos appear Courtesy of:
Vicwood Golf Links   (front)
Photo by John R. Johnson ©

Legion Memorial Golf Course   (back)
Photo provided by Golf Resources Northwest

1st Editon, April 1986	2nd Edition, May 1987
3rd Edition, May 1988	4th Edition, April 1989
5th Edition, March 1990	6th, Edition, March 1991
7th Edition, March 1992	8th Edition, March 1993
9th Edition, March 1994	10th Edition, March 1995
11th Edition, March 1996	12th Edition, April 1997
13th Edition, March 1998	14th Edition, March 1999

ISBN 1-878591-50-9 $11.95

Published by:
MAC Productions
P.O. Box 655; Carnation, Washington 98014 USA
Phone: (425) 880-4411; FAX: (425) 880-4450
e-mail address: waorgolf@concentric.net

Preface

In this the **fourteenth edition** of **"Golfing in Washington"** I hope it will be the most complete golf guide in the state published to date. The size is designed with the idea that the book will more easily fit in your glove box or golf bag. We have also provided small map inserts along with the driving directions to help you get to the golf facilities. As always you will find new courses, par 3's, and ranges just opened or due to open later in the season. Layouts, prices and yardage have been revised to reflect any changes that have occurred since last year. I hope you enjoy the book, see you on the links!

Acknowledgements

A special thanks to all the pros, owners and course managers who have been so helpful in providing us access to their courses and current information. Thanks to the Oregon Department of Transportation, Washington Department of Transportation and the Idaho Department of Transportation for the endless supply of maps needed in doing this project.

Jeff Shelley for his help and personal support on these projects. Without Jeffs help these projects would have not got out on time. Thanks Jeff!!!

Thanks to Bob Valentine and his personal touch on these projects over the years, Thanks Robert!!!

This book would not have been possible without the tremendous support of my entire family and my friends. I thank each and every one of them for the special interest they have shown in the golf books.

To my children Joshua Daniel, Sarah Gene and the newest addition Christian Rogers for showing me what really is important in life.

Thanks to my loving wife Kristi Gene. Words cannot express the love and support she has given me on this project. I feel blessed to have a wife whom provided a loving, caring, Christ like atmosphere in which to produce this book in. Thanks Kristi Gene. Most importantly my Lord Jesus, for his gentle hand and firm grip with my life and this company.

Daniel

Abbreviations 1
Washington Map...............2-5
Alderbrook Golf &
Yacht Club. 6
Allenmore Golf Club 7
Alta Lake Golf Course 8
Apple Tree Golf Course 9
Auburn Golf Course 10
Avalon Golf Club 11
Ballinger Park Golf Course .. 12
Banks Lake Golf Club 13
Battle Creek Golf Course 14
Beacon Rock Golf Course 15
Bear Creek Country Club 16
Bear Creek Golf Course 17
Bellevue Municipal G.C. 18
Bellingham Golf & C.C. 19
Big Bend Golf & C.C. 20
Birch Bay Village G.C. 21
Blue Boy West 22
Bowyer's Par 3 Golf, Inc. 23
Brae Burn Golf & C.C. 24
Broadmoor Golf Club 25
Brookdale Golf Course 26
Buckskin Golf Club .... 27 *New*
Camaloch Golf Club 28
Canterwood Golf & C.C 29
Canyon Lakes Golf Course .. 30
Capitol City Golf Club 31
Carey Lakes Golf Course 32
Carnation Golf Course 33
Cascade Golf Course 34
Cedarcrest Municipal G.C. ... 35
Cedars Golf Club 36
Centralia Public G.C. 37
Chevy Chase Golf Club 38
Chewelah Golf & C.C. 39
Christy's Range & Par 3 40
Clarkston Golf & C.C. 41
Classic Country Club 42
Clover Valley Golf Course ... 43
Club Green Meadows 44
Colfax Golf Club 45
Columbia Park Golf Course . 46

Columbia Point Golf Course. 47
Colville Elks Golf Course 48
Course @ Taylor Creek, The . 49
Creek @ Qualchan, The 50
Crescent Bar Resort 51
Crossroads Park G.C 52
New 9 Dakota Creek Golf & C.C. ... 53
Deer Meadows Golf Course . 54
Deer Park Golf & C. C. 55
Delphi Golf Course 56
Desert Aire Golf Course. 57
Desert Canyon Golf Resort .. 58
Downriver Golf Course 59
Druids Glen Golf Club 60
Dungeness Golf &C.C. 61
Eaglemont 62
Echo Falls Country Club 63
Elk Run Golf Course 64
Ellensburg Golf Club 65
Enumclaw Golf Course 66
Esmeralda Golf Course 67
Everett Golf & C.C. 68
Evergreen Golf Course 69
Fairway Village G.C. 70
Fairways @ W Terrace, The . 71
Fairwood Golf & C.C. 72
Family G.C. @ Tumwater ... 73
Fircrest Golf Club 74
Fisher Park Golf Course 75
Flowing Lake Golf Course ... 76
Fort Lewis Golf Course 77
Fort Steilacoom G.C. 78
Foster Golf Links 79
Gallery Golf Course 80
Gateway Golf Course 81
Gig Harbor Golf & C.C. 82
Glen Acres Golf & C.C. 83
Glendale Golf & C.C. 84
Gleneagle Golf Course 85
Gold Mountain GC...........86-87
Goldendale Country Club 88
Golfgreen Golf Center 89
Grandview Golf Course 90
Grays Harbor Country Club . 91

Green Lake Golf Course 92
Green Mountain Resort .... 93 *New*
Hangman Valley G.C. 94
Harbour Pointe Golf Club 95
Harrington Golf & C.C. 96
Hartwood Golf Course .... 97 *New*
Hat Island Golf Club 98
High Cedars Golf Club 99
High Valley Country Club.... 100
Highland Golf Course.......... 101
Highlands Golf Course 102
Holmes Harbor Golf Club 103
Homeplace Golf.................... 104
Homestead Golf & C.C. 105
Horn Rapids Golf & C.C. 106
Horseshoe Lake G.C. 107
Hot Springs Golf Course 108
Husum Hills Golf Course 109
Hylander Greens & P.C. 110
Indian Canyon Golf Course .. 111
Indian Summer Golf & C.C.. 112
Inglewood Golf Club 113
Interbay Family Golf Center 114
Ironwood Green Public G.C. 115
Island Greens 116
Jackson G.C. 117
Jade Greens G.C & D.R. 118
Jefferson G.C. 119
Kahler Glen Golf Course 120
Kayak Point Golf Course 121
Kenwanda Golf Course 122
Kitsap Golf & C.C. 123
Lake Chelan Golf Course 124
Lake Cushman Golf Course . 125
Lake Limerick C.C. 126
Lake Padden G.C. 127
Lake Spanaway G.C. 128
Lake Wilderness G.C. 129
Lake Woods Golf Course 130
LakeLand Village G & C.C.. 131
Lakeview Golf & C.C. 132
Lakeview Golf Challenge 133
Lams Golf Links 134
Latah Short Course 135

Leavenworth Golf Club 136
Legion Memorial G.C. 137
Lewis River Golf Course 138
Liberty Lake Golf Course 139
Linden Golf & C.C. 140
Lipoma Firs Golf Course 141
Lobo Country Club 142
Longview Country Club 143
Loomis Trail Golf Club 144
Lopez Island Golf Course 145
Lower Valley Golf Club 146
Lynnwood Municipal G.C. ... 147
M A 8 Golf 148
Madrona Links Golf Course . 149
Manito Golf & C.C. 150
Maple Grove Golf................. 151
Maplewood Golf Course 152
McCormick Woods 153
Meadow Park Golf Course ... 154
Meadow Springs C.C. 155
Meadowmeer Golf & C.C. ... 156
MeadowWood Golf Course.. 157
Meridian Greens GC &DR ... 158
Meridian Valley G. & C.C. .. 159
Meriwood Golf Course 160
Mill Creek Country Club 161
Mint Valley Golf Course 162
Monroe Golf Course 163
Moses Lake Golf & C.C. 164
New Moses Pointe Golf Resort 165
Mount Adams C.C. 166
Mount Si Golf Course 167
New World Pro Golf Center . 168
Newaukum Valley G.C. 169
Nile Golf & Country Club 170
Nisqually Valley G.C. 171
North Bellingham Public GC.172
North Shore Golf Course 173
Oakbrook Golf & C.C. 174
Oaksridge Golf Course 175
Oasis Park Par 3 176
Ocean Shores Golf Course ... 177
Odessa Golf Club 178
Okanogan Valley Golf Club . 179

Olympia Country & G.C. 180
Orcas Island Golf Course 181
Orchard Hills Golf & C.C. ... 182
Oroville Golf Club................ 183
Othello Golf Club 184
Overlake Golf & C.C. 185
Overlook Golf Course 186
Painted Hills Golf Club 187
Pasco Golfland..................... 188
Peaceful Valley G.C. 189
Pend Oreille Golf & C.C. 190
Peninsula Golf Club 191
Peninsula Golf Course 192
Pine Arces Par 3 G.C. 193
Pine Crest Golf Course 194
Plateau Golf & C.C............... 195
Pomeroy Golf Course 196
Port Ludlow Golf &
Meeting Retreat 197
Port Townsend Golf Course . 198
Potholes Golf Course 199
Quail Ridge Golf Course 200
Quincy Valley Golf 201
Rainier Golf & C.C............... 202
Raspberry Ridge G.C............ 203
Ritzville Muni Golf Course .. 204
Riverbend Golf Complex 205
Riverside Country Club 206
Riverside Golf Course 207
Riviera Golf & C.C............... 208
Rock Island Golf Club 209
Rolling Hills Golf Course 210
Royal City Golf Course 211
Royal Oaks Country Club 212
Sage Hills Golf Club 213
Sahalee Country Club 214
Saint John Golf & C.C.......... 215
San Juan Golf & C.C. 216
Sand Point Country Club 217
Sandy Point Golf Course 218
Scott Lake Golf Course 219
Sea Links 220
Seattle Golf Club 221
Semiahmoo Golf & C.C. 222

Serendipity Golf Course 223
Shelton Bayshore Golf Club . 224
Sheridan Greens G.C. 225
Shuksan Golf Club 226
Similk Beach Golf Course 227
Skagit Golf & C.C. 228
Skamania Lodge G.C............ 229
Skyline Golf Course 230
Snohomish Golf Course 231
Snoqualmie Falls G.C. 232
New Snoqualmie Ridge T.P.C.
Golf Club 233
Spokane Country Club 234
Sudden Valley G. & C.C.. 235
Sumner Meadows G.L........... 236
Sun Country Golf Resort 237
Sun Dance G.C. 238
Sun Willows 239
SunLand Golf & C.C. 240
Sunny Meadows Golf &
Four Season Resort 241
Suntides Golf Course 242
Surfside Golf Course 243
Tacoma Country & G.C. 244
Tall Chief Golf Course 245
Tam O' Shanter Golf & C.C .. 246
New Tanwax Greens 247
Tapps Island G.C. 248
Tekoa Golf Club 249
New The Golf Club @
Newcasttle.......................250-251
Three Lakes Golf Course 252
Three Rivers Golf Course 253
Touchet Valley G.C............... 254
Tri-City Country Club 255
Tri-Mountain Golf Course..... 256
New Trophy Lake Golf & C.C...... 257
Tumwater Valley G.C. 258
Twin Lakes Golf & C.C. 259
Twin Rivers Golf Course 260
Tyee Valley Golf Course 261
University Golf Club 262
Useless Bay Golf & C.C........ 263
Valley View Golf Course 264

Golf Courses (continued)

Vashon Island Golf & C.C. ... 265
Veterans Memorial Park G.C. 266
Vic Meyers Golf Course 267
Vicwood Golf Links .... 268 *New*
Village Greens G.C 269
Walla Walla Country Club 270
Walter E. Hall Memorial 271
Wandermere Golf Course ...... 272 *New*
Wayne Golf Course 273
Wellington Hills G.C. 274
Wenatchee Golf & C.C. 275
West Richland Municipal 276
West Seattle Golf Club 277
Westwood West 278
Whidbey Golf & C.C. 279
Whispering Firs Golf Club ... 280
Willapa Harbor Golf Club 281
Willows Run   *New 18, Exc. 9*
Golf Club 282-283
Wing Point Golf & C.C. 284
WSU Golf Course 285
Yakima Country Club 286
Yakima Elks Golf & C.C. 287

Driving Ranges &
Golf Learning Centers

Batstone Hill Driving Range 288
Beacon Hill Golf Center 288
Columbia Super Range 288
Desert Lakes Driving Range 288
Emerald Links D.R. 289
Evergreen Golf Center 289
Family Golf Center @ Kent . 289
Family Golf Center @ Lacey.289
Family G.C. @ Tacoma. 290
Gateway Golf Center 290
Gold Creek T. & S. Club 290
Golf Club, The 290
Grand Mound D.R. 291
H & H Driving Range 291
Harvest Valley Golf Center .. 291

Driving Ranges (continued)

Iron Eagle Sports Center 291
Kaddyshack Golf Center 292
Ken's Golf 292
Longshots Driving Range 292
Mulligan's Driving Range 292
North West Golf Range 293
Par IV Golf Learning Center. 293
ParFect Driving Range 293
Performance Golf Center 293
Puetz Golf Range 294
Rainbow Golf D.R. 294
Red Wood Golf Center 294
Rodarco Golf Range 294
Southcenter Golf 295
Steamboat Golf 295
Straight Arrow D. R. 295
Tour Fairways Golf Range ... 295
University of Wash. D.R. 296
Vanco Driving Range 296
Westside Golf Range 296
Woodalls World D.R 296

Golf Specialty Shops s 297-300

Weekend Getaways..........301-304

Geographical Index 305-309

LinksTime.com.................310-311
*New Internet Tee-Time Service
for Golfers*

Daniel MacMillan has been an avid golfer for the past 14 years. He enjoys researching and playing the various golf courses of the Pacific Northwest (if it were only that easy!!). *Golfing in Washington* was the brainchild of Daniel and his previous partner Mark Fouty who, one day while playing a round at Snohomish Golf Course, discussed finding a guide to use themselves. When no such guide was available this one was written. The book has taken on many stages. It was originally called *Golfing in Western Washington*, which encompassed only the more populous half of the state. In 1988 it expanded to *Golfing in Washington* (now in it's 14th edition). Meanwhile Mark pursued a career in New York so Daniel bought out Mark's share of the company. The company has therefore become a real family operation. Daniel drags his wife Kristi and their three children throughout the Pacific Northwest seeking information on new courses and facilities for upcoming publications. We hope all the thousands of miles and endless phone calls have paid off. This guide is designed to have all the information a golfer wants and needs to know about playing a course, and as a golfer Daniel has done just that.

Golfing in Oregon is the second book published by MAC Productions and written by Daniel. Now in its eighth edition it also is published on an annual basis. This book too has taken many forms it was originally called *Golfing in Oregon & Idaho*. In 1992 the book was changed to reflect the new format and now only includes the state of Oregon.

Golfing in Idaho & Montana is the third book published by MAC Productions and written by Daniel. The first edition of this book was called *Golfing In Idaho* and was published in 1994. The new book which came out in spring of 1996 includes the great state of Montana and is called *Golfing In Idaho & Montana* look for it in a pro shop or book store near you.

The Birdie Book is another one of MAC Productions titles that is a cooperative effort with newly formed Dornoch Publishing. It is a coupon book that offers the golfer nearly $2,500.00 worth of savings at many of Washington's finest golf facilities and learning centers. Hopefully in the future *The Birdie Book* will feature Oregon's finest golf courses and will cover the entire northwest region.

New territories are always being explored for writing golf course guides such as this. It takes many man hours and attention to detail to produce books of this nature. From start to finish a new book takes about two years to produce. Currently five more are in the works with many more in the initial planning stage. Look for the new publications at a pro shop or book store near you. Daniel's hope is that you will find this to be the best golf guide of its kind on the shelf.

Abbreviations, Explanatory notes and Disclaimers

Executive Course-An executive golf course is usually longer than a typical par 3 short course but shorter than a regulation course.

Private Course- A golf course that is not open to public play.

Semi-private- golf courses that are closed to the public at certain times during the week. Best to call ahead to reserve tee-times.

Tees: T-Tour; **C**-Championship; **M**-Men; **F**-Forward; **W**-Women. **W/D**-Weekday; **W/E**-Weekend.

N/A-Not available.

Course rating-This rates the degree of difficulty of course in the NorthWest and refers to the average number of shots per round a scratch golfer ought to shoot. It is figured by rating teams who factor in terrain, length and hazards of each course. The higher the rating the more difficult the course. Course ratings appear courtesy of the *Pacific Northwest Golf Association* and the *Oregon Golf Association.*

Slope-This is similar to the course rating but it considers other factors as well. The slope rating takes into consideration the playing difficulty of a course for handicaps above scratch. The higher the number, the more difficult the golf course. Slope ratings courtesy of the *Pacific Northwest Golf Association* and the *Oregon Golf Association.*

Greens fee- prices are subject to change at any time. Because a number of Eastern Washington courses close for the winter, the prices may reflect those of last year. When two prices are given, the first refers to the 18 hole fee, the second to the 9 hole fee. "Reciprocates" refers to the practice of private courses allowing members of other private courses to play their courses. However, because some courses only reciprocate with a limited number of other courses, it's best to call first.

Trail fee- the fee a course charges an individual to use their own power cart on the course.

Reservation policy- This refers to the maximum number of days the course allows reservations to made in advance under normal circumstances.

Winter condition- Dry, damp, wet refers to the club pro's opinion of the course's condition in rainy conditions.

Terrain- flat, flat some hills, relatively hilly, very hilly.

Tees- Grass or mats are the alternatives.

Spikes- many of the area golf courses are going to a soft spike policy during the peak golfing season. Be sure to check each course prior to play as the policies vary a great deal from course to course.

Course layouts/yardage- My intent is to show tees in relation to greens, obvious hazards and other holes. Some hazards may not be adequately represented, nor are trees shown. Use these layouts as a reference at the kind of golf course you are planning to visit. The more the hazards the more difficult the golf course will play.

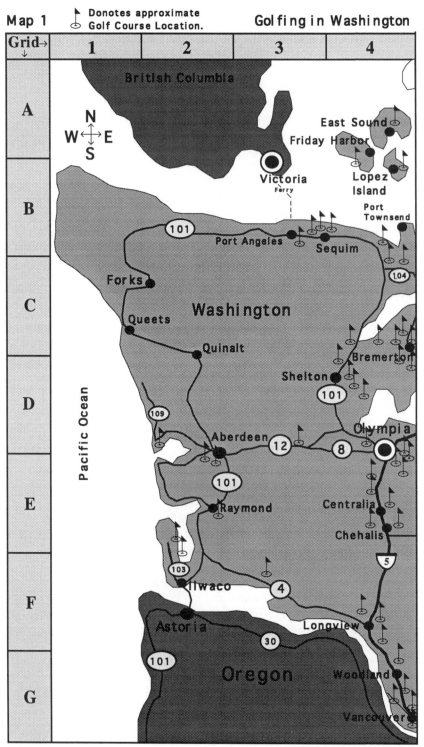

Map 1

Donotes approximate Golf Course Location.

Golfing in Washington

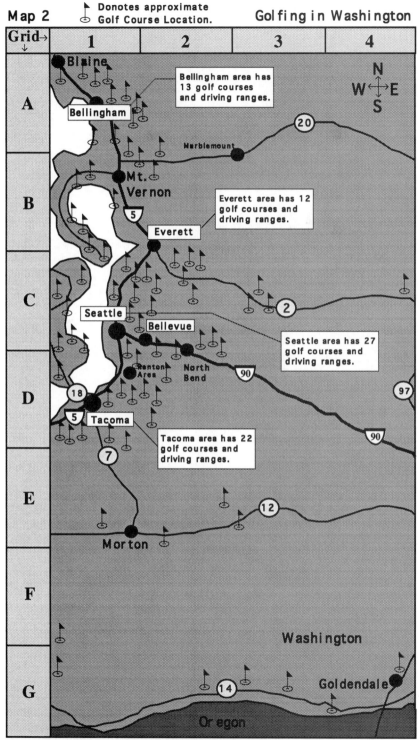

Map 2

Donotes approximate
Golf Course Location.

Golfing in Washington

Bellingham area has 13 golf courses and driving ranges.

Everett area has 12 golf courses and driving ranges.

Seattle area has 27 golf courses and driving ranges.

Tacoma area has 22 golf courses and driving ranges.

Washington

Oregon

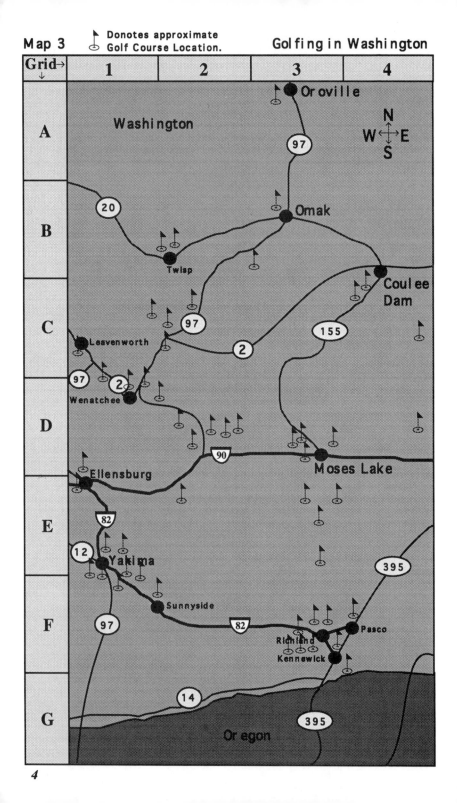

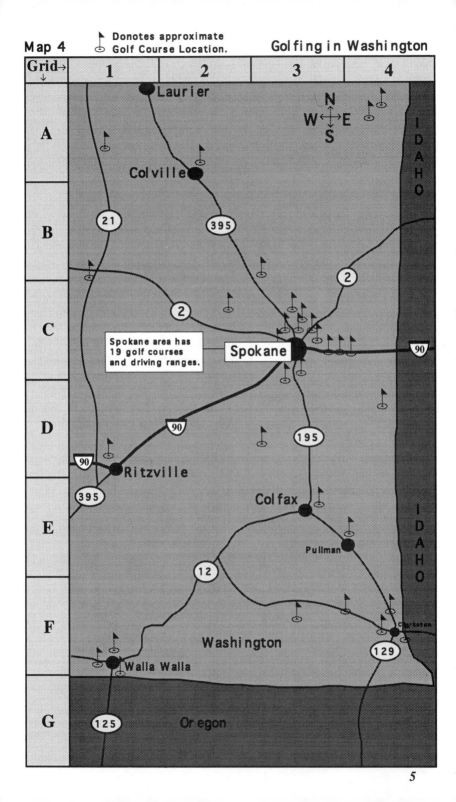

Alderbrook Golf & Yacht Club (semi-private, 18 hole course)

E 300 Country Club Drive East; Union,WA 98592

Phone:(360) 898-2560, 888-898-2560. FAX: (360) 898-2492.

Pro: Mike Fields, PGA. Supt.: Dwane Ehrich. Internet: http;//hood.hctc.com.

Rating/Slope: C 70.3/118; M 69.0/115; W 71.5/116. **Course record:** 64.

Green fees: W/D $25/$15; W/E $30/$18; Sr. rates $18 (M-F); M/C, VISA.

Power cart: $23/$13. **Pull cart:** $3/$1.50. **Trail fee:** $9 for personal carts.

Reservation policy: yes, 3 weeks for members & guests; 1 week for the public.

Winter condition: the golf course is open all year. Dry conditions, drains well.

Terrain: flat, some hills. **Tees:** all grass. **Spikes:** no metal spikes April-Oct.

Services: club rentals, lessons, snack bar, beer, pro shop, club fitting, tennis courts, driving range. **Comments:** Picturesque setting above Hood Canal and the beautiful Olympic Peninsula. Well stocked pro shop that will service all your golfing needs. The golf course has excellent drainage for winter play.

Directions: from I-5 N&S cut off for Highway 101 (exit 104) to Shelton/Port Angeles. Bypass Shelton, continuing approximately 5 miles to Twanoh State Park/Bremerton exit (Hwy 106). Follow for approximately 4 miles (along Hood Canal) to Union. The course will be on your right, across from the Alderbrook Inn on Hood Canal. Look for signs.

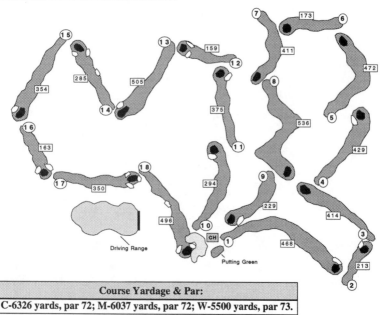

Course Yardage & Par:

C-6326 yards, par 72; M-6037 yards, par 72; W-5500 yards, par 73.

Allenmore Golf Club (public, 18 hole course)

2125 South Cedar; Tacoma, WA 98405
Phone:(253) 627-7211 or (877) 627-7211. FAX: none. Internet: none.
Pro: Don Mojean, PGA. Superintendent:: Arne Smith.
Rating/Slope: M 68.5/118; W 72.9/123. **Course record:** 60.
Green fees: $21/$15.50 all week long; Jr. & Sr. rates (M-F); VISA, M/C.
Power cart: $20/$10. **Pull cart:** $3/$2. **Trail fee:** $3 for personal carts.
Reservation policy: please call up to 1 week in advance for tee times.
Winter condition: the golf course is open all year long. Dry conditions.
Terrain: relatively hilly. **Tees:** all grass. **Spikes:** metal spikes permitted.
Services: club rentals, lessons, snack bar, pro shop, lockers, showers. No knob
shoes, 5-somes OK if they play fast. **Comments:** Great golf course for hosting
tournaments and special events. Good public course that gets a great deal of play
during the summer months so make your tee times well in advance for weekend
or holiday play. The course drains fairly well making this a good winter track.

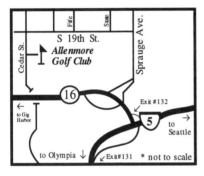

Directions: from I-5 N&S exit to Hwy
16W(Gig Harbor-Bremerton). Proceed
for a short distance to the Sprague Ave.
exit. Continue on Sprague for .4 miles to
S 19th St. Take a left on S 19th. Proceed
to Cedar St. left on Cedar Street. Golf
course entrance will be located on your
left. Look for signs marking your turn.

Course Yardage & Par:
C-6355 yards, par 71.
M-6064 yards, par 71.
W-5906 yards, par 75.

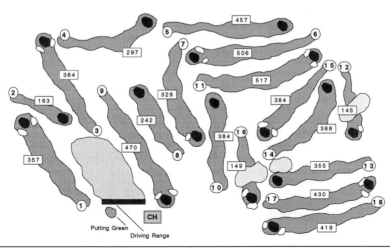

7

Alta Lake Golf Course (public, 18 hole course)

P.O. Box 85; Alta Lake Road; Pateros, WA 98846
Phone: (509) 923-2359. Fax: (509) 923-9467. Internet: none.
Owners: Don & Susan Barth. Pro: none.
Rating/Slope: C 71.3/125; M 69.5/121; W 69.9/118. **Course record:** 71.
Green fees: $22/$14 all week long; VISA, M/C.
Power cart: $20/$12. **Pull cart:** $3/$2. **Trail fee:** $5 for personal carts.
Reservation policy: yes, you may call ahead for a tee time, (a must in summer).
Winter condition: the golf course is closed from November to mid March.
Terrain: relatively hilly. **Tees:** all grass. **Spikes:** soft spikes only.
Services: club rentals, snack bar, beer, pro shop, motel on the 9th green.
Comments: links type course designed after the links of Scotland. Rolling
terrain and the desert framing each fairway make this course a special place to
play. Views of the Columbia River and Alta Lake can be seen from the course.

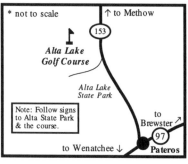

Directions: the golf course is located
southwest of Pateros, Washington.
From Highway 97 follow the signs to
Alta Lake State Park where the course
is located. (this is approximately 17
miles north of Lake Chelan).

Course Yardage & Par:
C-7028 yards, par 72.
M-6412 yards, par 72.
W-5748 yards, par 72.

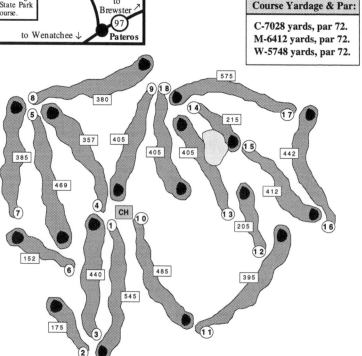

Apple Tree Golf Course (public, 18 hole course)
8804 Occidental Avenue; Yakima, WA 98903
Phone: (509) 966-5877. **Fax:** (509) 966-5537. **Internet:** www.appletreegolf.com
Manager: Cory Groves. **Pro:** Todd Capps. **Course record:** 64.
Rating/Slope: T 73.3/129; C 72.0/127; M 70.7/124; S 68.0/118; W 72.0/124.
Green fees: Monday thru Thursday $35 (+tax); Friday thru Sunday $50 (+ tax).
Power cart: $25 (plus tax). **Pull cart:** $4 (plus tax). **Trail fee:** $5 (+ tax).
Reservation policy: yes, please call ahead for your tee time info (30 days).
Winter condition: the golf course is open all year long, weather permitting.
Terrain: flat, some hills. **Tees:** all grass. **Spikes:** metal spikes not permitted.
Services: club rentals, lessons, snack bar & grill, pro shop, restaurant, banquet
facilities, beer, wine, driving range, putting & chipping greens, practice area.
Comments: Fantastic layout with an island green on the 17th hole in the shape
of a "Washington Apple". If you are looking for a course that is a pleasure to
play I highly recommend this top rate facility. This track is worth a special trip
so make sure you include Apple Tree in any eastern Washington golf vacation.

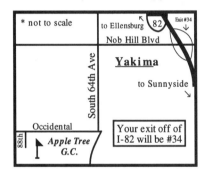

Directions: From I-82 take the Nob Hill
exit #34. Follow W Nob Hill westbound
to 64th Ave. Turn left on S 64th Ave.
Proceed on S 64th Ave. to Occidental
Ave. Turn right on Occidental Avenue.
Follow to 88th Avenue. Left to the
clubhouse. The golf course will be on
both sides of Occidental Avenue.

Course Yardage & Par:

T-6892 yards, par 72.
C-6618 yards, par 72.
M-6311 yards, par 72.
S-5857 yards, par 72.
F-5428 yards, par 72.

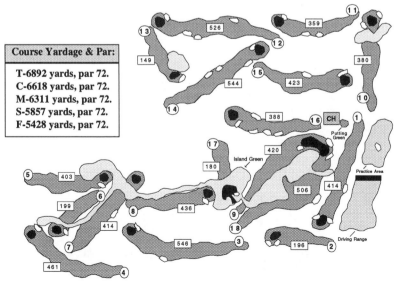

Auburn Golf Course (public, 18 hole course)
29630 Green River Road SE; Auburn, WA 98092
Phone: (253) 833-2350. **Fax: none. Internet: none.**
Pro: Doug Campbell, PGA. Superintendent: Kevin Van.
Rating/Slope: C 69.5/111; M 68.3/109; W 70.4/114. **Course record:** 62.
Green fees: W/D $20/$14.50; W/E $22/$15.25; Jr./Sr. rates (M-F).
Power cart: $20/$12. **Pull cart:** $3/$2. **Trail fee:** $5 for personal carts.
Reservation policy: yes, please call ahead up to 1 week in advance for times.
Winter condition: the golf course is open all year long. Wet conditions.
Terrain: flat, some hills. **Tees:** grass. **Spikes:** metal spikes permitted.
Services: club rentals, lessons, snack bar, beer, pro shop, putting green.
Comments: the golf course is pleasant to walk with a few hills throughout.
Water and sand comes into play on several holes. The front nine is fairly wide
open. The back nine is more hilly with trees coming into play throughout. The
well stocked pro shop will serve all your golfing needs. Fair public track.

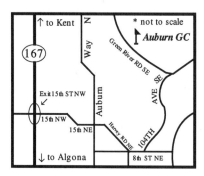

Directions: from I-5 N&S take exit #147
(S 272nd St.). Go east on S 272nd for 2.4
miles to Hwy 167 S. S for 2 miles to 15th
St NW exit. Go east on 15th NW for 1
mile to Harvey Rd. South for.5 miles to
8th NE. East for .4 mile to 104th SE. Go
north for .8 miles to SE 307th Pl-Green
River Road. Go for 1 mile to the course.

Course Yardage & Par:
C-6020 yards, par 71.
M-5571 yards, par 71.
W-5571 yards, par 73.

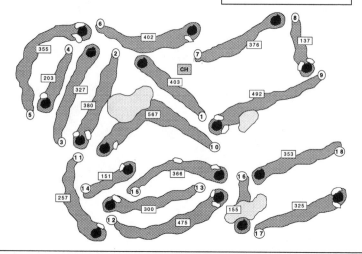

Avalon Golf Club (public, 27 hole course)

19345 Kelleher Road; Burlington, WA 98233   Internet: www.cybergolf.com
Phone: (360) 757-1900 or 1-800-624-0202. Fax: (360) 757-2555.
Pro: Brian Kruhlak, PGA. Superintendent: R. Letellier. Course record: 69.
Rating/Slope: South/North: T 73.1/132; C 71.3/127; M 69.6/124; W 73.2/127.
Green fees: M-Th. $32; Fri. $36; Sat.-Sun. Hol. $39/$24 (all+tax); M/C, VISA.
Power cart: $25. Pull cart: $3. Trail fee: $25 for personal carts.
Reservation policy: up to 7 days or no time limit if payment is by credit card.
Winter condition: the golf course is open all year long. No temporary greens.
Terrain: flat, some hills. Tees: all grass. Spikes: no metal spikes April to Oct.
Services: club rentals, lessons, restaurant, beer, wine, pro shop, driving range,
caddy service in season, putting green. Comments: First rate golfing facility.
This 27 hole Robert Muir Graves designed course offers spectacular views of the
Skagit Valley and surrounding countryside. If you are looking for top rate golf
course with a friendly staff try Avalon, you will not be disappointed. Great track.

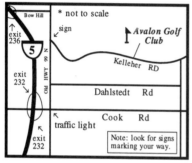

Directions: from I-5 N&S take exit #232
(Cook Road).Turn east and go for 1 block
to the traffic light. Turn left and go north
on old Hwy 99. When you reach Kelleher
Road turn right. Go beyond the Humane
Society and a make a left at the sign.

Rating/Slope:
North/South: T 73.1/132; C 71.3/127; M 69.6/124; W 73.2/127.
North/West: T 72.3/125; C 70.3/121; M 69.6/124; W 71.6/122.

Course Yardage & Par:
North: T-3428 yards, C-3201 yards, M-3001 yards, W-2726 yards, par 36.
South: T-3375 yards, C-3205 yards, M-3005 yards, W-2808 yards, par 36.
West: T-3201 yards, C-3001 yards, M-2797 yards, W-2510 yards, par 36.

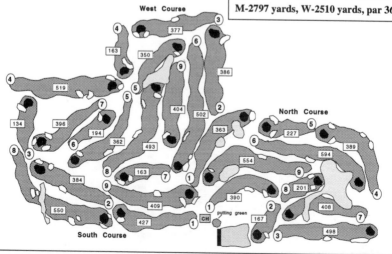

Ballinger Park Golf Course (public, 9 hole course)

23000 Lakeview Drive; Mountlake Terrace, WA 98043
Phone: (425) 775-6467. Fax: (425) 775-6468. Internet: none.
Managers: Jan Japar, Mimi Racicot. Superintendent: Matt Kimball.
Rating/Slope: M 64.2/100; W 66.9/105. Course record: 28.
Green fees: W/D $8.50; W/E $9; winter, twi-lite, Jr & Sr rates; VISA, MC.
Power cart: not available. Pull cart: $2. Trail fee: none (seasonal restrictions).
Reservation policy: yes, in summer all week long. Winter, weekends only.
Winter condition: the golf course is open all year long. Wet conditions.
Terrain: flat. Tees: grass & mats, off season only. Spikes: metal permitted.
Services: club rentals, restaurant, beer, wine, golf shop featuring discount golf
apparel & equipment. **Comments:** In 1999 Ballinger will go under a total
renovation and will be closed until June of the year 2000. The new Bill Overdorf
design promises to be outstanding. Improved drainage along with some of the
best green fee rates in western Washington will make Ballinger a must play.

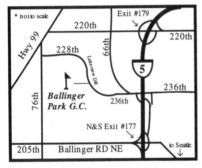

Directions: I-5 N take exit #177 to 236th
SW. Go west on 236th which becomes
Lakeview Dr. for .7 miles. I-5 S take
exit #179 to 220th SW. Go west on 220th
SW to 66th Ave. Go south for 1 mile to
Lakeview Dr. Go west on Lakeview Dr.
to the course.

Course Yardage & Par:
C-2740 yards, par 34.
M-2565 yards, par 34.
W-2330 yards, par 34.

New Layout for the year 2000.

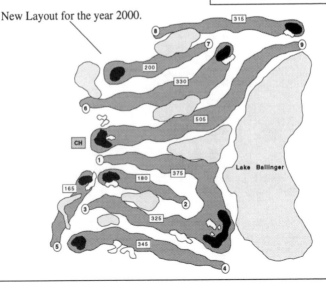

Banks Lake Golf Club (public, 9 hole course, dual tees)
Airport Road; P. O. Box 11; Grand Coulee, WA 99133
Phone: (509) 633-0163. Fax: (509) 633-0619. Internet: none.
Manager/Pro: John W Combs Jr. Superintendent: N/A.
Rating/Slope: M 68.1/103; W 70.2/110. **Course record:** 68.
Green fees: $16/$14 all week long; no special rates; VISA, M/C.
Power cart: $20/$12. **Pull cart:** $1. **Trail fee:** $5 for personal carts.
Reservation policy: yes, you may call in advance for a tee time, no restrictions.
Winter condition: the golf course is closed December through February.
Terrain: flat, some hills. **Tees:** grass. **Spikes:** metal spikes permitted.
Services: lessons, driving range, snack bar, beverages, pro shop, putting green.
Comments: rolling lush terrain situated in the midst of the "desert" in eastern
Washington. The golf course is relatively new and kept in excellent condition.
The course sports dual tees for those wanting a different look on the 2nd nine.
Good 9 hole tract that offers the golfer a very friendly atmosphere.

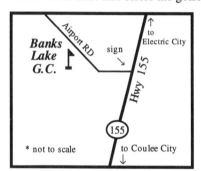

Directions: the golf course is located 2
miles south of Electric City off of Hwy
155. There is a sign on Highway 155
marking the turn to the golf course. The
golf course is located by the airport. You
will turn on Airport Road to the golf
course which will be located on your left
hand side of the road.

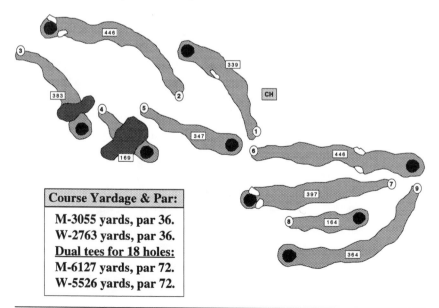

Course Yardage & Par:

M-3055 yards, par 36.
W-2763 yards, par 36.
<u>Dual tees for 18 holes:</u>
M-6127 yards, par 72.
W-5526 yards, par 72.

Battle Creek Golf Course (public 18 hole, 9 hole par 3).

6006 Meridian Avenue North; Marysville, WA 98271
Phone: 800-655-7931, (360) 659-7931. Fax: (425) 258-6755. Internet: none.
Pro: Jim Pulliam, PGA. Superintendent. Gene Connor.
Rating/Slope: C 71.2/121; M 69.3/116; W 70.5/121. **Record:** C 68; M 66.
Green fees: W/D $20/$14. W/E $25/$15; Jr. & Sr. rates (M-F); VISA, MC.
Green fees for the par 3 course: W/D $7; W/E $8.
Power cart: $21/$12. **Pull cart:** $3/$2. **Trail fee:** $9 for personal carts.
Reservation policy: yes, call up to 7 days in advance for your tee-times.
Winter condition: the golf course is open all year long. Dry, good drainage.
Terrain: some hills. **Tees:** all grass. **Spikes:** soft spikes preferred.
Services: club rentals, lessons, cafe, beer, wine, pro shop, grass tees in practice
area, driving range, club memberships. **Comments:** excellent, scenic golf course
that wanders thru woodlands and wetlands. Greens have improved dramatically
over the last few years so be sure to add Battle Creek to your weekend outings.

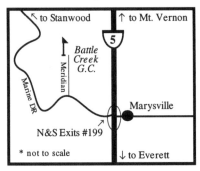

Directions: from I-5 N&S take exit #199
(Tulalip-Marysville). Go west on Marine
DR for 2.75 miles. Turn right on Meridian
Avenue. Travel north for .75 miles to the
course. Note: look for a sign at your turn.

Course Yardage & Par:
C-6575 yards, par 73.
M-6153 yards, par 73.
W-5286 yards, par 73.

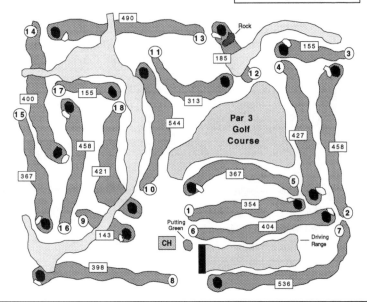

Beacon Rock Golf Course (public, 9 hole course)

Box 189; Highway 14; North Bonneville, WA 98639
Phone: (509) 427-5730, 800-428-5730. Fax: (509) 427-5710. Internet: none.
Owners: James & Linda Borup. Superintendent: James Borup.
Rating/Slope: M 67.5/115; W 69.7/109. **Course record:** 29.
Green fees: $22/$12 all week long; Senior rates Tuesday-Thursday; M/C, VISA.
Power cart: $10 per nine holes. **Pull cart:** $3/$2. **Trail fee:** $5.
Reservation policy: yes, you may call 7 days in advance for a tee times.
Winter condition: the golf course is open all year round. Drains very well.
Terrain: flat (easy walking). **Tees:** all grass. **Spikes:** metal spikes permitted.
Services: club rentals, restaurant, beer, beverages, pro shop, putting green.
Comments: this excellent walking golf course features tree lined fairways and spectacular views of the Columbia Gorge. Dual tees are available for a different look on your second nine. The course is playable throughout the entire year.

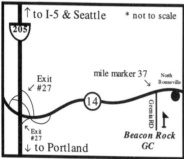

Directions: the golf course is located west of North Bonneville off of Hwy 14. Exit at Grenia Street to the course. Watch for a sign on the highway marking your way to the course. If coming from I-205 N&S be sure to exit to Hwy 14 (exit #27) going eastbound (Lewis & Clark Hwy).

Course Yardage & Par:
M-2753 yards, par 36.
W-2555 yards, par 36.
Dual tees for 18 holes:
M-5594 yards, par 72.
W-4984 yards, par 72.

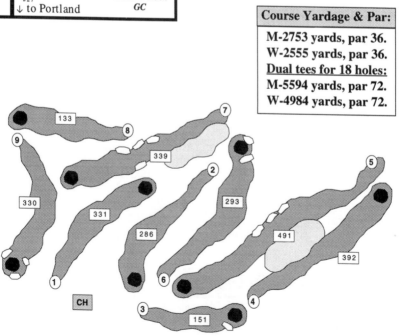

Bear Creek Country Club (private, 18 hole course)

13737 202nd Avenue NE; Woodinville, WA 98072
Phone: (425) 881-1350. **Fax:** (425) 869-0894. **Internet:** www.bearcreekcc.com
Pro: Rex Fullerton, PGA. **Supt.:** P. J. Patuzak. **Course record:** 68.
Rating/Slope: T 75.0/139; C 72.5/132; M 69.3/128; W 71.7/124.
Green fees: private club, members & guests only; Jr. rates; VISA, M/C.
Power cart: private club, members & guests only. **Pull cart:** members only.
Reservation policy: private club, members & guests of members only.
Winter condition: the golf course is open all year long. Dry conditions.
Terrain: relatively hilly. **Tees:** all grass. **Spikes:** soft spikes May-September.
Services: club rentals, lessons, snack bar, beer, wine, liquor, pro shop, lockers, showers, driving range, putting green. **Comments:** very difficult course where shot placement is a must. Hilly terrain gives the golfer a wide variety of lies. Out of bounds comes into play a nearly every hole. Excellent private course.

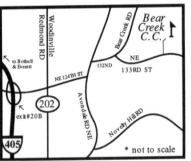

Directions: from I-405 N&S take exit #20B (NE 124th) to NE 124th. Travel eastbound for 4.25 miles to Avondale Road. Go North for .1 miles (your turn will come up quickly, veer left) to NE 132nd. Go east for .3 miles to NE 133rd. Go eastbound on 133rd until you reach 202ND Ave NE, take a left to the course.

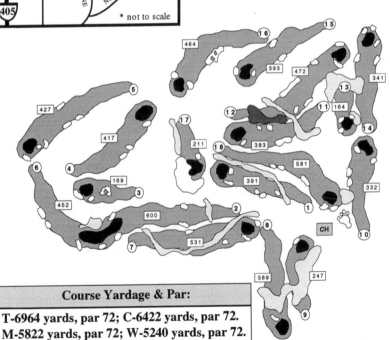

Course Yardage & Par:
T-6964 yards, par 72; C-6422 yards, par 72.
M-5822 yards, par 72; W-5240 yards, par 72.

Bear Creek Golf Course (public, 9 hole course)

Route 1, Box 275; off of Hwy 20; Winthrop, WA 98862
Phone: (509) 996-2284. Fax: (509) 996-3243. Internet: none.
Managers: Ashley & Linda Court. Superintendent: Ashley Court.
Rating/Slope: M 70.0/121; W 70.0/119. Course record: 65.
Green fees: W/D $19/$12; W/E $21/$13; M/C, VISA.
Power cart: $20/$10. Pull cart: $2. Trail fee: $2.50 for personal carts.
Reservation policy: yes, recommemded for weekends and holidays only.
Winter condition: the golf course is closed from November thru March.
Terrain: relatively hilly. Tees: all grass. Spikes: metal spikes permitted.
Services: club rentals, snack bar, beer, beverages, practice green, pro shop.
Comments: the course has beautiful views of the North Cascades. Fairways
are well-kept, lush and green. Water, and trees are the primary hazard from the
tee and on your approach shots. Versatility of placement on the back set of tees
makes you feel like you've played 18 holes. If you are looking for nice 9 hole
course in a great area of Washington try Bear Creek it will not disappoint you.

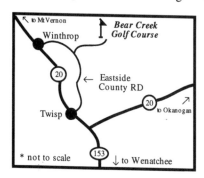

Directions: the golf course is located
north of Twisp and east of Winthrop.
From Hwy 20 go 7 miles north on
Eastside County Road. The golf course
is located 3/4 of a mile up the first paved
road on the right hand side. Look for
signs marking your way to the course.

Course Yardage & Par:
M-3114 yards, par 36.
W-2706 yards, par 37.
Dual tees for 18 holes:
M-6163 yards, par 72.
W-5309 yards, par 73.

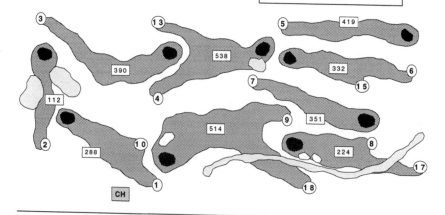

Bellevue Municipal Golf Course (public, 18 hole course)

5500 140th NE; Bellevue, WA 98005
Phone: (425) 452-7250. Fax: (425) 869-3857. Internet: none.
Pros: K. C. Anderson, PGA. Steve Hubbard, PGA. Supt.: Mark Blechen.
Rating/Slope: M 66.5/110; W 68.6/111. **Course record:** 60.
Green fees: W/D 21; W/E $24; Jr. & Sr. rates (M-F $14); no credit cards.
Power cart: $23/$14. **Pull cart:** $3. **Trail fee:** none.
Reservation policy: please call Monday for the entire weeks tee-times.
Winter condition: the golf course is open all year long. Wet conditions.
Terrain: flat, some hills. **Tees:** grass & mats. **Spikes:** metal spikes permitted.
Services: club rentals, lessons, snack bar, beer, wine, pro shop, driving range.
Comments: one of state's busiest golf courses. For being such a busy municipal course it can be found to be in excellent condition. Greens are generally in great shape during the peak season. Covered range for those wanting to practice.

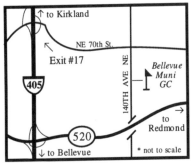

Directions: from I-405 N&S take exit #17 to NE 70th St. Proceed to 140th Ave. NE and turn left. Follow 140th Ave. NE until you reach the course, which will be on your left. From I-5 N&S take exit to Hwy 520 eastbound. Go east to 148th Ave. NE. Go north on 148th for .8 miles to NE 40th. West for .5 miles to 140th NE. Travel north for 1 mile to the course.

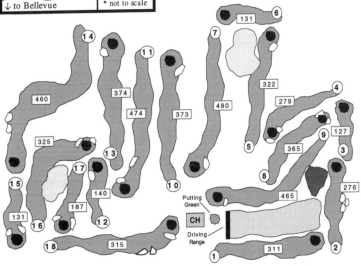

Course Yardage & Par:
M-5535 yards, par 71; W-5081 yards, par 71.

Bellingham Golf & Country Club (private, 18 hole course)
3729 Meridian; Bellingham, WA 98225
Phone: (360) 733-5381. Fax: (360) 676-9073. Internet: www.bellinghamgcc.com.
Pro: Dean Russell, PGA. Superintendent: Dave Bocci.
Rating/Slope: C 71.0/123; M 69.8/120; W 72.7/124. **Course record:** 65.
Green fees: private club, member & guests only; reciprocates; no credit cards.
Power cart: private club. **Pull cart:** private club. **Trail fee:** private club.
Reservation policy: private club, member & guests only. No Public play.
Winter condition: the golf course is open all year long. Dry conditions.
Terrain: flat, some hills. **Tees:** grass. **Spikes:** soft spikes only May thru Sept.
Services: lessons, lounge, beer, wine, liquor, pro shop, lockers, showers, range.
Comments: Excellent private facility for members and guests only. The course
features tree lined fairways, small well bunkered greens and lush conditions.

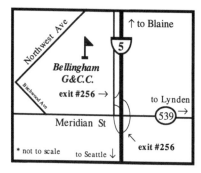

Directions: from I-5 N&S take exit #256
(Meridian St.) to Meridian St. Travel west
on Meridian Street for .2 miles to the golf
course which will be on your right hand
side. Golf course located right off of I-5.

Course Yardage & Par:
C-6473 yards, par 72.
M-6220 yards, par 72.
W-5781 yards, par 73.

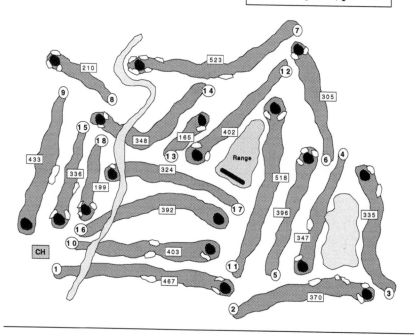

Big Bend Golf & Country Club (semi-private)

P.O. Box 162; Golf Course Road; Wilbur, WA 99185
Phone: (509) 647-5664. **Fax:** unavailable. **Internet:** golfpro@televar.com.
Pro: Kevin L. Wheeler, PGA. **Superintendent:** unavailable.
Rating/Slope: C 68.5/109; M 67.4/107; W 72.5/115. **Course record:** 30.
Green fees: W/D $14/$10; W/E $18/$14; All day $20, W/E's $25. VISA, MC.
Power cart: $18/$12. **Pull cart:** $3.50/$2. **Trail fee:** $5 for personal carts.
Reservation policy: yes, please call in advance for your tee times.
Winter condition: the golf course is open until the snow flies.
Terrain: flat, some hills. **Tees:** all grass. **Spikes:** metal spikes permitted.
Services: club rentals, snack bar, lounge, beer, wine, liquor, driving range,
pro shop, showers. **Comments:** well maintained. One of the best 9 hole golf
courses in the state with water and sand coming into play throughout. Lush
fairways. Two sets of tees provide a full 18 hole variation. Try Big Bend if you
are looking for quick 9 hole round on a beautiful golf course. Good golf course.

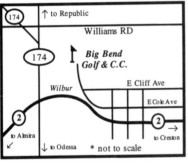

Directions: the course is located south
of the junctions of Hwys 2 and 174, just
northwest of Wilbur. The golf course is
on the east side of Hwy 21. Look for a
sign on the highway marking the way to
the course. If traveling from Spokane
take Highway 2 to Wilbur.

Course Yardage & Par:

M-2985 yards, par 36.
W-2875 yards, par 37.
Dual tees for 18 holes:
M-5942 yards, par 72.
W-5705 yards, par 74.

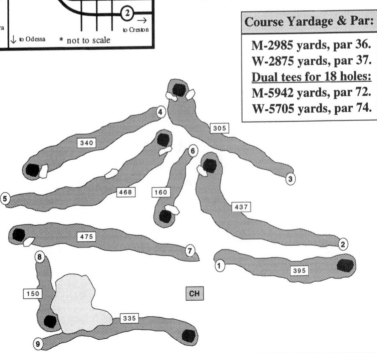

Birch Bay Village Golf Course (private, 9 hole course)
8169 Cowichan Road; Blaine, WA 98230
Phone: (360) 371-2026. **Fax:** (360) 371-3254. **Internet:** none.
Manager: Grant Wilson. **Superintendent:** Craig Swanson.
Rating/Slope: the golf course is not rated. **Course record:** 30.
Green fees: private golf course, members & guests only; no credit cards.
Power cart: members & guests only. **Pull cart:** private. **Trail fee:** not allowed.
Reservation policy: yes, no time limit. Must be a property owner or guest.
Winter condition: the golf course is closed from November to February.
Terrain: flat, some hills. **Tees:** all grass. **Spikes:** metal spikes permitted.
Services: club rentals, lessons, small pro shop, putting & chipping green.
Comments: the course reciprocates for club professionals. Adjacent to Birch Bay in Whatcom County, the course houses three ponds which are in play for the majority of the round. Greens are large with dual pin placements.

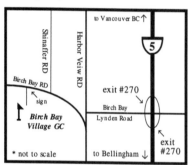

Directions: from I-5 N&S take exit 270 (Lynden-Birch Bay Road), to Lynden-Birch Bay Road. Travel west for 3.7 miles to Harbor View Road. Go south for .2 miles to the road paralleling the bay. Go north for 1.3 miles to the course entrance. Look for a sign marking your turn to the private entrance.

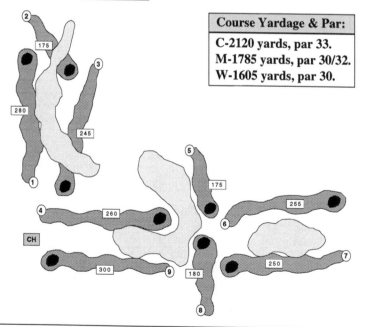

Course Yardage & Par:

C-2120 yards, par 33.
M-1785 yards, par 30/32.
W-1605 yards, par 30.

Blue Boy West (public, 9 hole course)

27927 Florence Acres Road; Monroe, WA 98272
Phone: (360) 793-2378. **Fax:** unavailable. **Internet:** none.
Managers: Ernie & Doug Smith. **Superintendents:** Ernie & Doug Smith.
Rating/Slope: M 61.2/98; W 64.2/109. **Course record:** 29.
Green fees: W/D $15/$9; W/E $17/$11; Jr. & Sr. rates (M thru F $13/$8).
Power cart: $10. **Pull cart:** $3/$2. **Trail fee:** personal carts are allowed.
Reservation policy: yes, please call ahead 1 day for tee times.
Winter condition: the golf course is open all year long. Damp conditions.
Terrain: flat, some rolling hills. **Tees:** grass. **Spikes:** metal spikes permitted.
Services: lessons (at the Iron Eagle Sports Center in Monroe (360) 794-0933),
snack bar, beverages, pro shop, full service clubhouse to serve all your needs.
Comments: beautiful scenery, many views of the mountains and flowers. This
short golf course is very challenging. Water comes into play on eight holes. If
you are looking for a course to take the whole family to, try Blue Boy West.

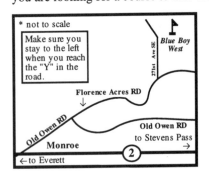

Directions: from Hwy 2 in Monroe, turn
up Old Owens Road. When you come to
a "Y" in the road veer to your left. This
will be Florence Acres Road. Proceed
for approximately 4 miles to the course.
The golf course will be located on the
left hand side of the road. Look for signs
that are posted indicating your turns.

Course Yardage & Par:
M-2199 yards, par 33.
W-1938 yards, par 33.

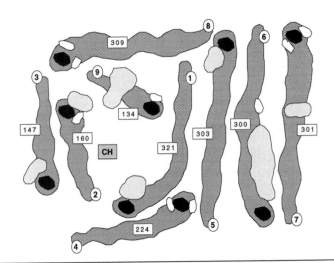

Bowyer's Par 3 Golf, Inc. (public, 9 hole par 3 course)
11608 NE 119th; Vancouver, WA 98662
Phone: (360) 892-3808. **Fax:** none. **Internet:** none
Owners: Mike & Bowyer. **Superintendent:** Mike Bowyer.
Rating/Slope: the golf course is not rated. **Course record:** 21.
Green fees: W/D$7; W/E $14/$7 Jr. & Sr. rates $11/$6; 13 years to 59 years $7 for the first 9, $6 for 2nd (Monday thru Friday); M/C, VISA, AMEX, DIS.
Power cart: not available. **Pull cart:** $1.50. **Trail fee:** not allowed.
Reservation policy: none. Tee-times are on a first come first served basis.
Winter condition: the golf course is open all year long. Damp conditions.
Terrain: flat (easy walking). **Tees:** mats. **Spikes:** metal spikes permitted.
Services: club rentals, snack bar, club memberships, small, limited pro shop.
Comments: this short par 3 course is well maintained with many fir trees towering above the fairways. Greens are of medium size and can challenge you at every turn. If you are looking for a course that challenges your iron play, try Bowyer's Par 3 Golf.

Directions: From I-205 N&S exit at NE 119th and travel eastbound on 119th to the golf course which will be located on your left hand side. Look for signs indicating your turn to the golf course.

Course Yardage & Par:
M-1015 yards, par 27.
W-1015 yards, par 27.

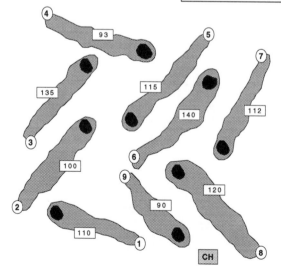

Brae Burn Golf & Country Club (private, 9 hole course)

2409 182nd Avenue NE; Redmond, WA 98052

Phone: (425) 881-0274. **Fax:** none. **Internet:** none.

Pro: none. **Superintendent:** Todd Tibke.

Rating/Slope: the golf course is not rated. **Course record:** 25.

Green fees: private club, members & guests only.

Power cart: none. **Pull cart:** none. **Trail fee:** not allowed.

Reservation policy: none. Private club, members & guests only.

Winter condition: the golf course is open all year long. Damp conditions.

Terrain: flat, some hills. **Tees:** grass. **Spikes:** metal spikes permitted.

Services: very limited services. Pool is for the property owners only.

Comments: a scenic executive golf course which is situated in a very attractive housing development . One creek and a few sand traps come into play throughout this short yet challenging track. Excellent greens during the peak season.

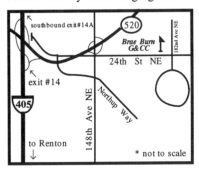

Directions: from I-405 N&S take exit #14 (northbound) 14A (southbound) to Hwy 520E. Take the 148th Avenue NE exit and turn left on NE 24th St. (It is the first light). Proceed on 24th St. to 182nd. Clubhouse is on your immediate left. There is a sign at the entrance to the golf course.

Course Yardage & Par:
M-1283 yards, par 28.
W-1216 yards, par 29.

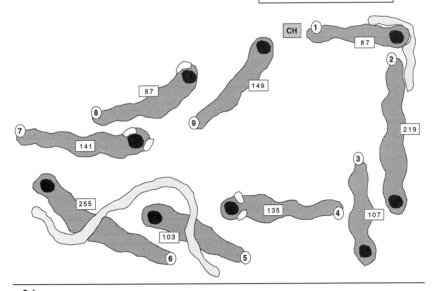

Broadmoor Golf Club (private, 18 hole course)

2340 Broadmoor Drive East; Seattle, WA 98112
Phone: (206) 325-8444. **Fax:** (206) 325-5607. **Internet:** www.broadmoorgolfclub.com.
Pro: Bill Tindall, PGA. **Superintendent:** Jerry Hilperts.
Rating/Slope: M 70.2/123; W 74.7/131. **Course Record:** 61.
Green fees: private club members & guests only; reciprocates, very limited.
Power cart: private club. **Pull cart:** complimentary. **Trail fee:** not allowed.
Reservations policy: private club, members & guests only.
Winter condition: the golf course is open all year long. Dry conditions.
Terrain: flat, some hills. **Tees:** grass. **Spikes:** no metal spikes April-October.
Services: lessons, snack bar, lounge, restaurant, beer, wine, liquor, pro shop,
lockers, showers, driving range. **Comments:** Course built in 1926. One of the
finest courses in the state. It is set among tree lined fairways and stately homes.
Greens are very fast, well bunkered, small and hard to hold. Great golf course.

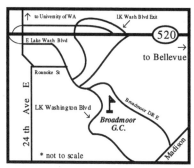

Directions: from I-5 N&S take exit 168B
to Hwy 520E. Exit at Montlake Blvd.
Travel east through the light to E Lake
Washington Blvd. Travel east for .5 miles
to Foster Island Road. Go left on Foster
Island Road to the course entrance which
will be on your right. **Note:** the course is
located near the arboretum. If coming
from Hwy 520 westbound take Montlake
Blvd exit and follow the above directions.

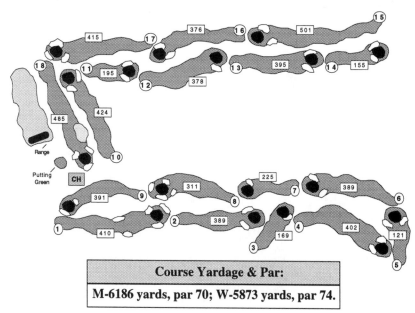

Course Yardage & Par:
M-6186 yards, par 70; W-5873 yards, par 74.

Brookdale Golf Course (public, 18 hole course)

1802 Brookdale Road E; Tacoma, WA 98445
Phone: 800-281-2428; (253) 537-4400. Internet: imbrookdale@msn.com
Director of Golf : Christine Brown-Jones. Pro: Doug Jones.
Superintendent: Steve Newman. Course record: 60.
Rating/Slope: C 70.3/119; M 69.2/117; W 73.1/120.
Green fees: $20/$12 every day; Jr./Sr. rates (M -F only $15/$10); M/C, VISA.
Power cart: $20/$12. **Pull cart:** $3. **Trail fee:** $5 for personal carts.
Reservation policy: yes, call up to 1 week in advance for your tee times.
Winter condition: the golf course is open all year long. Dry conditions.
Terrain: flat, some slight hills. **Tees:** all grass. **Spikes:** metal spikes permitted.
Services: club rentals, lessons, restaurant, beer, pro shop, lockers, showers.
Comments: the golf course's excellent drainage system provides dry play
during the dead of winter. Good greens and excellent fairways make this golf
course a local favorite. Outside tournaments are welcome so be sure to call.

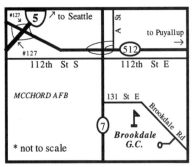

Directions: from I-5 N&S take exit #127
to Hwy 512E. Travel eastbound on Hwy
512 to Hwy 7. Exit at Hwy 7. Proceed
southbound on Hwy 7 for 1.3 miles to
131st Street. Go eastbound on 131st
Street for 1.3 miles to the golf course.
Note: 131st Street will be become
Brookdale Road. Look for signs marking
your way to the course.

Course Yardage & Par:
C-6435 yards, par 71.
M-6203 yards, par 71.
W-5833 yards, par 74.

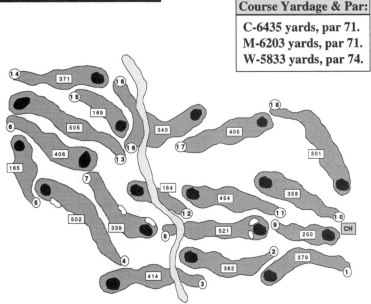

Buckskin Golf Club (public, 9 hole course)
2549 Aileron Street; P.O. Box 661; Richalnd,WA 99352
Phone: (509) 942-0888. Fax none. Internet: none.
Pro: Jeff Marcum, PGA. Superintendent: none.
Rating/Slope: the golf course is not rated yet. **Course record:** 33 (9 holes).
Green fees: $8 for 9 holes every day; M/C, VISA.
Power cart: $20/$10. **Pull cart:** $2. **Trail fee:** $5 for personal carts.
Reservation policy: walk-ons are welcome at any time.
Winter condition: the golf course is open all year long. Damp conditions.
Terrain: flat, easy walking. **Tees:** all grass. **Spikes:** soft spikes preferred.
Services: club rentals, lessons, pro shop, driving range, vending machine.
Comments: this new 9 hole executive course opened for play in late 1998. The
course features flat terrain medium size greens with few hazards. The resident
pro Jeff Marcum states that his course is playable and affordable for everyone.

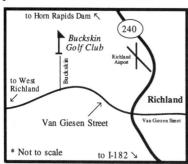

Directions: from Hwy 240 exit on Van
Giesen at the Van Giesen intersection.
Head westbound on Van Giesen to your
second right hand turn (this will be
Buckskin Street). Turn right on Buckskin. The pro shop is located 1000 yards
straight aheaaad. Look for signs.

Course Yardage & Par:
M-2600 yards, par 35.
W-2600 yards, par 35.
<ins>**Dual tees for 18 holes:**</ins>
M-4932 yards, par 67.
W-4932 yards, par 67.

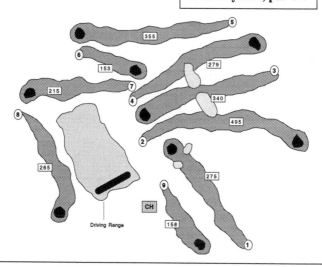

Camaloch Golf Club (public, 18 hole course, driving range)

326 NE Camano Drive; Camano Island, WA 98292
Phone: (360) 387-3084, 800-628-0469. Fax: (360) 387-9277. Internet: none.
PGA Director of Golf: Gary Schopf, PGA. Superintendent: Felix Rivera.
Rating/Slope: C 70.0/118; M 68.5/114; W 70.0/114. **Course record:** 65.
Green fees: W/D $19.75/$14.75; W/E & Hol. $27/$17.50; Jr/Sr rates (M-F).
Power cart: $20/$12. **Pull cart:** $3. **Trail fee:** $10 for personal carts. (add tax).
Reservation policy: reservations recommended, walk-ons are always welcome.
Winter condition: the course is open all year long. Dry, excellent drainage.
Terrain: 2 hills, very walkable. **Tees:** all grass. **Spikes:** metal spikes permitted.
Services: club rentals, lessons, cafe, beer/wine, pro shop, driving range.
Comments: This well maintained golf course lies in the sun belt of Washington
State. The area receives less rainfall than many places in western Washington. If
you want a dry course in winter, try Camaloch. Greens are well maintained and
putt very true. Great course that is worth the trip if in the area.

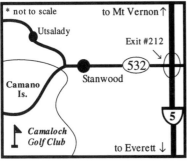

Directions: from I-5 N&S take exit #212
(Stanwood Hwy 532). Go west on Hwy
532 through Stanwood. Continue to the
golf course which will be on your left
hand side of the road. (The golf course
is located about 12 miles from I-5). The
course is very easy to find.

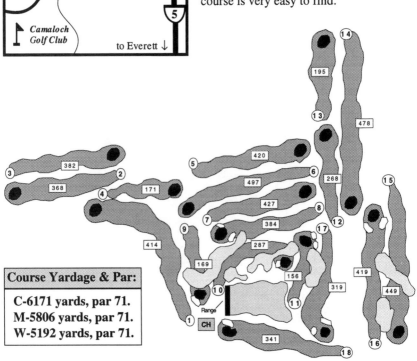

Course Yardage & Par:

C-6171 yards, par 71.
M-5806 yards, par 71.
W-5192 yards, par 71.

Canterwood Golf & Country -Club (private, 18 hole course)

4026 Canterwood Drive NW; Gig Harbor, WA 98335
Phone: (253) 851-1745. Fax: (253) 858-6329. Internet: cwgcc@earthlink.net
Pro: Mike Drake, PGA. Superintendent: Scott Young. Record: 64.
Rating/Slope: T 76.5/141; C 74.4/138; M 72.1/134; W 74.5/130.
Green fees: private club, members & guests only, reciprocates; VISA, MC.
Power cart: private club. **Pull cart:** private club. **Trail fee:** monthly basis.
Reservation policy: yes, members can call up to 1 week in advance.
Winter condition: the golf course is open all year long. Dry conditions.
Terrain: relatively hilly. **Tees:** all grass. **Spikes:** no metal spikes permitted.
Services: lessons, snack bar, restaurant, lounge, beer, wine, liquor, pro shop, lockers, showers, driving range, putting & chipping greens, banquet facilities.
Comments: very scenic, difficult golf course that has large undulating greens, bunkers and water hazards everywhere. This Robert Muir Graves designed track is nothing short of spectacular. Rated as one of the toughest courses in the state.

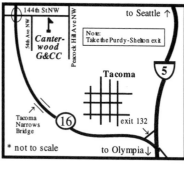

Directions: from I-5 N&S take exit #132 for Hwy 16W (Gig Harbor-Bremerton) Proceed to the Purdy exit and to 144th NW. Travel east for 1 mile to 54th. Turn south to the entrance to the Golf & Country Club. **Note:** look for signs to Canterwood G&CC indicating your turn.

Course Yardage & Par:

T-7175 yards, par 72.
C-6705 yards, par 72.
M-6245 yards, par 72.
W-5538 yards, par 73.

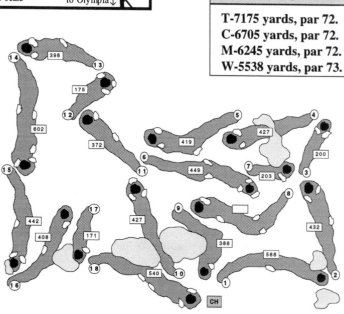

Canyon Lakes Golf Course (public, 18 hole course)
3700 West Canyon Lakes Drive; Kennewick, WA 99337
Phone: (509) 582-3736. **Fax:** (509) 585-0914. **Internet:** cybergolf/canyonlakes.com.
Dir. of Golf: Terry Graff, PGA. **Pros:** Wendy Rash PGA, Matt Mandell PGA.
Manager: Mike Lundgren. **Superintendent:** Kim Brock.
Rating/Slope: T 73.4/127; C 71.2/124; M 69.2/120; W 72.0/124. **Record:** 63.
Green fees: Mon.-Thur. $20; Fri. $25; W/E & Hol. $30. M/C, VISA, AMEX.
Power cart: $24/$12. **Pull cart:** $2. **Trail fee:** $8 for personal carts.
Reservation policy: please call up to 1 week in advance for your tee times.
Winter condition: course is open all year weather permitting. Dry conditions.
Terrain: relatively hilly. **Tees:** all grass. **Spikes:** no metal spikes permitted.
Services: club rentals, lessons, snack bar, restaurant, liquor, wine, beer, pro
shop, driving range, putting green. **Comments:** a links style course, Canyon
Lakes is set in the desert area of Eastern Washington. A challenging course
where water comes into play on many of the holes. One of the top ten public
courses in the Northwest that last year added an 18 hole putting course.
Be sure to make a special trip to Canyon Lakes, its simply a great golf course.

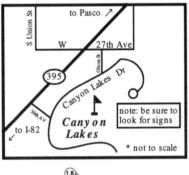

Directions: from Hwy 395S exit south
of Kennewick take 27th Street exit.
Proceed east to your second right and
the entrance to the golf course.

Course Yardage & Par:
T-6973 yards, par 72.
C-6505 yards, par 72.
M-6034 yards, par 72.
W-5565 yards, par 72.

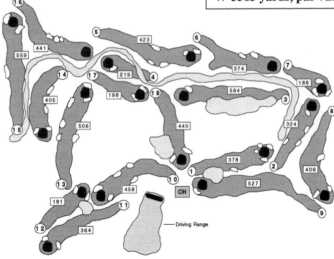

Capitol City Golf Club (public, 18 hole course)

5225 Yelm Highway SE; Lacey, WA 98513
Phone: (360) 491-5111. **Fax:** (360) 493-6067. **Internet: none.**
Manager: Darin Safford. Superintendent: Mark Biscay.
Rating/Slope: C 70.6/121; M 69.2/118; W 71.2/116. **Course record:** 62.
Green fees: W/D $18; W/E $23; Jr. & Sr. rates, (M-F). VISA, MC, AMEX.
Power cart: $22. **Pull cart:** $3. **Trail fee:** $8 for personal carts.
Reservation policy: yes, call up to 1 week in advance for all your tee-times.
Winter condition: the golf course is open all year long. Dry conditions.
Terrain: flat (easy walking). **Tees:** all grass. **Spikes:** metal spikes permitted.
Services: club rentals, lessons, lounge, beer, wine, pro shop, lockers, showers,
driving range, putting green. **Comments:** "One of the state's finest and driest
courses year round," beautiful view's of Mt. Rainier. Greens are kept in excellent condition throughout the season. Fantastic facility that is worth the trip.

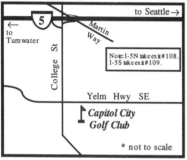

Directions: from I-5N exit #108 College
St. Proceed to College St. and take a right.
Follow College St. for 3 miles to the Yelm
Hwy. Take a left and follow for .4 miles
to the course which will be on your right.
From I-5S take exit #109. Take left on
College St. and follow the same directions.

Course Yardage & Par:
C-6536 yards, par 72.
M-6224 yards, par 72.
W-5510 yards, par 72.

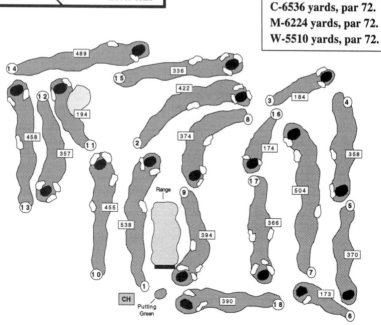

Carey Lakes Golf Course (public, 18 hole course)

1201 Umptanum Road; Ellensburg, WA 98926
Phone: (509) 962-5256. Fax: none. Internet: none
Manager: John W. Carey. Superintendent: John W. Carey.
Rating/Slope: the course has not been rated yet. **Course record:** 55.
Green fees: W/D $15/$9; W/E $15/$9; no credit cards.
Power cart: $10/$7.50. **Pull cart:** $2/$2. **Trail fee:** N/A.
Reservation policy: you may call ahead up to 7 days in advance.
Winter condition: the course is closed during the winter months.
Terrain: flat (easy walking). **Tees:** all grass. **Spikes:** soft spikes only.
Services: club rentals, lessons, snack bar, pro shop, driving range, state of the art practice facility. **Comments:** a friendly new course which promises to be a fast favorite with the locals. If you are making a quick trip through Ellensburg be sure to stop in at Carey Lakes for a quick round!

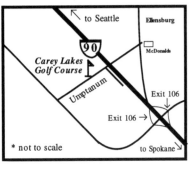

Directions: from I-90 take exit number 106. Proceed north 1/2 mile and turn left on Umptanum Road (road next to McDonalds). Travel west 1/2 mile to the course. Look for signs along the way.

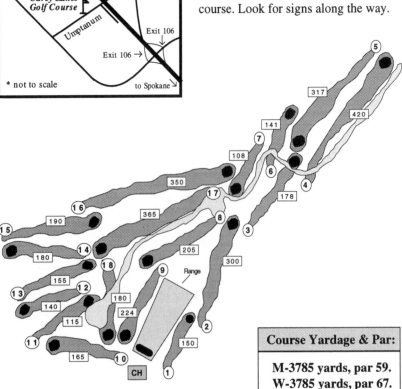

Course Yardage & Par:

M-3785 yards, par 59.
W-3785 yards, par 67.

Carnation Golf Course (public, 18 hole course)

1810 West Snoqualmie River Road NE; Carnation, WA 98014
Phone: (425)-333-4151, (206) 583-0314. Internet: www.carnationgolf.com
Director of Golf: Dan Tachell, PGA. Pro: Chad Tachell, PGA.
Tournament Director: Heidi Tachell. GM: Stephanie Tachell.
Rating/Slope: C 67.7/111; M 65.3/107; W 65.0/102. **Course record:** 64.
Green fees: W/D $22/$14; W/E. $25; Jr/Sr rates, Mon.-Friday; VISA, MC.
Power cart: $20/$12. **Pull cart:** $3. **Trail fee.** $5 for personal carts.
Reservation policy: yes, no time limit. Please call in advance for tee-times
Winter condition: the golf course is open all year long. Damp conditions.
Terrain: flat (easy walking). **Tees:** all grass. **Spikes:** metal spikes permitted.
Services: club rentals, lessons, driving range, restaurant, beer, wine, pro shop,
catering, memberships. **Comments:** the course is flat, easy to walk and in good
condition. It sits in a peaceful setting along the Snoqualmie River. Very friendly.

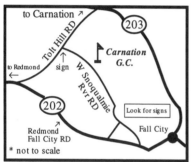

Directions: from I-5 N&S exit to 168B
(Hwy 520E). Proceed eastbound on Hwy
520 to Hwy 202 in Redmond (Redmond-
Fall City RD). Go east on Hwy 202 for 8
miles to Tolt Hill RD. Turn left on Tolt
Hill RD. Proceed for 2.5 miles. Take a
right on W Snoqualmie River Road NE.
The golf course will be located on your
left. Look for signs that are posted.

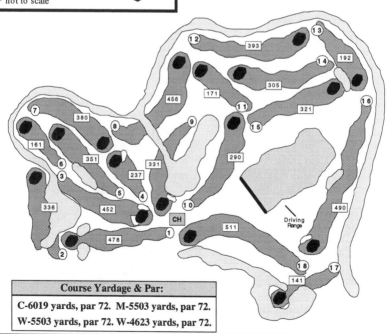

Course Yardage & Par:		
C-6019 yards, par 72. M-5503 yards, par 72.		
W-5503 yards, par 72. W-4623 yards, par 72.		

Cascade Golf Course (public, 9 hole course)
14303 436th Avenue SE; North Bend, WA 98045
Phone: (425) 888-0227. Fax: (425) 888-6600. Internet: none.
Owner/Manager/Superintendent: Leroy Jorgenson.
Rating/Slope: M 63/94; W 67.2/103. **Course record:** M 69; W 84.
Green fees: Weekdays $21/$13.50; Weekends $23/$15.50;
Jr. & Sr. rates $18/$11; winter rates $15/$10; M/C, VISA.
Power cart: $20/$12. **Pull cart:** $3. **Trail fee:** no charge personal carts.
Reservation policy: tee-times suggested March to October. Walk-ons welcome.
Winter condition: the course is open all year with extremely dry conditions.
Terrain: flat (easy walking). **Tees:** all grass. **Spikes:** metal spikes permitted.
Services: club rentals, restaurant, beer, snacks, beverages, espresso.
Comments: Excellent drainage provides dry fairways and greens for winter play. A friendly golf course where you can usually walk on during the week. Home of the "Tony Burger." Great family, beginner to intermediate course

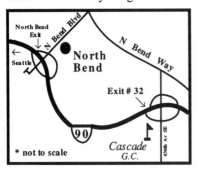

Directions: from I-90 E&W take exit #32 to 436th SE. Proceed for .1 mile to the course which will be on your right. The golf course is located 2 miles east of the city of the North Bend.

Course Yardage & Par:
Red Tees-2331 yards, par 36.
White Tees-2595 yards, par 36.
Blue Tees-2712 yards, par 36.
<u>**Dual tees for 18 holes:**</u>
Red Tees-4662 yards, par 72.
White Tees-5190 yards, par 72.
Blue Tees-5424 yards, par 72.

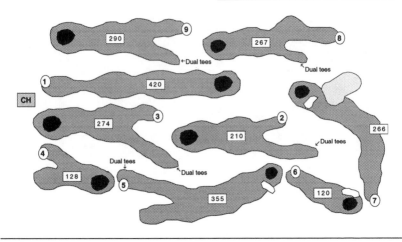

Cedarcrest Municipal Golf Course (public, 18 hole course)

6810 84th Street NE; Marysville, WA 98270
Phone: (360) 659-3566. Fax: none. Internet: none.
Pro: Don Shaw, PGA. Superintendent: Michael Robinson.
Rating/Slope: C 67.0/114; M 65.0/109; W 66.6/112 **Course record:** 63.
Green fees: $22/$16; Sr. rates $16/$12 (M-F); Jr. rates $10 (M-F).
Power cart: $20. **Pull cart:** $3. **Trail fee:** $7 for personal carts.
Reservation policy: yes, please call up to 1 week in advance for your tee-times.
Call Saturday for next Saturday & Sunday tee-times. A must during the summer.
Winter condition: the golf course is open all year long. Dry conditions.
Terrain: flat, some hills. **Tees:** all grass. **Spikes:** metal spikes permitted.
Services: club rentals, lessons, lockers, showers, pro shop. The restaurant will
be opening soon. **Comments:** well conditioned course that can offer a wide
variety of fairway lies and approach shots to greens. The golf course has been
remodeled and is much improved over the previous design. Great public track.

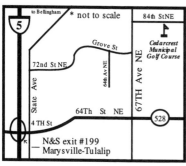

Directions: from I-5 N&S take exit
#199 (Marysville-Tulalip) to Hwy
528E (4th St.). Continue on 4th St
which becomes 64th St. NE. Proceed
to 67th Avenue NE. Turn left on 67th
Ave. Travel north on 67th until you
reach 84th St NE. Turn right on 84th.
The golf course will be on your right.

Course Yardage & Par:
C-5811 yards, par 70.
M-5381 yards, par 70.
W-4846 yards, par 70.

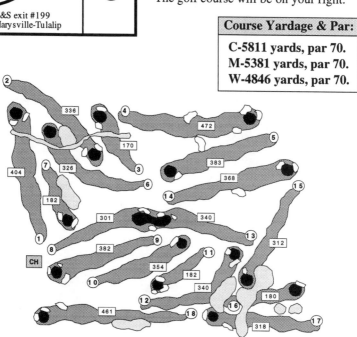

Cedars Golf Club (public, 18 hole course)

15001 NE 181 Street; Brush Prairie, WA 98606
Phone: (360) 687-4233. Fax: (360) 687-1554. Internet: none.
Pro: Ron Blum, PGA. Superintendent: Steve Brown.
Rating/Slope: C 71.3/127; M 69.9/125; W 71.7/117. **Course record:** 68.
Green fees: W/D $22/$12; W/E $24/$13; M/C, VISA.
Power cart: $22/$12. **Pull cart:** $2/$1.50. **Trail fee:** not allowed.
Reservation policy: yes, call up to 1 week in advance for your tee-times.
Winter condition: the golf course is open all year long. Wet conditions.
Terrain: flat, some slight hills. **Tees:** all grass. **Spikes:** metal spikes permitted.
Services: club rentals, lessons, restaurant, bar, lockers, showers, pro shop,
driving range, putting & chipping greens. **Comments:** picturesque setting, cedar
trees, lakes and trout stream surround challenging golf. Greens are well bunkered
and can putt very tough at times. Good course that can get very busy in summer.

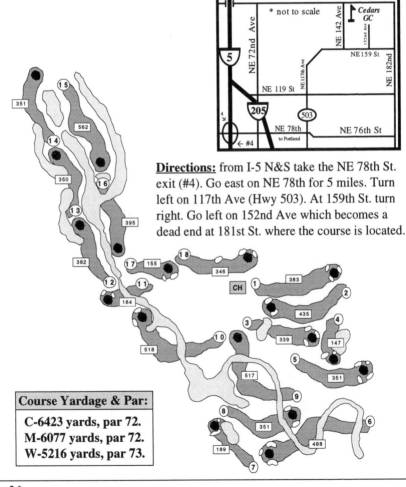

Directions: from I-5 N&S take the NE 78th St.
exit (#4). Go east on NE 78th for 5 miles. Turn
left on 117th Ave (Hwy 503). At 159th St. turn
right. Go left on 152nd Ave which becomes a
dead end at 181st St. where the course is located.

Course Yardage & Par:

C-6423 yards, par 72.
M-6077 yards, par 72.
W-5216 yards, par 73.

Centralia Public Golf Course (public, 9 hole course)

1012 Duffy Street; Centralia, WA 98531
Phone: (360) 736-5967. Fax: (360) 736-6909. Internet: none.
Owners: Michel & Renee Rey. Superintendent: Pete Holmstedt.
Rating/Slope: M 67.4/118; W 71.9/125. **Course record:** 32 (9 holes).
Green fees: W/D $10/$7; W/E $13/$10; Jr. rates $5; M/C, VISA.
Power cart: $16/$10. **Pull cart:** $2. **Trail fee:** $4 for personal carts.
Reservation policy: please call ahead for your tee-times. No time limit.
Winter condition: the golf course is open all year long. Dry conditions.
Terrain: relatively hilly, walkable. **Tees:** grass. **Spikes:** metal permitted.
Services: club rentals, beer, wine, liquor, restaurant, snack bar, limited pro shop.
Comments: tight fairways puts an emphasis on your shot placement. The golf course offers a dual tee layout for 18 hole play. Creeks come into play on several holes. Course is much improved with a new pond on the 8th hole.

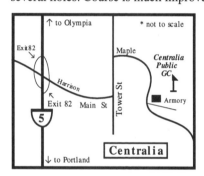

Directions: from I-5 N&S take the Centralia/Harrison Ave/Mellen Street. (exit #82) Follow the city center signs. Proceed to Tower Street and turn left (east). When you reach E Maple Street turn right. Go up the hill on Seminary Road, thru the intersection at the Armory, and down the hill to the golf course. Look for signs that are posted along the way.

Course Yardage & Par:
M-2826 yards, par 36.
W-2897 yards, par 37.
Dual tees for 18 holes:
M-5728 yards, par 72.
W-5405 yards, par 74.

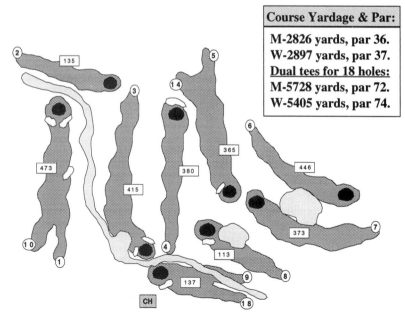

Chevy Chase Golf Club (public, 18 hole course)

7401 Cape George Road; Port Townsend, WA 98368
Phone: (360) 385-0704, 1-800-385-8722. Internet: www.chevychasegolf.com
Pro: to be determined. Superintendent: Scott Westwood.
Rating/Slope: C 71.5/120; M 68.1/113; W 69.2/111. **Record:** 68.
Green fees: W/D $22/$15; W/E $25/$17; twilight rates, Jr.& Sr. rates.
Power cart: $21/$15. **Pull cart:** $3/$2. **Trail fee:** $10. VISA, M/C is honored.
Reservation policy: yes, you may call 14 days in advance for your tee time.
Winter condition: the golf course is open all year long. Dry conditions.
Terrain: flat, some hills. **Tees:** all grass. **Spikes:** metal spikes permitted.
Services: club rentals, lessons, snack bar, beer, banquet room, pro shop, lockers, waterfront rental cabins, driving range. **Comments:** "one of the oldest courses in the state". The course recently opened its "Forest Nine" in May of 1997 to complement its "Farm Nine" and provides you with a challenging but user friendly course that is located in one of the most beautiful and peaceful settings in the "Sun Belt" of the Olympic Peninsula. With the historic Pt. Townsend and all of its victorian homes located just 7 miles away it is a perfect weekend spot.

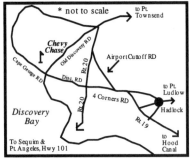

Directions: from the Hood Canal Bridge, go 5 miles. Turn right off Route 104 onto Route 19 at signs to Chimacum, Port Ludlow and Pt. Townsend. Go through Chimacum to Four Corners Rd. Take left on Four Corners Rd. Go straight to stop sign & Junction with Route 20 (Four Corners Store) Proceed straight ahead for 1 mile and take left at Cape George Rd. to the Chevy Chase Complex.

Course Yardage & Par:

C-6642 yards, par 72.
M-5925 yards, par 72.
W-5185 yards, par 72.

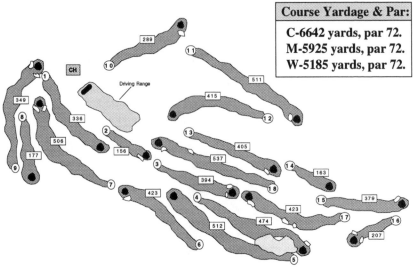

Chewelah Golf & Country Club (semi-private, 18 hole course)

P.O. Box 407; Sand Canyon Road; Chewelah, WA 99109
Phone: (509) 935-6807. Fax: (509) 935-8522. Internet: none.
Pro: Kim Walker, PGA. Superintendent: Bob McBride.
Rating/Slope: C 70.9/125; M 69.9/123; W 72.7/120. **Course record:** 64.
Green fees: W/D $14\$10; W/E $16/$12; Jr & Sr rates; M/C, VISA.
Power cart: $22/$12. **Pull cart:** $3. **Trail fee:** $4 for personal carts.
Reservation policy: call up to 7 days in advance for your tee times.
Winter condition: the golf course is closed from mid November to March.
Terrain: flat. **Tees:** all grass. **Spikes:** no metal spikes permitted.
Services: club rentals, lessons, snack bar, pro shop, beverage cart, driving range
putting green, tennis courts, RV park. **Comments:** narrow fairways, numerous
sand traps trees, and three ponds make this course play difficult. Well run golf
course that offers a real challenge for every caliber of golfer. Worth a trip.

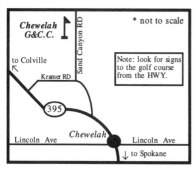

Directions: from Spokane travel on
Hwy 395N for approximately 45 miles
to Chewelah Washington. When in
Chewelah look for and follow signs to
the golf course.

Course Yardage & Par:
C-6531 yards, par 72.
M-6161 yards, par 72.
W-5637 yards, par 74.

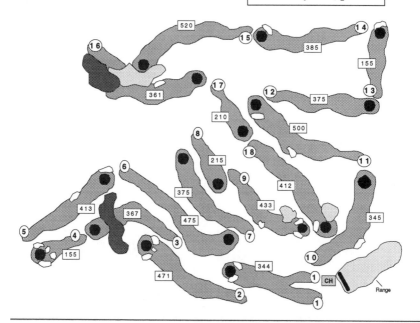

Christy's Golf Range & Par 3 (public, 9 hole par 3 course)

37712 28th Avenue South; Federal Way, WA 98003
Phone: (253) 927-0644. **Fax:** none. **Internet:** none.
Pros: Robert & Dave Christy. **Superintendent:** N/A.
Rating/Slope: the golf course is not rated. **Course record:** 24.
Green fees: W/D $11/$6; W/E $13/$7; Sr rates.
Power cart: not available. **Pull cart:** $1.50. **Trail fee:** not allowed.
Reservation policy: tee times are on a first come first served basis.
Terrain: flat, some hills. **Tees:** grass and mats. **Spikes:** metal spikes permitted.
Services: club rentals, lessons, full service pro shop, excellent driving range.
Comments: challenging par 3 golf course that is great for the whole family.
Great course to practice your short irons on. Excellent on course pro shop that
will service all your golfing needs. The facility also includes a lighted and
covered driving range that is open seven days a week.

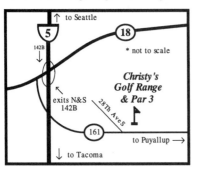

Directions: from I-5 N&S take exit 142B.
Proceed westbound for .2 miles to Hwy
161S. Turn south for 1.6 miles to 28th
Avenue South. Turn left on 28th Avenue
South to the golf course. Look for a sign.

Course Yardage & Par:
M-905 yards, par 27.
W-905 yards, par 27.

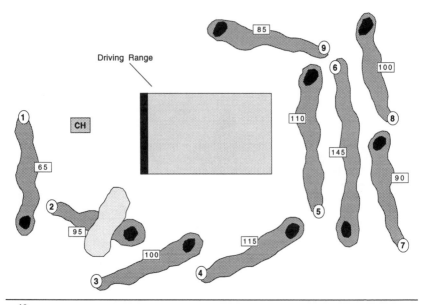

Clarkston Golf & Country Club (private, 18 hole course)
1676 Elm Street; Clarkston, WA 99403
Phone: (509) 758-7911. Fax: (509) 751-9229. Internet: none.
Pro: Vicki Mallea, PGA. Superintendent: Mike Waisanen.
Rating/Slope: C 72.0/120; M 71.3/118; W 71.1/120. **Course record:** 63.
Green fees: private club, members & guests only; reciprocates; VISA, M/C.
Power cart: private club, members only. **Pull cart:** private. **Trail fee:** private.
Reservation policy: yes, please call up to 1 week in advance for members.
Winter condition: the golf course is open weather permitting. Dry conditions.
Terrain: flat, some hills. **Tees:** all grass. **Spikes:** metal spikes not permitted.
Services: club rentals, lessons, restaurant, lounge, beer, wine, liquor, lockers, showers, driving range. **Comments:** beautiful setting along the Snake River with the Palouse Mountains nearby. Water, trees and well bunkered greens abound. This well kept private facility will test your skill at every turn.

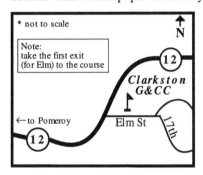

Directions: travel to Clarkston via Hwy 12. The golf course is located north of Clarkston near Hwy 12 which parallels the golf course. Take the first exit (for Elm Street) to the golf course.

Course Yardage & Par:
T-6650 yards, par 72.
C-6470 yards, par 72.
M-5920 yards, par 72.
W-5432 yards, par 72.

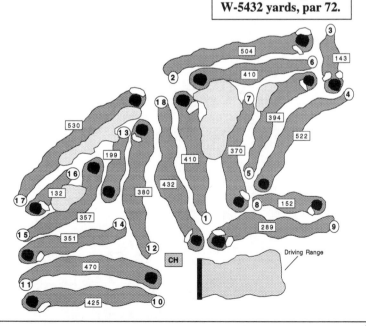

Classic Country Club (public, 18 hole course, driving range)
4908 208th Street East; Spanaway, WA 98387; Internet: classiccc@att.net
Phone: (253) 847-4440; (206) 622-4653. Fax: (206) 846-9868.
Manager/Pro: Russ Olsen, PGA. Superintendent: Pete Echols.
Rating/Slope: C 72.8/135; M 71.2/131; W 72.7/128. **Course record:** 67.
Green fees: April 1st to Sep. 30th W/D $30/$15, W/E & Holidays $45/$25.50;
October to March 31st W/D $20/$15; W/E & Holidays $30/$15; Twilight $15,
Jr. & Sr. rates $18 (Monday through Wednesday), AMEX, MC, VISA.
Power cart: $25/$15. **Pull cart:** $5/$3. **Trail fee:** $25/$15 for personal carts.
Reservation policy: yes, please call 7 days in advance for your tee times.
Winter condition: the golf course is open all year long. Dry conditions.
Terrain: flat, some hills. **Tees:** all grass. **Spikes:** soft spikes preferred.
Services: club rentals, lessons, snack bar, restaurant, beer, wine, pop, pro shop,
lockers, showers, excellent driving range, putting green & chipping green.
Comments: *Golf Digest* magazine rated the Classic Country Club #7 in the state
of Washington on their list of America's best 500 places to play in 1996. This
course is worth a special trip at anytime during the year. Excellent golf course.

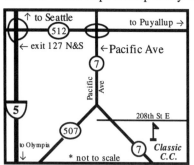

Directions: from I-5 N&S take exit #127
to Hwy 512. Follow Hwy 512 to Hwy 7.
Exit to Hwy 7 southbound. Follow Hwy 7
south until you reach 208th St. E go left.
The course is located 2 miles ahead on the
right.

Course Yardage & Par:
C-6793 yards, par 72.
M-6387 yards, par 72.
M-6008 yards, par 72.
W-5580 yards, par 72.

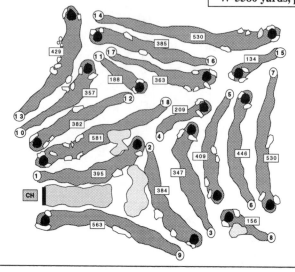

Clover Valley Golf Course (public, 18 hole course)

5180 Country Club Way SE; Port Orchard, WA 98366
Phone: (360) 871-2236. Fax: none. Internet: none.
Pro: to be determined. Superintendent: to be determined.
Rating/Slope: M 64.9/102; W 66.8/106. Course record: 63.
Green fees: W/D $12.50/$9; W/E $16/$11; Jr. and Sr. rates; VISA, MC.
Power Cart: $18/$10. Pull Cart: $3. Trail fee: none.
Reservation policy: yes, call in advance for a tee time (no restrictions).
Winter Condition: the golf course is open all year long. Wet conditions.
Terrain: flat with some hills. Tees: grass. Spikes: metal spikes permitted.
Services: banquet hall, snack bar, beer, pro shop, driving range, putting green.
Comments: located near Bremerton in Port Orchard on the Olympic Peninsula. Water comes into play on several holes throughout the course. Very friendly course that has improved every year. The facility now sports an on course range. The 9th hole, a 228 yard par 3 is one of the toughest par 3's you will ever find.

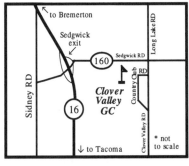

Directions: from Hwy 16 take the Port Orchard-Sedgwick Road (Hwy 160) exit. Proceed 3 miles on Sedgwick Road until you reach Long Lake Road then turn right. While on Long Lake Road take your first right onto Country Club Way to the golf course. **Note:** look for signs from Hwy 16 indicating the exit to the golf course.

Course Yardage & Par:

M-5341 yards, par 69.
W-4824 yards, par 70.

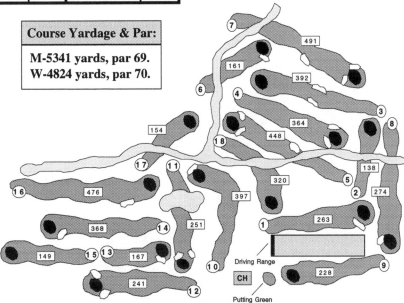

Club Green Meadows (private, 18 hole course)

7703 NE 72nd Avenue; Vancouver, WA 98661
Phone: (360) 256-1510, (503) 230-1461. Fax: (360) 256-1596.
Pro: Ross Thurik, PGA. Superintendent: Phil Taylor.
Rating/Slope: C 70.9/119; M 70.0/117; W 73.4/125. **Course record:** 63.
Green fees: private club, members & guests only; reciprocates.
Power cart: private club. **Pull cart:** private club. **Trail fee:** private club.
Reservation policy: private club, reservations for members & guests only.
Winter condition: the golf course is open all year long. Damp conditions.
Terrain: flat (easy walking). **Tees:** all grass. **Spikes:** metal spikes permitted.
Services: lessons, snack bar, lounge, restaurant, beer, wine, liquor, pro shop.
Comments: course has narrow tree lined fairways with ponds and greenside
bunkers coming into play on nearly every hole. Athletic club is on site.

Directions: from I-5 N&S take exit #4
to NE 78th. Go east on NE 78th to NE
72nd Ave. Go south on NE 72nd Ave.
While on NE 72nd Ave. turn east to the
golf course. From I-205 N&S take exit
#32. Go west on NE 83rd. Take a left on
Andersen RD. When you reach NE 78th
St. turn left. Proceed to 72nd Avenue NE
turn right.

Course Yardage & Par:

C-6486 yards, par 72.
M-6246 yards, par 72.
W-5831 yards, par 76.

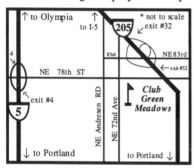

Colfax Golf Club (public, 9 hole course)
off Cedar Street; Route 1, Box 46-A; Colfax, WA 99111
Phone: (509) 397-2122. **Fax:** none. **Internet:** none.
Pro: Craig Gronning. **Superintendent:** Mark Black.
Rating/Slope: M 67.9/117; W 70.9/115. **Course record:** M/63; W/73.
Green fees: $18/$12 all week long; $12 Mondays (all day); no credit cards.
Power cart:$18/$10. **Pull cart:** $1.50. **Trail fee:** $5 for personal carts.
Reservation policy: yes, for weekend play only. Call 1 week in advance.
Winter condition: the golf course is open all year long, dry conditions.
Terrain: flat (easy walking). **Tees:** grass. **Spikes:** no metal spikes permitted.
Services: club rentals, lessons, pro shop, driving range net, putting green.
Comments: easily walked golf course. The atmosphere is friendly and
casual. Dual tees available for a full 18 hole round. The Palouse River
borders the course. Be straight off the tee as out of bounds borders nearly
every hole on this golf course.

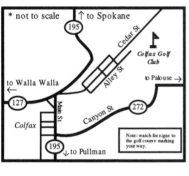

Directions: from Hwy 195 take the Cedar
Street exit and travel east bound to the
golf course. The golf course is located
slightly north of the city of Colfax,
Washington. **Note:** look for signs from
the Highway indicating your turn to the
golf course.

Course Yardage & Par:

M-3010 yards, par 35.
W-2817 yards, par 36.
Dual tees for 18 holes:
M-5907 yards, par 70.
W-5556 yards, par 72.

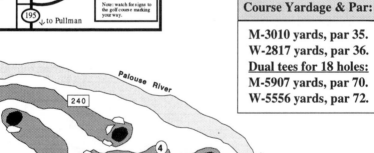

Columbia Park Golf Course (public, 18 hole course)

Physical address: 2701 West Columbia Drive; Kennewick, WA 99336
Mailing address: 505 South Authur Place; Kennewick, WA 99336
Phone: (509) 585-4423. **Fax:** none. **Internet:** none.
Pro: Dale Schoner, PGA. **Superintendent:** Dale Schoner.
Rating/Slope: M 51.1/079; W 51.1/079. **Course record:** 47.
Green fees: W/D $10/$7; W/E $11/$8; Jr. & Sr. rates; no credit cards.
Power cart: not available. **Pull cart:** $2. **Trail fee:** not allowed.
Reservation policy: yes, taken for weekends, 1 week in advance.
Winter condition: the course is open weather permitting. Dry conditions.
Terrain: very flat. **Tees:** grass and mats. **Spikes:** metal spikes permitted.
Services: club rentals, driving range, pro shop, lessons, snack bar.
Comments: the course is near the Columbia River which can be seen from nearly every tee. Greens are on the small size and are firm. The golf course is flat & easy to walk. Great course for seniors or to practice your iron play.

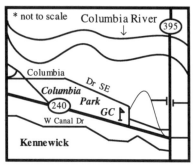

Directions: from Hwy 395 take the Columbia Park exit. Go to Columbia Drive and turn left. Proceed for 1 mile to the course which will be on your left. If you are coming from I-82 take the Columbia Park exit and proceed to the golf course. Look for signs marking your way to the golf course.

Course Yardage & Par:
M-2682 yards, par 55.
W-2682 yards, par 55.

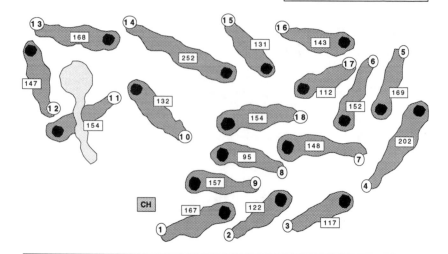

Columbia Point Golf Course (public, 18 hole course)

225 Columbia Point Drive; Richland, WA 99352

Phone: (509) 946-0710. **Fax:** (509) 946-1930. **Internet:** cybergolf.com/columbiapoint/.
Pro: Joe Creager, PGA. **Superintendent:** Bob Weitz.
Rating/Slope: T 70.0/121; C 67.1/114; M 64.2/105; W 65.9/107. **Record:** 65.
Green fees: M-Th $20; Fri. $25; W/E $30; W/D 9/twilight $15;
W/E 9/twilight $20; Jr.'s $14/$8 (M-Th); Sr.'s $16/$10 (M-Th); after 3pm W/E).
Power cart: $12/$8. **Pull cart:** $3/$2. **Trail fee:** $8 for personal carts.
Reservation policy: please call up to 10 days in advance for your tee time.
Winter condition: the course is open weather permitting. Dry conditions.
Terrain: flat some hills. **Tees:** grass. **Spikes:** metal spikes not permitted.
Services: club rentals, lessons, lounge, restaurant, beer, wine, liquor, pro shop,
lockers, driving range, putting green. **Comments:** Columbia Point features
beautifully manicured fairways and greens. With a staff dedicated to player
satisfaction this course is sure to please. This championship 18 hole course,
beautiful clubhouse, and practice facility is a perfect setting to enjoy great golf
and nearly 300 days of sunshine a year. Worth a trip if in the Tri-City area.

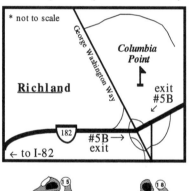

Directions: When in Richland exit off
of either Hwy 182 or Hwy 240 on to
George Washington Way. At the first
stop light turn right on Columbia Point
Drive. The clubhouse is 1 mile up on
your right. From I-82 take exit #5-B and
head north on George Washington Way.
Then follow the above directions

Course Yardage & Par:

T-6555 yards, par 72.
C-6038 yards, par 72.
M-5365 yards, par 72.
W-4651 yards, par 72.

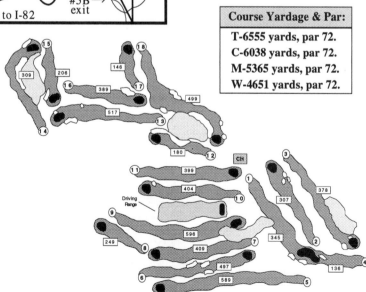

Colville Elks Golf Course (public, 9 hole course)
1861 East Hawthorne; P. O. Box 367; Colville, WA 99114
Phone: (509) 684-5508. Fax: none. Internet: none.
Pro: Andy Hite, PGA. Superintendent: Ron Arnold.
Rating/Slope: M 69.3/115; W 73.6/122. **Course record:** 62.
Green fees: $14/$10 all week long; no special rates; no credit cards.
Power cart: $20/$10. **Pull cart:** $2.50. **Trail fee:** $2 for personal carts.
Reservation policy: tee-times are on a first come first served basis.
Winter condition: the golf course is closed from November 1st until thaw.
Terrain: flat, some hills. **Tees:** all grass. **Spikes:** metal spikes permitted.
Services: club rentals, lessons, snack bar, beer, restaurant, lounge, pro shop,
lockers, showers, driving range. **Comments:** This eastern Washington course
is well conditioned and plays much tougher than the yardage would indicate.
The golf course will be expanding to 18 holes in the future. Alternating tees.

Directions: from Spokane travel N on
Hwy 395 through Chewelah to Colville.
Go east on Hawthorne Avenue. While
traveling on Hawthorne Avenue you will
go up a hill then you will proceed to the
golf course. Look for signs marking your
way to the golf course.

Course Yardage & Par:

M-3125 yards, par 36.
W-2865 yards, par 36.
Dual tees for 18 holes:
M-6330 yards, par 72.
W-5990 yards, par 73.

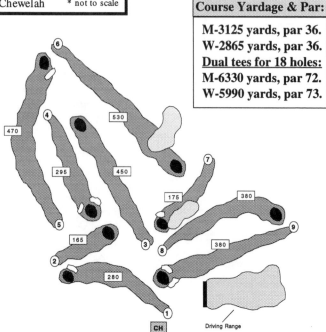

Course at Taylor Creek, The (public, 9 hole course)
21401 244th Avenue SE; Maple Valley, WA 98038
Phone: (425) 413-1900. **Fax:** (425) 432-1456. **Internet: none.**
Manager: Brad Habenicht. **Superintendent:** Brett Ticehurst.
Rating/Slope: C 66.6/122; M 63.6/109; W 62.8/105. **Course record:** 63.
Green fees: W/D $22/$14; W/E $28/$16; Jr. & Sr. $18/$12; twilight $10.
Power cart: $10/$5 per person. **Pull cart:** $3. **Trail fee:** $5 for personal carts.
Reservation policy: please call in advance for a tee time. Walk-ons welcome.
Winter condition: the course is open all year long. Very dry conditions.
Terrain: rolling hills. **Tees:** all grass. **Spikes:** no spike restrictions.
Services: restaurant, pro shop, covered and heated 16 stall driving range.
Comments: This 9-hole Scottish-links designed course plays exceptionally dry all year round. This unique layout features picturesque grass mounding and requires a variety of different shots. The golf course surrounds the Olson Mansion, a King County Historical Landmark built in 1908, which is available for receptions and business meeting functions. Excellent newer golf course.

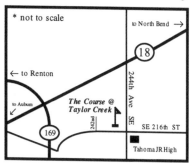

Directions: from Hwy 18 northbound (toward North Bend) or southbound (toward Auburn) turn eastbound on 244th Avenue SE. Proceed to the golf course entrance that will be located on your right hand side. Look for signs.

Course Yardage & Par:
C-2705 yards, par 35.
M-2437 yards, par 35.
W-2130 yards, par 35.

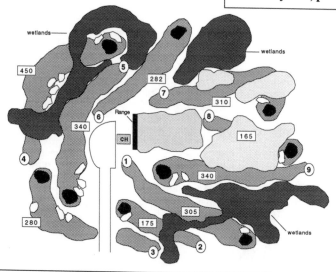

Creek at Qualchan, The (public, 18 hole course)

301 East Meadow Lane Road; Spokane, WA 99204
Phone: (509) 448-9317. Fax: none. Internet: none.
Pro: Mark Gardner, PGA. Superintendent: Mark Nord.
Rating/Slope: C 71.6/127; M 69.9/123; W 72.3/126. **Course record:** 66.
Green fees: $22/$16 all week long; $16 with discount card; Jr & Sr rates M-F.
Power cart: $22. **Pull cart:** $2. **Trail fee:** $9 for personal carts.
Reservation policy: W/D call 1 day in advance. W/E call 1 week in advance.
Winter condition: the course is closed during winter. November to March.
Terrain: very hilly. **Tees:** all grass. **Spikes:** soft spikes preffered.
Services: club rentals, lessons, restaurant, beer, wine, pro shop, driving range.
Comments: the facility opened in spring of 1993. The golf course features
bunkers, 5 ponds, and a creek wandering through. Excellent newer golf course
that will challenge you at every turn. Worth a trip if in the Spokane area.

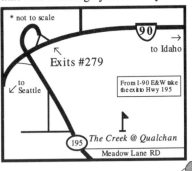

Directions: From I-90 E&W (#279) exit
to Hwy 195 and proceed southbound.
Turn eastbound on Meadow Lane Road.
Follow this to the golf course. Look for
signs that are posted along the way.

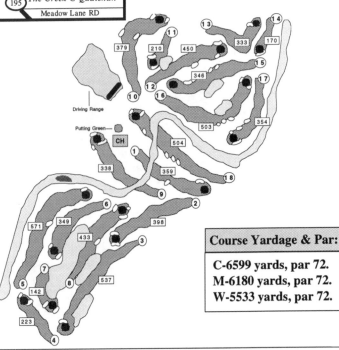

Course Yardage & Par:

C-6599 yards, par 72.
M-6180 yards, par 72.
W-5533 yards, par 72.

Crescent Bar Resort (public, 9 hole course)

8894 Crescent Bar Road NW; Suite 1; Quincy, WA 98848
Phone: (509) 787-1511, 1-800-824-7090. Fax: none. Internet: none.
Manager: Gil Stewart. Superintendent: unavailable.
Rating/Slope: C 68.8/108; M 68.4/107; W 72.4/118. **Course record:** 67.
Green fees: $22/$17 all week long; Sr rates (Mondays only); VISA, M/C.
Power cart: $21/$16. **Pull cart:** $4/$3. **Trail fee:** $5; seasonal rates available.
Reservation policy: please call up to 1 week in advance for tee times.
Winter condition: the golf course is open all year long weather permitting.
Terrain: flat, easy walking. **Tees:** all grass. **Spikes:** soft spikes only.
Services: club rentals, lessons, restaurant, cafe, lounge, store, pro shop, driving range, tennis courts, marina, campground. **Comments:** well-designed course with bunkers, water and rough. Accommodates both low and high handicappers. Good eastern Washington course set on an island in the Columbia River.

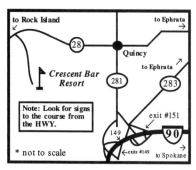

Directions: from I-90 E&W take exit #149 to Hwy 281 to Quincy. When you reach Hwy 28 turn left and go west on Hwy 28. Proceed on Hwy 28 for 7.1 miles to Crescent Bar RD and turn left. **Note:** look for the sign on the highway marking your turn to the course.

Course Yardage & Par:
C-3034 yards, par 35.
M-2944 yards, par 35.
W-2844 yards, par 36.
<u>Dual tees for 18 holes:</u>
C-6068 yards, par 70.
M-5978 yards, par 70.
W-5788 yards, par 72.

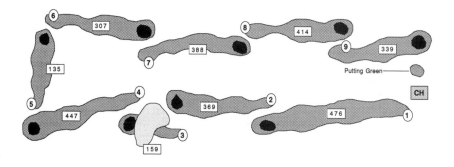

Crossroads Park Golf Course (public, 9 hole par 3 course)
16000 NE 10th; Bellevue, WA 98008
Phone: (425) 452-4875. **Fax:** none. **Internet:** none.
Pro: Joe Torrontegui. **Manager:** Ted Mittelstaedt.
Rating/Slope: the golf course is not rated. **Course record:** 21.
Green fees: $5 for 9 holes all week long; Jr & Sr rates (weekdays only).
Power cart: not available. **Pull cart:** not available. **Trail fee:** not available.
Reservation policy: none needed, all times are on a first come first served basis.
Winter condition: the golf course is closed December 1st through February 1st.
Terrain: flat, some slight hills. **Tees:** all mats. **Spikes:** metal spikes permitted.
Services: club rentals, lessons, snack machines, pop, putting/chipping green.
Comments: good golf course to take a young family member to learn the game
of golf. The atmoshpere is very casual with no pressure on having to play fast.
Holes range from 64 to 107 yards and is not overly difficult.

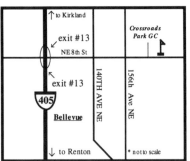

Directions: from I-405 N&S take the NE
8th exit eastbound. Follow NE 8th to
160th Avenue NE and turn left. The pro
shop is located inside of the Community
Center at the end of 160th Avenue NE,
just east of the Crossroads Mall. Look for
signs indicating your turn to the course.

Course Yardage & Par:
M-837 yards, par 27.
W-837 yards, par 27.

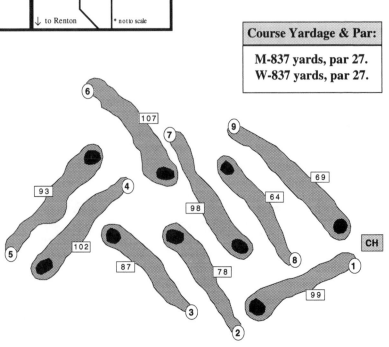

Dakota Creek Golf & Country Club (public, 18 hole course)
3258 Haynie Road; Custer, WA 98240
Phone: (360) 366-3131. **Fax:** unavailable. **Internet:** none.
Owner: Pam Foster. **Superintendent:** Jamie Boyer.
Rating/Slope: M 64.3/103; W 67.5/112. **Course record:** 67.
Green fees: W/D $15/$10; W/E $20/$12; M/C, VISA.
Power cart: $16/$8. **Pull cart:** $1.50. **Trail fee:** no charge.
Reservation policy: call ahead during the summer months.
Winter condition: the golf course is open all year long. Dry conditions.
Terrain: some hills. **Tees:** all grass. **Spikes:** metal spikes permitted.
Services: snack bar, pro shop, chipping green. **Comments:** tough, challenging and fun, all holes different. Casual atmosphere track that opened new 9 holes in July 1998. The new 9 is playable for all levels of golfers. Excellent, well kept golf course that is worth the trip. You will not be disappointed.

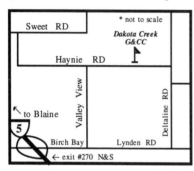

Directions: from I-5 N&S exit #270 to Birch Bay-Lynden Road turn right go for 100' and turn left on Valley View. Follow Valley View until you reach Haynie Road. Turn right on Haynie Road and proceed to the golf course.

Course Yardage & Par:
M-5185 yards, par 71.
W-4803 yards, par 71.

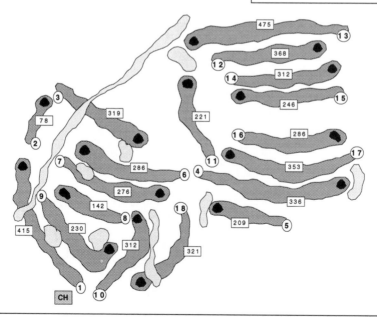

Deer Meadows Golf Course (public, 9 hole course)

Route 1; Box 203; Davenport, WA 99122
Phone: (509) 725-8488. **Fax:** none. **Internet:** none.
Manager: Charles Spencer. **Superintendent:** N/A.
Rating/Slope: M 68.8/112; W 68.1/113.
Green fees: W/D $12/$9; W/E $12/$9; call for special green fee rates.
Power cart: $20/$15. **Pull cart:** $2. **Trail fee:** not allowed.
Reservation policy: please call up to 1 day in advance for tee times.
Winter Condition: the golf course is closed from November to March.
Terrain: flat, some hills. **Tees:** grass. **Spikes:** metal spikes permitted.
Services: club rentals, pro shop, driving range. **Comments:** newer 9 hole course that opened the 1st 9 in April of 1995. The course offers the golfer modest length and challenging terrain. Plans include an additional 9 holes (due to open sometime in 2000) a clubhouse and other services in the future. Very friendly facility.

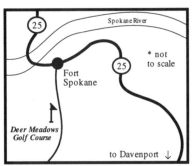

Directions: the golf course is located south of Fort Spokane off of Hwy 25. From Davenport follow Hwy 25 north toward Fort Spokane. When in Fort Spokane turn southboound on Miles Creston Road. The course will be located on your right hand side. Look for a sign marking your turn to the golf course.

Course Yardage & Par:
M-3082 yards, par 36.
W-3000 yards, par 36.

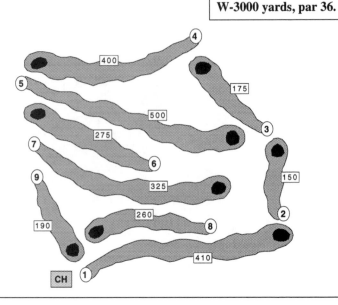

Deer Park Golf Club (semi-private, 18 hole course)
N 1201 Country Club Drive; Deer Park, WA 99006
Phone: (509) 276-5912. **Fax:** (509) 276-5806. **Internet:** none.
Pro: Craig Schuh. **Superintendent:** Jim Jenson. **Course record:** 61.
Rating/Slope: C 71.2/114; M 69.0/110; W 69.9/110.
Green fees: Monday-Thur. $16/$10; Friday & W/E's $21/$14.
Power cart: $23/$12. **Pull cart:** $2. **Trail fee:** $7 for personal carts.
Reservation policy: call Saturday to make your T-time for the following week.
Winter Condition: golf course is closed from November to February or March.
Terrain: flat, some hills. **Tees:** all grass. **Spikes:** soft spikes preferred.
Services: club rentals, lessons, lounge, restuarant, snack bar, beer, wine, liquor, pro shop, driving range. **Comments:** new desert design with 4 lakes, ponds and streams. Waste bunkers and other traps are in play on nearly every hole. Very scenic course that will be enjoyable for all. Great course, worth a special trip.

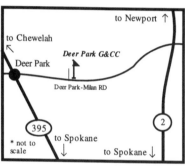

Directions: from I -90 take the exit for Hwy 395 (Division Street) Proceed north on Hwy 395 toward Deer Park. When you get to Crawford turn east. Proceed to Country Club Drive where you will turn north to the course. Look for signs.

Course Yardage & Par:
C-6750 yards, par 72.
M-6340 yards, par 72.
W-5615 yards, par 72.

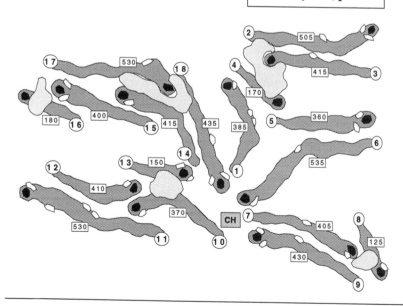

Delphi Golf Course (public, 9 hole course)

6340 Neylon Drive SW; Olympia, WA 98512
Phone: (360) 357-6437. Fax: none. Internet: none.
Manager: Rich Williams. Superintendent: David Thietje.
Rating/Slope: M 61.4/102; W 61.8/102. **Course record:** 27 (9 holes).
Green fees: W/D $15/$10; W/E $16.50/$11; Jr. & Sr. rates are available,
twlight rates are available; VISA, M/C, AMEX, Discover.
Power cart: $15/$10. **Pull cart:** $2.50. **Trail fee:** $5 for personal carts.
Reservation policy: yes, reservations are taken, no time limit.
Winter Condition: the golf course is open all year long, drains very well.
Terrain: a few hills, but the course is very walkable. **Tees:** all grass.
Spikes: metal spikes permitted. **Services:** club rentals, pro shop.
Comments: residential course. Beautiful setting with narrow tree-lined fairways
on every hole. This track is in excellent condition throughout the season. Lots of
new drainage adds to the playability during the winter months. Fun course.

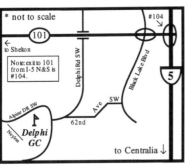

Directions: from I-5 N&S exit to Hwy
101 (exit #104) in Olympia. Follow 101
and exit at Black Lake Blvd. (which
becomes 62nd Ave. SW). Go south on
Black Lake Blvd to Delphi Road. Turn
left on Delphi Road to Alpine Dr. SW,
right to the golf course. Look for signs.

Course Yardage & Par:
M-1937 yards, par 32.
W-1789 yards, par 34.

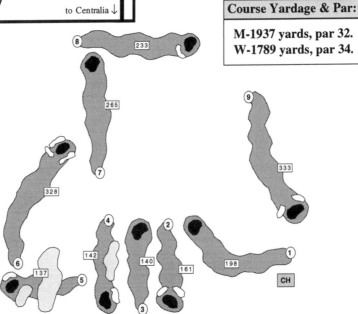

Desert Aire Golf Course (semi-private, 18 hole course)

505 Clubhouse Way West; Desert Aire, WA 99349
Phone: (509) 932-4439. **Fax:** (509) 932-5844. **Internet:** none.
Pro: Bo Krause. **Superintendent:** James Crudy.
Rating/Slope: M 69.0/111; W 71.9/111. **Course record:** M 65/ W 75.
Green fees: W/D $20/$16; W/E $24/$16; Sr. & twilight rates (May-September).
Power cart: W/D $24/$14; W/E $24/$14. **Pull cart:** $3/$2. **Trail fee:** $5.
Reservation policy: yes, please call 7 days in advance for tee-times.
Winter condition: dry conditions. The course is usually open during the winter.
Terrain: flat, some hills. **Tees:** all grass. **Spikes:** soft spikes only.
Services: club rentals, snack bar, pro shop, driving range, beer, wine, lessons, RV spots, memberships are available. **Comments:** the course is fairly wide open with a beautiful view of the Columbia River and surrounding countryside. The golf course can play very difficult if the wind picks up. Fair golf course.

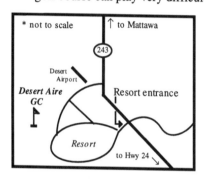

Directions: from I-90 E&W take exit to Hwy 243S towards Mattawa. The course is located 5 miles south of Mattawa off of Hwy 243. Go through the resort to Clubhouse Way. Turn right on Clubhouse Way and proceed to the clubhouse and the golf course. Look for signs marking your way.

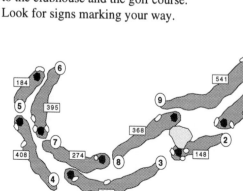

Course Yardage & Par:
M-6501 yards, par 72.
W-5786 yards, par 73.

Desert Canyon Golf Resort (public, resort 18 hole course)
1201 Desert Canyon Boulevard; Orondo, WA 98843
Phone:(509) 784-1111, 800-258-4173. **Fax:** (509) 784-2701.
Dir. of Golf: Jack Frei. Pro: Von Smith, PGA. Internet: www.desertcanyon.com.
Rating/Slope: T 74.0/127; C 72.4/121; M 68.2/108; W 67.5/104. **Record:** 65.
Green fees: July 1st-Oct. 14th Mon.-Th. $65, Friday-Sunday $75; M/C, VISA.
Power cart: included in green fee. **Pull cart:** none. **Trail fee:** not allowed.
Reservation policy: yes, please call 7 days in advance for all your tee-times.
30 days in advance with pre payment made by a major credit card.
Winter condition: the golf course is open, weather permitting.
Terrain: rolling hills. **Tees:** all grass tees. **Spikes:** soft spikes required.
Services: club rentals, full service resort facilities, driving range, pro shop.
Comments: This is a desert style, links course with spectacular views of the
Columbia River. The facilty was recently ranked #2 in the state of Washington
by *Golf Digest*. It was also ranked #35 in Americas top 75 upscale golf courses
to play. This is simply a must play and is well worth the price of admission.

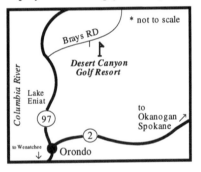

Directions: the course is located on the
east side of the Columbia River off of
Hwy 97 (not Alt. Hwy 97 on the
westside), 6.5 miles north of Orondo.
From Hwy 97 turn eastbound on Brays
Road. Go 3/4 of a mile to the entrance.

Course Yardage & Par:
T-6923 yards, par 72.
C-6894 yards, par 72.
M-6181 yards, par 72.
W-5515 yards, par 72.

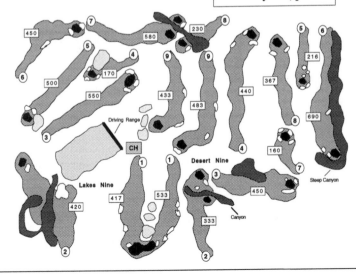

Downriver Golf Course (public, 18 hole course)

3225 Columbia Circle; Spokane, WA 99205
Phone: (509) 327-5269. **Fax:** none. **Internet:** none.
Pro: Steve Conner, PGA. **Superintendent:** Bob Mielke.
Rating/Slope: M 68.8/115; W 72.8/118. **Course record:** 60.
Green fees: $18.50/$13.50 all week long; Jr.'s $8; VISA, M/C.
Power cart: $23. **Pull cart:** $3. **Trail fee:** $8 for personal carts.
Reservation policy: weekdays call 1 day in advance, weekends-previous Sat.
Winter condition: the golf course is closed during the winter months.
Terrain: flat, some hills. **Tees:** all grass. **Spikes:** soft spikes preferred.
Services: club rentals, lessons, restaurant, snack bar, beer, wine, beverages,
pro shop, lockers, showers, driving range, putting & chipping greens.
Comments: tree-lined fairways are a challenge on this course. If you are
looking for a good public golf course at a very affordable price try Downriver.

Directions: from I-90 eastbound take
exit #280 (westbound #280A) to Maple
Street Bridge. Go north on Maple St.
until you reach Northwest Blvd. Turn
left on Northwest Blvd. and follow to
Euclid St. Turn left on Euclid. Follow
this to the golf course. The course is
located about 1 mile off NW Blvd.

Course Yardage & Par:
M-6021 yards, par 71.
W-5992 yards, par 73.

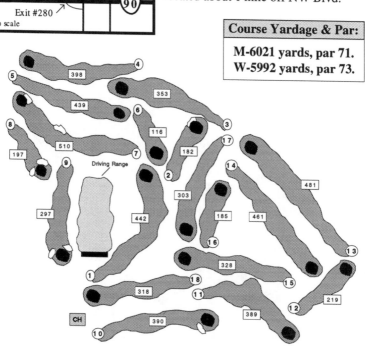

Druids Glen Golf Club (public, 18 hole course)
29925 207th Avenue SE; Kent, WA 98042
Phone: (253) 638-1200. **Fax:** (253) 638-1440. **Internet:** www.druidsglengolf.com.
Director of Golf: Travis Cox, PGA. **Pro:** Eric Berry, PGA.
Rating/Slope: T 74.8/137; C 71.8/131; M 68.9/123; W 70.6/121 **Record:** 67.
Green fees: Monday thru Thursday $43; Friday thru Sunday & Holidays. $53;
lower winter rates; twilight & early bird rates; Jr. & Sr. rates (M-F); M/C, VISA.
Power cart: $28. **Pull cart:** $5. **Trail fee:** personal carts not allowed.
Reservation policy: Call up to 1 week in advance. Advance reservations a must.
Winter condition: the golf course is open all year long. Course drains very well.
Terrain: flat, some hills. **Tees:** all grass. **Spikes:** soft spikes preffered.
Services: club rentals, lessons, liquor, pro shop, driving range, putting green.
Comments: 7000 + yard championship golf course. Fantastic layout that opened
July 14th 1997. This new course will challenge you at nearly every turn. Druids
Glen is a must play for any Northwest golfer. Be sure to call ahead for tee times.

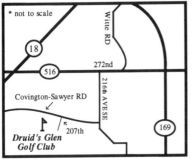

Directions: from I-405 N&S, exit at
Maple Valley (Hwy 169) to Four Corners.
Take a right on Kent Kangley (272nd).
Proceed for about 2 miles, then take a
left at 216th. Turn right on Covington -
Sawyer Rd., then a left on 207th to the
golf course. Look for signs along the way.

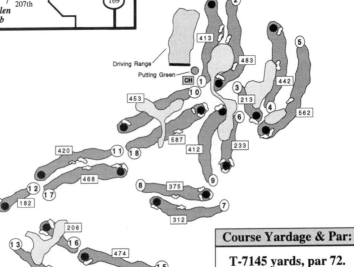

Course Yardage & Par:

T-7145 yards, par 72.
C-6574 yards, par 72.
M-6004 yards, par 72.
W-5354 yards, par 72.

Dungeness Golf & Country Club (public, 18 hole course)

1965 Woodcock Road: Sequim, WA 98382 Internet: www.dungenessgc.com
Phone: (360) 683-6344; 800-447-6826. **Fax:** (360) 683-1709.
Pro: Robert Bourns, PGA. **Superintendent:** Robert Schoessler.
Rating/Slope: C 70.1/123; M 68.5/120; W 70.3/119. **Course record:** 64.
Green fees: M-Thur. $22/$16; Friday-Sun. $26/$17; winter rates; M/C, VISA.
Power cart: $22/$14. **Pull cart:** $3/$2. **Trail fee:** $11/$6 (all prices + tax).
Reservation policy: call up to 60 days in advance for your tee-times.
Winter condition: the golf course is open all year long. Very dry conditions.
Terrain: flat, some hills. **Tees:** all grass. **Spikes:** soft spikes preferred.
Services: pro shop, driving range, club rentals, lessons, restaurant and lounge, beer, wine, liquor, showers, putting & chipping greens. **Comments:** has an excellent golf package with the Red Ranch Inn. One of the finest and friendliest golf courses in Washington. Worth a special trip to Olympic Peninsula.

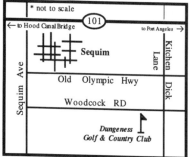

Directions: from Seattle take the Edmonds or Winslow ferry. Follow signs to the Hood Canal Bridge and Hwy 104. From Hwy 104 follow to Hwy 101. Proceed on Hwy 101 to Sequim. At the first light (Sequim Ave.) turn right. Go for 3 miles to Woodcock Road. Turn left on Woodcock Road. Proceed for 3 miles, the course will be on your right. Note signs marking your turn.

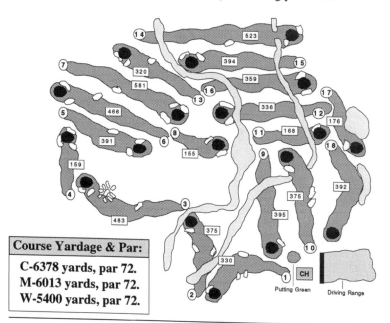

Course Yardage & Par:
C-6378 yards, par 72.
M-6013 yards, par 72.
W-5400 yards, par 72.

Eaglemont (semi-private, 18 hole course)

4127 Eaglemont Drive; Mount Vernon, WA 98273 Internet: www.eaglemont.com
Phone: (360) 424-0800; 1-800-368-8876. Fax: (360) 424-0790
Pro: Mike O'Laughlin, PGA. Superintendent: Charles Fisher.
Rating/Slope: T 73.4/134; C 71.6/129; M 70.5/126; M 69.4/124; W 70.7/124.
Green fees: W/D $42; W/E $54; w/ cart; earlybird $32; M/C, VISA, AMEX.
Power cart: included. **Pull cart:** not available. **Trail fee:** not allowed.
Reservation policy: yes, please call in advance for all your reservations.
Winter condition: the golf course is open all year long. Dry conditions.
Terrain: very hilly. **Tees:** all grass. **Spikes:** soft spikes preferred.
Services: the golf course offers a full service clubhouse and pro shop, range.
Comments: This John Steidel designed golf course is of championship caliber, featuring ponds, tree lined fairways and bunkers galore. Excellent newer course that can play very tough. Shot placement off the tee is a must at Eaglemont.

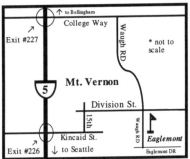

Directions: From I-5 N&S take exit #227 (College Way). Proceed eastbound on College Way until you reach Waugh Road. Turn right on Waugh Road. Proceed on Waugh Road to Eaglemont Drive where you will turn left to the golf course. Look for signs marking the way.

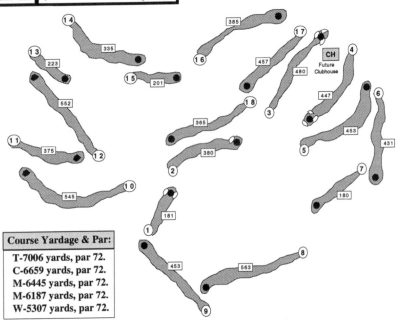

Course Yardage & Par:

T-7006 yards, par 72.
C-6659 yards, par 72.
M-6445 yards, par 72.
M-6187 yards, par 72.
W-5307 yards, par 72.

Echo Falls Country Club (semi-private, 18 hole course)
20414 121st Avenue SE; Snohomish, WA 98296
Phone: (206) 362-3000; (360) 668-3030. Fax: (360) 668-3733
Pro: Dave Shelton, PGA. Supt.: Rich Jahnke. Internet: none.
Rating/Slope: C 69.4/132; M 67.4/120; W 64.6/118. **Course record:** 65.
Green fees: Mon.-Thur. $36; Fri.-Sun. $46; twilite rates; VISA, M/C, AMEX.
Power cart: $13 per person. **Pull cart:** $3. **Trail fee:** not allowed.
Reservation policy: please call 7 days in advance for your tee-times.
Winter condition: the golf course is open all year long. Good winter drainage.
Terrain: relatively hilly. **Tees:** all grass. **Spikes:** soft spikes only April-Nov.
Services: club rentals, lessons, full service pro shop, clubhouse, restuarant, beer, wine, driving range, putting & chipping greens. **Comments:**18th hole is an island green that is spectacular. Shot placement is a must in order to score well. Greens are large, undulating and well bunkered. The staff at Echo Falls wants you to feel that this facility is "The Public's Country Club". Excellent track.

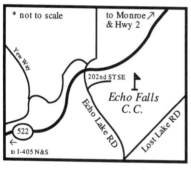

Directions: If traveling on I-405 N&S exit to Hwy 522 eastbound. Proceed for 7.1 miles to Echo Lake Road. Turn right on Echo Lake Road. Proceed to your first left (202nd Ave SE) and turn left. Proceed for 1/4 of a mile to the course entrance on your right hand side. Look for signs to mark your way to the golf course.

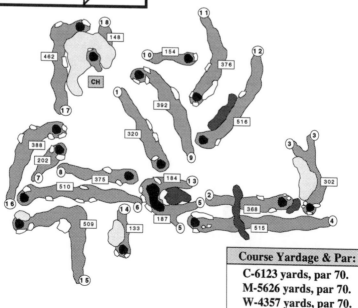

Course Yardage & Par:
C-6123 yards, par 70.
M-5626 yards, par 70.
W-4357 yards, par 70.

Elk Run Golf Course (public, 18 hole course)

22500 SE 275th Place; Maple Valley, WA 98038
Phone: (425) 432-8800. Fax: (425) 432-1907. Internet: none.
Director of Golf: Steve Dubsky, PGA. Head Golf Pro: Doug Eisele, PGA.
Manager: Roy Humphreys. Superintendent: Tony Bubenas.
Rating/Slope: M 67.8/117; W 70.4/115. **Course record:** 62.
Green fees: W/D $26/$16; W/E $30/$20; Sr.'s $22/$15 (M-Th); M/C, VISA.
Power cart: $22. **Pull cart:** $3. **Trail fee:** $7 for personal carts.
Reservation policy: yes, please call 5 days in advance for your tee-times.
Winter condition: the golf course is open all year long. Dry conditions.
Terrain: flat, some slight hills. **Tees:** grass. **Spikes:** soft spikes optional.
Services: club rentals, lessons, restaurant, coffee shop, pro shop, lighted driving
range, call for seasonal hours. **Comments:** one of the driest golf courses in
the Northwest. The new 9 is a real challenge with fairways that are narrow and
tree-lined. Numerous bunkers and ponds guard tricky undulating greens. If you
are looking for great course for your company tournament give Elk Run a try.

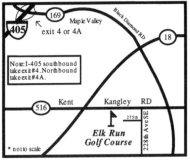

Directions: from I-405 N&S take exit
#4 (southbound) #4A (northbound) to
Hwy 169 (Maple Valley-Black Diamond
Road). Proceed to the Kent-Kangley
Road and turn right. Proceed for 1 mile
to 228th SE. Turn left on 228th SE and
follow to the golf course. Look for signs
marking your turn to the course the way
is well marked.

Course Yardage & Par:

M-5724 yards, par 71.
W-5189 yards, par 71.

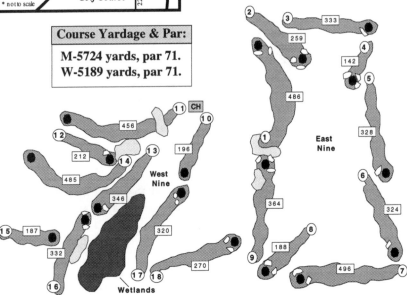

Ellensburg Golf Club (semi-private, 9 hole course)
3231Thorp Road South; Ellensburg, WA 98926
Phone: (509) 962-2984. Fax: none. Internet: none.
Pro: Rich Farrell, PGA. Superintendent: Frank Crimp.
Rating/Slope: M 69.4/115; W 72.3/120. Course record: 29/62.
Green fees: W/D $16/$9; W/E $18/$10; M/C, VISA.
Power cart: $20/$10. Pull cart: $1.50. Trail fee: $5 for personal carts.
Reservation policy: you may call ahead to make a tee time.
Winter condition: golf course is closed from mid November to March.
Terrain: flat (easy walking). **Tees:** grass. **Spikes:** soft spikes preferred.
Services: club rentals, lessons, restaurant, snack bar, lounge, beer, wine, liquor, pro shop, lockers, showers, driving range, putting green. **Comments:** sand traps and water make this 9 hole course a real challenge. Fairways are fairly wide giving you ample room off the tee. Dual tees available for 18 hole play. Course does limit outside play at certain times so be sure call ahead for your tee time.

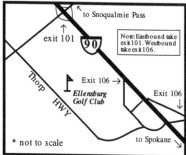

Directions: from I-90 eastbound take Thorp Hwy exit #101 and go for 2 miles to the golf course. From westbound I-90 take exit #106 the West Interchange by the KOA campground. Cross the bridge over the Yakima River onto Thorp Road and proceed for 2 miles to the golf course.

Course Yardage & Par:
M-2988 yards, par 35.
W-2807 yards, par 36.
Dual tees for 18 holes:
M-5974 yards, par 70.
W-5597 yards, par 73.

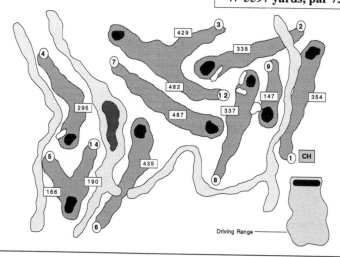

Driving Range

Enumclaw Golf Course (public, 18 hole course)
45220 288th SE; Enumclaw, WA 98002
Phone: (360) 825-2827. **Fax:** none. **Internet:** none.
Pro: John McGregor, PGA. **Superintendent:** Chad Chevalier.
Rating/Slope: M 66.0/105; W 68.6/109. **Course record:** 61.
Greens fee: $17/$12; Jr. & Sr. rates (Monday thru Friday only); M/C, VISA.
Power cart: $20/$10. **Pull cart:** $3. **Trail fee:** no charge for personal carts.
Reservation policy: yes, call up to one week in advance for tee-times.
Winter condition: the golf course is open all year long. Wet conditions.
Terrain: relatively hilly. **Tees:** grass & mats. **Spikes:** metal spikes permitted.
Services: club rentals, lessons, snack bar, restaurant, beer, wine, chipping &
putting greens. **Comments:** The golf course has beautiful views of the sur-
rounding countryside. Boise Creek winds through the golf course and is a factor
on many of the holes. The course itself can play much longer than the yardage
would indicate. Be sure to call ahead for tee times during the summer.

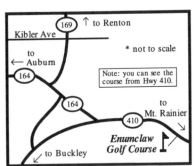

Directions: from I-5 N&S take exit 142
to Hwy 18E. East to Auburn Way S/Hwy
164 E exit. Go east on Hwy 164 for 13.8
miles to Hwy 410 (SE 448th). Proceed
eastbound for 1 mile to the golf course.
Note: You can see the golf course when
driving on Hwy 410. Look for signs
indicating your turn to the golf course.

Course Yardage & Par:
M-5561 yards, par 70.
W-5211 yards, par 71.

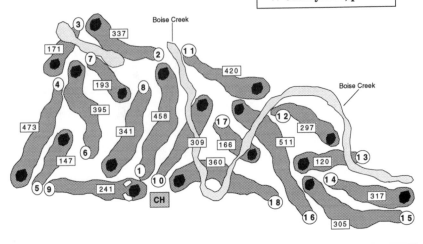

Esmeralda Golf Course (public, 18 hole course)

East 3933 Courtland; Spokane, WA 99207
Phone: (509) 487-6291. Fax: none. Internet: none.
Pro: Bill Warner, PGA. Superintendent: Morgan Boyce.
Rating/Slope: C 68.7/108; M 67.7/106; W 70.8/113. **Course record:** 62.
Green fees: $18.50/$13.50 all week long; Jr. & Sr. rates W/D's $8; VISA, M/C.
Power cart: $22/$11. **Pull cart:** $2. **Trail fee:** $7 for personal carts.
Reservation policy: yes, 1 day for weekdays, 1 week for the weekends.
Winter condition: the course open weathering permitting. Dry conditions.
Terrain: flat, some hills. **Tees:** all grass. **Spikes:** soft spikes preferred.
Services: club rentals, lessons, restaurant, beer, wine, pro shop, driving range, putting green. **Comments:** large, quick greens and fairly flat terrain make for a pleasant round. Fairways are wide giving the golfer ample room off the tee. Excellent public course with tree lined fairways and few hazards.

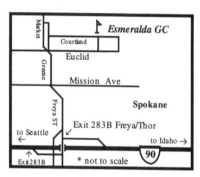

Directions: from I-90 E&W take the Freya/Thor exit #283B. Go northbound for 3 miles to Euclid Avenue. Go right on Euclid Avenue for 3 blocks to Freya. Turn left on Freya to the golf course. Look for signs indicating your turn to the course.

Course Yardage & Par:
C-6249 yards, par 70.
M-6015 yards, par 70.
W-5594 yards, par 72.

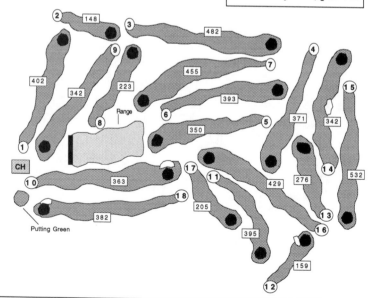

Everett Golf & Country Club (private, 18 hole course)

1500 52nd Street; P.O. Box 2300; Everett, WA 98203
Phone: (425) 259-1214. Fax: (425) 355-4570. Internet: none.
Pro: Bob Borup, PGA. Superintendent: Randy White.
Rating/Slope: C 70.0/126; M 69.2/124; W 73.1/126. **Course record:** 62.
Green fees: private course, members & guests only; reciprocates.
Power cart: private club. **Pull cart:** private club. **Trail fee:** not allowed.
Reservation policy: private club, members only. No public play allowed
Winter condition: The golf course is open all year long. Dry conditions.
Terrain: flat, some hills. **Tees:** grass. **Spikes:** soft spikes preferred.
Services: lessons, lounge, restaurant, beer, wine, liquor, lockers, showers,
pro shop, driving range. **Comments:** the golf course is fairly flat with tree lined
fairways with small well bunkered greens. This private track was built in 1910
and gives the golfer many outstanding views of the surrounding countryside.

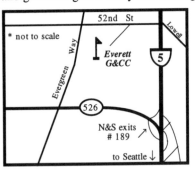

Directions: from I-5 N&S take exit #189
to Hwy 526E for .5 miles to Evergreen
Way. Turn right (north) on Evergreen
Way and proceed for 2 miles to 52nd
Street. Turn right (east) on 52nd Street.
Proced to the golf course.

Course Yardage & Par:
C-6087 yards, par 72.
M-6073 yards, par 72.
W-5731 yards, par 72.

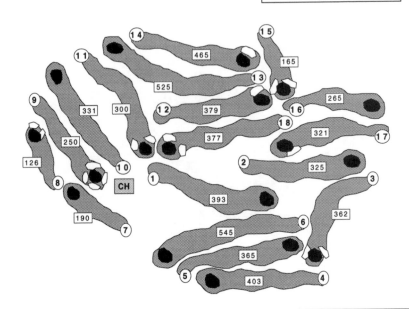

Evergreen Golf Course (public, 9 hole course)

P.O. Box 156; 413 East Main Street; Everson, WA 98247
Phone: (360) 966-5417. Fax: none. Internet: none.
Owner: Jerry McBeth. Superintendent: none.
Rating/Slope: the golf course is not rated. **Course record:** 28, 9 holes.
Green fees: $12/$8 all week long; Jr. & Sr. rates $10/$6; no credit cards.
Power cart: none available for use. **Pull cart:** $2. **Trail fee:** no charge.
Reservation policy: none. Times are on a first come first served basis.
Winter condition: the golf course is closed during the winter months.
Terrain: flat, some slight hills. **Tees:** grass. **Spikes:** metal spikes permitted.
Services: club rentals, snack bar, beer, wine, limited pro shop, putting green.
Comments: family owned executive course with narrow tree lined fairways.
A creek which wanders throughout the course comes into play on a number
of holes. Fairly rustic course that is very friendly and has a laid back feel.

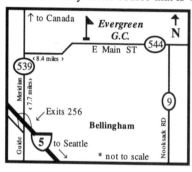

Directions: from I-5 N&S take exit #256 to Guide Meridian St. Go northbound on Meridian (Hwy 539) for 7.7 miles to Hwy 544E. Turn eastbound on Hwy 544 for 8.4 miles to the golf course. Look for signs marking your way to the entrance of the golf course.

Course Yardage & Par:
M-2145 yards, par 31.
W-2145 yards, par 31.

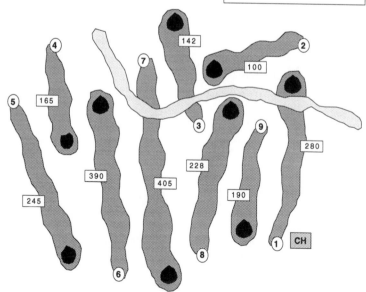

Fairway Village Golf Course (public, 9 hole course)
15503 SE Fernwood Drive; Vancouver, WA 98684
Phone: (360) 254-9325. **Fax:** (360) 253-5525. **Internet: none.**
Manager: Russ Dixon. Superintendent: Cris Carley.
Rating/Slope: M 64.5/107; W 64.3/106. **Course record:** 29.
Green fees: $19/$12 all week long; Sr. rates weekdays $9; M/C, VISA.
Power cart: $18/$12. **Pull cart:** $2. **Trail fee:** $5 for personal carts.
Reservation policy: yes, call up to 1 week in advance for your tee-times.
Winter condition: the golf course is open all year long. Dry conditions.
Terrain: flat, some hills. **Tees:** grass. **Spikes:** soft spikes preferred..
Services: lessons, pro shop, vending machines. **Comments:** this well bunkered
short and narrow golf course was designed by Bunny Mason and dedicated by
Sam Snead. If you want to play early in the morning try the Early Bird Special
Saturday & Sunday before 9am. Greens and fairways are kept in excellent
condition with the course playing tight in certain area's. Great little golf course.

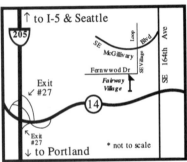

Directions: from I-5 N&S exit to I-205
N&S. Exit from I-205 to Hwy 14 going
eastbound. Proceed east to exit #8 (SE
164th). Turn left on SE 164th and
proceed for 1 mile to SE McGillivary
(2nd light). Turn left for .2 miles to SE
Village Loop. At SE Village Loop turn
left and then follow this to the course.

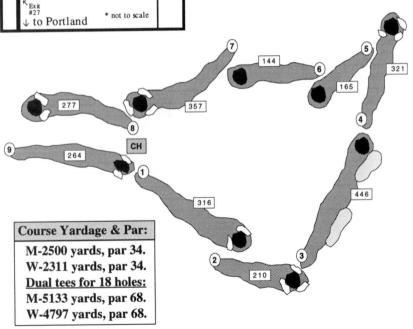

Course Yardage & Par:

M-2500 yards, par 34.
W-2311 yards, par 34.
Dual tees for 18 holes:
M-5133 yards, par 68.
W-4797 yards, par 68.

Fairways at West Terrace, The (public, 18 holes)

W 9810 Melville Road; Cheney, WA 99004
Phone: (509) 747-8418. **Fax:** (509) 455-8403. **Internet: none.**
Pro: Jerry Zink, PGA. Superintendent: Chris Becker.
Rating/Slope: C 69.0/117; M 67.5/114; W 71.4/125; W 68.9/120. **Record: 61.**
Green fees: W/D $15; W/E $18/$11; Jr & Sr rates $13; M/C, VISA.
Power cart: $22/$11. **Pull cart:** $2. **Trail fee:** $7 for personal carts.
Reservation policy: yes. Call up to 1 week in advance for tee-times.
Winter condition: the golf course is open weather permitting. Drains well.
Terrain: flat, some hills. **Tees:** all grass. **Spikes:** metal spikes permitted.
Services: club rentals, lessons, snack bar, restaurant, beer, wine, liquor, driving
range, pro shop, putting & chipping greens. **Comments:** home of the "Lilac
City Invitational Tournament." The course has numerous sand traps and 6 ponds
which come in to play. Great golf course that can play very tough.

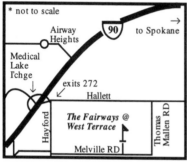

Directions: from I-90 E&W take exit #272 (Medical Lake). Go south to 4-way stop (West Bow Road). Turn right. Go to Hayford Road. turn left. Go to Melville Road turn left. The course will be on your left side of the road.

Course Yardage & Par:

C-6459 yards, par 72.
M-6138 yards, par 72.
W-5650 yards, par 72.
W-5142 yards, par 72.

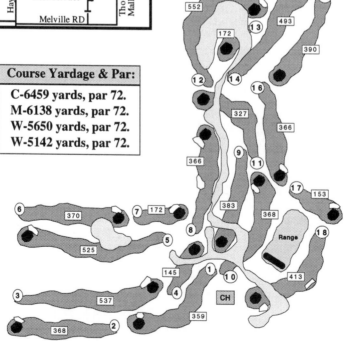

Fairwood Golf & Country Club (private, 18 hole course)

17070 140th SE; Renton, WA 98055
Phone: (425) 226-7890. **Fax:** (425) 226-1737. **Internet:** none.
Pro: Chris Johnson, PGA. **Superintendent:** Greg Hall.
Rating/Slope: C 71.1/127; M 69.5/124; W 72.4/123. **Course record:** 63.
Green fees: private club, members and guests only, limited reciprocation.
Power cart: private club. **Pull cart:** private club. **Trail fee:** not allowed.
Reservation policy: yes, call on Thursday for the following week.
Winter condition: the golf course is open all year long. Dry conditions.
Terrain: relatively hilly. **Tees:** all grass. **Spikes:** soft spikes preferred.
Services: lessons, lounge, beer, wine, liquor, lockers, showers, sauna, pro shop,
driving range, chipping & putting green. **Comments:** OB on both sides of each
hole puts a premium on accuracy off the tee. Undulating greens, bunkers and
length make this golf course difficult. Excellent private facility built in 1972.

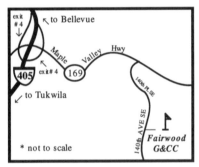

Directions: from I-5 N&S exit to
I-405 N&S. From I-405 N&S take exit
#4 to Hwy 169S. Proceed on Hwy 169
until you reach 140th PL SE. Turn
right on 140th PL SE. Travel up the
hill until 140th PL SE turns into 140th
St SE. The golf course will be on your
left. Note the clubhouse is beyond
the main entrance.

Course Yardage & Par:
C-6306 yards, par 71.
M-5944 yards, par 71.
W-5396 yards, par 71.

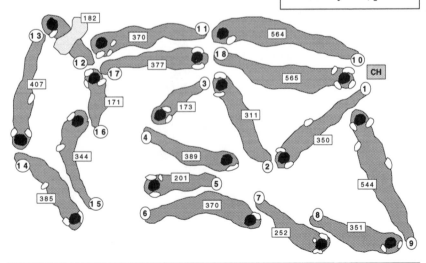

Family Golf Center @ Tumwater (public, 9 hole course)

8080 Center Street SW; Tumwater, WA 98501
Phone: (360) 786-8626. Fax: (360) 786-1848. Internet: www.familygolf.com
Pro: Mike Foswick, PGA. Superintendent: Rusty Sauls.
Manager: Eric Rowe. Teaching Pro: LeAnne Hine, LPGA
Rating/Slope: M 28.9/89. Course record: 27.
Green fees: $13/$10 all week long; winter rates.
Power cart: not allowed. **Pull cart:** $2. **Trail fee:** personal carts not allowed.
Reservation policy: call ahead up to 7 days in advance for a tee time.
Winter condition: the golf course is open all year around. Dry conditions.
Terrain: flat (easy walking). **Tees:** grass. **Spikes:** soft spikes preferred.
Services: club rentals, lessons, club repair, pro shop, driving range that is covered and has heated stalls, club memberships, putting & chipping green.
Comments: Very challenging executive golf course. Great place to sharpen your scoring iron play. The course layout facilitates using all the clubs in your bag. The driving range is open 8am- 9pm during the winter and from dawn to dusk during the summer months. Be sure to give Family Golf Center a try.

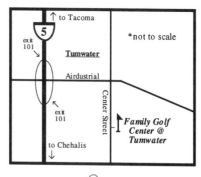

Directions: from I-5 N&S take exit #101 (Airdustrial). Proceed eastbount to the first stoplight. Right on Center Street. Proceed for 1/2 mile, the course is on the left side of the street. Look for signs.

Course Yardage & Par:
M-1737 yards, par 29.
W-1401 yards, par 30.

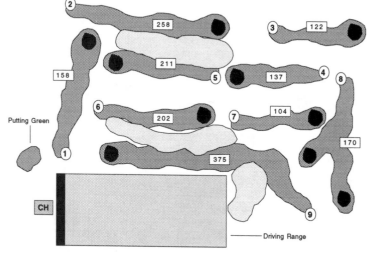

Fircrest Golf Club (private, 18 hole course)
1500 Regents Boulevard; Fircrest, WA 98466
Phone: (253) 564-5792, 564-6756. **Fax:** (253) 565-1880. **Internet:** none.
Pro: Glenn Malm, PGA. **Superintendent:** Mike Etchemendy.
Rating/Slope: C 72.6/131; M 71.8/128; W 74.8/131. **Course record:** 62.
Green fees: private, members only; very limited reciprocation; no credit cards.
Power cart: private club. **Pull cart:** private club. **Trail fee:** not allowed.
Reservation policy: none. Private club members only no outside play allowed.
Winter condition: the golf course is open all year long. Dry conditions.
Terrain: relatively hilly. **Tees:** all grass. **Spikes:** soft spikes preferred.
Services: lessons, snack bar, lounge, restaurant, beer, wine, liquor, lockers,
showers, pro shop, practice range, club memberships, dress code, putting green.
Comments: Established in 1923, this course's fairways are surrounded by trees
which makes the course play tight. Greens are very fast and well bunkered. This
older private club is rich in golf tradition and feel. Excellent, demanding course.

Directions: from I-5 N&S take exit #132
to SR16 Westbound. Take the Fircrest-
Center Street exit off of SR16. Turn right
onto Center Street. Center Street becomes
Regents Blvd. in Fircrest. Look for your
turn to the facility.

Course Yardage & Par:

C-6685 yards, par 71.
M-6440 yards, par 71.
W-5985 yards, par 75.

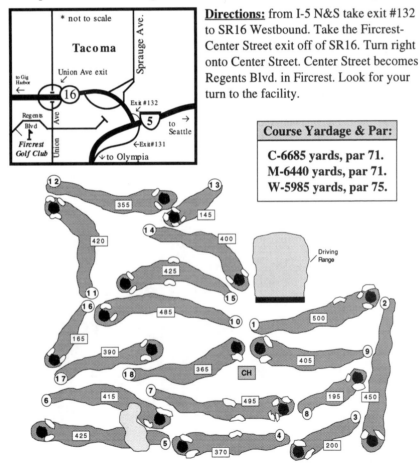

Fisher Park Golf Course (public, 9 hole par 3 course)
2301 Fruitvale Boulevard; Yakima, WA 98901
Phone: (509) 575-6075. Fax: none. Internet: none.
Manager: Doty Hodgson. Teaching Pro: Bob Hoag.
Rating/Slope: the golf course has not been rated. **Course record:** 23.
Green fees: W/D $10/$6; W/E & Holidays $9/$6; Jr & Sr rates $8/$5.
Power cart: none available. **Pull cart:** $2. **Trail fee:** no personal carts allowed.
Reservation policy: tee-times are on a first come first served basis.
Winter condition: the course is closed from November 15th to February 15th.
Terrain: flat, some slight hills. **Tees:** grass. **Spikes:** metal spikes permitted.
Services: club rentals, lessons, snack bar, beverages, putting green.
Comments: Economical course golf course run by the City of Yakima Parks
Department. This par 3 golf course can play long at times with holes ranging
from 118 to 191 yards. You will use every iron in your bag.

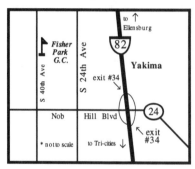

Directions: From I-82 take the Nob
Hill exit #34 and proceed westbound.
At 40th Avenue turn right and proceed
to the golf course. The golf course will
be located on your right hand side.
Look for signs.

Course Yardage & Par:
M-1354 yards, par 27.
W-1354 yards, par 27.

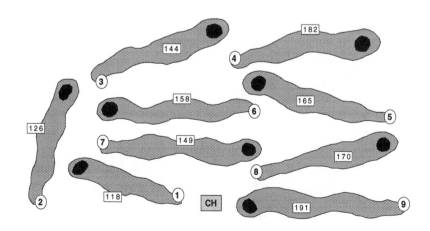

Flowing Lake Golf Course (public, 18 hole course)
5001 Weber Road; Snohomish, WA 98290
Phone: (360) 568-2753. Fax: none. Internet: none.
Manager: Gary Laz. Superintendent: Gary Laz.
Rating/Slope: the golf course has not been rated. **Course record:** 63.
Green fees: W/D $16/$11; W/E $20/$15; M/C, VISA.
Power cart: $25/$12.50. **Pull cart:** $3/$1.50. **Trail fee:** $5.
Reservation policy: yes, please call 1 week in advance for a tee time.
Winter condition: course closed from November 15th to February 15th.
Terrain: flat, some hills. **Tees:** all grass. **Spikes:** metal spikes permitted.
Services: club rentals, snack bar, putting green, pro shop.
Comments: newer family run golf course that can play very tight in spots.
This is a beautiful country course with spectacular views of the Cascades from many of the tees and fairways. The track has improved every year as the layout and greens have had a chance to mature. Water is a major factor on many holes.

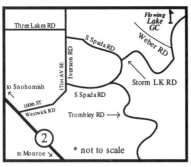

Directions: from Hwy 2 exit at 100th St. SE (which is east of Snohomish). Follow to Spada Road. Right on Spada. Proceed to Storm Lake Road. Right on Storm Lake Road to Weber Road where you will turn left. The golf course entrance is located ahead on your right. Look for signs.

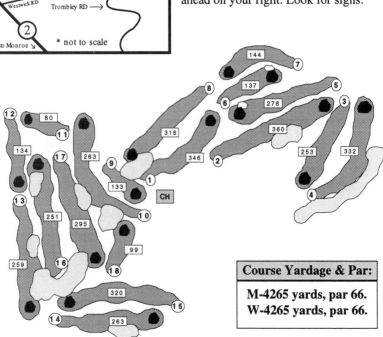

Course Yardage & Par:

M-4265 yards, par 66.
W-4265 yards, par 66.

Fort Lewis Golf Course (military-private, 27 hole course)

P.O. Box 33175; Fort Lewis Army Base; Fort Lewis, WA 98433
Phone: (253) 967-6522. Fax: (253) 964-2789. Internet: none.
Pro: James Barnhouse. Superintendent: John Ford. Course record: 64.
Rating/Slope: Red/Blue C 72.6/125; M 70.4/121; W 73.3/120.
Green fees: military & guests only, sliding fee scale based on rank.
Power cart: private course. **Pull cart:** private course. **Trail fee:** not allowed.
Reservation policy: please call ahead and ask for tee-time policy.
Winter condition: the golf course is open all year long. Dry conditions.
Terrain: relatively hilly. **Tees:** grass. **Spikes:** spikeless only May-October.
Services: club rentals, lessons, snack bar, beer, lockers, showers, two driving
ranges, pro shop, putting green. **Comments:** Mature trees, ponds and sand
traps make this 27 hole layout a very difficult course to score on. Most tees are
elevated leaving the golfer very little room off the tee. Excellent military track.

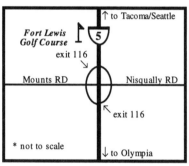

Directions: from I-5 N&S take exit
#116 (Mounts Rd.-Nisqually). Proceed
west for .1 miles to the golf course.
Note: the golf course is adjacent to I-5.

Course Yardage & Par:
Red/Blue: C-6855 yards, par 72.
Red/Blue: M-6388 yards, par 72.
Red/Blue: W-5822 yards, par 74.

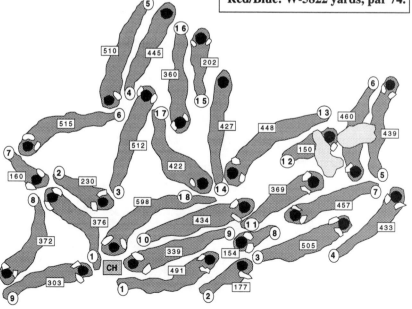

Fort Steilacoom Golf Course (public, 9 hole course)
Box 97325; 8202 87th SW; Tacoma, WA 98498
Phone: (253) 588-0613. Fax: none. Internet: none.
Pro: Craig W. Price. Superintendent: Scott Tyson.
Rating/Slope: M 62.8/098; W 66.8/105. **Course record:** 54.
Green fees: $15.75/$10.25; Jr & Sr rates $11/$7.25; twilight rate; M/C, VISA.
Power cart: $14/$8. **Pull cart:** $3. **Trail fee:** $5 for personal carts.
Reservation policy: yes, please call in advance for your tee times.
Winter condition: golf course is open all year long. Dry conditions.
Terrain: very flat. **Tees:** grass & mats. **Spikes:** soft spikes preferred.
Services: club rentals, lessons, pro shop, pop, vending machines, hot & cold sandwiches, snacks, putting & chipping green, club memberships available.
Comments: golf course is not overly long so its an excellent course to practice your short irons on. Dual tees are available for those wanting to play a full 18 hole round. Fairways are tree lined and fairly wide leaving room off the tee.

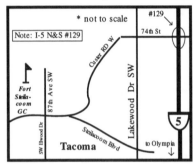

Directions: from I-5 N&S take exit #129 to S 74th. Turn west on S 74th and proceed 2.2 miles to Custer Road W. Go south for 1 mile to Steilacoom Blvd. Turn west on Steilacoom Blvd. for 1.1 miles to 87th Ave. SW. Turn north on 87th Ave. SW for .2 miles to the golf course driveway. Look for signs marking your turn to the course.

Course Yardage & Par:
M-2518 yards, par 34; W-2410 yards, par 34.
Dual tees for 18 holes:
M-4928 yards, par 68; W-4928 yards, par 68.

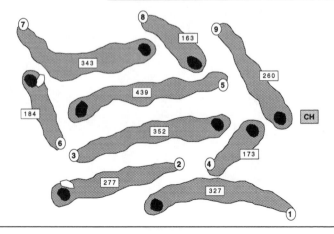

Foster Golf Links (public, 18 hole course)
13500 Interurban Avenue; Tukwila, WA 98168
Phone: (206) 242-4221. Fax: (206) 246-4064. Internet: none.
Pro: Marty O'Brien, PGA. Superintendent: Chuck Morris.
Rating/Slope: M 62.3/94; W 66.6/101. **Course record:** 59.
Green fees: $19/$15; Jr & Sr rates (weekdays) $15.50/$13; VISA, MC.
Power cart: $20/$12. **Pull cart:** $3/$1.50. **Trail fee:** $7 for personal carts.
Reservation policy: yes, call up to 1 week in advance for tee times.
Winter condition: the golf course is open all year long. Dry conditions.
Terrain: flat, some hills. **Tees:** grass & mats. **Spikes:** soft spikes optional.
Services: club rentals, restaurant, beer, wine, pop, liquor, pro shop.
Comments: the course is easy to walk and a favorite of seniors. This track has been undergoing changes the last two years to enhance its playability. If you are looking for a change of pace from the 6000+ yards golf course, give Foster a try.

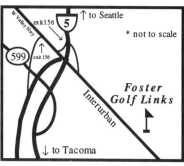

Directions: from I-5 N&S take exit #156 (Tukwila) to Interurban South. Proceed south for .4 miles to the golf course which will be on your left hand side. Look for a sign indicating your turn into the parking lot.

Course Yardage & Par:
M-4930 yards, par 69.
W-4695 yards, par 70.

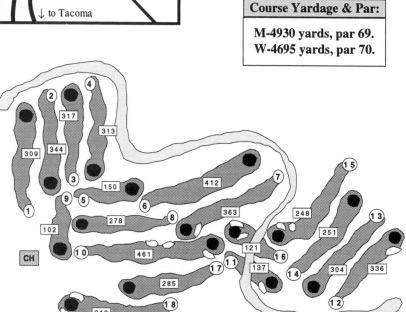

Gallery Golf Course (military, open to public, 18 hole course)
MWR Golf; NAS Whidbey Island; Oak Harbor, WA 98278
Phone: (360) 257-2178. **Fax:** (360) 277-6585. **Internet:** none.
Golf Course General Manager: Christopher M. Braun.
Rating/Slope: C 70.1/121; M 69.0/120; W 70.7/123. **Course record:** 66.
Green fees: Monday-Thursday $20; Friday-Sunday & Holidays $22;
sliding fee scale for military based on rank; VISA, M/C, DIS, AMEX.
Power cart: $14. **Pull cart:** $3. **Trail fee:** $10 for personal carts.
Reservation policy: yes, please call in advance for all tee-times.
Winter condition: the golf course is open all year long. Dry conditions.
Terrain: flat, some hills. **Tees:** grass. **Spikes:** soft spikes preffered.
Services: club rentals, lessons, restaurant, lounge, beer, wine, beverages, liquor,
lockers, pro shop, driving range, short practice chipping green, putting green.
Comments: a very scenic and demanding layout located at the Whidbey Island
Naval Air Station. Gallery Golf Course features well bunkered greens that can
get very fast in the summer months. The golf course is now open for public play.

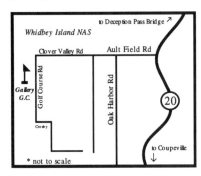

Directions: from I-5 N&S take exit 230
to Hwy 20 W. Travel west to Whidbey
Island and exit at Ault Field Road.
Continue beyond NAS to Clover Valley
Road to the golf course. **Note:** the golf
course is located right outside the military
base. Look for signs indicating your way
to the base.

Course Yardage & Par:
C-6351 yards, par 72.
M-6101 yards, par 72.
W-5454 yards, par 74.

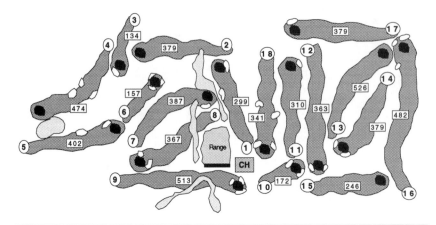

Gateway Golf Course (public, 9 hole course)
839 Fruitdale Road; Sedro Woolley, WA 98284
Phone: (360) 856-0315. Fax: none. Internet: none.
Pro: Wellington Lee. Superintendent: Rudy Franulovich.
Rating/Slope: C 68.8/122; M 68.2/120; W 68.0/115. **Course record:** 31.
Green fees: W/D $13/$9; W/E & Hol. $16/$13; Sr. rates M-F; no credit cards.
Power cart: $15/$10. **Pull cart:** $3/$2. **Trail fee:** $1 per 9 holes.
Reservation policy: no, play happens on a first come first served basis.
Winter condition: the course is open all year, weather permitting. Damp.
Terrain: relatively hilly. **Tees:** grass, mats. **Spikes:** soft spikes preffered.
Services: club rentals, lessons, snack bar, beer, pro shop, chipping area, putting
green, club memberships. **Comments:** ditches, ponds and creeks come into play
throughout the course. Fairways have generous landing areas giving the golfer
room off the tee. Peek a boo views of the Cascades from many tees and fairways.

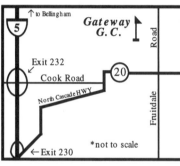

Directions: from I-5 N&S take exit
#232 to Cook Road. Travel east for 4.4
miles to Hwy 20 E. Turn east for .7
miles to Fruitdale Road. Proceed on
Fruitdale Road to the golf course. Look
for signs locating the turn to the course.

Course Yardage & Par:
C-3050 yards, par 36.
M-2914 yards, par 36.
W-2500 yards, par 36.

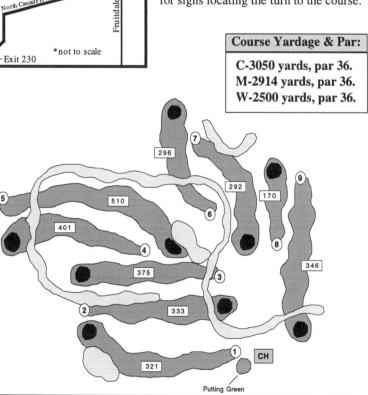

Gig Harbor Golf & Country Club (semi-private 9 hole course)
6909 Artondale Drive. NW; Gig Harbor, WA 98335
Phone: (253) 851-2378. Fax: (253) 858-2917. Internet: none.
Pro: Mark Holden, PGA. Superintendent: Todd Lupkes.
Rating/Slope: M 65.6/109; W 68.8/114. **Course record:** 64.
Green fees: Mon.-Thur. $20/$14; Fri.-Sun. $22/$16; Jr./Sr. rates; M/C, VISA.
Power cart: $20/$13. **Pull cart:** $5/$3. **Trail fee:** $10 for personal carts.
Reservation policy: please call in advance for your tee times.
Winter condition: the golf course is open all year long. Dry conditions.
Terrain: relatively hilly. **Tees:** all grass. **Spikes:** soft spikes preffered.
Services: club rentals, lessons, snack bar, beer, wine, lounge (members only),
lockers, pro shop, driving range, custom built clubs-Zevo Fitting System.
Comments: beautiful views of Mount Rainier and the surrounding countryside
from many holes. A friendly staff and some of the best greens in the northwest
can be found at Gig Harbor Golf & Country Club. Worth a visit if in the area.

Directions: from I-5 N&S take exit
#132 to Highway 16 West. Proceed on
Highway 16 West to the Gig Harbor City
Center exit. Turn south off exit onto
Pioneer Way. Proceed for 2 miles to
Artondale Road where you will turn right.
Proceed for .3 miles to the golf course
located on your right hand side.

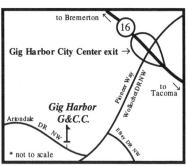

Course Yardage & Par:

M-2702 yards, par 35.
W-2614 yards, par 35.
<u>Dual tees for 18 holes:</u>
M-5420 yards, par 70.
W-5095 yards, par 70.

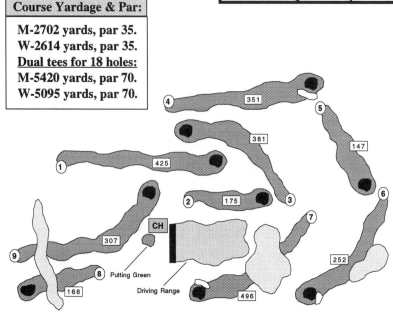

Glen Acres Golf & Country Club (private, 9 hole course)

1000 South 112th Street; Seattle, WA 98168
Phone: (206) 244-3786. **Fax:** (206) 439-9952. **Internet:** www.cybergolf.com/glenacres.
Pro: Bart Turchin, PGA. **Supt.:** Daniel Kukla. **GM:** Randall Gudanowski.
Rating/Slope: M 69.5/122; W 73.2/127. **Course record:** 61.
Green fees: private club, members & guests only; limited reciprocation.
Power cart: private club. **Pull cart:** private club. **Trail fee:** private club.
Reservation policy: yes, call up to 1 week for tee-times. No public play.
Winter condition: the golf course is open all year long. Wet conditions.
Terrain: flat to hilly terrain. **Tees:** grass. **Spikes:** soft spikes preferred.
Services: club rentals, lessons, snack bar, lounge, restaurant, beer, wine, liquor, pro shop, lockers, showers, social memberships, driving range, putting green.
Comments: the fairways are narrow and tree lined leaving very little room off the tee. All greens are well bunkered, elevated and have huge undulations. Good, older private club that is kept in excellent condition throughout the golfing year. Be sure to call and inquire about what memberships they offer. This is Glen Acres Homeowners Assoc. Facility managed by G. R. NW.

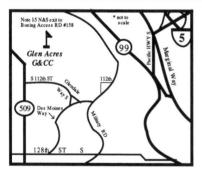

Directions: from I-5 N&S take exit 158B. Go west on Boeing Access Road for .4 miles to Pacific Hwy S. Travel south for 1.2 miles to S 128th. West for 1 mile to Des Moines Way. Go north for .5 miles and veer left to Glendale Way S. Proceed north for .7 miles to the course.

Course Yardage & Par:
M-3060 yards, par 36.
W-2828 yards, par 36.
Dual tees for 18 holes:
M-6088 yards, par 72.
W-5652 yards, par 72.

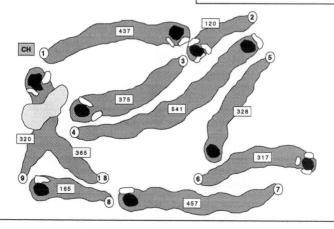

Glendale Golf & Country Club (private, 18 hole course)
13440 Main Street; Bellevue, WA 98005
Phone: (425) 746-7377. Fax: (425) 746-7660. Internet: none.
Pro: Stan Hyatt, PGA. Superintendent: Stephen Kealy.
Rating/Slope: C 71.5/135; M 70.2/132; W 73.1/131. **Course record:** 65.
Green fees: private club, members only; limited reciprocation; no credit cards.
Power cart: private club. **Pull cart:** private club. **Trail fee:** not allowed.
Reservation policy: yes, call up to 1 week in advance for weekends only.
Winter condition: the golf course is open all year long. Dry (drains well).
Terrain: relatively hilly. **Tees:** all grass. **Spikes:** soft spikes preferred.
Services: lessons, snack bar, lounge, restaurant, beer, wine, liquor, pro shop,
lockers, showers, club memberships, driving range, putting & chipping greens.
Comments: tough, well-trapped, woodsy layout that has fast greens and trouble
off the tees. This private facility has hosted the Washington State Open
Championship. A well maintained track that will challenge any level of golfer.

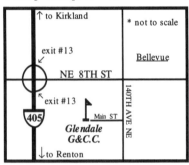

Directions: from I-405 N&S take exit
#13 to NE 8th St eastbound. Travel east
for 1.6 miles to 140th Ave. Turn south
(right) and proceed for 1 mile to Main
St. When you reach Main St. turn west
(right) on Main St. and proceed to the
golf course. **Note:** small sign just before
the entrance to the facility.

Course Yardage & Par:
C-6568 yards, par 72.
M-6274 yards, par 72.
W-5706 yards, par 72.

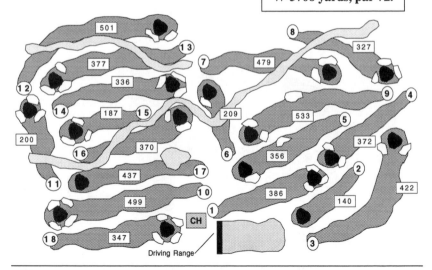

Driving Range

Gleneagle Golf Course (public, 18 hole course)
7619 Country Club Drive; Arlington, WA 98223
Phone: (360) 435-6713. Fax: none. Internet: www.americangolf.com.
Pro: John Pinardi, PGA. Superintendent: Paul Peterson.
Rating/Slope: C 69.8/129; B 67.0/123; M 65.6/121; F 64.2/118. **Record:** 66.
Green fees: W/D $23; W/E $29; twilight rates; M/C, VISA, AMEX.
Power cart: W/D $11, W/E $12 per person. **Pull cart:** $3. **Trail fee:** $10.
Reservation policy: please call 7 days in advance for your tee times.
Winter condition: the golf course is open all year long, weather permitting.
Terrain: flat, some hills. **Tees:** all grass. **Spikes:** metal spikes permitted.
Services: club rentals, pro shop, driving range, snack bar, full service clubhouse
with restaurant. **Comments:** The course features tree lined fairways, ponds and
well bunkered greens. Homes line most of the fairways as Gleneagle is part of a
master planned development. The 1st 9 holes has been open for play since 1993,
with the 2nd nine opening up 2 years later. Good course that plays very tight.

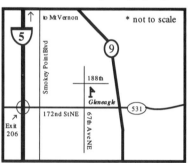

Directions: From I-5 N&S take exit
#206 and proceed eastbound on 172nd
ST NE until you reach 67th Ave. NE. At
67th Ave. proceed straight through up
the hill to Gleneagle Dr. where you will
turn left. Proceed on Gleneagle Dr. to the
course. Look for signs along the way.

Course Yardage & Par:
C-6010 yards, par 70.
B-5498 yards, par 70.
M-4828 yards, par 70.
F-4318 yards, par 70.

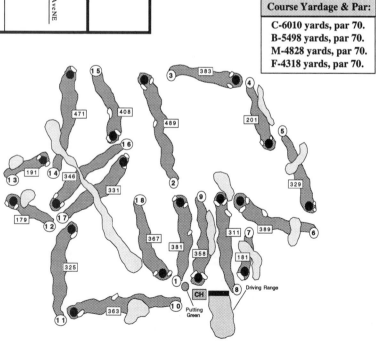

Gold Mountain Golf Complex (public, 36 hole course)
Physical address: 7263 West Belfair Valley Road; Gorst, WA 98337
Mailing address: P.O. Box 4130; Bremerton, WA 98312
Phone numbers: (360) 451-5432; or call toll free 1-800-249-2363
Fax number: (360) 451-6880. Internet: none available.
Director of Golf: Scott Alexander, PGA. Superintendent: Edward Faulk.
Pros: Cascade: Joe Purdue, PGA. Olympic: Daryl Matheny, PGA
Rating/Slope: C 71.6/120; M 68.6/116; W 69.9/116. **Record:** 63 Cas 67 Oly.
Green fees: Cascade Course: W/D $22/$15; W/E $26/$18; M/C, VISA.
Jr. rates $8.50; Sr. rates $18 W/D's only. Twilight rates are available.
Green fees: Olympic Course: W/D $32/$19; W/E $36/$23; M/C, VISA.
Jr. $18.50 & Sr. $27 rates are available weekdays only. Twilight rates available.
Power cart: $24/$15. **Pull cart:** $3. **Trail fee:** $15 for personal carts.
Reservation policy (Cascade): 1 week in advance at 11am for tee-times.
Reservation policy (Olympic): 1 month in advance w/ credit card no discounts.
Winter condition: the golf course is open all year long. Dry conditions.
Terrain: flat, some steep hills. **Tees:** grass. **Spikes:** spikeless April-September.
Services: club rentals, lessons, snack bar, lounge, restaurant, beer, wine, pop,
lockers, well stocked pro shop, driving range, putting & chipping greens.
Comments: the course is well manicured, bunkered and long. The complex
opened an additional 18 holes in September of 1996. The new course features
extensive mounding, varied terrain and tree-lined fairways. Water will comes
into play on some holes leaving the golfer many challenges from the fairway.
The Olympic Course has received great reviews from many national golf
magazines and is worth a special trip. Gold Mountain is one of the finest public
courses in the state of Washington.

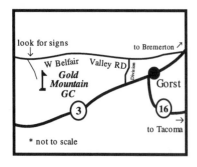

Directions: from I-5 N&S take exit 132 to Hwy 16W. Travel west to Hwy 3S. Go straight ahead on Sam Christopherson Ave. to W. Belfair Valley Road. Turn left and follow for 2.3 miles to the course on your left. From the Bremerton Ferry veer left to 1st for 1 block to Burwell (Hwy 304W). Follow signs to Shelton to Hwy 3S. Turn south on 3S to Sam Christopherson Ave. Turn right to W. Belfair Valley Rd. Turn left and go 2.3 miles.

The Cascade Course	The Olympic Course
Course Yardage & Par:	**Course Yardage & Par:**
C-6708 yards, par 71.	T-7003 yards, par 72.
M-6059 yards, par 71.	C-6474 yards, par 72.
W-5306 yards, par 74.	M-6003 yards, par 72.
	W-5220 yards, par 72.

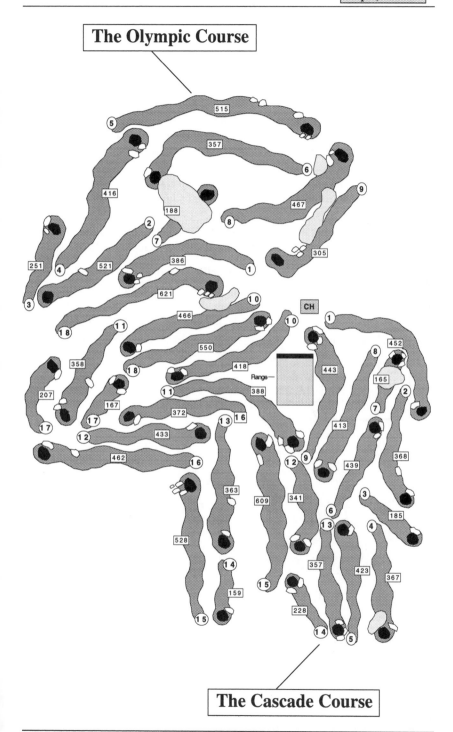

The Olympic Course

The Cascade Course

Goldendale Country Club (semi-private, 9 hole course)

1901 North Columbus; P.O. Box 1026; Goldendale, WA 98620
Phone: (509) 773-4705. Fax: none. Internet: none.
Pro: Steve Welker, PGA. Superintendent: N/A.
Rating/Slope: M 66.2/107; W 69.4/114. **Course record:** 66.
Green fees: W/D $18/$13; W/E $20/$15; winter rates; no credit cards.
Power cart: $20/$11. **Pull cart:** $2. **Trail fee:** $5 for personal carts.
Reservation policy: please call up to 1 week in advance for tee times.
Winter condition: the course is sometimes closed in December and February.
Terrain: flat, some hills. **Tees:** grass tees. **Spikes:** soft spikes preferred.
Services: club rentals, lessons, pro shop, putting green, chipping area.
Comments: the course is open to men only after 1 pm on Wednesday. This track offers dual tees for those wanting to play a full 18 hole round. Beautiful mountain and territorial views abound from this golf course. A creek comes into play on two holes with sand bunkers dotting some fairways. Good 9 hole course.

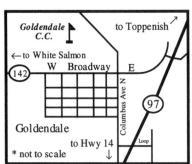

Directions: from Hwy 97 N&S follow to city center to Columbus St. (flashing light). Turn right and travel 1.5 miles to the golf course. **Note:** the golf course is located on the north edge of the city. Look for signs indicating your turn.

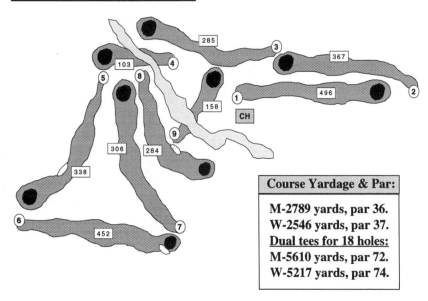

Course Yardage & Par:

M-2789 yards, par 36.
W-2546 yards, par 37.
Dual tees for 18 holes:
M-5610 yards, par 72.
W-5217 yards, par 74.

Golfgreen Golf Center (public, 9 hole par 3 course)

P.O. Box 1123; 561 7th Avenue; Longview, WA 98632
Phone: (360) 425-0450, 800-424-0450. Fax: (360) 501-4045.
Manager: Skip Manke. Superintendent: none. Internet: none.
Rating/Slope: the golf course is not rated. Course record: 21.
Green fees: W/D $10/$5.25; W/E's & Holdays $10.50/$5.50; no credit cards.
Power cart: not available. Pull cart: $1. Trail fee: not allowed.
Reservation policy: none, tee times are on a first come first served basis.
Winter condition: the golf course is open all year long.
Terrain: flat, very walkable. Tees: grass. Spikes: metal spikes permitted.
Services: club rentals $3, coffee shop, full service pro shop, miniature golf.
Comments: good hole variation. Yardage ranges from 55 yards to almost 200.
A great course to practice your short and long iron game on. Good golf course
for family golf or the first time golfer. Very easy course to walk so it is great for
the senior golfer. If you are looking for a change of pace try Golfgreen.

Directions: From I-5 N&S take exit #36
(Hwy 423) and travel westbound on Hwy
432 for .7 mile. Turn left at your first
available left at 9th Avenue to the golf
course. Look for signs indicating your
turn to the golf course. (The course is
located across from the drive in theater).

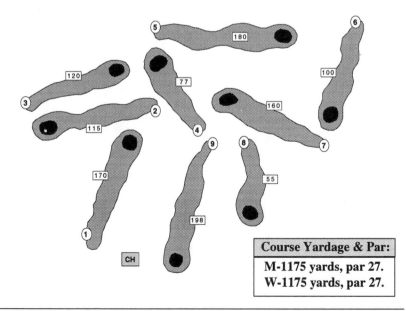

Course Yardage & Par:
M-1175 yards, par 27.
W-1175 yards, par 27.

Grandview Golf Course (public, 18 hole course)
7738 Portal Way; Custer, WA 98240
Phone: (360) 366-3947. **Fax:** none. **Internet:** none.
Manager: Thomas Okuma. **Superintendent:** Paul Booterbaugh.
Rating/Slope: C 69.9/117; M 68.2/113; W 71.2/120. **Course record:** 67.
Green fees: W/D $19/$14; W/E $22/$15; Jr/Sr rates (M-F); VISA, M/C, DIS.
Power cart: $22/$16. **Pull cart:** $3. **Trail fee:** $8 for personal carts.
Reservation policy: yes, please call 7 days in advance for your tee times.
Winter condition: the golf course is open all year long. Dry conditions.
Terrain: flat (easy walking). **Tees:** all grass. **Spikes:** soft spikes preferred.
Services: club rentals, snack bar, beer, wine, pro shop, lockers, putting green.
Comments: a very flat easy to walk course where water comes into play on numerous holes. Bunkers guard medium size greens on many of your approach shots. The golf course is fast becoming a top rate facility with added upgrades to enhance its playability. The golf course has great freeway access.

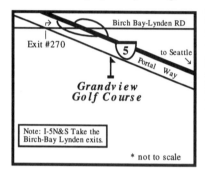

Directions: from I-5 N&S take exit #270 (Lynden-Birch Bay) to the west. Travel west for .2 miles to Portal Way. Turn south for 1.4 miles to the golf course. **Note:** the golf course can be seen from Interstate 5. Look for signs marking your way to the golf course.

Course Yardage & Par:
C-6425 yards, par 72.
M-6119 yards, par 72.
F-5422 yards, par 72.

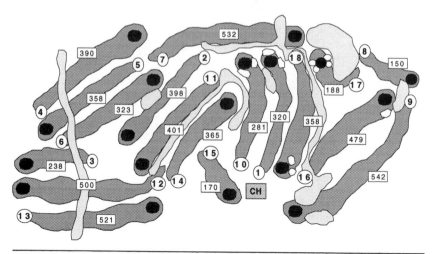

Grays Harbor Country Club (private, 9 hole course)
5300 Central Park Drive; Aberdeen, WA 98520
Phone: (360) 532-1931. Fax: (360) 533-3252. Internet: none.
Pro: Keith Liedes, PGA. Supertindent: Don Scott.
Rating/Slope: M 67.1/111; W 71.6/119. **Course record:** 62.
Green fees: private club, members & guest only; reciprocates.
Power cart: private club. **Pull cart:** private club. **Trail fee:** private club.
Reservation policy: yes, minimum call 1 day in advance for tee times.
Winter condition: the golf course is open all year long. Dry (drains well).
Terrain: flat, some hills. **Tees:** grass. **Spikes:** soft spikes preferred.
Services: club rentals, lessons, snack bar, lounge, restaurant, beer, wine, liquor, lockers, pro shop, showers, club memberships, driving range, putting green.
Comments: a variety of shots are required on this course. Greens are medium to large in size and have few hazards fronting them. Challenging holes abound from this 9 holer. Great course that plays much longer and harder than it looks.

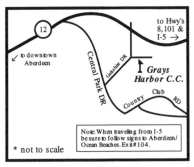

Directions: from I-5 N&S take exit #104 (Ocean Beaches) to Hwy 12 to Aberdeen/Hoquiam. Exit (left) in Central Park on Central Park Drive. Travel .75 miles to the golf course.

Course Yardage & Par:
M-2915 yards, par 35.
W-2884 yards, par 36.
Dual tees for 18 holes:
M-5779 yards, par 70.
W-5644 yards, par 72.

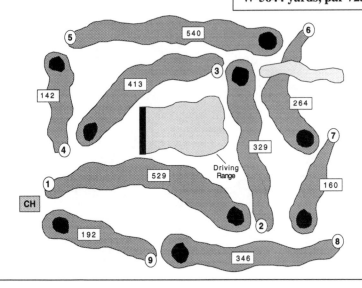

Green Lake Golf Course (public, 9 hole par 3 course)
5701 West Greenlake Way North; Seattle, WA 98103
Phone: (206) 632-2280. Fax: none. Internet: none.
Manager: Marlene Taitch. Pro: none. Superintendent: none.
Rating/Slope: the golf course is not rated. **Course record:** 22.
Green fees: $4/$2 additional 9 holes (all week long); Jr. & Sr. rates.
Power cart: none. **Pull cart:** $1. **Trail fee:** no personal carts allowed.
Reservation policy: tee times are on a first come first served basis.
Winter condition: the golf course is closed during the winter months.
Terrain: very, flat. **Tees:** all mats. **Spikes:** metal spikes permitted.
Services: club rentals, lessons, vending machines, small pro shop.
Comments: the course is located at Green Lake in north Seattle. Excellent for practice on your short iron play. If you are looking for a course for the first time golfer Green Lake is sure to fit the bill.

Directions: From I-5 N&S take exit 159 to NE 50th. Go westbound for 1.3 miles to Green Lake Way N. North for .8 miles to the golf course (located at the southern tip of Greenlake).

Course Yardage & Par:
M-705 yards, par 27.
W-705 yards, par 27.

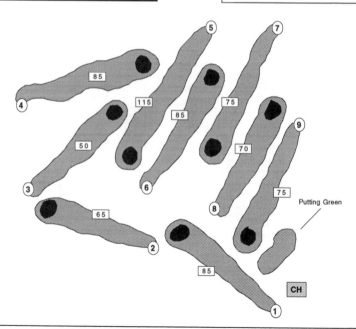

Green Mountain Resort (public, 18 hole course)

off NE Ingle & Goodwin Roads; Orchards, WA 98662
Phone: not available. **Fax:** not available. **Internet:** none.
General Manager: Paul DeBoni. **Superintendent:** to be determined.
Rating/Slope: the golf course is not yet rated. **Course record:** N/A.
Green fees: to be determined; call for information on credit card usage.
Power cart: to be determined. **Pull cart:** to be determined. **Trail fee:** N/A.
Reservation policy: you may call ahead for a tee time.
Winter condition: the golf course is open all year long. Weather permitting.
Terrain: flat some hills. **Tees:** all grass. **Spikes:** soft spikes required.
Services: club rentals, lessons, snack bar, beer, pro shop, driving range.
Comments: this easy walking course is due to open 9 holes sometime in June or July of 1999. The additional 9 will open shortly thereafter. Short and sporty for the ladies Green Mountain requires careful driving for the long hitter. The par fours are not overly long but the par 3's are a strong test from the back tees. Five par 5's are mixed through the layout giving a little something for everyone.

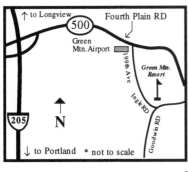

Directions: From I-205 N&S take the Orchards exit to Hwy 500. Proceed east on Hwy 500 (Fourth Plain Road) until you reach 199th Ave. (just beyond the Green Mtn. Airport) turn right on 199th. Follow this until you reach the intersection of Ingle Rd. & Goodwin Road where the golf course is located.

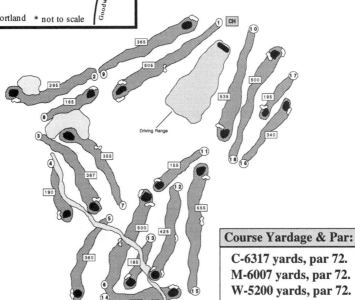

Course Yardage & Par:

C-6317 yards, par 72.
M-6007 yards, par 72.
W-5200 yards, par 72.

Hangman Valley Golf Club (public, 18 hole course)
2210 E Hangman Valley Road; Spokane, WA 99223
Phone: (509) 448-1212. Fax: (509) 448-7612. Internet: none.
Pro: Steve Nelke, PGA. Superintendent: Mike Barber.
Rating/Slope: C 71.9/126; M 69.4/119; W 72.2/124. **Course record:** 64.
Green fees: $22/$16 all week long; Jr. & Sr. rates (M-F); M/C, VISA.
Power cart: $23/$11.50. **Pull cart:** $3. **Trail fee:** $6 for personal carts.
Reservation policy: call ahead up to 1 week in advance for times.
Winter condition: the golf course is closed from November until mid March.
Terrain: relatively hilly. **Tees:** all grass. **Spikes:** metal spikes permitted.
Services: club rentals, lessons, restaurant, snack bar, beer, wine, beverages, pro
shop, driving range, putting green, club memberships, handicapping service.
Comments: a challenging course featuring elevated tees, many trees, and well
bunkered greens. Hangman Creek comes into play on seven holes and is a major
factor. Excellent public golf course that is well maintained throughout the year.

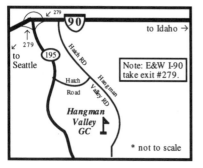

Directions: from I-90 east and west, take
the exit for Hwy 195 S. Proceed for 4.5
miles to the Hatch Road exit. Turn left
on Hatch Road for .2 miles to Hangman
Valley Road. Turn right on Hangman
Valley Road. The golf course will be
located five miles ahead. Look for signs.

Course Yardage & Par:
C-6951 yards, par 72.
M-6409 yards, par 72.
W-5603 yards, par 72.

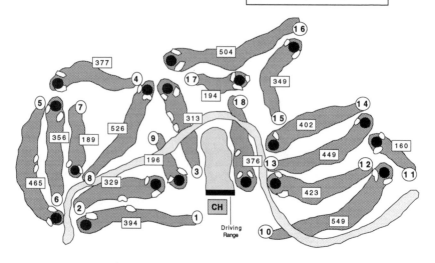

Harbour Pointe Golf Club (public, 18 hole course)

11817 Harbour Point Boulevard; Mukilteo, WA 98275
Phone: 800-233-3128, (425) 355-6060. Fax: (425) 347-2200.
Pro: Mark Rhodes, PGA. Supt.: Keith Coleman. Internet: none.
Rating/Slope: T 72.9/137; C 71.6/129; M 69.5/118; W 68.8/118. **Record:** 64.
Green fees: Mon.-Th. $60; Fri.- Sun. $72 (peak rates) the course offers lower rates during the off season and off times; twilight, early bird rates; M/C, VISA.
Power cart: $13/$9 per player. **Pull cart:** $3. **Trail fee:** not allowed.
Reservation policy: yes, call up to 5 days in advance for tee-times.
Winter condition: the golf course is open all year long. Dry conditions.
Terrain: flat, some hills. **Tees:** all grass. **Spikes:** soft spikes preferred.
Services: club rentals, lessons, restaurant, lounge, beer, wine, liquor, pro shop, driving range, practice area. **Comments:** outstanding layout with water and sand coming into play on nearly every hole. This track is challenging and demanding. Breathtaking view of Puget Sound from the 11th hole. Excellent golf course.

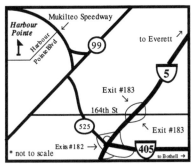

Directions: from I-5 or I-405 exit onto Mukilteo to Hwy 99. Turn right on Hwy 99. At the first stop light turn left onto the Mukilteo Spdwy. Once on the Mukilteo Spdwy go to the second light and turn left onto Harbour Pointe Blvd. Proceed to the course on the right side. I-5 south should exit at 164th St. and proceed to 99 northbound and proceed to the Mukilteo Speedway. Follow the above directions.

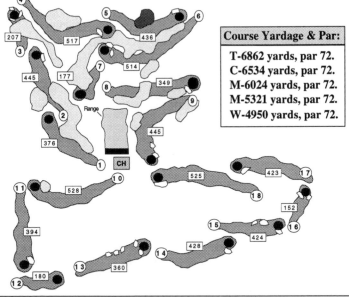

Course Yardage & Par:
T-6862 yards, par 72.
C-6534 yards, par 72.
M-6024 yards, par 72.
M-5321 yards, par 72.
W-4950 yards, par 72.

Harrington Golf & Country Club (semi-private , 9 hole course)

700 South 2nd; P. O. Box 191; Harrington, WA 99134
Phone: (509) 253-4308. **Fax:** none. **Internet:** none.
Pro: Bud Drake, PGA. **Superintendent:** Jim Gilliland.
Rating/Slope: M 70.1/119; W 74.6/126. **Course record:** 66.
Green fees: W/D $14/$10; W/E $16/$11; Sr rates (weekdays); M/C, VISA.
Power cart: $20/$12. **Pull cart:** $3.00. **Trail fee:** not available.
Reservation policy: please call in advance for your starting times.
Winter condition: the golf course is open all year long, if playable.
Terrain: relatively hilly. **Tees:** grass. **Spikes:** soft spikes preferred.
Services: club rentals, restaurant, snack bar, lounge (members and guests), beer, wine, liquor, pro shop, driving range, putting green. **Comments:** the course is one of the finest 9 holers in the state. This course is situated in the midst of rolling, beautiful wheat fields. Excellent golf course that has wide open fairways and large, well bunkered greens. You will truely enjoy your round at Harrington.

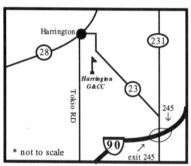

Directions: from I-90 east & west exit to Hwy 231, #245 and head northbound. Hwy 231 will intersect with Hwy 23. Follow Hwy 23 to Harrington. When in Harrington exit to Hwy 28. From Hwy 28 exit on Main Street and proceed south to the golf course.

Course Yardage & Par:
M-3166 yards, par 36.
W-2983 yards, par 36.
Dual tees for 18 holes:
M-6348 yards, par 72.
W-5988 yards, par 72.

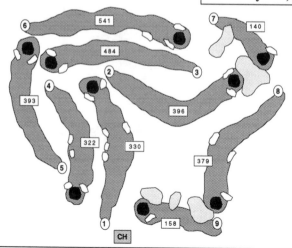

Hartwood Golf Course (public, 9 hole executive course)

12506 NE 152nd Avenue; Brush Prairie, WA 98606
Phone: (360) 896-6041. Fax: none. Internet: none.
Manager: Sue Hart. Superintendent: none.
Rating/Slope: golf course is not rated. **Course record:** 25.
Green fees: $8/$9 all week long; Jr. & Sr. rates; M/C, VISA, AMEX, DIS.
Power cart: not available. **Pull cart:** $2. **Trail fee:** not allowed.
Reservation policy: tee times are on a first come first served basis.
Winter condition: the golf course is closed November thru February.
Terrain: flat. **Tees:** grass & mats. **Spikes:** soft spikes only.
Services: club rentals, pro shop, snack bar, putting green.
Comments: beautiful views of Mount St. Helens and Mount Hood from the open fairways, old oak and fir trees surround the course. This is a fun, friendly executive course that is enjoyable for both beginners and experienced golfers.

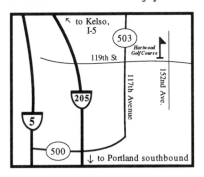

Directions: from I-5 N&S take SR/500 Orchards exit. Follow SR500 until it intersects with 4th Plain. Continue straight across 4th Plain onto 117th Avenue headed north. Turn right (east) onto 119th Street. Proceed 2 miles then turn left (north) onto 152nd Ave. Course is 1/4 mile on the west side of 152nd.

Course Yardage & Par:
M-1588 yards, par 29.
W-1464 yards, par 29.

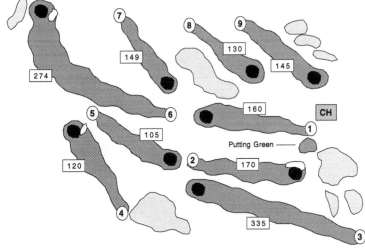

Hat Island Golf Course (private, 9 hole course)
1016A 14th Street; Everett, WA 98201
Phone: no phone listing. Fax: none. Internet: none.
Manager: Jan Coleman. Superintendent: none.
Rating/Slope: golf course is not rated. **Course record:** 32.
Green fees: private club, property owners and their guests $10/$5.
Power cart: private club. **Pull cart:** private club. **Trail fee:** private club.
Reservation policy: private club, members & guests only.
Winter condition: the golf course is open for play open, weather permitting.
Terrain: very flat. **Tees:** all grass. **Spikes:** metal spikes permitted.
Services: private club, members and guests only.
Comments: the golf course is very flat and easy to walk. Holes are very narrow with many trees surrounding fairways and greens. Tight golf course.

Directions: Hat Island golf course is located in Puget Sound just west of Everett and southeast of Camano Island.

Course Yardage & Par:
M-2335 yards, par 35.
W-2335 yards, par 35.
Dual tees for 18 holes:
M-4805 yards, par 70.
W-4805 yards, par 70.

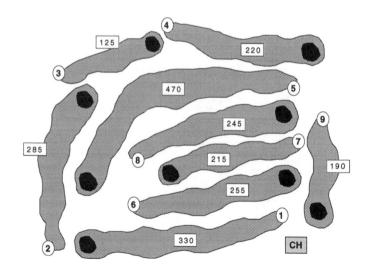

High Cedars Golf Club (public 18 & 9 hole course)
14604 149th Court East; Box 490; Orting, WA 98360
Phone: (253) 845-1853. Fax: (253) 848-6849. Internet: none
General Manager: Darin Thompson. Superintendent: Greg Williams.
Rating/Slope: C 69.7/114; M 68.6/111; W 70.7/115. **Course record:** 64.
Green fees: W/D $22.50/$17.25; W/E $32/$22; M/C, VISA.
Power cart: $22$15. **Pull cart:** $4/$2.50. **Trail fee:** $15 for personal carts.
Reservation policy: call ahead up to 1 week in advance for tee-times.
Winter condition: the golf course is open all year long weather permitting.
Terrain: flat (easy walking). **Tees** all grass. **Spikes:** soft spikes preferred.
Services: club rentals, lessons, snack bar, beer, pro shop, large driving range,
outdoor barbecue. **Comments:** towering cedar trees, great restaurant, and
beautiful flowers make for a fantastic day of golf. This one is a favorite with
the locals. The facility has a 18 hole all grass putting course, fees are $5.

Directions: From I-5 S exit to I-405 N to
Hwy 167S. Proceed southbound on Hwy
167 and exit at Hwy 410E. Proceed east
on Hwy 410E to the Orting exit (Hwy
162). Turn right on Hwy 162 and proceed
for 5 miles to the golf course. From I-5 N
take exit #127 to Hwy 512E. Travel east
to the Pioneer Ave exit. Turn right on
Hwy 162 and travel 4 miles to the golf
course. **Note:** Sign on Hwy 410.

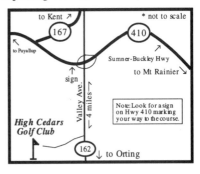

Executive Course Yardage & Par:
C-1566 yards, par 28.
M-1538 yards, par 28.
W-1326 yards, par 28.

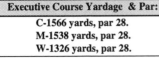

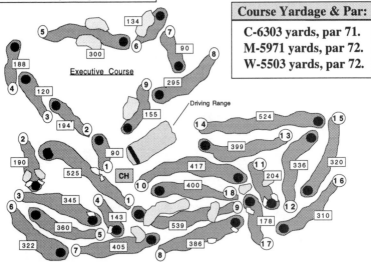

Course Yardage & Par:
C-6303 yards, par 71.
M-5971 yards, par 72.
W-5503 yards, par 72.

High Valley Golf Course (private, 9 hole course)

633 Cannon Road, Box 427; Packwood, WA 98361
Phone: (360) 494-8431. **Fax:** none. **Internet:** none.
Manager: Carol Beaty. **Superintendent:** Wright VanderWegen.
Rating/Slope: M 58.2/83; W 59.1/87. **Course record:** 29.
Green fees: guests fees W/D $5 all day rate; W/E $10 all day rate.
Power cart: limited. **Pull cart:** limited. **Trail fee:** none.
Reservation policy: none, private club members and guests only.
Winter condition: closed November to February depending on the weather.
Terrain: flat (easy walking). **Tees:** all grass. **Spikes:** soft spikes preferred.
Services: club rentals, limited pro shop, vending machines, pool, putting green.
Comments: a very scenic private club near Mount Rainier and right on the
Cowlitz River. Fairways are tree lined with few other hazards coming into play.
The course can play tough if the wind begins to blow. Good private course.

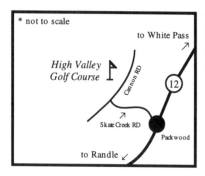

Directions: from Hwy 12 exit on Skate
Creek Road (north in Packwood). Travel
east, just over the river (.5 miles). Turn
right on Cannon Road. Proceed 2 miles
to the golf course.

Course Yardage & Par:
M-1728 yards, par 31.
W-1728 yards, par 33.

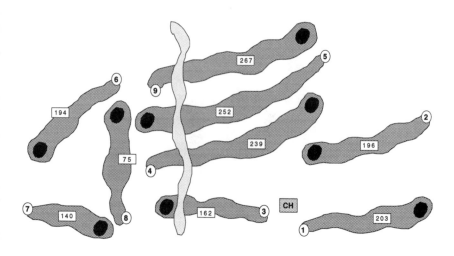

Highland Golf Course (public, 18 hole course)

300 Yard Drive; P.O. Box 542; Cosmopolis, WA 98537
Phone: (360) 533-2455. **Fax:** none. **Internet:** none.
Pro: Joe Golia, PGA. **Superintendent:** Mike Strada.
Rating/Slope: C 67.4/108; M 65.7/105; W 63.0/100. **Course record:** 62.
Green fees: W/D $15/$10; W/E & Holidays $17/$12; credit cards accepted.
Power cart: $20/$10. **Pull cart:** $1.50. **Trail fee:** $5 for personal carts.
Reservation policy: please call in advance for all your tee times.
Winter condition: the golf course is open all year long. Dry conditions.
Terrain: relatively hilly. **Tees:** grass. **Spikes:** metal spikes permitted.
Services: club rentals, lessons, snack bar, beer, wine, pro shop, driving range.
Comments: established in 1929 this course has many mature trees with which
one must contend to score well. Greens are large and well bunkered. This good
public track is worth a try when visiting the Grays Harbor area.

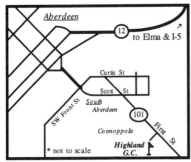

Directions: from I-5 north & south take
exit #104 and follow Hwy 12 to Aberdeen Proceed to Hwy 101. The golf
course is located 2 miles south of the
Aberdeen city limits. Turn westbound to
the golf course. Look for signs marking
your way to the golf course.

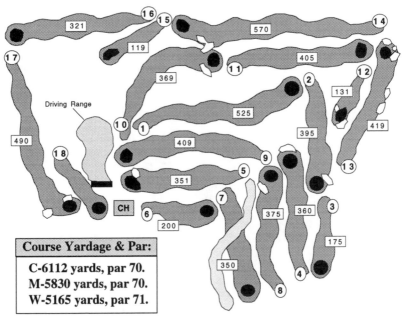

Course Yardage & Par:

C-6112 yards, par 70.
M-5830 yards, par 70.
W-5165 yards, par 71.

Highlands Golf Course (public, 9 hole course)
1400 Highlands Parkway North; Tacoma, WA 98406
Phone: (253) 759-3622. **Fax:** none. **Internet:** none.
Manager: Jerry Brugler. **Superintendent:** Clyde Strampher.
Rating/Slope: golf course is not rated. **Course record:** 9 holes 23, 18 holes 52.
Green fees: $13/$8.50 all week long; Jr. & Sr. rates $11/$7.50 (Monday thru
Friday); punch cards & yearly rates available; M/C, VISA.
Power cart: not allowed. **Pull cart:** $3. **Trail fee:** not allowed.
Reservation policy: please call up to 1 week in advance for tee times.
Winter condition: the golf course is open all year long, dry, excellent drainage.
Terrain: flat, some hills. **Tees:** grass. **Spikes:** soft spikes preffered.
Services: club rentals, pro shop, club memberships, putting green.
Comments: kept in good condition, two water holes, lots of bunkers, and
challenging golf is what you will find at Highlands. Excellent executive length
golf course that will be worth the trip if you are looking for a change of pace.

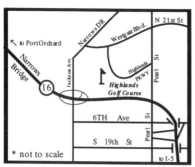

Directions: from I-5 N&S take exit #132
to Hwy 16W. From Hwy 16W exit at the
Jackson Avenue exit. Turn north to N
17th. Turn right on N 17th. Proceed to
Highlands Parkway where you will turn
right. Note: You can see the golf course
from Hwy 16. Look for signs.

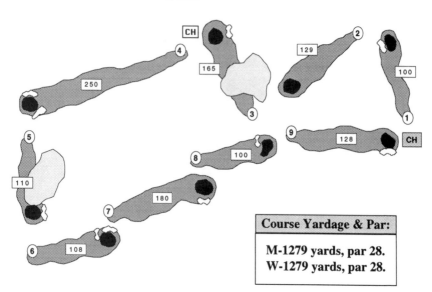

Course Yardage & Par:
M-1279 yards, par 28.
W-1279 yards, par 28.

Holmes Harbor Golf Club (public, 18 hole course)

5023 Harbor Hills Drive; Freeland, WA 98249
Phone: (360) 331-2363. **Fax:** (360) 331-2366. **Internet:** www.hhgc@whidbey.co
Pro: Rich Kirkl. **Superintendent:** Don Stin.
Rating/Slope: C 62.0/109; M 61.0/107; W 62.9/110. **Course record:** 57.
Green fees: Monday-Thursday $18; Friday thru Sunday & holidays $25;
Jr. & Sr. rates available; twilight rates available; M/C, VISA.
Power cart: $9 per player. **Pull cart:** $2. **Trail fee:** $12 for personal carts.
Reservation policy: please call ahead for tee times. No time limit.
Winter condition: the golf course is open all year long. Dry conditions.
Terrain: flat, some hills. **Tees:** all grass. **Spikes:** soft spikes preffered.
Services: club rentals, lessons, lounge, restaurant, snack bar, beer, wine, liquor,
pro shop. **Comments:** very scenic newer course with views of the Cascades,
Olympics, and Holmes Harbor from many of the tees and greens. The golf
course has rolling fairways well bunkered greens and excellent conditions.

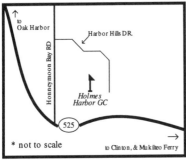

Directions: take the Mukilteo ferry to
Clinton. Travel 10.1 miles on Hwy 525.
Turn right on Honeymoon Bay Road.
Travel 1.3 miles. Turn right on Harbor
Hills Dr. and follow directly to the
parking lot of the golf course (this is
where the road ends). Look for signs.

Course Yardage & Par:
C-4371 yards, par 64.
M-4035 yards, par 64.
W-3565 yards, par 64.

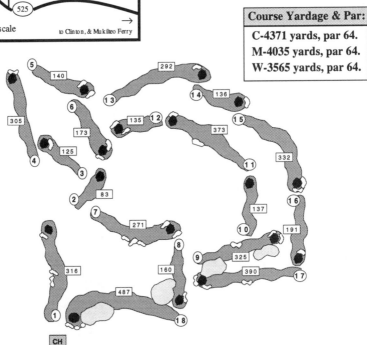

Homeplace Golf (public, 9 hole course)

6404 Kimber; Cashmere, WA 98815
Phone: (509) 782-GOLF (4653). Fax: (509) 782-1024. Internet: none.
Owners: Paul & Edna Hansen. Superintendent: Paul Hansen.
Rating/Slope: the golf course is not yet rated.
Green fees: $20/$12 all week long; no credit cards.
Power cart: $10. **Pull cart:** $3. **Trail fee:** $3.
Reservation policy: you may call ahead up to 6 days in advance.
Winter condition: the golf course is closed from November to February.
During the winter months the golf course opens for cross country skiing.
Terrain: relatively hilly. **Tees:** all grass. **Spikes:** metal spikes permitted.
Services: club rentals, lessons, snack bar, pro shop, driving range.
Comments: the fairways at Homeplace are bordered by apple and cherry trees.
The course is set among beautiful hills and orchards. Be sure to call ahead for
your tee-times as the course can be busy during the summer months. RV parking
is available at the Chelan County Fairground for those spending the night.

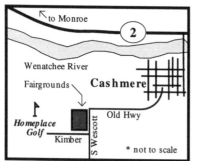

Directions: the course is located through
Cashmere. Follow Old Highway West
(approximately 1 mile). Look for "Fairgrounds" signs. The course is located .25
miles west of the Fairgrounds at the end
of Kimber Road.

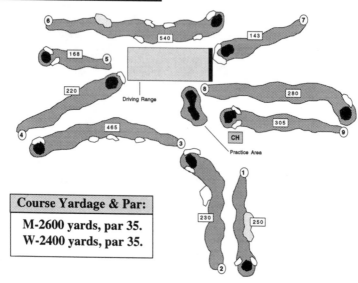

Course Yardage & Par:
M-2600 yards, par 35.
W-2400 yards, par 35.

Homestead Golf & Country Club (semi-private, 18 holes)

115 E Homestead Boulevard P.O. Box 707; Lynden, WA 98264

Phone: 800-354-1196. Fax: (360) 354-5614. Internet: www.cybergolf.com/homestead

Pro: Bill Chrysler, PGA. Superintendent: Mick O'brien.

Rating/Slope: T 73.6/129; C 71.9/125; M 69.9/117; W 72.9/123. **Record:** 66.

Green fees: May-Sept. W/D $35; W/E $40; winter rates, Jr. & Sr. (M-Thur).

Power cart: $10 per person. **Pull cart:** $3/$2. **Trail fee:** not allowed.

Reservation policy: please call up to 1 week in advance for tee-times.

Winter condition: the golf course is open all year long. Dry conditions.

Terrain: flat, some mounds. **Tees:** all grass. **Spikes:** soft spikes required.

Services: club rentals, lessons, driving range, full service clubhouse with restaurant, beer, wine, beverages, pro shop. **Comments:** this Bill Overdorf design is a challenge to all golfers. All 18 holes opened in the spring of 1995 and has fast become a favorite of the local golfers. Signature hole is the par 5 eighteenth hole that will test your nerve. This course is worth a trip.

Directions: from I-5 northbound take exit #256, Hwy 539 (Guide Meridian) to Lynden (10 miles). Turn eastbound on Hwy 546 for 1.5 miles to Depot RD. Turn south on Depot RD for 1/4 mile to the course. From I-5 southbound exit off of I-5 at Birch Bay-Lynden #270 and follow to Lynden. Turn northbound on Hwy 539 and follow the above directions to the golf course. Look for signs along the way.

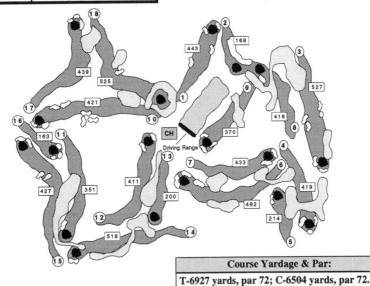

Course Yardage & Par:
T-6927 yards, par 72; C-6504 yards, par 72.
M-6033 yards, par 72; W-5570 yards, par 72.

Horn Rapids Golf & Country Club (public, 18 hole course)

2800 Clubhouse Lane; P. O. Box 840; Richland, WA 98352
Phone: (509) 375-4714. Fax: (509) 375-7494. Internet: none.
Manager: Nick Rodrigues. Superintendent: Dave Bock.
Rating/Slope: C 73.6/130; M 71.0/122; W 70.4/117. F 69.0/118. **Record:** 62.
Green fees: Monday-Thur. $18/$13; Friday $23/$16; W/E & Holidays $28/$20.
Power cart: $24/$14. **Pull cart:** $4/$2. **Trail fee:** $7 for personal carts.
Reservation policy: you may call 1 week in advance for tee times.
Winter condition: dry, the golf course open all year weather permitting.
Terrain: flat, some rolling hills. **Tees:** grass. **Spikes:** soft spikes only.
Services: club rentals, lessons, snack bar, beer, wine, pro shop, driving range.
Comments: the golf course is a desert style track emphasizing shot placement (target golf). Greens are large undulating and tricky to putt. If you are looking for change and want a challenge try Horn Rapids it will not disappoint.

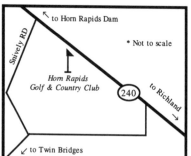

Directions: the golf course is located on Highway 240 2 miles west of Richland Washington (the Vantage Highway). From I-182/Hwy12 in Richland, WA take exit #4 and proceed northbound to the golf course which is located 2.3 miles north. Look for signs indicating your turn to the golf course.

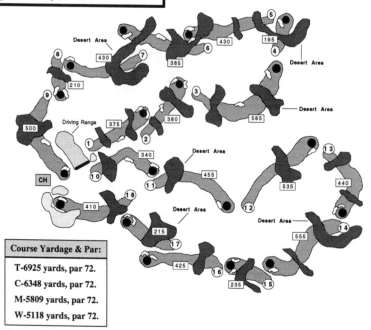

Course Yardage & Par:
T-6925 yards, par 72.
C-6348 yards, par 72.
M-5809 yards, par 72.
W-5118 yards, par 72.

Horseshoe Lake Golf Course (public, 18 hole course)
1250 S.W. Clubhouse CT ; Port Orchard, WA 98367
Phone: 800-843-1564, (253) 857-3326. Fax: (253) 857-4352. Internet: none.
Pro: Chris Morris, PGA. Superintendent: Scott Brooke.
Rating/Slope: C 69.1/114; M 67.0/109; W 68.1/110. **Course record:** 64.
Green fees: W/D $27*/$16; W/E 31*/$19 (*includes cart on back 9);
Jr. and Sr. rates (Monday through Friday); M/C, VISA, AMEX, DISCOVER
Power cart: 9 hole fee $5 per person. **Pull cart:** $3. **Trail fee:** not allowed.
Reservation policy: yes, please call up to 7 days in advance for tee-times.
Or you can call up to one month in advance with credit card conformation.
Winter condition: the golf course is open all year. Very dry conditions.
Terrain: front 9, flat; back 9 very hilly. **Tees:** grass. **Spikes:** no policy.
Services: club rentals, driving range, full service clubhouse, restaurant, lessons.
Comments: Excellent on course restaurant, and challenging golf course is
worth a special trip. You will have fantastic views of the countryside and the
Olympic Mountains from nearly every tee. Challenging course that can be tough.

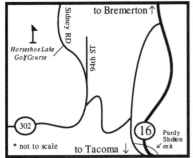

Directions: from Hwy 16 take the Purdy
exit. Take Hwy 302 across the Purdy
Bridge to the top of the hill (approximately 2 miles). Turn right on 94th Ave.
The golf course is located 1.2 miles on
the left hand side. Look for signs.

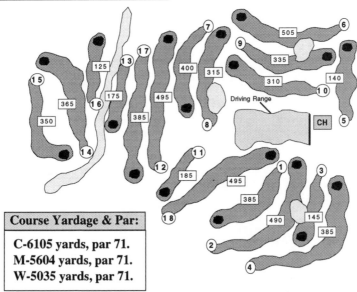

Course Yardage & Par:

C-6105 yards, par 71.
M-5604 yards, par 71.
W-5035 yards, par 71.

Hot Springs Golf Course (public, 18 hole course)
Saint Martin Road; P.O. Box 370; Carson, WA 98610
Phone: (509) 427-5150. Fax: none. Internet: none.
Manager: John Broughten. Superintendent: Bob Henrdricksen.
Rating/Slope: C 72.1/125; M 70.4/122; W 68.9/116. **Course record:** 73.
Green fees: W/D $16/$9; W/E $19/$11; Sr. & winter rates available.
Power cart: $20/$10. **Pull cart:** $3.50/$2.50. **Trail fee:** no charge.
Reservation policy: yes, accepted for weekend tee-times, please call ahead.
Winter condition: the golf course is open all year long. Dry conditions.
Terrain: flat, some hills. **Tees:** all grass. **Spikes:** soft spikes preferred.
Services: snacks, beer, pro shop, driving range, putting & chipping greens.
Comments: Gentle rolling terrain and wind that roles through the tree lined
fairways characterize this golf course. Bunkered fairways along with water
come into play off the tee and approach shots. Greens are medium in size and
are well bunkered. Course plays much longer than the yardage would indicate.

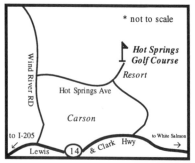

Directions: the golf course is located 1
mile north of Hwy 14 on the east side of
Carson. From Hwy 14 turn northbound
toward Carson, Washington. Turn right
on Hot Springs Avenue to the golf
course. Look for signs along the way.

Course Yardage & Par:
C-6559 yards, par 73.
M-6150 yards, par 73.
W-5365 yards, par 73.

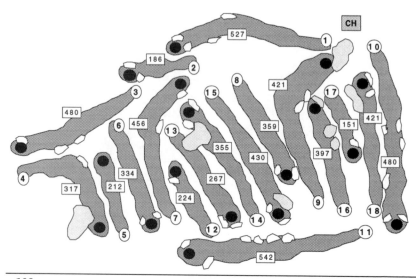

Husum Hills Golf Course (public, 9 hole course)

820 Highway 141, White Salmon, WA 98672
Phone: (509) 493-1211, 800-487-4537. Fax: (509) 493-1014. Internet: none.
Pro: Gary Tamietti, PGA. Superintendent: none.
Rating/Slope: 63.7/96; W 67.6/104. Course record: 31.
Green fees: $20/$12 all week long; credit cards are accepted.
Power cart: $20/$10. **Pull cart:** $4/$2. **Trail fee:** $5 for personal carts.
Reservation policy: yes, call up to 7 days in advance but are not necessary.
Winter condition: the golf course is open when playable. Fair conditions.
Terrain: flat to very hilly. **Tees:** grass. **Spikes:** soft spikes preferred.
Services: club rentals, restaurant, pro shop, wine, beer, putting/chipping green.
Comments: The course is well treed, with beautiful views of Mount Adams.
Grass bunkers abound which create some difficult lies. Good nine hole track
that can challenge any level of golfer. Course is adding new hazards as well as
rebuilding some tees to lengthen some holes. This should improve playability.

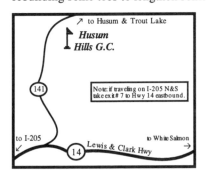

Directions: from I-5S take exit #7 to
I-205S. Travel southbound to exit #27 to
Hwy14E. Proceed eastbound to Hwy 141
and exit at Hwy 141. Go northbound on
Hwy 141 for 5.5 miles to the golf course.
Look for signs that are posted marking
your turn to the golf course.

Course Yardage & Par:
C-2631 yards, par 35.
M-2458 yards, par 35.
W-2390 yards, par 35.

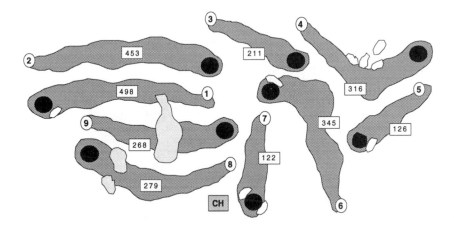

Hylander Greens Golf Practice Center (public, 9 hole course)

1475 East Nelson Road; Moses Lake, WA 98837
Phone: (509) 766-1228. **Fax:** none. **Internet:** none.
Pro: Bill Porter, PGA. **Superintendent:** none.
Rating/Slope: the golf course is not rated. **Course record:** 25.
Green fees: W/D $10/$6; W/E $12/$7; Jr. & Sr. rates; no credit cards.
Power cart: $12/$7. **Pull cart:** $2/$1. **Trail fee:** no charge for personal carts.
Reservation policy: reservations are not needed, first come first served.
Winter condition: the golf course is closed December 1st to February 7th.
Terrain: flat, easy walking. **Tees:** all grass. **Spikes:** soft spikes only in summer.
Services: pro shop, club repair, club rentals, driving range, putting green.
Comments: a very well maintained 9 hole executive course. The areas best driving range featuring an elevated tee with high quality range balls. Golf professional Bill Porter is available to help you with all your golf needs. A new clubhouse and continued course improvements are planned in 1999.

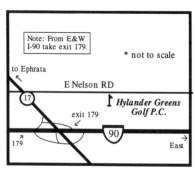

Note: From E&W I-90 take exit 179.

* not to scale

to Ephrata

E Nelson RD

17

exit 179

Hylander Greens Golf P.C.

90

179

East

Directions: from I-90 E&W take the Moses Lake/ Highway 17 exit #179. Go northbound on Highway 17. Stay to your right when the road splits. Turn right on East Nelson Road and proceed to the golf course. Look for signs to the course.

Course Yardage & Par:
M-1720 yards, par 29.
W-1720 yards, par 29.

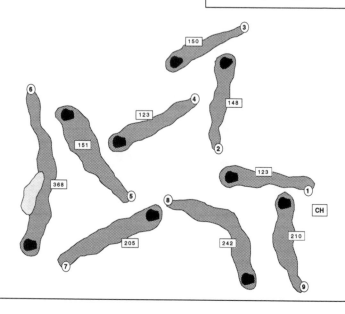

Indian Canyon Golf Course (public, 18 hole course)
West 4304 West Drive; Spokane, WA 99204
Phone: (509) 747-5353. Fax: unavailable. Internet: none.
Pro: Gary Lindeblad, PGA. Superintendent: Don Nelson.
Rating/Slope: C 70.7/126; M 69.3/123; W 73.9/132. **Course record:** 62.
Green fees: $16/$13 with discount card; $22/$16 without discount card. The fees listed are all week long fees; Jr. & Sr. rates are available; VISA, M/C.
Power cart: $23. **Pull cart:** $3. **Trail fee:** $9 for personal carts.
Reservation policy: yes, W/D 1 day in advance, W/E 1 week in advance.
Winter condition: the golf course is closed from November to March.
Terrain: very hilly. **Tees:** all grass. **Spikes:** soft spikes preferred.
Services: club rentals, lessons, restaurant, snack bar, beer, wine, pro shop, driving range. **Comments:** consistently rated in the top 75 public courses by *Golf Digest.* Greens are large and well bunkered. This golf course is extremely well maintained and is worth a special trip if you are in the Spokane area.

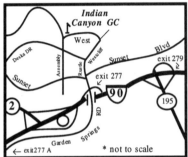

Directions: from I-90 eastbound & westbound take the Garden Springs exit. #277 or #277A. Proceed north on Rustle Street to the Sunset Hwy where you will turn left. Proceed to Assembly Street and turn right. Follow this to the golf course. Look for signs marking your way.

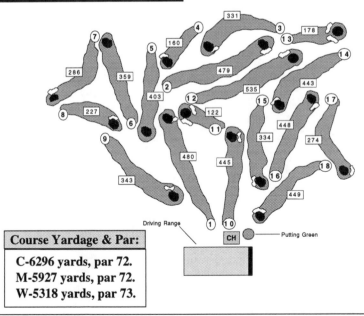

Course Yardage & Par:
C-6296 yards, par 72.
M-5927 yards, par 72.
W-5318 yards, par 73.

Indian Summer Golf & Country Club (private, 18 hole course)

5900 Troon Lane SE; Olympia, WA 98501
Phone: (360) 459-3772. **Fax:** (360) 923-9037. **Internet:** none.
Pro: Kevin Bishop, PGA. **Superintendent:** Bob Pearsall.
Rating/Slope: T 75.1/142; C 73.3/136; M 71.5/128; W 71.1/125. **Record:** 64.
Green fees: private club, members & guests of members only.
Power cart: $25. **Pull cart:** private club. **Trail fee:** private club, not allowed.
Reservation policy: have your golf pro call for recprocity. Private club
Winter condition: the golf course is open all year long. Dry conditions.
Terrain: flat, some hills. **Tees:** all grass. **Spikes:** soft spikes April- October.
Services: full service clubhouse, restaurant, snack bar, lounge, pro shop, lockers, driving range, putting & chipping greens. **Comments:** championship caliber course. The back 9 winds through Pacific Northwest old growth timber stands and bordering wetlands. The front 9 features wide open, rolling terrain and water on 7 holes. Home of the Pacific NW PGA offices. Great course.

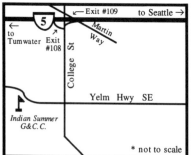

Directions: from I-5S exit #108 College St. Proceed to College St. and turn right. Follow College St. for 3.4 miles to the Yelm Hwy. Turn right and follow for 1/2 mile to the golf course which will be on your left. From I-5N take exit #109. Take left on College St. and follow the same directions. Look for signs at your turn.

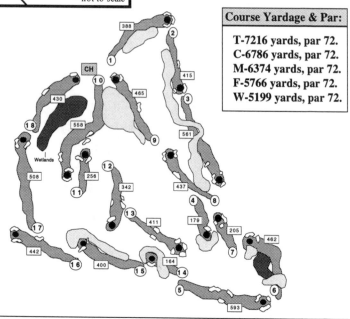

Course Yardage & Par:
T-7216 yards, par 72.
C-6786 yards, par 72.
M-6374 yards, par 72.
F-5766 yards, par 72.
W-5199 yards, par 72.

Inglewood Golf Club (private, 18 hole course)

6505 Inglewood Road NE; P. O. Box 70; Kenmore, WA 98028
Phone: (425) 488-7000. Fax: (425) 488-1783. Internet: none.
Pro: N/A. Superintendent: Tom McCarthy.
Course record: 63. **Competitive course record:** 64.
Rating/Slope: T 72.9/131; C 71.6/128; M 70.0/124; W 74.9/127.
Green fees: private club members & guests only; reciprocates; no credit cards.
Power cart: private club. **Pull cart:** private club. **Trail fee:** not allowed.
Reservation policy: private club members & guests only. Reciprocates call.
Winter condition: the golf course is open all year long. Damp conditions.
Terrain: very hilly. **Tees:** all grass. **Spikes:** no metal spikes in summer.
Services: club rentals, lessons, snack bar, restaurant, lounge, beer, wine, liquor, shower, lockers, pro shop, driving range. **Comments:** past home of the Senior PGA event the "GTE Northwest Classic". Past host to the "Fred Couples Invitational". Hilly terrain gives a wide variety of fairway lies. Good course.

Directions: from I-5S take exit 177 to Hwy 104E (Forest Park Drive). Travel east 2.5 miles to Hwy 522 E (Bothell Way). Turn east for 1.3 miles to 68th NE-Juanita Dr. Turn south for .4 miles to NE 170th. Turn west to the golf course. From I-5N take exit 175 to NE 145th. Travel east for 1.5 miles to Bothell Way NE. Turn left and travel 3.1 miles to 68th-Juanita Dr. Turn right. Proceed .4 miles to NE 170th. Turn right to course.

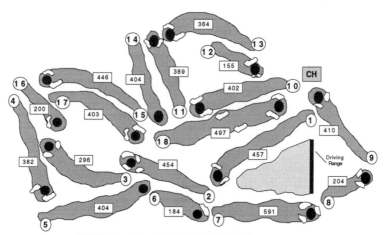

Course Yardage & Par:
T-6731 yards, par 73; C-6460 yards, par 73.
M-6150 yards, par 73; W-5176 yards, par 73.

Interbay Family Golf Center (public, 9 hole course)

2501 15th Avenue West; Seattle, WA 98199
Phone: (206) 285-2200. Fax: (206) 285-0239. Internet: familygolf.com.
Pro: Steve Wozniak, PGA. Manager: Bill Meyer. Course record: N/A.
Rating/Slope: the golf course is not rated.
Green fees: W/D $11; W/E $13; Jr. & Sr. rates; VISA, M/C, AMEX, DINERS.
Power cart: $10. **Pull cart:** $2.50. **Trail fee:** $10.
Reservation policy: tee-times may be made 1 week in advance.
Winter condition: the golf course will be opened all year around.
Terrain: some hills. **Tees:** grass. **Spikes:** soft spikes preferred.
Services: club rentals, lessons, restaurant, beer, wine, pro shop, driving range.
Comments: this Golden Bear designed golf course is a fantastic layout for the first time golfer or the experienced linksman. Extensive mounding and large greens make the golf course user friendly. Great change of pace golf course.

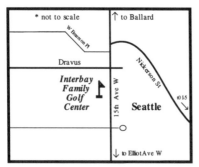

Directions: from I-5 N&S take exit #167 to Mercer Street. Follow arterial to Westlake (far right lane), turn right. Follow for 2.3 miles (it becomes Nickerson) to City Center exit. Proceed south on 15th Avenue to Gilman Drive. Turn right to course and range.

Course Yardage & Par:
M-1327 yards, par 28.
W-1204 yards, par 28.

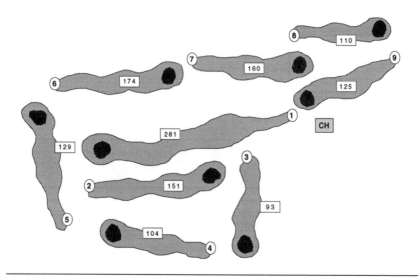

Ironwood Green Public Golf Course (public, 9 hole course)
8138 U.S. Highway 12; Glenoma, WA 98336
Phone: (360) 498-5425. Fax: none. Internet: none.
Owners: Jim & Alice Redmon. Superintendent: Jim Redmon.
Rating/Slope: the golf course is not rated. **Course record:** 28.
Green fees: $7.50/$5.50; Sr. rates $6.50 all week long; no credit cards.
Power cart: $15/$8. **Pull cart:** $2. **Trail fee:** $7.50 for personal cart.
Reservation policy: not needed. Times on a first come first served basis.
Winter condition: the golf course is open all year long. Damp conditions.
Terrain: flat (easy walking). **Tees:** all grass. **Spikes:** metal spikes permitted.
Services: club rentals, pro shop, convenience store, RV park for overnighters.
Comments: Nestled in the foothills of the Cascade Mountains this tree lined executive course is an excellent test for your iron skills. A friendly family owned course. Flat and only 1500 yards it is very walker and senior friendly. Small bentgrass greens are a challenge for all who play. For those traveling in an RV there is an RV park along the 9th fairway.

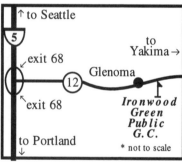

Directions: from I-5 N&S take exit #68 onto Hwy 12. Proceed eastbound 47 miles to Glenoma. The golf course is located just off Hwy 12 on the right.

Course Yardage & Par:
M-1512 yards, par 30.
W-1500 yards, par 31.

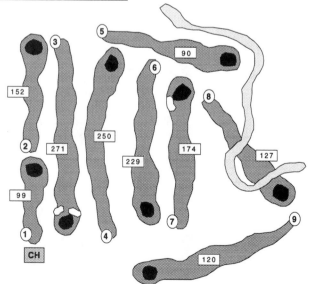

Island Greens (public, 9 hole par 3 course)
3890 East French Road; Clinton, WA 98236
Phone: (360) 579-6042. Fax: (360) 579-2248. Internet: none.
Owners: Dave & Karen Anderson.
Rating/Slope: the golf course is not rated. **Course record:** 25.
Green fees: W/D $6; W/E $7 (honor system @ times); no credit cards.
Power cart: not available. **Pull cart:** $1. **Trail fee:** no private carts.
Reservation policy: no policy, tee times are on a first come first serve basis.
Winter condition: the golf course is open all year long. Fair conditions.
Terrain: gently rolling terrain that is very walkable. **Tees:** grass & mats.
Services: club rentals, vending machines. **Spikes:** metal spikes permitted.
Comments: this challenging par 3 course features rolling terrain, tree lined
fairways and well manicured greens. With three ponds, bunkered greens and a
good variety of hole lengths Island Greens can be a handful. Excellent course
that is especially worth a trip during the months of April thru June when the
Rhodys are in bloom. Great change of pace from the 6500 + yard back breaker.

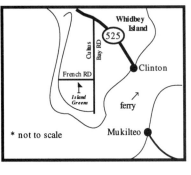

Directions: take the Mukilteo-Clinton
ferry to Clinton. Follow Hwy 525 2
miles to Cultus Bay Road. Left on
Cultus Bay for 2 miles to French Road.
Right on French Road, golf course is .5
miles ahead. Look for signs.

Course Yardage & Par:
C-1355 yards, par 27.
M-1135 yards, par 27.
W-859 yards, par 27.

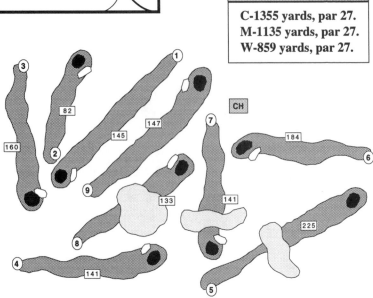

Jackson Golf Club (public, 18 hole course, 9 hole par 3)
1000 NE 135th; Seattle, WA 98125
Phone: (206) 363-4747; Tee-Times: 301-6472. **Fax: (206) 361-6636.**
Pro: Mark Granberg, PGA. Superintendent: Don Hellstrom.
Rating/Slope: C 67.3/113; M 66.3/111; W 70.7/118. **Course record:** 61.
Green fees: $18.50 all week long; Jr. & Sr. rates (Mon. thru Fri.); M/C, VISA.
Power cart: $20/$13. **Pull cart:** $3.50. **Trail fee:** $10 for personal carts.
Reservation policy: up to 7 days ahead in person. Up to 6 days ahead by phone.
Winter condition: the golf course is open all year long. Damp conditions.
Terrain: very hilly. **Tees:** all grass. **Spikes:** soft spikes preferred.
Services: club rentals, lessons, snack bar, lounge, restaurant, beer, wine, lockers, pro shop. **Comments:** few hazards, wide open. Very busy during the peak golfing season so be sure call ahead to obtain your tee times. The course has a well stocked pro shop for all your golfing needs. Much improved course.

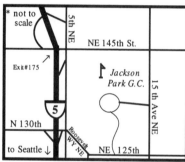

Directions: from I-5 N&S take exit #175 to NE 145th. Travel east for .5 miles to 15th Ave NE. Turn southbound on 15th Ave NE and proceed for .5 miles to NE 135th. Turn west on 135th and go up the hill to the entrance to the golf course which will be on your right. Look for signs marking your turn into Jackson Park.

Course Yardage & Par:
C-5946 yards, par 71.
M-5720 yards, par 71.
W-5495 yards, par 74.

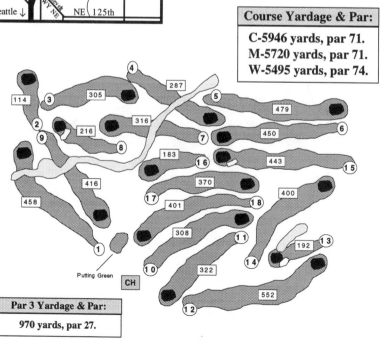

Par 3 Yardage & Par:
970 yards, par 27.

Jade Greens Golf Course (public, 9 holes w/dual pin placements)

18330 SE Lake Holm Road; Auburn, WA 98092
Phone: (253) 931-8562. **Fax:** (253) 931-0549. **Internet:** golfprojoe@aol.com
Pro: Joesph Bauman. **General Manager:** Jim Hawk Jr.
Rating/Slope: C 65.9/113; M 65.0/110; W 62.1/103 . **Course record:** 61.
Green fees: W/D $20/$13; W/E $22/$15; Jr. & Sr. $14/$9 (M-F); M/C VISA.
Power cart: $18/$13. **Pull cart:** $2. **Trail fee:** $5/$2.50 for personal carts.
Reservation policy: yes, call up to 1 week in advance for your tee-times.
Winter condition: the golf course is open all year long. Dry conditions.
Terrain: flat, some hills. **Tees:** all grass. **Spikes:** soft spikes preferred.
Services: club rentals, lessons, deli, beer, wine, pro shop, lighted driving range.
Comments: course surrounds natural wetlands which adds to the natural beauty of this well taken care of track. Excellent drainage for winter play. Course has a 25 stall, covered & lighted driving range for those wanting to practice.

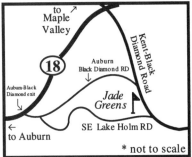

Directions: from I-5 take exit exit #142 (Hwy 18). Proceed eastbound on Hwy 18 to Auburn. Proceed just past the city limits on Hwy 18 where you will exit on the Auburn Black Diamond Road. Proceed for .5 miles to SE Lake Holm RD where you will turn right to the and proceed for 3.2 miles to the golf course.

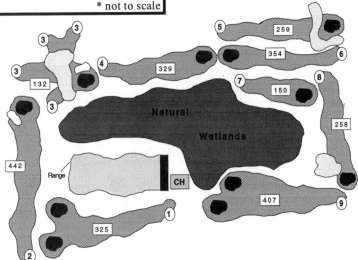

Course Yardage & Par:
C-2656 yards, par 34; M-2531 yards, par 34; W-2232 yards, par 35.
Dual tees for 18 holes:
C-5348 yards, par 69; M-5099 yards, par 69; W-4501 yards, par 71.

Jefferson Golf Club (public, 18 hole course, 9 hole par 3)

4101 Beacon Avenue South; Seattle, WA 98108
Phone: (206) 762-4513; T-Times: (206) 301-0472. Fax: (206) 762-2312.
Pro: Peter J. Guzzo, PGA. Superintendent: James Weir.
Rating/Slope: C 68.3/112; M 67.0/110; W 70.2/116. **Course record:** 62.
Green fees: $18.50 all week long; Jr. & Sr. rates (M-F) $13.50; M/C, VISA.
Power cart: $20/$13. **Pull cart:** $3.50. **Trail fee:** $10 for personal carts.
Reservation policy: up to 7 days ahead in person. Up to 6 days ahead by phone.
Winter condition: the golf course is open all year long. Damp conditions.
Terrain: relatively hilly. **Tees:** grass & mats. **Spikes:** soft spikes preferred.
Services: club rentals, lessons, snack bar, restaurant, beer, wine, lockers, pro
shop, lighted and covered driving range, putting green, executive golf course.
Comments: Jefferson has a flat front nine and a relatively hilly back nine.
Greens are large with a few greenside bunkers coming into play on your
approach shots. Many lovely views of the Seattle skyline can be seen from
several holes. Well stocked pro shop, and great lesson center.

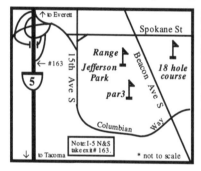

Directions: from I-5 N&S take exit #163
to Columbia Way. Turn left at the light
and travel .3 miles to Beacon Avenue S.
Turn southbound for .2 miles to the golf
course on your left hand side. The pro
shop will be located on your right hand
side next to the driving range.

Course Yardage & Par:

C-6182 yards, par 70.
M-5857 yards, par 70.
W-5430 yards, par 73.

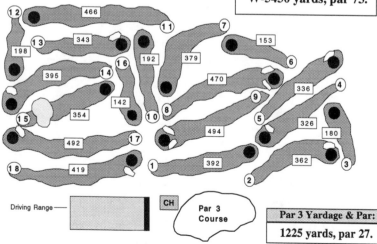

Par 3 Yardage & Par:
1225 yards, par 27.

Kahler Glen Golf Course (public, 18 hole course)

20700 Clubhouse Drive Leavenworth, WA 98826
Phone: (509) 763-4025. Fax: (503) 763-5030. Internet: www.kahlerglen.com.
Pro: Ed Paine, PGA. Office Manager: Dellas Herring.
Rating/Slope: M 65.7/115; W 67.1/114. **Course record:** 63.
Green fees: Monday thru Thursday $20/$12; Friday thru Sunday $28/$16.
Power cart: $24/$12. **Pull cart:** $5/$3. **Trail fee:** $10 for personal carts.
Reservation policy: yes, please call up to 2 weeks ahead for a tee time.
Winter condition: the golf course closed during the winter months.
Terrain: flat, some hills. **Tees:** all grass. **Spikes:** soft spikes only.
Services: club rentals, lessons, full service resturant & lounge, pro shop, driving range, putting green. **Comments:** located in Lake Wenatchee State Park this course is surrounded by trees and sports very narrow fairways. The greens are medium to large giving the golfer ample room to manoeuvre the ball. This definitely is a shot makers course. Great location for a quick golf getaway.

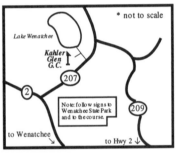

Directions: on Hwy 2 the course is located 15 miles west of Leavenworth. Turn in at Lake Wenatchee State Park where the golf course is located. Make sure you look for signs along the way. A brown and white golf sign is on Hwy 2 marking your turn off of the Hwy.

Course Yardage & Par:

C-6105 yards, par 70.
M-5682 yards, par 70.
W-4994 yards, par 70.

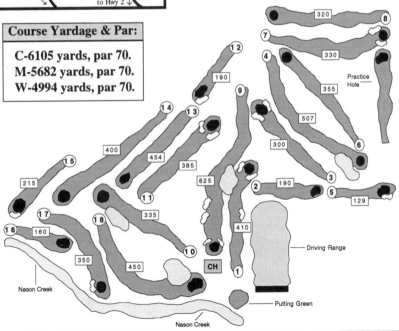

Kayak Point Golf Course (public, 18 hole course)

15711 Marine Drive; Stanwood, WA 98292   Internet: www.kayakgolf.com
Phone: (360) 652-9676; 1-800-562-3094. Fax: (360) 652-3812
Director of Golf: Rob Lindsey, PGA. Supt.: Randy Vander Vaate
Rating/Slope: C 72.9/138; M 70.2/127; W 71.1/125. Course record: 67.
Green fees: Monday-Friday $26/$14; Saturday-Sunday & Holidays $30/$16;
Jr. & Sr. & winter rates (Monday-Friday no holidays); M/C, VISA, AMEX.
Power cart: $27. **Pull cart:** $3.25. **Trail fee:** $13.50. (*add tax on all fees).
Reservation policy: up to 1 week in advance for W/D tee times. Call 5 days in
advance for W/E tee times. 1 month in advance with credit card payment.
Winter condition: open, dry, golf course has excellent drainage for winter play.
Terrain: very hilly (consider a cart). **Tees:** grass. **Spikes:** metal permitted.
Services: club rentals, lessons, snack bar, restaurant, liquor, lounge, beer, wine,
pop, pro shop, driving range, putting & chipping greens, practice bunker.
Comments: one of the NW's most beautiful and difficult golf courses.
Tree-lined fairways demand accuracy off the tee. Greens are medium to large
and well bunkered. This course is worth a special trip any time of year.

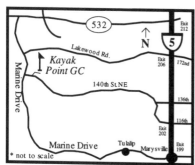

Directions: from I-5 N&S take exit
199 (Marysville-Tulalip) to Hwy 528W.
Travel west on Hwy 528W for approximately 14 miles to the golf course
entrance which will be on your right.
Follow the road up the hill to the golf
course. **Note:** Look for a sign on the
Hwy marking your turn to the course.

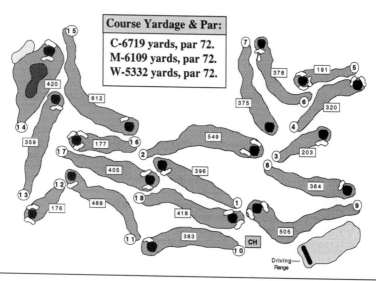

Course Yardage & Par:
C-6719 yards, par 72.
M-6109 yards, par 72.
W-5332 yards, par 72.

Kenwanda Golf Course (public, 18 hole course)
14030 Kenwanda Drive; Snohomish, WA 98290
Phone: (360) 668-1166. **Fax:** none. **Internet:** none.
Manager: Curtis Creighton.
Rating/Slope: M 65.3/106; W 70.4/126. **Course record:** 63.
Green fees: $20/$14 all week long; VISA, M/C.
Power cart: none. **Pull cart:** $2.50. **Trail fee:** no charge, weather restrictions.
Reservation policy: yes, call 7 days a week, up to 1 week in advance.
Winter condition: the golf course is open all year round. Dry conditions.
Terrain: relatively hilly. **Tees:** all grass. **Spikes:** metal spikes permitted.
Services: club rentals, coffee shop, beer, beverages, pro shop.
Comments: atop Fiddlers Bluff, Kenwanda boasts beautiful views of Mount Baker, Snohomish Valley, and the North Cascades. The course has very small greens, wide sloping fairways lined by trees. Accuracy is a must at Kenwanda.

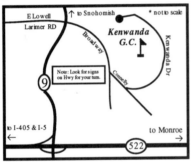

Directions: from Hwy 9 turn right on Broadway/131st Street. Follow approximately 1/2 mile to Connelly St. and turn left. Go .2 miles to Kenwanda Dr. Turn left. The clubhouse is at the top of the hill and will be on your left hand side. From I-405 take exit #23 to Hwy 522. Follow Hwy 522 to Hwy 9 and follow the above directions. **Note:** Look for a sign on marking your way to the course.

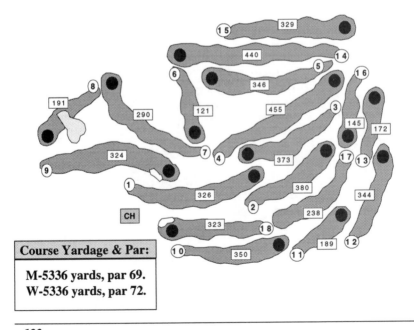

Course Yardage & Par:

M-5336 yards, par 69.
W-5336 yards, par 72.

Kitsap Golf & Country Club (private, 18 hole course)

3885 NW Golf Club Hill Road; Bremerton, WA 98312
Phone: (360) 373-5101. Fax: (360) 373-0685. Internet: none.
Pro: Mark Sivara, PGA. Supt.: Joel Kachamarek. 18 hole course.
Rating/Slope: C 70.1/120; M 69.6/118; W 72.0/122. **Course record:** 62.
Green fees: private club members and guests only; reciprocates.
Power cart: private club. **Pull cart:** private club. **Trail fee:** private club.
Reservation policy: yes, up to 2 days in advance. Members only.
Winter condition: the golf course is open all year long. Dry conditions.
Terrain: relatively hilly. **Tees:** all grass. **Spikes:** soft spikes preferred.
Services: coffee shop, dining room, ballroom, lounge, beverages, pro shop,
driving range, lessons, putting & chipping green, club memberships available.
Comments: very demanding layout with tricky doglegs and well bunkered, fast
greens. Fairways are tree lined and can be very narrow in spots. You must be
accurate off the tee to score well. This private track is always in great condition.

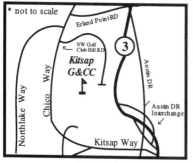

Directions: from Hwy 3 take the exit for
Austin-Kitsap Lake. Turn right on Austin
Road and proceed for 1.1 miles to Erland
Point Road. Turn left and proceed for .5
miles to Chico Way. Turn Left and
proceed for .3 miles to NW Golf Club Hill
Road. Proceed to the golf course on NW
Golf Club Hill Road. Look for a small
sign marking your turn to the course.

Course Yardage & Par:

C-6329 yards, par 71.
M-6153 yards, par 71.
W-5590 yards, par 73.

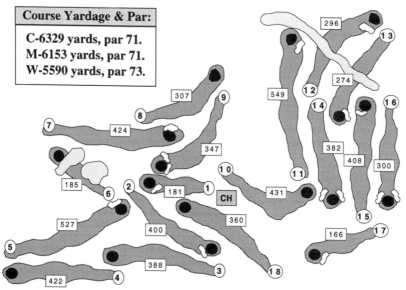

Lake Chelan Golf Course (public, 18 hole course)

1501 Golf Course Drive; P.O. Box 1669; Chelan, WA 98816
Phone: (509) 682-8026 or 1-800-246-5361. Fax: none.
Pro: Jim Oscarson, PGA. Superintendent: Don Hensley.
Rating/Slope: C 70.6/121; M 69.2/118; W 70.7/116. **Course record:** 65.
Green fees: $25/$15 all week long; VISA, M/C is accepted.
Power cart: $22/$12. **Pull cart:** $3/$2. **Trail fee:** $10 for personal carts.
Reservation policy: yes, call up to 1 week in advance for your tee-times.
Winter condition: the course is closed during the winter November to March.
Terrain: flat, some hills. **Tees:** grass. **Spikes:** soft spikes preferred.
Services: lessons, club rentals, snack bar, beer, wine, pro shop, driving range,
putting green. **Comments:** this is a beautiful course situated in a favorite
summer spot of weekend vacationers. This course is set atop a hill over looking
Lake Chelan and the surrounding landscape. Greens are small to medium in size
but can become very firm and fast in the summer months. Great course for the
summer golfer. The golf course has improved over the last few years.

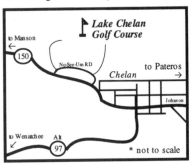

Directions: follow Hwy 150 through
Chelan toward Manson. About 1/4 mile
beyond the City Trailer Park take the
right fork of the No-See-Um Road to
the golf course. Look for signs to the
golf course on the Manson Highway
marking your turn.

Course Yardage & Par:
C-6440 yards, par 72.
M-6152 yards, par 72.
W-5501 yards, par 73.

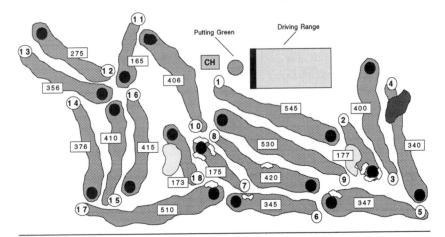

Lake Cushman Golf Course (public, 9 hole course)

North 210 West Fairway Drive; Hoodsport, WA 98548
Phone: (360) 877-5505. Fax: (360) 877-6713. Internet: none.
Pro/Manager: Scott Wadewitz, PGA. Superintendent: N/A.
Rating/Slope: M 67.7/107; W 70.5/110. **Course record: 62.**
Green fees: W/D $16/$11; W/E & Holidays $19/$15; tightwad Tuesday $12/$6.
Power cart: $20/$12. **Pull cart:** $2. **Trail fee:** $5 for personal carts.
Reservation policy: yes, call ahead 14 days for tee-times (advised in summer).
Winter condition: damp conditions. The course is open weather permitting.
Terrain: flat, some hills. **Tees:** all grass. **Spikes:** soft spikes preferred.
Services: club rentals, snack bar, small pro shop, practice range, putting green,
club memberships. **Comments:** a very challenging 9 hole course set in the
beautiful Olympic Mountains. Fairways are tree-lined with few hazards coming
into play around the greens. Excellent on course range so plan to practice.

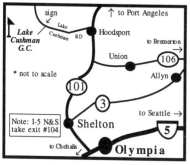

Directions: from I-5 N&S take exit 104
to Hwy 101. Follow to Hoodsport.
At the north end of Hoodsport turn left to
the Lake Cushman Resort. Follow for 2.8
miles to Fairway Village. Left, then right
to the golf course. Look for signs.

Course Yardage & Par:
C-2848 yards, par 35.
M-2957 yards, par 35.
W-2674 yards, par 35.
__Dual tees for 18 holes:__
C-5696 yards, par 70.
M-5914 yards, par 70.
W-5348 yards, par 70.

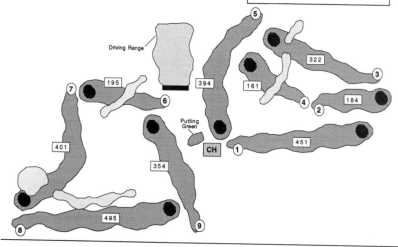

Lake Limerick Country Club (semi-private, 9 hole course)
E 790 Saint Andrews Drive; Shelton, WA 98584
Phone: (360) 426-6290. Fax: none. Internet: none.
Pro: Terry O'Hara. Superintendent: Steve Cox.
Rating/Slope: M 67.2/114; W 70.9/120. Course record: 67.
Green fees: W/D $15/$10; W/E $18/$13; M/C, VISA, AMEX.
Power cart: $21/$13. **Pull cart:** $3/$2. **Trail fee:** $5 for personal carts.
Reservation policy: yes, call up to one week in advance for tee times.
Winter condition: the golf course is open all year long. Damp conditions.
Terrain: flat, some hills. **Tees:** all grass. **Spikes:** soft spikes preferred.
Services: club rentals, restaurant, beer, wine, snack bar, pro shop, putting green.
Comments: narrow tree lined fairways and tricky greens makes this course a real test of golf. Greens are medium in size and fairly flat. Perfect golf course for a quick 9 holes on a weekend to the Olympic Peninsula. Do not let the lack of yardage fool you this course plays very tough in spots. Well kept golf course.

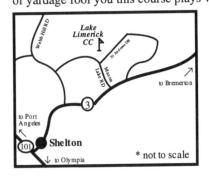

Directions: on Hwy 3 go 5 miles north of Shelton to Mason Lake Road. Turn left on Mason Lake Road and travel approximately 3 miles to the Lake Limerick entrance. Turn left on St. Andrews Drive and follow for 1 mile to the golf course. Look for signs marking your way to the golf course.

Course Yardage & Par:
M-2898 yards, par 36.
W-2658 yards, par 36.
Dual tees for 18 holes:
M-5779 yards, par 72.
W-5424 yards, par 72.

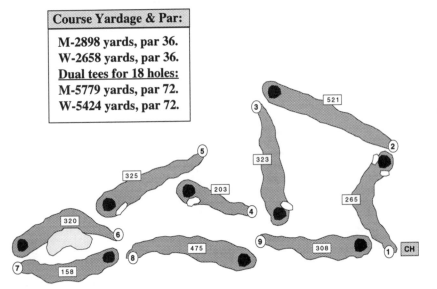

Lake Padden Golf Course (public, 18 hole course)

4882 Samish Way; Bellingham, WA 98226
Phone: (360) 676-6989. **Fax:** (360) 738-7303. **Internet: none.**
Pro: Kene Bensel, PGA. **Superintendent:** James Howes.
Rating/Slope: C 72.0/124; M 69.9/120; W 71.9/122. **Course record:** 63.
Green fees: $17/$13 Monday thru Friday; Sat. thru Sunday. including hol. $22;
Jr. & Sr. $13 (M-F); twilight rates $17 (M-F); VISA, M/C, AMEX.
Power cart: $22/$13. **Pull cart:** $3. **Trail fee:** $5 for personal carts.
Reservation policy: yes, up to 1 week in advance. Advised during the summer.
Winter condition: the golf course is open all year long. Damp conditions.
Terrain: relatively hilly. **Tees:** grass. **Spikes:** soft spikes only May-October.
Services: club rentals, lessons, snack bar, beer, driving range, pro shop.
Comments: Lake Padden's primary difficulty lies in the towering evergreens
surrounding every fairway. This course is well maintained and is a true pleasure
to play any time of year. Popular public course located in a recreational area.

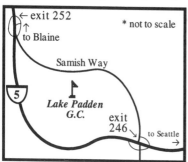

Directions: from I-5 southbound take exit
#252 to Samish Way. Travel east for 2.4
miles to the golf course which will be on
your right. If traveling on I-5 northbound
take exit #246 to Samish Way and proceed
2.5 miles to the golf course. The golf
course will be on your left hand side.

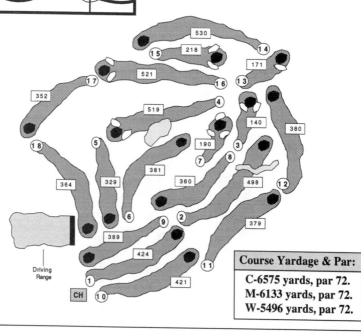

Course Yardage & Par:

C-6575 yards, par 72.
M-6133 yards, par 72.
W-5496 yards, par 72.

Lake Spanaway Golf Course (public, 18 hole course)

15602 Pacific Avenue; Tacoma, WA 98444
Phone: (253) 531-3660. Fax: (253) 531-7759. Internet: none.
Pro: Keith Johnson, PGA. Superintendent: Andy Soden.
Rating/Slope: C 71.8/121; M 70.0/118; W 73.4/123. **Course record:** 63.
Green fees: $20/$14 all week long; M/C, VISA, DISCOVER.
Power cart: $20/$12. **Pull cart:** $3. **Trail fee:** $5 for personal carts.
Reservation policy: public can call up to 7 days in advance after 11:00 am.
Winter condition: the course is open all year. Dry, excellent drainage.
Terrain: flat, some hills. **Tees:** all grass. **Spikes:** soft spikes preferred.
Services: club rentals, lessons, snack bar, restaurant, beer, wine, pro shop,
putting green, covered driving range. **Comments:** the course is kept in excellent
condition all year long. The length, many bunkers, ponds, and trees will chal-
lenge you at every turn. Shot placement off the tee is very important. Good track.

Directions: from I-5 N&S take exit
#127 to Hwy 512 eastbound. Proceed
east on 512 to Hwy 7 S. Exit to Hwy 7
southbound. Proceed south on Hwy 7 for
2.8 miles to the golf course which will
be on your right hand side. Look for
signs marking your way to the course.

Course Yardage & Par:
C-6810 yards, par 72.
M-6405 yards, par 72.
W-5935 yards, par 74.

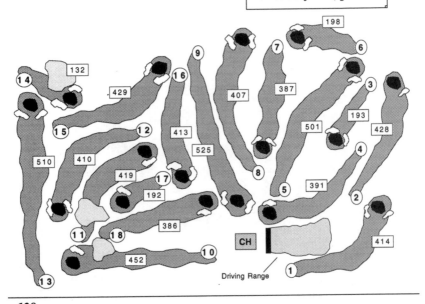

Lake Wilderness Golf Course (public, 18 hole course)

25400 Witte Road SE; Maple Valley, WA 98038
Phone: (425) 432-9405. Fax: (425) 432-2185. Internet: none.
Manager: Kelly Beymer. Superintendent: Martin Giannini.
Rating/Slope: C 66.1/118; M 64.7/116; W 66.6/117. **Course record:** 64.
Green fees: W/D $20/$13; W/E $25; Jr/Sr, twi-lite rates; VISA, M/C, AMEX.
Power cart: $20/$12. **Pull cart:** $4. **Trail fee:** $7.50 for personal carts.
Reservation policy: yes, call up to 1 week in advance for your tee-times.
Winter condition: the golf course is open all year long. Dry conditions.
Terrain: relatively hilly. **Tees:** all grass. **Spikes:** soft spikes preferred.
Services: club rentals, lessons, snack bar, lounge, restaurant, beer, wine, liquor,
club memberships, pro shop. **Comments:** new layout is not long but yet is very
demanding. Out of bounds comes into play on every hole. Challenging course.

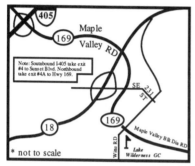

<u>Directions:</u> from I-5 N&S exit to I-405 to
Renton. Take exit #4 for Hwy 169. Take
Hwy 169 going south. Upon entering
Maple Valley (about 15 minutes), take a
right at the 4th stoplight onto Witte Road
SE. Go approximately 1 mile. You will
pass the 18th fairway on your left. You
will take the 2nd left to the golf course.
From I-90 exit to I-405 southbound.
Proceed south and exit to Hwy 169 and
follow the above directions.

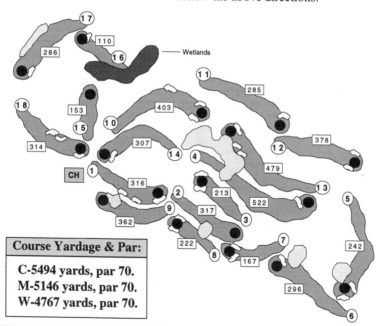

Course Yardage & Par:

C-5494 yards, par 70.
M-5146 yards, par 70.
W-4767 yards, par 70.

Lake Woods Golf Course (public, 9 hole course)

240 State Park Road; P.O. Box 427; Bridgeport, WA 98813
Phone: (509) 686-5721. Fax: none. Internet: none.
Manager: Dick Field. Superintendent: Cliff Pins.
Rating/Slope: M 66.7/115; W 67.8/115. Course record: 63.
Green fees: W/D $15/$10; W/E $17/$11; Jr. & Sr. rates; VISA, M/C.
Power cart: $18/$11. Pull cart: $2.50. Trail fee: $2.50.
Reservation policy: advance tee-time reservations are not required.
Winter condition: course is closed October to April, depending on weather.
Terrain: flat, some hills. **Tees:** all grass. **Spikes:** metal spikes permitted.
Services: club rentals, restaurant, beer, pro shop, putting green, driving range.
Comments: the course runs partially along the Columbia River although it does not come into play. Small, sloping well bunkered greens make approach shots very difficult. Campground near the course for those wanting to spend the night.

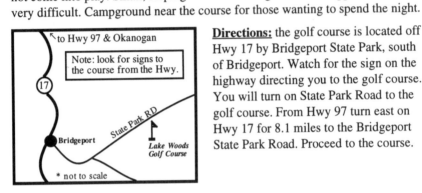

Directions: the golf course is located off Hwy 17 by Bridgeport State Park, south of Bridgeport. Watch for the sign on the highway directing you to the golf course. You will turn on State Park Road to the golf course. From Hwy 97 turn east on Hwy 17 for 8.1 miles to the Bridgeport State Park Road. Proceed to the course.

Course Yardage & Par:

M-2845 yards, par 35.
W-2543 yards, par 35.
<u>Dual tees for 18 holes:</u>
M-5646 yards, par 70.
W-5091 yards, par 70.

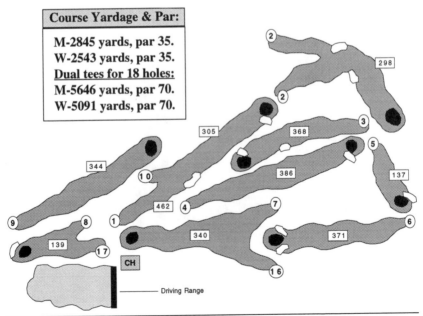

LakeLand Village Golf & Country Club (semi-private, 27 hole course)
E 200 Old Ranch Road; P. O. Box 670; Allyn, WA 98524
Phone: (360) 275-6100. Fax: (360) 275-0266. Internet: none.
Pro: Randy Jensen, PGA. Superintendent: Steve Anderson.
Rating/Slope I/II: C 68.5/117; M 67.7/114; W 69.6/119. **Course record:** 62.
Green fees: W/D $20/$14; W/E $25/$15; Sr. rates Mondays & Thursday only.
Power cart: $24. **Pull cart:** $3. **Trail fee:** personal carts are not allowed.
Reservation policy: yes, please call 7 days in advance for tee times.
Winter condition: the golf course is open all year long. Damp conditions.
Terrain: flat, some hills. **Tees:** all grass. **Spikes:** soft spikes preferred.
Services: club rentals, lessons, snack bar, restaurant, beer, wine, liquor,
pro shop, club memberships, two driving ranges (full woods), putting green.
Comments: well maintained, this beautiful layout sports 14 water hazards to
challenge any golfer. Good golf course that is much improved over last year.

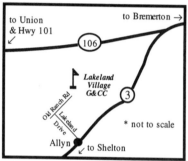

Directions: from the Bremerton ferry
veer left to 1st St. for 1 block to Pacific.
Turn right. Travel 1 block to Burwell
(Hwy 304 W). Turn left and follow signs
to Shelton to Hwy 3 S. Turn south on
Hwy 3 S to Allyn. Turn right on Lakeland Drive and proceed to the golf course.
The golf course is located just off of Hwy
3 toward Shelton or Bremerton.

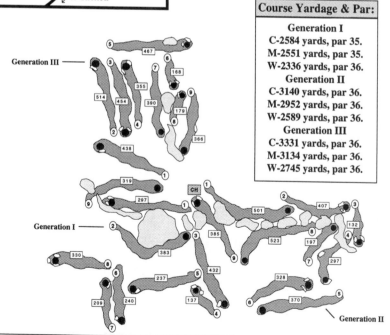

Course Yardage & Par:
Generation I
C-2584 yards, par 35.
M-2551 yards, par 35.
W-2336 yards, par 36.
Generation II
C-3140 yards, par 36.
M-2952 yards, par 36.
W-2589 yards, par 36.
Generation III
C-3331 yards, par 36.
M-3134 yards, par 36.
W-2745 yards, par 36.

Lakeview Golf & Country Club (private, 18 hole course)
52 Golf Club Road; Soap Lake, WA 98851
Phone: (509) 246-0336. **Fax:** none. **Internet:** none.
Pro: Don Tracy, PGA. **Superintendent:** Dave Paulson.
Rating/Slope: C 70.9/114; M 69.5/111; W 72.4/117. **Course record:** 62.
Green fees: private club; members only; reciprocates; no credit cards.
Power cart: private club. **Pull cart:** private club. **Trail fee:** private club.
Reservation policy: private club members only. No public play is allowed.
Winter condition: the golf course is open all year long. Dry conditions.
Terrain: very flat. **Tees:** all grass. **Spikes:** soft spikes preferred.
Services: club rentals, lessons, restaurant, snack bar, lounge, beer, wine, liquor, pro shop, showers, lockers, putting green and chipping green, driving range.
Comments: the course is unique in as much as there are no adjoining fairways. Greens are medium to large in size well bunkered and fast. Tree's dot the landscape and can be a major factor off the tee. Excellent private facility.

Directions: from Hwy 17, take the 19th NW exit south of Soap Lake. Proceed 2 blocks and turn right to the course. From I-90 Take the Ephrata exit and follow Hwy 583 to Ephrata. Proceed to Road 19 NW and turn westbound to the course.

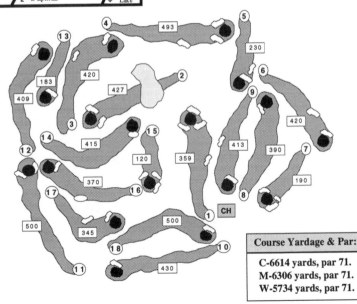

Course Yardage & Par:

C-6614 yards, par 71.
M-6306 yards, par 71.
W-5734 yards, par 71.

Lakeview Golf Challenge (public, 9 hole par 3 course)
2425 NW 69th Street; Vancouver, WA 98665
Phone: (360) 693-9116. Fax: (360) 699-6197. Internet: none.
Manager: Charley Greene. Superintendent: Charley Greene.
Rating/Slope: the golf course is not rated. **Course record:** 54 for 18 holes.
Green fees: $11/$6 all week long; Sr. rates $9/$5; no credit cards.
Power cart: not available. **Pull cart:** $1. **Trail fee:** not allowed.
Reservation policy: reservations are not required. First come first served.
Winter condition: the golf course is open all year long. Damp conditions.
Terrain: very flat. **Tees:** grass & mats. **Spikes:** metal spikes permitted.
Services: club rentals, small pro shop, beverages, putting green.
Comments: difficult golf course that will challenge you at every turn. The course sports sloping well bunkered greens. Water comes into play on several holes and is a major factor. If you are looking for change of pace try Lakeview.

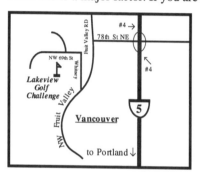

Directions: I-5 N&S take exit for 78th St. Travel west to the end of the road. Turn left (on Fruit Valley Road) and travel .7 miles. Turn right (sharp) Whitney Road which becomes 69th St. Proceed on 69th Street to the golf course. Look for signs marking your turn to the facility.

Course Yardage & Par:
M-833 yards, par 27.
W-833 yards, par 27.
Dual tees for 18 holes:
M-1836 yards, par 54.
W-1836 yards, par 54.

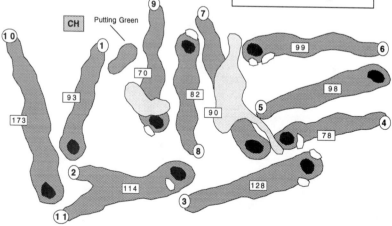

Lams Golf Links (public, 9 hole course)
585 West Ducken Road; Whidbey Island, WA 98277
Phone: (360) 675-3412. Fax: none. Internet: none.
Manager: Bill Lam. Superintendent: Bill Lam.
Rating/Slope: the golf course is not rated. **Course record:** 26.
Green fees: W/D $8/$5; W/E $9/$6; Sr. rates; no credit cards.
Power cart: none available. **Pull cart:** $3. **Trail fee:** not allowed.
Reservation policy: reservations are not needed, first come first served.
Winter condition: the golf course is closed from December through March.
Terrain: flat (easy to walk). **Tees:** grass. **Spikes:** metal spikes permitted.
Services: very limited services, vending machines, putting green.
Comments: executive length golf course located on scenic Whidbey Island just
south of the Deception Pass Bridge. Golf course has an honor box for green fees
if the clubhouse is not open. Very easy to just walk on for a quick 9 holes.

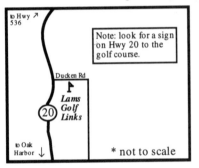

Directions: the course is located 1 mile
south of Deception Pass off Hwy 20.
Turn left on Ducken Road to the golf
course. **Note:** Look for a sign on Hwy
20 marking the turn to the golf course.

Course Yardage & Par:
M-1347 yards, par 28. **W-1347 yards, par 28.**

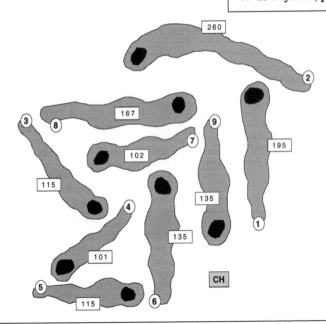

Latah Short Course (public, 9 hole par 3 course)
5840 Meadowlane Road; Spokane, WA 99204
Phone: (509) 443-9751. **Fax:** none. **Internet:** none.
Manager: Terry Kelly. **Superintendent:** Chris Becker.
Rating/Slope: the golf course is not rated. **Course record:** 21.
Green fees: Adults: $7; Seniors: $6; Juniors $5; Each additional 9 $3.
Power cart: none. **Pull cart:** $2. **Trail fee:** no personal carts.
Reservation policy: call and reserve tee times 1 week in advance.
Winter condition: the golf course is closed from December to February.
Terrain: flat. **Tees:** grass. **Spikes:** metal spikes permitted.
Services: club rentals, snack bar, beer, wine, lessons, night golf, free clinics.
Comments: a well maintained Par 3 with a lake and a stream running through the course layout. The course sits among four old barns and gives the track some character. Great course for the first time or beginner golfer.

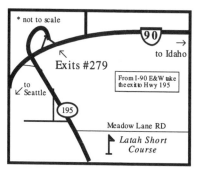

Directions: From I-90 E&W (#279) exit to Hwy 195 and proceed southbound. Turn eastbound on Meadow Lane Road. Follow this to the golf course. Look for signs that are posted along the way.

Course Yardage & Par:
M-730 yards, par 27.
W-730 yards, par 27.

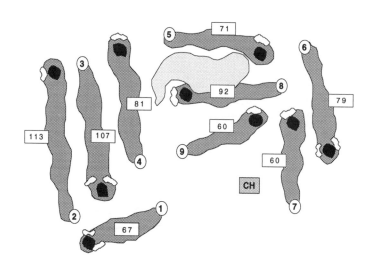

Leavenworth Golf Club (semi-private, 18 hole course)

9101 Icicle Road; P.O. Box 247; Leavenworth, WA 98826
Phone: (509) 548-7267. Fax: none. Internet: www.leavenworthgolf.com
Pro: Jim Van Tuyl, PGA. Superintendent: Michael Snyder.
Rating/Slope: M 67.0/110; W 69.6/112. Course record: 61.
Green fees: W/D $22/$15; W/E $25/$16; M/C, VISA, DIS, AMEX.
Power cart: $22. **Pull cart:** $2.50. **Trail fee:** $5 for personal carts.
Reservation policy: call Monday to book the week (Monday to Monday).
Winter condition: the golf course is closed from mid November to March.
Terrain: flat, some slight hills. **Tees:** grass. **Spikes:** soft spikes only.
Services: club rentals, snack bar, beer, wine, lessons, pro shop, putting green.
Comments: a beautiful setting in the heart of the Cascade Mountains. Many
trees, sand traps, and the Wenatchee River come into play on a number of holes.
Fairways are tree-lined and can be narrow in spots. The town of Leavenworth
and the Bavarian Village alone are worth the trip. Some restricted tee times,
Sunday AM men members only; Wednesday AM women members only.

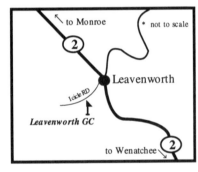

Directions: golf course located 1 mile
west of Leavenworth. From Hwy 2 go
south on Icicle Road for 0.6 miles to the
golf course which will be on your left
hand side. **Note:** Look for a sign on the
Hwy marking your turn to the course.

Course Yardage & Par:
M-5711 yards, par 71.
W-5343 yards, par 71.

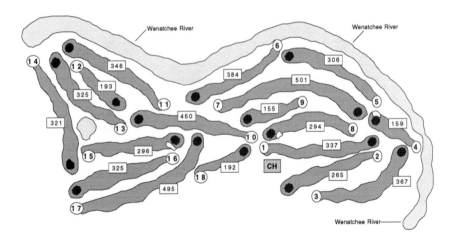

Legion Memorial Golf Course (public, 18 hole course)

144 W Marine View Drive; Everett, WA 98201
Phone: (425) 259-4653. **Fax:** (425) 259-8165. **Internet:** www.cybergolf.com/legion
Pro: Mike Coury, PGA. **Superintendent:** Edward Phelps.
Rating/Slope: C 71.2/116; M 70.0/113; W 65.9/100. **Course record:** 66.
Green fees: Everett resident $21.50/$15.25; non-res. $30/$21.50; Jr/Sr rates.
Power cart: $20/$12. **Pull cart:** $3. **Trail fee:** $5 for personal carts.
Reservation policy: W/D 1 week in advance. Call Monday 9am for W/E times.
Winter condition: the golf course is open all year long. Damp conditions.
Terrain: flat, some hills. **Tees:** grass. **Spikes:** metal spikes permitted.
Services: newly remodeled clubhouse featuring the Greenside Grill and beverage cart service, pro shop, club rentals, lessons, lockers, showers, putting green.
Comments: The course was renovated with all 18 holes open in September 1998. The "new" course is expected to become one of the driest winter courses in western Washington. Water hazards and sand bunkers add beauty, challenge and playability to the course. Managed by Golf Resources Northwest.

Directions: from I-5 N take exit 195. Turn left on Marine View Drive and follow for 2.1 miles to the golf course. From I-5 S take exit 194. Go west for .1 mi to Walnut. Go north for 1.2 miles to Marine View Drive and turn west for 1.3 miles to golf course. Look for signs.

Course Yardage & Par:
T-6900 yards, par 72.
C-6627 yards, par 72.
M-6111 yards, par 72.
W-4805 yards, par 72.

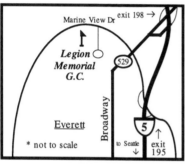

Lewis River Golf Course (public, 18 hole course)

3209 Lewis River Road; Woodland, WA 98674
Phone: (360) 225-8254. Fax: (360) 225-5869. Internet: oregongolf.com.
Pro: Dick Smith, PGA. Superintendent: Terry Vanderstoop.
Rating/Slope: C 70.1/123; M 68.1/118; W 69.7/119. **Course record:** 62.
Green fees: Monday thru Thursday $25/$13; Friday $28/$15;
Saturday thru Sunday $32/$17; Jr/Sr rates $18 (Monday-Friday); M/C, VISA.
Power cart: $24/$12. **Pull cart:** $2. **Trail fee:** $8 for personal carts.
Reservation policy: yes, please call up to 1 week in advance.
 Winter condition: the golf course is open all year long. Very dry conditions.
Terrain: flat, some hills. **Tees:** all grass. **Spikes:** metal spikes permitted.
Services: club rentals, lessons, snack bar, lounge, restaurant, beer, wine, liquor,
driving range, pro shop, club memberships, putting and chipping greens.
Comments: Lewis River sports the longest golf hole in Washington, a 649
yard par 5. Great winter & summer course. Course can play very tough with
water and sand coming into play on several holes. Excellent course that is worth
a special trip. Play golf and take in Mount Saint Helens in the same day.

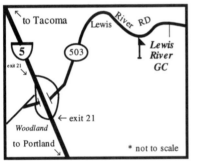

Directions: the golf course is located east of Woodland. From I-5 N&S take exit #21. Travel east for 4.7 miles to the golf course which will be located on your right hand side of the road. This golf course has great freeway access. Look for signs.

Course Yardage & Par:
C-6352 yards, par 72.
M-5903 yards, par 72.
W-5260 yards, par 73.

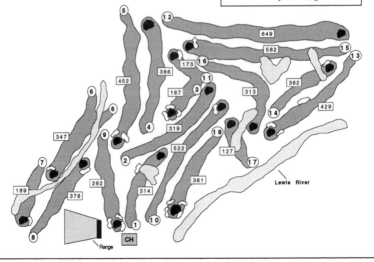

Liberty Lake Golf Course (public, 18 hole course)

24403 E Sprague Avenue; Liberty Lake, WA 99019
Phone: (509) 255-6233. Fax: (509) 255-5105. Internet: none.
Pro: Kit DeAndre. Superintendent: Mike Kingsley.
Rating/Slope: C 69.8/121; M 68.7/118; W 72.6/125. **Course record:** 61.
Green fees: resident $16/$12; non $22/$15.50; Jr/Sr rates (Mon.-Fri.).
Power cart: $23/$11.50. **Pull cart:** $3. **Trail fee:** $6.
Reservation policy: yes, call Tuesday to make your upcoming tee-times.
Winter condition: dry. The golf course is closed during inclement weather.
Terrain: flat, some hills. **Tees:** all grass. **Spikes:** soft spikes preferred.
Services: club rentals, lessons, restaurant, snack bar, beer, wine, pro shop,
driving range, putting green. **Comments:** the golf course is easy to walk with
many well-trapped greens. Liberty Lake can play much tougher than the layout
indicates. Shot placement from the tee is a must. This is one of the finest public
golf courses in the state of Washington. Worth a trip if in the Spokane area.

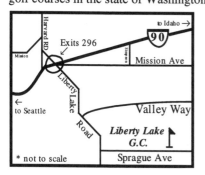

Directions: the golf course is located
east of Spokane. From I-90 eastbound
and westbound take exit #296 and go
south to Sprague Avenue. Turn left on
Sprague Avenue and continue to the
golf course. Look for signs marking
your turn to the golf complex.

Course Yardage & Par:
C-6398 yards, par 70.
M-6153 yards, par 70.
W-5886 yards, par 74.

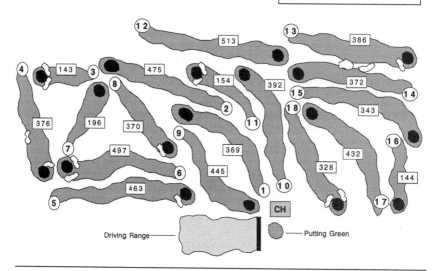

Linden Golf & Country Club (private, 18 hole course)

2519 Main Avenue East; Puyallup, WA 98371
Phone: (253) 845-2056. Fax: none. Internet: none.
Pro: David Leon Jr, PGA. Superintendent: Dean Hanson.
Rating/Slope: M 69.7/120; W 74.1/123. **Course record:** 62.
Green fees: private club members & guests only; no credit cards.
Power cart: private club. **Pull cart:** private club. **Trail fee:** private club.
Reservation policy: private club members only. No public play is allowed.
Winter condition: the golf course is open all year long. Dry conditions.
Terrain: flat, some hills. **Tees:** grass. **Spikes:** soft spikes preferred.
Services: lessons, pro shop, lockers, showers, club memberships, putting green.
Comments: private 9 hole course with separate tee boxes for 18 hole play.
Rolling terrain small greens and bunkers enhance this interesting course design.
The course is well kept with water coming into play on two holes.

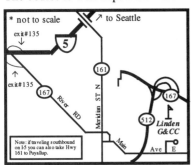

Directions: from I-5 N&S take exit
135 to Hwy 167 N. Turn north and
travel 5.3 miles to Meridian Street N.
Turn south for .4 miles to Main Avenue
E. Proceed east for 1.5 miles to the golf
course on your left hand side.

Course Yardage & Par:
M-3120 yards, par 36.   **W-3110 yards, par 37.**   **Dual tees for 18 holes:**   **M-6112 yards, par 72.**   **W-6017 yards, par 73.**

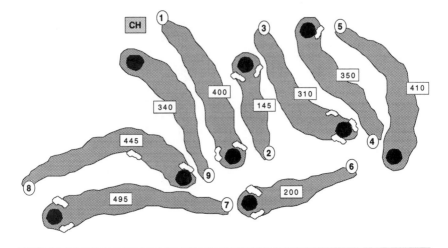

Lipoma Firs Golf Course (public, 27 hole course)
18615 110th Avenue East; Puyallup, WA 98374
Phone: (253) 841-4396; 1-800-649-4396. Fax: none. Internet: none.
Pro: Joe Stroberger. Supertintendent: Rod Ragsdale.
Rating/Slope: C 72.5/124; M 70.2/120; M 69.5/118; W 71.0/117. **Record:** 68.
Green fees: W/D $19/$12; W/E $24/$15; Jr. & Sr., twilight rates; M/C, VISA.
Power cart: $20/$12. **Pull cart:** $3. **Trail fee:** $6 for personal carts.
Reservation policy: yes, call up to 1 week in advance for your tee times.
Winter condition: the golf course is open all year long. Dry conditions.
Terrain: flat, some hills, **Tees:** all grass. **Spikes:** soft spikes only (summer).
Services: club rentals, lessons, snack bar, beer, wine, beverages, pro shop,
grass tee driving range, 2 practice greens, practice bunkers, club memberships.
Comments: the course is always in good condition, excellent drainage provides
good winter play. Fairways are tree lined and narrow in certain areas. You must
be able to position your ball in the right place off the tee in order to score well.

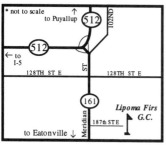

Directions: from I-5 N&S take the exit
for Hwy 512E. Travel 8 miles to Hwy
161S. Proceed 6 miles to 187th. The
course will located on your left hand side.

Course Yardage & Par:	
Green Course	**Gold Course**
C-3302 yards, par 36.	C-3420 yards, par 36.
M-3123 yards, par 36.	M-3094 yards, par 36.
W-2716 yards, par 36.	W-2760 yards, par 36.

Course Yardage & Par:
Blue Course
C-3385 yards, par 36.
M-3051 yards, par 36.
W-2757 yards, par 36.

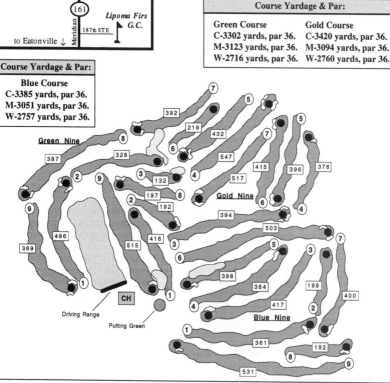

Lobo Country Club (public, 9 hole par 3 course)
12015 84th Street SE; Snohomish, WA 98290
Phone: (360) 568-1638. **Fax: none. Internet: none.**
Owners: Gordon & Fedora Loth.
Rating/Slope: the golf course is not rated. **Course record:** 25.
Green fees: $14/$8 all week long; Sr. rates $13/$7 (weekdays); no credit cards.
Power Cart: $12/$8. **Pull Cart:** $2. **Trail fee:** not available.
Reservation policy: advance tee times are not required.
Winter condition: the golf course is closed December & January.
Terrain: flat, some hills. **Tees:** all grass. **Spikes:** metal spikes permitted.
Services: club rentals, clubhouse, vending machines, chipping & putting greens.
Comments: friendly family owned course, surrounded by a beautiful country
setting. If you are looking for a place to take the first time golfer try Lobo CC.

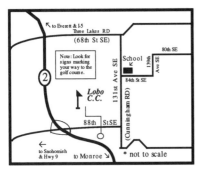

Directions: from Hwy 2 exit at the
Snohomish 88th Street SE exit eastbound.
Proceed on 88th Street to 123rd Avenue
SE turn north to the course. Look for signs
marking your turn to the golf course.

Course Yardage & Par:
M-1014 yards, par 27.
W-1005 yards, par 27.

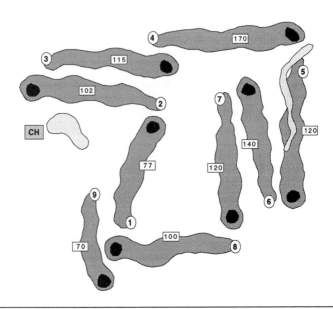

Longview Country Club (private, 18 hole course)

41 Country Club Drive; Longview, WA 98632
Phone: (360) 425-3132. Fax: none. Internet: none.
Pro: Jeff Bartleson, PGA. Superintendent: Ben Davis.
Rating/Slope: M 69.2/122; W 70.6/118. **Course record:** 64.
Green fees: private club, members only; reciprocates; VISA, M/C.
Power cart: private club. **Pull cart:** private club. **Trail fee:** not allowed.
Reservation policy: private club, members only. No public play allowed.
Winter Condition: the golf course is open all year long. Damp conditions.
Terrain: relatively hilly. **Tees:** all grass. **Spikes:** soft spikes preferred.
Services: club rentals, lessons, snack bar, restaurant, beer, wine, liquor, pro
shop, lockers, showers, club memberships, practice range, putting green.
Comments: course has newly redesigned three holes that are now in excellent
condition. Challenging, well maintained greens are this course's trademark.

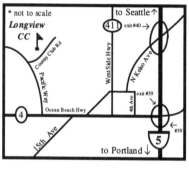

Directions: from I-5 take exit # 39
and follow to the Ocean Beach Hwy,
continuing to Pacific Hwy. Travel north
on Pacific Hwy to Country Club Road.
Turn right on Country Club Road to the
golf course.

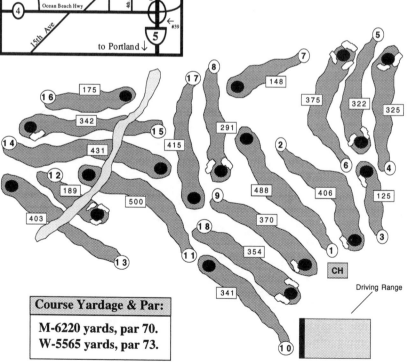

Course Yardage & Par:

M-6220 yards, par 70.
W-5565 yards, par 73.

Loomis Trail Golf Club (private, 18 hole course)
4342 Loomis Trail Road; Blaine, WA 98230
Phone: (360) 332-8138. Fax: (360) 332-2232. Internet: none.
Pro: Keith Henderson, PGA. Superintendent: Stan Becker.
Rating/Slope: T 74.9/139; C 72.3/133; 69.4/125; W 72.4/129. **Record:** 64.
Green fees: private club. For membership information call (360) 332-1608.
Power cart: members only. **Pull cart:** members only. **Trail fee:** not allowed.
Reservation policy: private club, members only. No public play allowed
Winter condition: the golf course is open all year long. Dry conditions.
Terrain: flat, some hills. **Tees:** all grass. **Spikes:** metal spikes not permitted.
Services: pro shop, restaurant, lodging for members & guests, memberships.
Comments: Open since 1993, the course was rated 3rd best new private course
by *"Golf Digest"*. This 18 hole layout was also ranked #3 best course in the
Washington State. This tough track sports numerous bunkers, ponds and tree
lined fairways. Excellent private facility that is nothing short of spectacular.

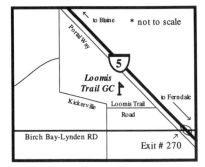

Directions: from I-5 N&S take exit #270
(Birch Bay - Lynden Rd.). Travel W on
Birch Bay-Lynden Rd. for 2.1 miles to
Kickerville Rd. Turn N on Kickerville Rd.
for .8 mile to Loomis Trail Rd. Turn W on
Loomis Trail Rd. to the course.

Course Yardage & Par:
T-7137 yards, par 72.
C-6611 yards, par 72.
M-6167 yards, par 72.
W-5475 yards, par 72.

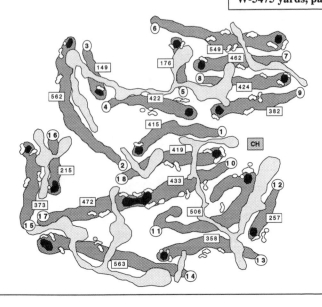

Lopez Island Golf Course (public, 9 hole course)

Airport Road; Box 124; Lopez Island, WA 98261
Phone: (360) 468-2679. Fax: none. Internet: none.
Pro Shop Manager: L. Holmes. Superintendent: none.
Rating/Slope: C 65.2/110; M 62.8/105; W 67.0/114. **Course record:** 68.
Green fees: $20/$14 all week long; Jr rates; no credit cards.
Power cart: power carts are not available. **Pull cart:** $1. **Trail fee:** no charge.
Reservation policy: advance tee times are not required.
Winter Condition: the golf course is open all year long. Damp conditions.
Terrain: relatively hilly, walkable. **Tees:** grass. **Spikes:** soft spikes preferred.
Services: club rentals, pro shop. **Comments:** situated in the scenic San Juan Islands this course is easy to walk with few hazards. Good course in a very beautiful part of Washington. If in the islands make sure to bring your clubs.

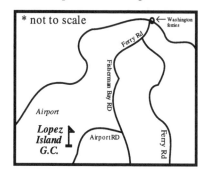

Directions: from I-5 N&S take exit #230 to Hwy 20W to Anacortes and the San Juan ferry terminal. Board the ferry for Lopez Island. From the Lopez ferry landing proceed south on Ferry Road on to Fisherman Bay Road. Turn right on Airport Road. Proceed for .5 miles and turn left to the golf course which will be on your right hand side. Look for signs that will be posted indicating your turn.

Course Yardage & Par:
M-2711 yards, par 35. **W-2427 yards, par 35.**

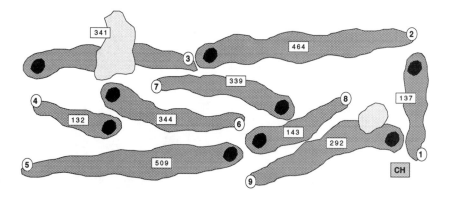

Lower Valley Golf Club (public, 18 hole course)

31 Ray Road; Sunnyside, WA 98944
Phone: (509) 837-5340. Fax: (509) 837-5340. Internet: none.
Pro: Craig Thomas, PGA. Superintendent: John Tucker.
Rating/Slope: C 70.2/112; M 68.4/108; W 70.6/111. Course record: 64.
Green fees: W/D $18/$12; W/E & Holidays $20/$12; M/C, VISA.
Power cart: $22/$11. Pull cart: $3. Trail fee: $5 for personal carts.
Reservation policy: you may call ahead 1 week in advance for tee times.
Winter condition: dry conditions. Course is open all year, weather permitting.
Terrain: flat (easy walking). **Tees:** all grass. **Spikes:** soft spikes only.
Services: club rentals, Henry-Griffits club fitting, lessons, pro shop,
practice range, vending machines, beverages, putting & chipping green.
Comments: this course is an excellent facility which added a new nine in spring
of 1995. This track is a challenging golf course that is easy to walk and demand-
ing. Water comes into play on 10 holes and the greens are of varing sizes.

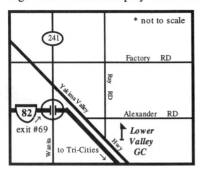

Directions: from I-82 eastbound take
exit # 69 (Sunnyside). Travel north on
Wanita to the Yakima Valley Hwy. Turn
eastbound. Proceed 1.5 miles to Ray Rd.
and the golf course. Look for signs.

Course Yardage & Par:
C-6664 yards, par 72.
W-6271 yards, par 72.
W-5618 yards, par 72.

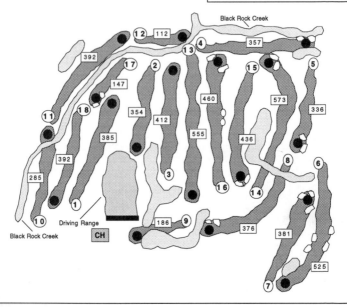

*Lynnwood Municipal Golf Course (public, 18 hole course)

20200 68th Avenue West; Box 5008; Lynnwood, WA 98036
Phone: (425) 672-4653. Fax: (425) 712-8554. Internet: none.
Pro: Dan Smith, PGA. Superintendent: Gary Stormo.
Rating/Slope: M 62.9/107; W 63.5/105. **Course record:** M 59; W 65.
Green fees: $20/$15; Jr. & Sr. rates Monday thru Friday $2 discount.
Power cart: $20/$10. **Pull cart:** $3. **Trail fee:** not allowed.
Reservation policy: please call up to Seven days in advance for Monday thru
Friday tee-times. Call up to Five days in advance for Saturday & Sunday times.
Winter condition: the golf course is open all year long. Dry conditions.
Terrain: flat, some hills. **Tees:** all grass. **Spikes:** soft spikes optional.
Services: club rentals, lessons, restaurant, pro shop, driving range, lessons,
putting green. **Comments:** Excellent, short length golf course that is very
demanding off the tee. Tree lined fairways, bunkers and ponds make this track a
challenge. If you are looking for a change of pace from the standard 6000+ yard
golf course, try Lynnwood Municipal it will not disappoint. Good golf course.

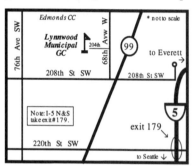

Directions: from I-5 N&S take exit
179 and travel west on 220th St. SW.
Proceed to Hwy 99 and turn right
(north). Follow to 208th St. SW and turn
left. Then take the immediate right on
68th Ave. W. The entrance to the golf
course is on 68th and 204th. The golf
course is located adjacent to the
Edmonds Community College campus.
Look for signs indicating your turns.

Course Yardage & Par:

M-4741 yards, par 65.
W-4094 yards, par 65.

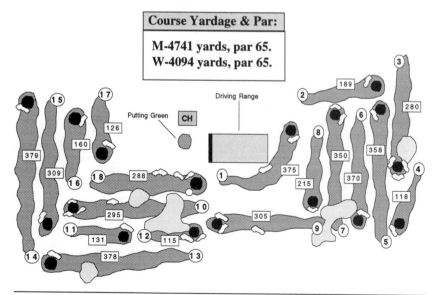

147

M A 8 Golf (public, 9 hole course)
453 Wapato Lake Road; Manson, WA 98831
Phone: (509) 687-6338. Fax: none. Internet: none.
Manager: Garrey Hayes. Pro: none.
Rating/Slope: the golf course is not rated. **Course record:** 30.
Green fees: $22/$12 all week long; Jr. rates (Monday-Friday) $18/$10.
Power cart: none available. **Pull cart:** $4. **Trail fee:** not allowed.
Reservation policy: yes, please call ahead for tee-times. No time limit.
Winter condition: the course is closed in the winter November to March.
Terrain: flat, some hills. **Tees:** all grass. **Spikes:** soft spikes preferred.
Services: club rentals, snack bar, driving range, putting & chipping green.
Comments: the course is fairly flat and easy to walk. Although not overly long the course can play tough if the wind blows. This track has large greens with few traps that hold shots well. Those vacationing in the Chelan area might want to take a chance and play a course off the beaten path.

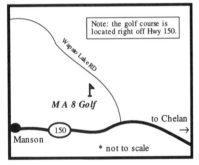

Note: the golf course is located right off Hwy 150.

Directions: the golf course is located near the Manson Hwy. From Lake Chelan on Hwy 150 proceed westbound for 6 miles. Turn right on Wapato Lake Road and proceed to clubhouse. The golf course is located right next to the Hwy.

Course Yardage & Par:
M-1881 yards, par 30.
W-1881 yards, par 30.

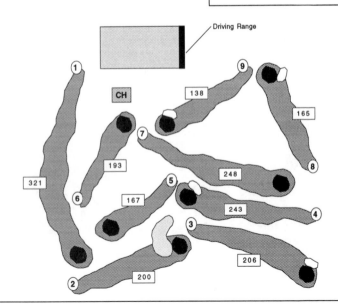

Madrona Links Golf Course (public, 18 hole course)
3604 22nd Avenue NW; Gig Harbor, WA 98335
Phone: (253) 851-5193. Fax: (253) 851-3844. Internet: none.
Pro: Bradley C. Dally, PGA. Superintendent: Chad Niedermeier.
Rating/Slope: C 65.5/110; M 63.7/107; W 65.6/110. **Course record:** 59.
Green fees: Monday thru Thursday $21/$15; M/C, VISA.
Friday thru Sunday & Holidays $23/$17; Jr & Sr rates $17/$12 (M-F).
Power cart: $22/$13. **Pull cart:** $2.50. **Trail fee:** $8 for personal carts.
Reservation policy: yes, call up to 1 week in advance for tee times.
Winter condition: the golf course is open all year long. Dry conditions.
Terrain: flat, some hills. **Tees:** grass. **Spikes:** metal spikes permitted.
Services: club rentals, lessons, snack bar, lounge, restaurant, beer, wine, liquor,
beverages, pro shop, club memberships, driving range, putting green.
Comments: friendly, well kept, tree-lined course. Great golf course that is
worth a special trip. If you are looking for a quality course that is excellent for
tournaments and company outings try Madrona. This course will not disappoint.

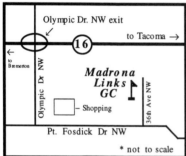

Directions: from Hwy 16 take the exit
for Olympic Dr. Follow Olympic Dr. to
Pt. Fosdick Dr. NW and turn left. Travel
.9 miles to 36th Avenue NW. Turn left
(it is not well marked). The golf course
is located .4 miles ahead on your left.

Course Yardage & Par:
C-5602 yards, par 71.
M-5193 yards, par 71.
W-4737 yards, par 73.

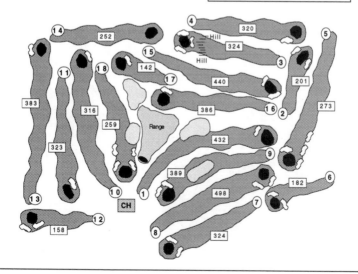

Manito Golf & Country Club (private, 18 hole course)

5303 South Hatch Road; Spokane, WA 99203
Phone: (509) 448-5829. Fax: (509) 448-9607. Internet: none.
Pro: Steve Prugh, PGA. Superintendent: Tim Ansett.
Rating/Slope: C 70.0/123; M 69.2/120; W 72.3/125; W 69.2/118. **Record:** 60.
Green fees: private club members & guests only; reciprocates.
Power cart: private club. **Pull cart:** private club. **Trail fee:** not allowed.
Reservation policy: private club members & guests only. No outside play.
Winter condition: the golf course is closed during winter months.
Terrain: flat . **Tees:** all grass. **Spikes:** no metal spikes are permitted.
Services: club rentals, lessons, restaurant, snack bar, lounge, beer, wine, liquor, showers, pro shop, driving range, putting and chipping greens, memberships.
Comments: premium put on accuracy due to many sand traps, well bunkered greens and tight tree-lined fairways. Holes 9 and 18 on an island and are very demanding. Excellent private facility that is very hard to score on.

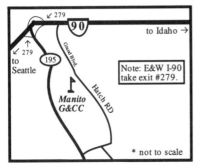

Note: E&W I-90 take exit #279.

* not to scale

Directions: from I-90 E&W take the exit for Hwy 195S southbound #279. Travel for approximately 4.5 miles to the Hatch Road exit. Proceed eastbound uphill for 2 miles to the stop sign (stay left at the fork). Turn left at the stop sign and proceed to the golf course 1/2 mile ahead on the right hand side of the road.

Course Yardage & Par:
C-6378 yards, par 70.
M-6153 yards, par 71.
W-5678 yards, par 72.
W-5401 yards, par 72.

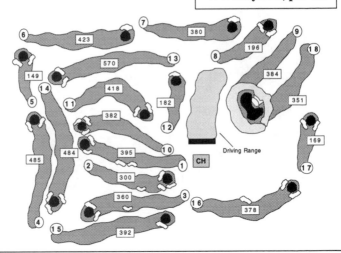

Maple Grove Golf (public, 9 hole course)

Hwy 12 & Cispus Road; P. O. Box 205; Randle, WA 98377
Phone: (360) 497-2741. **Fax:** none. **Internet:** none.
Owner: Earl Brischle. **Superintendent:** none.
Rating/Slope: M 53.7/72; W55.2/76. **Course record:** 26.
Green fees: $10/$7.50; all day $14; Jr. & Sr. rates (weekdays); M/C, VISA.
Power cart: none available. **Pull cart:** $2. **Trail fee:** no charge.
Reservation policy: for tournaments only. Everyone else first come first served.
Winter condition: the golf course is open all year long. Dry conditions.
Terrain: flat, some hills. **Tees:** all grass. **Spikes:** metal spikes permitted.
Services: club rentals, snack bar, beer, wine, pro shop, driving range, RV parking and hook-ups. **Comments:** course situated in Maple Grove Park. Short course that has medium sized greens with few hazards. The course is wide open with few hazards coming into play. Good track for the senior or first time golfer.

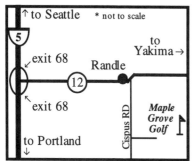

Directions: from I-5 N&S cut-off eastbound on Highway 12 exit #68 toward Randle, Washington. Turn right on Cispus Road (Hwy 131 South). Proceed to the golf course which will be located on your left hand side. Look for signs marking your way to the golf course.

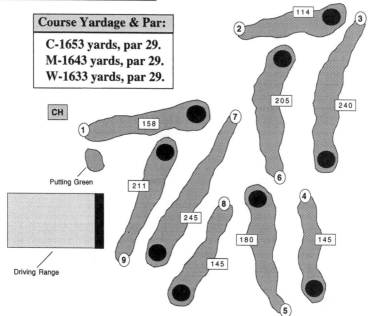

Course Yardage & Par:

C-1653 yards, par 29.
M-1643 yards, par 29.
W-1633 yards, par 29.

Maplewood Golf Course (public, 18 hole course)

4000 SE Maple Valley Highway; Renton, WA 98055
Phone: (425) 277-4444. Fax: (425) 271-7773. Internet: none.
Pro: Gordy Graybeal, PGA. Superintendent: Brad Barnes.
Rating/Slope: C 67.4/112; M 66.1/110; W 68.7/114. **Course record:** 62.
Green fees: W/D $20/$15; W/E $25/$15; Jr/Sr (M-Th. $15/$12); M/C, VISA.
Power cart: $22/$14. **Pull cart:** $3/$2. **Trail fee:** $6 for personal carts.
Reservation policy: yes, call up to 1 week in advance for weekday times, call
Monday for the following weekend. (Be sure to call ahead during the summer).
Winter condition: the golf course is open all year long. Drains fairly well.
Terrain: flat, some hills. **Tees:** grass & mats. **Spikes:** soft spikes preferred.
Services: club rentals, lessons, restaurant, lounge, beer, wine, liquor, pro shop,
club memberships, 30 stall driving range (covered & heated), banquet rooms.
Comments: measuring nearly 6,000 yards in length, the course's wide variety of
holes provides a good test for all level of golfers. The front side has water on
seven of the nine holes and the back side will challenge even the straightest
drivers with tight tree lined fairways. The course can get very busy in summer.

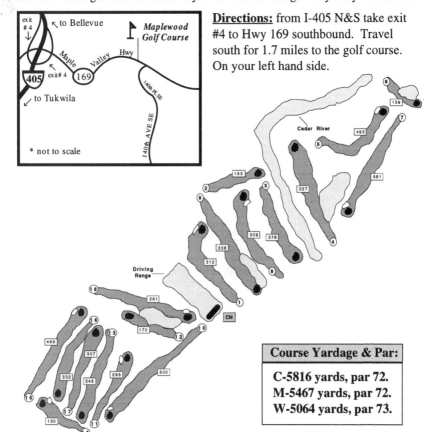

Directions: from I-405 N&S take exit
#4 to Hwy 169 southbound. Travel
south for 1.7 miles to the golf course.
On your left hand side.

Course Yardage & Par:

C-5816 yards, par 72.
M-5467 yards, par 72.
W-5064 yards, par 73.

McCormick Woods (public, 18 hole course)

5155 McCormick Woods Drive SW; Port Orchard, WA 98366
Phone numbers: (360) 895-0130 or 1-800-323-0130.
Fax: (360) 876-2254. **Internet:** www.mccormickwoodsgolf.com
Pro: Scott Ashworth, PGA. **Supt.:** Howard Sisson. **Record:** 64.
Rating/Slope: T 74.6/136; C 72.6/131; M 70.5/125; W 73.6/131; E 66.6/115.
Green fees: Monday thru Thursday $40/$25; Friday thru Sun. & Holidays $55;
Early Bird (B-4 8am) Monday-Thursday $25; VISA, M/C, Discover, AMEX.
Power cart: $26/$16. **Pull cart:** $4/$3. **Trail fee:** personal carts not allowed.
Reservation policy: recommended, call up to 5 days in advance for tee times.
Winter condition: the course is open all year long. Dry, excellent drainage.
Terrain: flat, some hills. **Tees:** all grass. **Spikes:** metal spikes permitted.
Services: club rentals, lessons, snack bar, beer, wine, restuarant, lounge, pro
shop, driving range. **Comments:** ranked in the top 50 public golf courses by
Golf Digest Magazine. Golfweek voted McCormick Woods the #1 course in
Washington State. Championship caliber track. Well bunkered by grass and
sand bunkers. Great golf course that is worth a special trip. You will often see
deer walking down your fairway so if you are in the area don't miss this course.

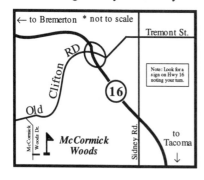

Directions: from I-5 N&S take the exit
for Hwy 16 westbound. Follow Hwy
16 to the Old Clifton/Tremont exit.
Turn left and proceed 1.8 miles to the
entrance located on your. **Note:** look
for signs on Hwy 16 to the course.

Course Yardage & Par:
T-7040 yards, par 72.
C-6658 yards, par 72.
M-6165 yards, par 72.
W-5758 yards, par 72.
Exc-5299 yards, par 72.

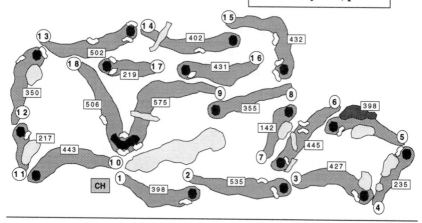

Meadow Park Golf Course (public, 18 hole, 9 hole par 3 course)
7108 Lakewood Drive West; Lakewood, WA 98499
Phone: (253) 473-3033. Fax: (253) 471-9266. Internet: none.
Pro: Gerry Mehlert, PGA. Superintendent: Chris Goodman.
Rating/Slope: C 68.9/116; M 67.3/11; W 70.2/115. Course record: 64.
Green fees: W/D $20/$14; W/E $24/$15; Jr./Sr. rates (M-Friday); VISA, M/C.
Green fees for Williams 9: $12/$8 all week long; Jr. & Sr. rates (M-Friday).
Power cart: $20/$12. Pull cart: $2.50. Trail fee: $6 for personal carts.
Reservation policy: yes, call up to 1 week in advance for your tee times.
Winter condition: the golf course is open all year long. Dry conditions.
Terrain: flat, some hills. **Tees:** all grass. **Spikes:** metal spikes permitted.
Services: club rentals, lessons, snack bar, lounge, restaurant, pro shop,
beverages, club memberships, covered driving range, putting & chipping greens.
Comments: the golf course has been completely revamped with a stunning new
layout. Greens are large with bunkers coming onto play on several holes.
Fairways are fairly wide giving the golfer room off the tee. Good winter course.

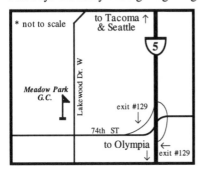

Directions: from I-5 N&S take exit #129
to S 74th St. Travel westbound for 2.1
miles to Lakewood Drive W. Turn north.
The golf course is located .1 miles ahead
on your left hand side. Look for signs.

Course Yardage & Par:
C-6093 yards, par 71.
M-5763 yards, par 71.
W-5225 yards, par 71.

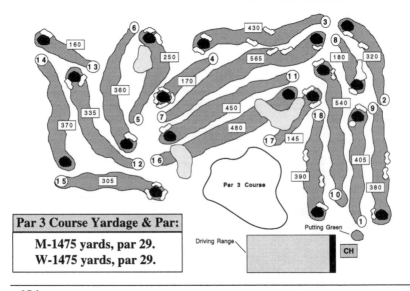

Par 3 Course Yardage & Par:
M-1475 yards, par 29.
W-1475 yards, par 29.

Meadow Springs Country Club (private, 18 hole course)

700 Country Club Place; Richland, WA 99352
Phone: (509) 627-2321. Fax: (509) 6274022. Internet: none.
Pro: Greg Moore, PGA. Superintendent: Mark Dalton.
Rating/Slope: C 73.3/132; M 71.3/127; M 68.9/123; W 69.2/120. **Record:** 63.
Green fees: private club; members & guests only; reciprocates; M/C, VISA.
Power cart: private club. **Pull cart:** private club. **Trail fee:** private club.
Reservation policy: private club; members & guests only. No outside play.
Winter condition: the golf course open all year long weather permitting, dry.
Terrain: relatively hilly. **Tees:** all grass. **Spikes:** metal spikes not permitted.
Services: lessons, restaurant, lounge, beer, wine, liquor, lockers, driving range,
pro shop, putting green. **Comments:** a very challenging course featuring well-
placed traps, elevated greens and a fair amount of water. Meadow Springs is
the host course for the Nike Tri-Cities Open. Excellent well balanced layout.

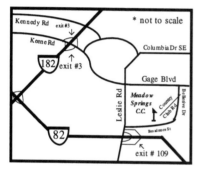

Directions: from I-182 take the exit for
Keene Road #3. Continue to Gage Blvd.
You will run right in to Gage Blvd. Turn
left on Bellerive Drive to Country Club
Place and proceed to the golf course.
From I-82 take exit #109 to Leslie Road.
Proceed to Broadmore Street and turn
right. Proceed to Bellerive Drive and
turn left to Country Club Place. Turn left
and proceed to the clubhouse. Look for
signs to the clubhouse.

Course Yardage & Par:

C-6957 yards, par 72.
M-6537 yards, par 72.
M-5940 yards, par 72.
W-5471 yards, par 72.

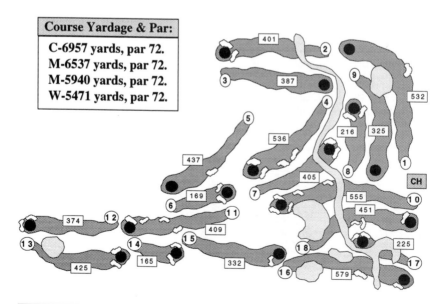

Meadowmeer Golf & Country Club (semi-private, 9 holes)

8530 Renny Lane NE; Bainbridge Island, WA 98110
Phone: (206) 842-2218. Fax: (206) 842-4771. Internet: none.
Pro: Tom Mueller, PGA. Supterintendent: Gary Duffner.
Rating/Slope: M 66.7/119; W 69.6/119. **Course record:** 62.
Green fees: Monday thru Thursday $19/$14.50; Friday thru Sunday &
Holidays $23/$17; Jr & Sr rates (Monday thru Thursday only); M/C, VISA.
Power cart: $21.50/$13. **Pull cart:** $3/$2. **Trail fee:** $7 for personal carts.
Reservation policy: up to 1 week in advance, public play is restricted at times.
Winter condition: the golf course is open all year long. Dry conditions.
Terrain: flat, some hills. **Tees:** grass. **Spikes:** soft spikes optional.
Services: club rentals, lessons, snack bar, beer, pro shop, club memberships.
Comments: the course is just 35 minutes from Seattle on the Winslow-Seattle
ferry. Good winter golf course. Easy to walk on even during the summer, so
if you are looking to play golf on your visit to the Olympic Peninsula try
Meadowmeer. The layout can play much longer than the scorecard states.

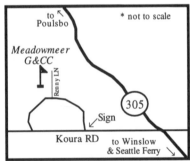

Directions: from the Seattle-Winslow
ferry terminal in Winslow take Hwy 305
northbound to Koura Road. Turn left on
Koura Road. 1/4 mile up you will see
signs for the golf course on your right
hand side. Follow the signs to the golf
course. **Note:** Look for signs marking
your way to the golf course from state
highway 305.

Course Yardage & Par:

M-2824 yards, par 35.
W-2765 yards, par 38.
Dual tees for 18 holes:
M-5589 yards, par 71.
W-5170 yards, par 74.

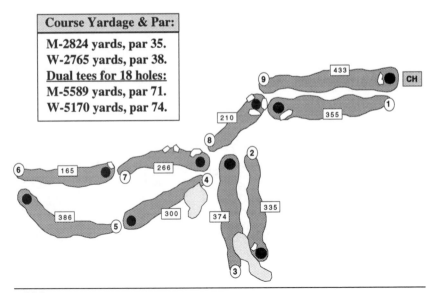

MeadowWood Golf Course (public, 18 hole course)

E 24501 Valley Way; Liberty Lake, WA 99019
Phone: (509) 255-9539. **Fax:** none. **Internet:** none.
Pro: Bob Scott, PGA. **Superintendent:** Mike Kingsley.
Rating/Slope: C 72.1/126; M 70.7/122; W 73.5/137. **Course record:** 64.
Green fees: non-resident: $22/$16; resident: $16/$12.
Power cart: $23/$11.50. **Pull cart:** $3. **Trail fee:** $6 for personal carts.
Reservation policy: yes, call in advance on Tuesday for the rest of the week.
Winter condition: the golf course is closed from November to March.
Terrain: rolling terrain. **Tees:** all grass. **Spikes:** metal spikes permitted.
Services: club rentals, lessons, restaurant, snack bar, beer, wine, pro shop,
driving range, putting green, club memberships. **Comments:** designed by
Robert Muir Graves this course is one of the nicest public play courses in
eastern Washington. A links-type course, MeadowWood features mounds,
water, and sand bunkers. A **Four-Star** golf course that is worth a special trip.

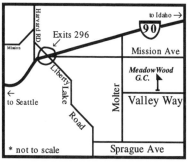

Directions: from I-90 E&W take exit
296. Go through the stoplight 1 mile
to Molter Road. Turn right on Molter
Road. Proceed for 1 mile and turn left
on Valley Way. Proceed to the golf
course. Look for signs marking your
way to the complex.

Course Yardage & Par:

C-6874 yards, par 72.
M-6429 yards, par 72.
W-5880 yards, par 72.

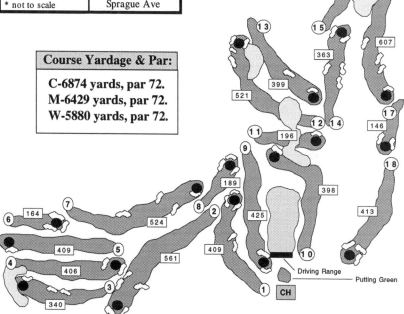

Meridian Greens G. C. & D. R. (public 9 hole par 3 course)
9705 136th Street East; Puyallup, WA 98373
Phone: (253) 845-7504. **Fax:** none. **Internet:** none.
Pro: Rusty Fancher, PGA. **Superintendent:** Cort Gould.
Rating/Slope: course ratings not available. **Course record:** 25.
Green fees: W/D $12/$8; W/E $13/$9; Jr & Sr rates (M-F) $9/$5; VISA, M/C.
Power cart: not allowed. **Pull cart:** $2. **Trail fee:** not allowed.
Reservation policy: calls up to 1 week in advance, have priority.
Winter condition: the golf course is open all year long.
Terrain: flat (easy walking). **Tees:** all grass. **Spikes:** metal spikes permitted.
Services: lessons, club rentals, pro shop, covered and lighted driving range.
Comments: flat course which is easy to walk. Mount Rainier comes into view on several of the holes. Great course for every level of golfer. The golf course also has a practice putting green and a lighted, covered driving range.

Directions: from I-5 N&S take exit #127 to Hwy 512 eastbound. Travel east to the 9th St. SW exit, turn right at the first light and proceed 2 miles south on 9th St. SW. **Note:** (9th St. SW changes to 94th Ave. E) to 136th St. E where you will turn left to the course. You may also travel a little farther east on Hwy 512 to the South Hill/ Eatonville exit. Turn right on Meridian E (Hwy 161). Follow to 136th and turn right to the course. **Note:** Look for the sign on (Hwy 161, Meridian) marking your turn.

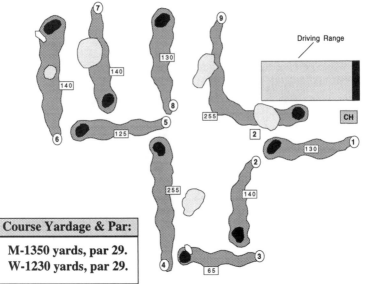

Course Yardage & Par:
M-1350 yards, par 29.
W-1230 yards, par 29.

Meridian Valley Golf & Country Club (private, 18 hole course)

24830 136th Avenue SE; Kent, WA 98042
Phone: (253) 631-3133. **Fax:** (253) 631-9014. **Internet:** none.
Pro: Greg Manley, PGA. **Superintendent:** Craig Benson.
Rating/Slope: C 71.9/127; M 70.5/123; W 73.7/127. **Record:** M 64, W 62.
Green fees: private club members & guests of members only; reciprocates.
Power cart: private club. **Pull cart:** private club. **Trail fee:** not allowed.
Reservation policy: private club members only. No outside play allowed.
Winter condition: the golf course is open all year long. Damp conditions.
Terrain: relatively hilly. **Tees:** grass. **Spikes:** no metal spikes permitted.
Services: lessons, lounge, restaurant, beer, wine, liquor, pro shop, driving range, lockers, showers, club memberships. **Comments:** home of the LPGA Safeco Classic. Demanding layout with well-trapped greens, tree-lined fairways and water. This private course is challenging from every tee. Great private course.

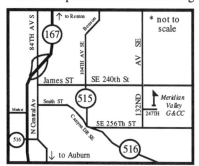

Directions: from I-5 N&S take exit # 149 to Hwy 516 eastbound. Travel eastbound for 7.7 miles (through Kent) to 132nd Avenue SE. Turn north and proceed 1.4 miles to SE 247th. Turn east for .1 mile to 136th Avenue SE. Turn south to the golf course.

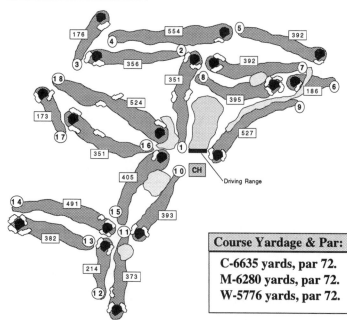

Course Yardage & Par:

C-6635 yards, par 72.
M-6280 yards, par 72.
W-5776 yards, par 72.

Meriwood Golf Course (public, 18 hole course)

4550 Meriwood Drive; Lacey, WA 98516 Internet: www.cybergolf.com/meriwood
For Tee-times: 1-800-55-TEE IT. (360) 412-0495. Fax: (360) 491-9091.
Dir. of Golf: Ron Coleman. Pro: Kevin Meyers. Supt.: Kirk Anderson.
Rating/Slope: T 75.1/135; C 72.6/129; M 70.2/123; W 73.0/127. **Record:** 65.
Green fees: Monday thru Thursday $43 includes cart; Friday thru Sunday
& Hol. $49 includes cart; winter, Jr./Sr., twilight rates; M/C, VISA, AMEX.
Power cart: included in green fee. **Pull cart:** $5. **Trail fee:** not allowed.
Reservation policy: please call up to 7 days in advance for tee times.
Winter condition: the golf course is open all year long. Good conditions.
Terrain: flat, some rolling hills. **Tees:** grass. **Spikes:** spikeless April thru Sept.
Services: club rentals, lessons, lounge, coffee shop, beer, pro shop, driving
range, putting green. **Comments:** newer golf course that has been well received
by all. This track features rolling terrain, tree lined fairways and well bunkered
greens. Excellent course that will challenge you at every turn. Worth a special
trip at any time. Professionally managed by Golf Resources Northwest.

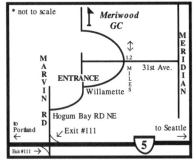

Directions: from the north take exit #111
from I-5. Turn right at the light. Go
approximately 125 yards and turn right
on Hogum Bay Rd. Go .3 miles to
Meridian Campus Entrance at Willamette
Dr., go 2.2 miles to the golf course. From
the south take exit #111 from I-5. Turn
left at the light and go over the freeway.
Proceed through stop light and follow the
above directions.

Course Yardage & Par:
C-7170 yards, par 72.
M-6579/6159 yards, par 72.
W-5707/5600 yards, par 72.

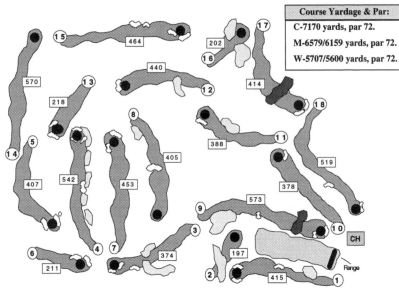

Mill Creek Country Club (private, 18 hole course)

15550 Country Club Drive; Mill Creek, WA 98012

Phone: (425) 743-5664. **Fax:** (425) 338-7025. **Internet:** none.

Pro: Tom Sursley, PGA. **Superintendent:** Paul Hoffman.

Rating/Slope: C 70.8/128; M 69.8/124; W 73.0/126; W 71.7/123. **Record:** 62.

Green fees: members only; some reciprocation; no credit cards.

Power cart: private club. **Pull cart:** private club. **Trail fee:** not allowed.

Reservation policy: private club members only. No outside play allowed.

Winter condition: the golf course is open all year long. Damp conditions.

Terrain: relatively hilly. **Tees:** all grass. **Spikes:** no metal spikes in summer.

Services: club rentals, lessons, lounge, restaurant, beer, wine, liquor, pro shop, driving range, lockers, showers, club memberships. **Comments:** rolling terrain, tree-lined fairways and many hazards put emphasis on shot placement. Greens are fairly large with undulations throughout. Excellent well kept private facility.

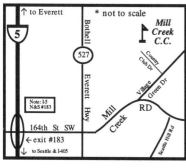

Directions: from I-5 N&S take exit #183 to Martha Lake Road (164th St. SW). Travel eastbound for 2 miles to Mill Creek Road. Turn left and travel .3 miles to Village Green Drive. Turn left and proceed .3 miles to Country Club Drive. Turn left to the golf course.

Course Yardage & Par:

C-6331 yards, par 72.
M-6022 yards, par 72.
W-5560 yards, par 72.

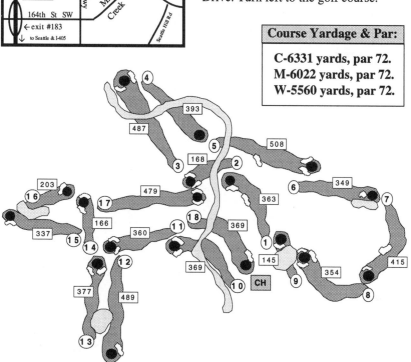

Mint Valley Golf Course (public, 18 hole course)
4002 Pennsylvania Street; Longview, WA 98632
Phone: (360) 577-3395, 1-800-928-8929. Fax: none. Internet: none.
Pro: Mahlon Moe, PGA. Superintendent: Dave MacDonald.
Rating/Slope: C 69.4/114; M 67.2/109; W 69.0/109. **Course record: 63.**
Green fees: Weekdays $16/$12; Weekends $21/$16; Sr. rates $12.50/$10
(Monday thru Friday); winter rates and twilight rates are available. Jr. rates
$11.50/$9.50 or a Jr. can play for $1 after 1pm with a paid adult on the W/E.
Power cart: $24/$13. **Pull cart:** $3. **Trail fee:** $10 for personal carts.
Reservation policy: yes, call up to 1 week in advance for tee times.
Winter condition: the golf course open all year long. Fair conditions.
Terrain: flat, very easy to walk. **Tees:** grass. **Spikes:** soft spikes preferred.
Services: club rentals, lessons, snack bar, beer, pro shop, driving range.
Comments: not overly long, strategically placed bunkers and lakes challenge
any golfers shot making. Greens are in excellent condition and putt well. The
course does play longer than the yardage would indicate. If you are looking for
a course that is not a back breaker try Mint Valley it will not disappoint.

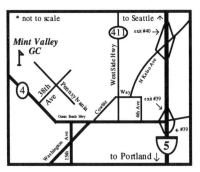

Directions: from I-5 N&S take exit # 39
or any other Longview/Kelso exit and
proceed west to Highway 4 (Ocean
Beach). Turn right on 38th, then turn left
on Pennsylvania and proceed to the golf
course. Look for signs marking your turns
to the golf course the way is well marked.

Course Yardage & Par:
C-6304 yards, par 71.
M-5800 yards, par 71.
W-5214 yards, par 71.

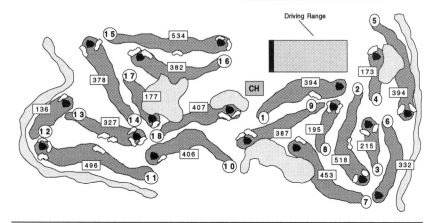

Monroe Golf Course (public, 9 hole course)

22110 Old Owen Road; Monroe, WA 98272
Phone: (360) 794-8498. Fax: none. Internet: none.
Pro/Manager:Ray Bloom, PGA. Superintendent: none.
Rating/Slope: M 61.8/100; W 66.9/110. **Course record:** 27.
Green fees: W/D $15/$10; W/E $17/$12. Sr. rates on power carts $13/$6.50.
Power cart: $17/$8.50. **Pull cart:** $4. **Trail fee:** $6 per 9 holes.
Reservation policy: yes, please call in advance for tee-times. No time limit.
Winter condition: the golf course is open all year long. Dry conditions.
Terrain: flat, some slight hills. **Tees:** grass. **Spikes:** metal spikes permitted.
Services: club rentals, snack bar, pro shop, lockers, club memberships, picnic
area, putting green. **Comments:** golf course can play tight due to many trees
lining most fairways. Friendly staff and good food in the club house can make
up for any bad day on the course. Great family golf course.

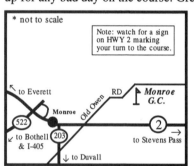

Directions: from I-405 N&S take
the exit for 522 eastbound to Hwy 2
eastbound. Travel east to Old Owen
Road, (the third light in the town of
Monroe) to the golf course. The golf
course will be on your right. **Note:** Look
for a sign on the Hwy 2 marking your
turn to the golf course.

Course Yardage & Par:
M-2451 yards, par 33; W-2451 yards, par 33.

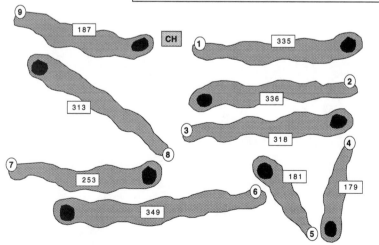

Moses Lake Golf & Country Club (private, 18 hole course)
P.O. Drawer G; West Highway 90; Moses Lake, WA 98837
Phone: (509) 765-5049. Fax: (509) 765-5371. Internet: none.
Pro: Mike Eslick, PGA. Superintendent: Carl Thompson.
Rating/Slope: C 69.5/111; M 68.5/109; W 72.5/120. **Course record:** 63.
Green fees: private club members & guests only; reciprocates; no credit cards.
Power cart: private club. **Pull cart:** private club. **Trail fee:** private club.
Reservation policy: private club members & guests only. No outside play.
Winter condition: the golf course is closed from December to January.
Terrain: flat, some hills. **Tees:** all grass. **Spikes:** no metal spikes permitted.
Services: lessons, restaurant, lounge, beer, wine, pro shop, driving range.
Comments: beautiful lush green fairways and excellent putting surfaces
make this a very enjoyable course. Greens are large and well bunkered. Fairways are generous and forgiving off the tee. The course is very easy to walk.

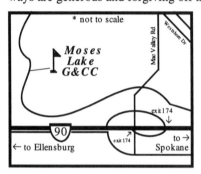

Directions: from I-90 eastbound and westbound take the first Moses Lake exit #174. Travel north to the golf course.

Course Yardage & Par:

C-6436 yards, par 71.
M-6187 yards, par 71.
W-5852 yards, par 74.

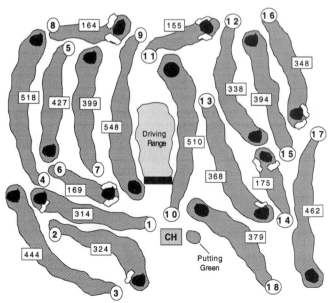

Moses Pointe Golf Resort (semi-private, 18 hole course)
4524 Westshore Drive; Moses Lake, WA 98837
Phone: (509) 764-2275. Fax: (509) 764-0831. Internet: none.
Manager: Mike Moore. Pro: to be named later.
Rating/Slope: the golf course has not been rated. **Course record:** N/A.
Green fees: W/D $30/$20; W/E $40/$30; VISA, M/C, AMEX.
Power cart: $20/$15. **Pull cart:** $5/$3. **Trail fee:** $10 for personal carts.
Reservation policy: yes, call up to 7 days in advance for tee times.
Winter condition: the golf course open all year long. Very dry conditions.
Terrain: flat, some hills. **Tees:** all grass. **Spikes:** soft spikes only.
Services: club rentals, lessons, full service restaurant, snack bar, beer, wine, liquor, pro shop, lockers, driving range, putting green, tennis courts.
Comments: this new course is set to open in June of 1999 and promises to be one the bright spots on the eastern Washington golf scene. The course sports generous landing areas off the tee. Greens will be firm and fast. With views of Moses Lake the Cascade Mt.'s and plenty of sunshine this track is sure to please.

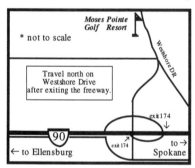

Directions: from I-90 eastbound and westbound take the first Moses Lake exit #174 (Mae Valley). Travel northbound for approximately 3 miles up Westshore Drive to the golf course.

Course Yardage & Par:
T-7428 yards, par 72.
C-6889 yards, par 72.
M-6342 yards, par 72.
W-5807 yards, par 72.

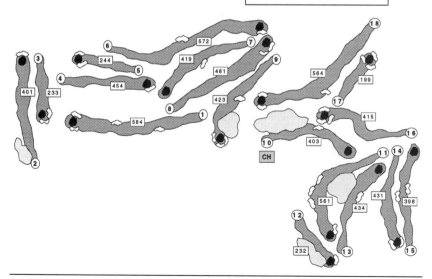

Mount Adams Country Club (semi-private, 18 hole course)
1250 Rocky Ford Road; Toppenish, WA 98948
Phone: (509) 865-4440. **Fax:** none. **Internet:** none.
Pro: Scott Galbraith, PGA. **Superintendent:** Rick Cullen.
Rating/Slope: C 70.6/121; M 74.1/126; W 73.9/124. **Course record:** 65.
Green fees: $17.50/$12; Jr. rates, weekdays only; VISA, M/C.
Power cart: $21/$11. **Pull cart:** $2.50/$1.25. **Trail fee:** $3.
Reservation policy: yes, you may call ahead for a tee time. Call prior Thursday
for your weekend reservations. Some other times are restricted by member play.
Winter condition: the golf course is open all year long. Dry conditions.
Terrain: flat (easy walking). **Tees:** all grass. **Spikes:** soft spikes preferred.
Services: lessons, restaurant, lounge, beer, wine, pro shop, driving range.
Comments: the course features semi-wide fairways and small quick bent grass
greens that are the best greens you might putt anywhere. This Eastern Washington course has beautiful views of Mount Adams and the surrounding countryside
from many spots on the golf course. Very enjoyable golf course to play.

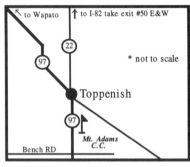

Directions: from I-82 eastbound take
the exit for Highway 97 southbound to
Toppenish. Continue 2 miles south of
Toppenish to the golf course. The golf
course will be located on your left hand
side. Look for signs.

Course Yardage & Par:
C-6524 yards, par 72.
M-6292 yards, par 72.
W-5831 yards, par 73.

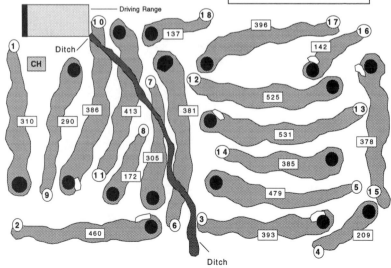

Mount Si Golf Course (public, 18 hole course)

9010 Boalch Avenue SE; P.O. Box 2020; Snoqualmie, WA 98065
Phone: (425) 391-4926 or 888-1541. Fax (425) 888-7079. Supt: Mike Moore.
Pros: Gary Barter PGA , John Sanford PGA, Matt Campbell PGA.
Rating/Slope: C 68.5/116; M 67.4/113; W 68.8/108. **Course record:** 62.
Green fees: W/D $26/$15; W/E $31/$18; Jr /Sr $21/$14 (M-Th) & winter rates.
Power cart: $24/$14. **Pull cart** $3/$2. **Trail fee:** $3 for personal carts.
Reservation policy: yes, please call ahead for your T-time. No restrictions.
Winter condition: the golf course is open all year long. Dry conditions.
Terrain: flat, some hills. **Tees:** grass . **Spikes:** metal spikes permitted.
Services: club rentals, lessons, snack bar, restaurant, beer, wine, liquor, lockers, showers, pro shop, club memberships, driving range, putting & chipping green.
Comments: Scenic setting near the base of Mt. Si. Course offers a full service restaurant with fantastic views. Greens are well kept, large and putt well. If you are looking for a good course with a friendly staff Mount Si is sure to please.

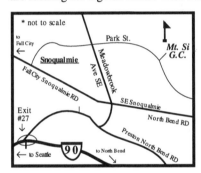

Directions: From I-90 eastbound take exit #27. At the stop sign turn left and go 1 mile to a left turn lane for "Snoqualmie Falls". Turn left, following the "Snoqualmie Falls" sign until you reach a traffic light. Continue straight through the light, past Mount Si High School to Park Street. Turn right onto Park Street. The course will be 1 mile ahead on your left.

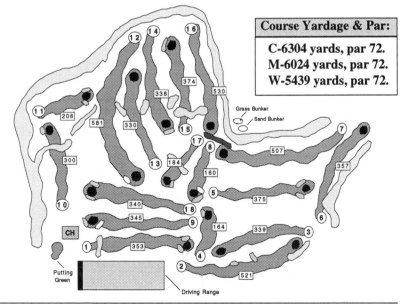

Course Yardage & Par:

C-6304 yards, par 72.
M-6024 yards, par 72.
W-5439 yards, par 72.

New World Pro Golf Center (public, 9 hole par 3 course)
5022 Guide Meridian; Bellingham, WA 98226
Phone: (360) 398-1362. **Fax:** none. **Internet:** none.
Pro: none. **Superintendent:** none.
Rating/Slope: the golf course is not rated. **Course record:** 22.
Green fees: $8/$6 all week long; no credit cards.
Power cart: none. **Pull cart:** $1. **Trail fee:** personal carts are not allowed.
Reservation policy: advance reservations not required, first come first served.
Winter condition: the golf course is closed from November to March.
Terrain: flat, some slight hills. **Tees:** all grass. **Spikes:** metal spikes permitted.
Services: club rentals, limited pro shop, pop, covered driving range.
Comments: fair par 3 golf course with medium to small sized greens. A creek runs through 2 and 9 and does present some challenges. The complex also has a covered driving range for those wanting to practice their short or long irons.

Directions: From I-5 N&S take exit #256 to Meridian Street. Proceed north on Hwy 539N for 2 miles to the golf course on your right hand side of the highway. Look for a sign indicating your turn.

Course Yardage & Par:
M-947 yards, par 27.
W-947 yards, par 27.

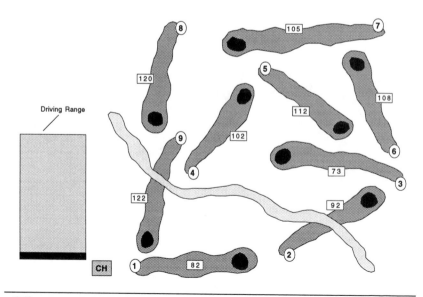

Newaukum Valley Golf Course (public, 27 hole course)

3024 Jackson Highway; Chehalis, WA 98532
Phone: (360) 748-0461. **Fax: none. Internet: none.**
Pro: Scott Date, PGA. Superintendent: John Date.
Rating/Slope: West/South C 69.9/113; M 68.0/108; W 70.6/112. **Record:** 66.
Green fees: W/D $17/$12; W/E $22/$17; Sr. & Jr. rates; M/C, VISA.
Power cart: $20/$10. **Pull cart:** $2/$1. **Trail fee:** $5 for personal carts.
Reservation policy: call in advance for tee times from March to September.
Winter condition: the golf course is open all year long. Dry conditions.
Terrain: flat, some hills. **Tees:** all grass. **Spikes:**soft spikes preferred.
Services: club rentals, lessons, restaurant, beer, wine, pro shop, driving range.
Comments: A full irrigation system keeps the course in great shape all year
round. Good public golf course that expanded to 27 holes in March of 1996.
Greens are large and have very good putting surfaces. This new layout is much
more user freindly and enjoyable. Good public track at very affordable prices.

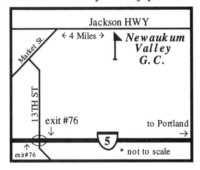

Directions: from I-5 N&S take exit # 76
to 13th St. Go east on 13th to Market St.
Turn right on Market which becomes
Jackson Highway. Follow for 4 miles to
the golf course. Look for signs.

Course Yardage & Par:
West Course: C-3268 yards, M-3087 yards, W-2847 yards, par 36.
South Course: C-3223 yards, W-2981 yards, W-2672 yards, par 36.
East Course: C-2945 yards, M-2813 yards, W-2440 yards, par 36.

Rating/Slope:
South/East: C 68.5/109; M 66.8/105; W 68.3/108.
East/West: C 68.4/109; M 67.0/105; W 68.9/110.

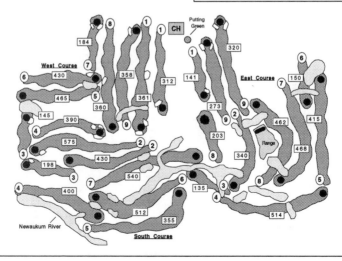

Nile Golf & Country Club (semi-private, 18 hole course)
6601 204th SW; Mountlake Terrace, WA 98043
Phone: (425) 776-5154. Fax: (425) 672-1833. Internet: none.
Pro: Randy Puetz, PGA. Superintendent: David Korsmoe.
Rating/Slope: M 67.3/119; W 70.7/124. **Course record:** 64.
Green fees: Shriners $16/$10; guests $25/$15; M/C, VISA, carts/merchandise.
Power cart: $22/$12. **Pull cart:** $2. **Trail fee:** $5 for personal carts.
Reservation policy: members may call up to 1 week in advance for tee times.
The public may call ahead 3 days and reserve times on a "space available basis".
Winter condition: the golf course is open all year long. Good drainage.
Terrain: very hilly. **Tees:** all grass. **Spikes:** soft spikes preffered.
Services: lessons, well stocked pro shop, club repair, putting green.
Comments: short, but a test of skill for all players. This beautifully tree-lined
well bunkered course is a joy to play. The new layout has no two holes that are
the same. Be sure to play the Nile while the public is allowed to play.

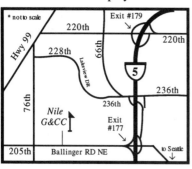

Directions: from I-5 N&S take exit # 177
to 244th SW-205th St-Hwy 104W. Travel
westbound for .3 miles to the golf course
entrance, which will be on your right.
Note: Look for the Nile Temple entrance
and this will take you into the grounds of
the golf course and clubhouse

Course Yardage & Par:
M-5000 yards, par 68.
W-5000 yards, par 69.

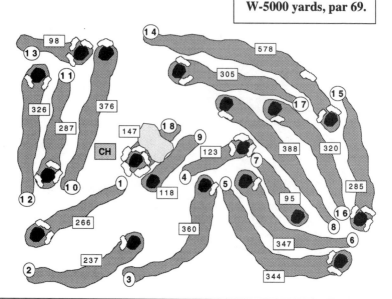

Nisqually Valley Golf Course (public, 18 hole course)
15425 Mosman Street; Box Q; Yelm, WA 98597
Phone: (360) 458-3332, 800-352-2645. Fax: none. Internet: none.
Pro: Eric Olsen, PGA. Superintendent: Al Simpson
Rating/Slope: C 68.0/113; M 67.1/111; W 71.4/115. **Course record:** 62.
Green fees: W/D $17/$10; W/E $20; Jr & Sr rates $10/$5 (M-F).
Power cart: $15/$8. **Pull cart:** $2. **Trail fee:** none.
Reservation policy: yes, up to 2 weeks in advance, for weekends times only.
Winter condition: the golf course is open all year long. Fair conditions.
Terrain: flat, some hills. **Tees:** all grass. **Spikes:** soft spikes preferred.
Services: club rentals, lessons, lounge, restaurant, beer, wine, liquor, pro shop.
Comments: very dry and easy to walk golf course that has very few hazards.
Very scenic course with beautiful views of Mount Rainier and the surrounding
countryside. Good public golf course that has excellent greens all year round.

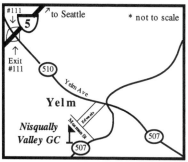

Directions: from I-5 N&S take exit
111 onto Hwy 510 and travel southeast
toward the town of Yelm. When Yelm
turn right on Edwards Street (at
McDonalds). Proceed on Edwards Street
for .6 miles to Mosman Street where you
will turn to the golf course. Look for
signs indicating your turn to the course.

Course Yardage & Par:
C-6007 yards, par 72.
M-5815 yards, par 72.
W-5751 yards, par 72.

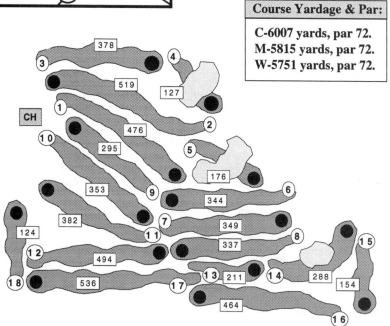

North Bellingham Public Golf Course (public, 18 hole course)
205 West Smith Road; Bellingham, WA 98226
Phone: (360) 398-8300; 888-322-6242. Fax: (360) 398-2523.
Pro: Nathan Vickers, PGA. **Superintendent:** Duane Zander.
Rating/Slope: C 72.2/125; M 69.1/119; 68.9/112. **Course record:** 67.
Green fees: W/D $27.83/$16.70; W/E $32.47/$24.20; Jr. & Sr., winter rates.
Power cart: $10.20/$7.42 (per person). **Pull cart:** $2.50. **Trail fee:** not allowed.
Reservation policy: please call up to 1 week in advance for tee times.
Winter condition: the course is open all year long, weather permitting. Dry.
Terrain: flat, some rolling hills. **Tees:** grass. **Spikes:** soft spikes April-October.
Services: club rentals, lessons, lounge, restaurant, beer, wine, liquor, pro shop,
driving range, putting green. **Comments:** newer public golf course. The course
is of championship caliber and length. From the back tees the course plays 6800
yards and is demanding. Ponds, grass and sand bunkers dot the entire course.

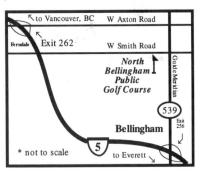

Directions: from I-5 N take exit #256
(Guide Meridian, Hwy 539). Proceed
north on Hwy 539 until you reach W
Smith Road. Turn left on W Smith Road
and proceed to course entrance on your
left hand side. From I-5 S take exit #262
W Axton Rd. Proceed east on W Axton
Road to Guide Meridian Hwy 539. Turn
right on Hwy 539. Proceed to W Smith
Road where you will turn right to the golf
course located on your left hand side.

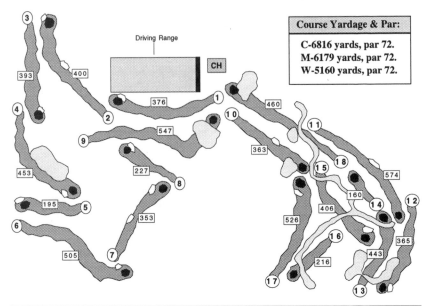

Course Yardage & Par:

C-6816 yards, par 72.
M-6179 yards, par 72.
W-5160 yards, par 72.

North Shore Golf Course (public, 18 hole course)

4101 North Shore Boulevard NE; Tacoma, WA 98422
Phone: (253) 927-1375, 800-447-1375. Fax: (253) 838-5898.
Pro: David Wetli, PGA. Superintendent: Michael Tight.
Rating/Slope: C 70.3/129; M 69.1/126; W 71.4/123. Course record: 65.
Green fees: Mon.-Tues. $20/$12.33*; Wed.-Thur. $25/$15*; Fri.-Sun. $30*;
no 9 hole rate on Fri. thru Sun.; twi-lite rates $18*; VISA, M/C, AMEX.
Power cart: $22/$11*. **Pull cart:** $3*. **Trail fee:** $22/$11* (add tax to all fees).
Reservation policy: yes, call up to 1 week in advance for your tee-times.
Winter condition: the golf course is open all year long. Dry conditions.
Terrain: relatively hilly. **Tees:** all grass. **Spikes:** soft spikes preferred.
Services: club rentals, lessons, snack bar, lounge, restaurant, beer, wine, liquor,
well stocked pro shop, lighted and covered driving range, banquet, tournament
facilities available. **Comments:** sand bunkers, water hazards and undulating
terrain make this course a true challenge. Greens are medium to large in size.
This golf course is worth a special trip anytime. The Northshore pro shop was
voted for the ninth straight year as one of the countries top pro shops by Golf
Shop Operations magazine. Excellent golf course that is well run.

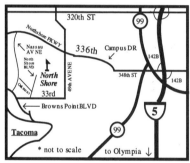

Directions: from I-5 N&S take exit
142B. Travel westbound for 5 miles.
Turn left on Nassau Avenue. Travel for
1/2 mile to Oakmont. Turn left. Take the
next left onto Northshore Blvd. The golf
course will be 1/10 mile ahead on your
right hand side. Look for signs the roads
to the golf course are well marked.

Course Yardage &Par:

C-6305 yards, par 71.
M-6039 yards, par 71.
W-5442 yards, par 73.

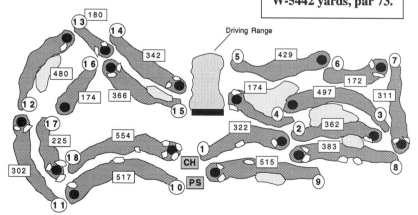

Oakbrook Golf & Country Club (private, 18 hole course)

8102 Zircon Drive SW; Tacoma, WA 98498
Phone: (253) 584-8770. Fax: (253) 581-3397. Internet: none.
Pro: Tad Davis, PGA. Superintendent: Jay Griswold.
Rating/Slope: B 71.6/125; W 69.8/121; Y 73.3/124; R 70.4/117. **Record:** 60.
Green fees: private club, members & guests only; reciprocates.
Power cart: private club. **Pull cart:** private club. **Trail fee:** not allowed.
Reservation policy: private club members & guests only. No outside play.
Winter condition: the golf course is open all year long. Dry conditions.
Terrain: flat, some hills. **Tees:** grass. **Spikes:** no metal spikes permitted.
Services: club rentals, lessons, lounge, beer, wine, liquor, lockers, showers,
pro shop, driving range. **Comments:** narrow tree-lined fairways and many
sand bunkers routinely challenge any golfer's game. Greens tend to get firm in
the summer months and can be hard to hold. Excellent private golf course.

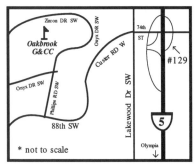

Directions: from I-5 N&S take exit #129
to S 74th. Go west for 2.3 miles, then S
74th will become Custer Road. Continue
to 88th St. Turn right on 88th. 88th
becomes Steilacoom. At your second light
turn right on Phillips. Stay on Phillips until
you come to the end of the arterial (sign).
Turn left on Turquoise. At the first stop
sign turn right on Zircon. Stay on Zircon
and this should lead to the clubhouse.

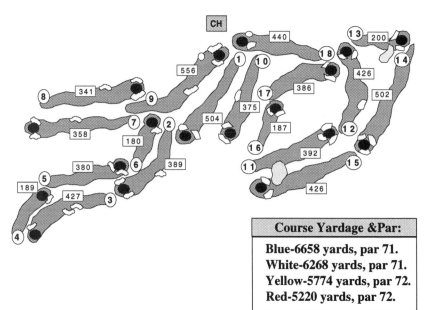

Course Yardage &Par:

Blue-6658 yards, par 71.
White-6268 yards, par 71.
Yellow-5774 yards, par 72.
Red-5220 yards, par 72.

Oaksridge Golf Course (public, 18 hole course)
1052 Monte-Elma Road; Elma, WA 98541
Phone: (360) 482-3511. Fax: (360) 482-5060. Internet: none.
Pro: Rich Walker, PGA. Superintendent: N/A.
Rating/Slope: M 65.3/100; W 68.9/108. **Course record:** 61.
Green fees: $15/$9 all week long; Jr. & Sr. rates $12/$6 (M-F); VISA, MC.
Power cart: $16/$9. **Pull cart:** $2. **Trail fee:** $5 for personal carts.
Reservation policy: yes, taken for weekends and holidays only.
Winter condition: the golf course is open all year long, weather permitting.
Terrain: flat. **Tees:** all grass. **Spikes:** metal spikes permitted.
Services: club rentals, lessons, pro shop, driving range, club memberships.
Comments: course is easy to walk and has few hazards. Fairways are tree-lined and fairly wide. For the senior golfer this course is very friendly. During the week it offers discounted rates on green fees to all seniors and juniors.

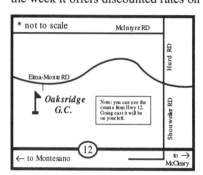

Directions: from I-5 N&S take exit # 104 to Hwy 101 and continue to Hwy 8 westbound. Proceed to Highway 12 westbound. Follow past the town of Elma and turn right on Schouweiler Road. (watch for your turn because it can come up very quickly). At Monte-Elma Road turn west to the golf course which will be located on your left.
Note: you will be able to see the course from highway 12.

Course Yardage & Par:
M-5643 yards, par 70. **W-5423 yards, par 72.**

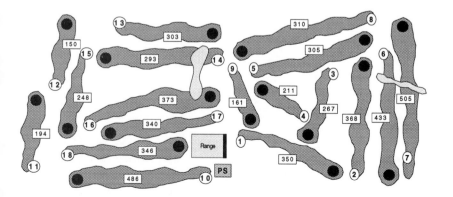

Oasis Park Par 3 (public, 9 hole par 3 course)
2541 Basin SW; Ephrata, WA 98823
Phone: (509) 754-5102. Fax: none. Internet: none.
Owners: Mike & Patti Donovan.
Rating/Slope: the golf course is not rated. **Course record:** 23.
Green fees: $4; all day pass $7; Jr & Sr rates.
Power cart: not available. **Pull cart:** $1.50. **Trail fee:** not allowed.
Reservation policy: reservations are not needed or required.
Winter condition: the golf course is closed from November to mid-March.
Terrain: flat, some hills. **Tees:** grass. **Spikes:** metal spikes permitted.
Services: club rentals, vending machines, limited pro shop.
Comments: Treed, well groomed & challenging par 3 course. Holes are fairly
short in length. RV parking is available for those wanting to stay at the park.

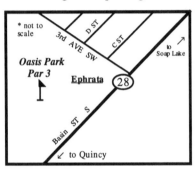

Directions: the course is located 1 mile
south of Ephrata on the west side of Hwy
28. Look for signs to the golf course.

Course Yardage & Par:
M-930 yards, par 27.
W-930 yards, par 27.

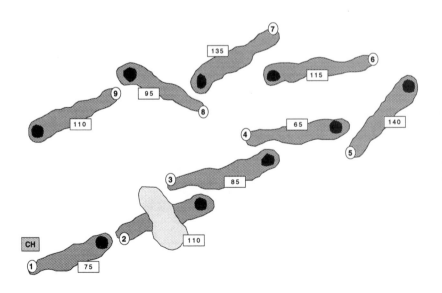

Ocean Shores Golf Course (public, 18 hole course)

Box 369; 500 Canal Drive; Ocean Shores, WA 98569
Phone: (360) 289-3357. Fax: (360) 289-0149. Internet: none.
Pros: Ronnie Espedal, PGA, Curt Zander, PGA.
Rating/Slope: C 70.2/115; M 68.8/113; W 69.6./115. **Course record:** 66.
Green fees: $25/$15 everday; Sr. rates $17/$10 (M-F); winter rates; M/C, VISA.
Power cart: $22/$14. **Pull cart:** $3. **Trail fee:** $7.50/$5 for personal carts.
Reservation policy: call in advance for tee times. No time limit on reservations.
Winter condition: the golf course is open all year long. Dry conditions.
Terrain: flat (easy walking). **Tees:** all grass. **Spikes:** metal spikes permitted.
Services: club rentals, lessons, snack bar, beer, wine, liquor, pro shop, club
memberships, putting & chipping greens. **Comments:** back nine very wooded,
front nine winds by the ocean, a very distinctive setting. The golf course can play
very tough at times especially if the wind picks up. Excellent facility that is very
popular with the summer crowd that vacations at the ocean. Ocean Shores is a
fantastic winter course because it drains well and stays very dry.

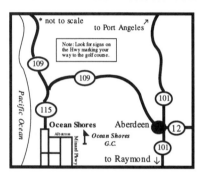

Directions: from I-5 N&S take exit
#104 to Hwy 101. Follow Hwy 101 to
Aberdeen/Ocean Beaches. Proceed to
Hwy 109. Exit to Hwy 115 southbound
and follow the signs to the golf course.
The course is located on the Washington
coast. **Note:** keep following the signs to
Ocean Beaches and this will get you to
Aberdeen then Ocean Shores.

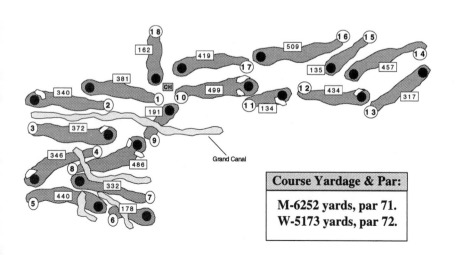

Grand Canal

Course Yardage & Par:
M-6252 yards, par 71.
W-5173 yards, par 72.

Odessa Golf Club (public, 9 hole course)
off of Highway 28; Box 621; Odessa, WA 99159
Phone: (509) 982-0093. Fax: none. Internet: none.
Manager: Gary Valenta. Superintendent: Gary Valenta.
Rating/Slope: M 68.8/113; W 72.3/112. **Course record:** 67.
Green fees: Weekdays $15/$10; Weekends & Holidays $17.50/$11;
All day rates: Weekdays $18, W/E's & Holidays $20 all day; M/C, VISA, DIS.
Power cart: $5 per person per 9 holes. **Pull cart:** $2. **Trail fee:** $5.
Reservation policy: yes, you may call ahead for a tee time, no restrictions.
Winter condition: the golf course is closed from Novemeber to February.
Terrain: relatively hilly. **Tees:** grass. **Spikes:** metal spikes permitted.
Services: club rentals, snack bar, beer, pro shop, putting green, discounted
RV hook-ups for golfers. **Comments:** a tough medium length golf course
with elevated greens and wide fairways. This track has excellent greens during
the peak golfing season. Adjacent to the golf course is RV parking with power,
and water. Odessa is a great bargin for those wanting to stay and play!!!

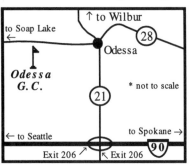

Directions: from I-90 take the exit #206
for Hwy 21 northbound to Odessa. Travel
north to Odessa and once in Odessa exit
to Hwy 28 westbound to the golf course.
The golf course is located west of the city
limits on Hwy 28. Look for signs.

Course Yardage & Par:
M-3070 yards, par 36.
W-2894 yards, par 37.
Dual tees for 18 holes:
M-6248 yards, par 72.
W-5885 yards, par 74.

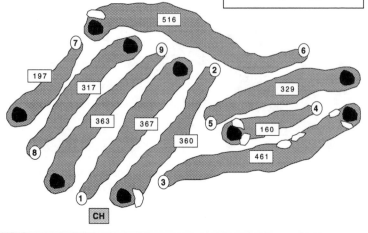

Okanogan Valley Golf Club (semi-private, 9 hole course)

Golf Course Drive; Box 1692; Omak, WA 98841
Phone: (509) 826-6937. Fax: (509) 826-4043. Internet: none.
Pro: Bill Sproule, PGA. Superintendent: none.
Rating/Slope: M 69.2/117; W 72.7/125. **Course record:** 65.
Green fees: W/D 15/$10; W/E $20/$15; no credit cards.
Power cart: $20/$11. **Pull cart:** $1.50. **Trail fee:** no charge.
Reservation policy: yes, call 4 days in advance for a tee times.
Winter condition: the course is closed from mid-October to mid-March.
Terrain: flat, some hills. **Tees:** grass. **Spikes:** soft spikes preferred.
Services: club rentals, lessons, snack bar, beer, pro shop, putting/chipping green.
Comments: closed to the public Wednesday, men only, Thursday am women
only. Rated by the *National Golf Foundation* as one of the top 9 hole courses in
the state. Well layed out track with water and sand coming into play throughout.
Greens are on the small size with tricky undulations. Great eastern Wa. course.

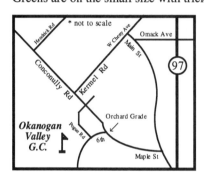

Directions: the golf course is located
between Omak and Okanogan. From
southbound Hwy 97 take the Hwy 215
exit and enter Omak. Note the signs and
turns to the course southwest of town.

Course Yardage & Par:
M-3040 yards, par 35.
W-2955 yards, par 38.
<u>**Dual tees for 18 holes:**</u>
M-6152 yards, par 70.
W-5880 yards, par 76.

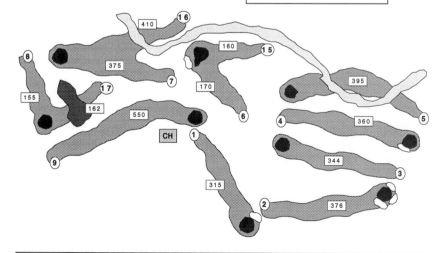

Olympia Country & Golf Club (private, 18 hole course)

3636 Country Club Drive NW; Olympia, WA 98502
Phone: (360) 866-9777. Fax: (360) 866-9790. Internet: none.
Pro: Scott Smith, PGA. Superintendent: Robert Pearsall.
Rating/Slope: C 69.6/116; M 68.6/114; W 70.7/123. **Course record:** 63.
Green fees: private club members & guests only; reciprocates.
Power cart: private club. **Pull cart:** private club. **Trail fee:** not allowed.
Reservation policy: members only club no public is allowed.
Winter condition: the golf course is open all year long. Damp conditions.
Terrain: very hilly. **Tees:** all grass. **Spikes:** soft spikes preferred.
Services: lessons, lounge, restaurant, beer, wine, liquor, beverages, pro shop,
showers, club memberships, driving range, chipping and putting greens.
Comments: the front nine is short and tricky demanding shot placement from
the tee. The back nine is long and more difficult. Greens are well bunkered and
can be hard to hold and fast in peak season. Excellent private facility.

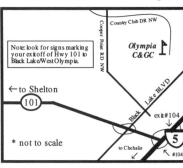

Directions: from I-5 N&S take exit
#104 to Hwy 101 to the Port Angeles-
Aberdeen. Follow to the Black Lake-
West Olympia exit. Turn right off the
exit to Cooper Point Road. Turn left
and travel 4 miles to the golf course.

Course Yardage & Par:
C-6048 yards, par 71.
M-5801 yards, par 71.
W-5265 yards, par 74.
W-5313 yards, par 75.

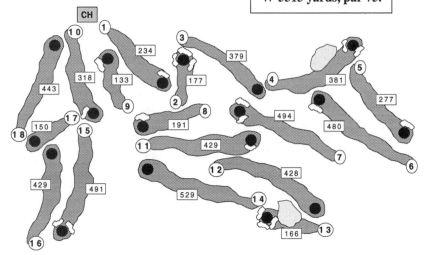

Orcas Island Golf Course (public, 9 hole course)

Route 1, Box 85; East Sound, WA 98245
Phone: (360) 376-4400. Fax: (360) 376-7100. Internet: http//www.orcasisle.com/golf/.
Owner/Manager: Robert Blake. Superintendent: Beatrice vonTobel.
Rating/Slope: M 67.5/116; W 70.7/119. **Course record: 65.**
Green fees: $28/$18 all week long; no special rates; M/C, VISA.
Power cart: $20/$15. **Pull cart:** $3. **Trail fee:** $5 for personal carts.
Reservation policy: yes, call in advance, no restrictions on tee times.
Winter condition: the golf course is open all year long. Dry, drains well.
Terrain: relatively hilly. **Tees:** grass. **Spikes:** soft spikes preferred.
Services: club rentals $8, snack bar, pro shop, club memberships, putting green.
Comments: the golf course is set in the scenic San Juan Islands, a very popular area for vacationers in the summer months. The track features hilly terrain, water and bunkers. One of the best kept secrets in the entire northwest region.

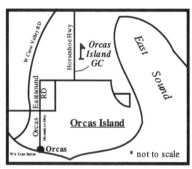

Directions: take the Anacortes ferry to Orcas Island. From the terminal in Orcas follow Horseshoe Hwy toward Eastsound. The golf course is approximately 10 minutes from the ferry landing. Turn right at Sunderland Road for the entrance to the golf course.

Course Yardage & Par:
M-3060 yards, par 36.
W-3000 yards, par 37.
<u>Dual tees for 18 holes:</u>
M-5803 yards, par 71.
W-5464 yards, par 73.

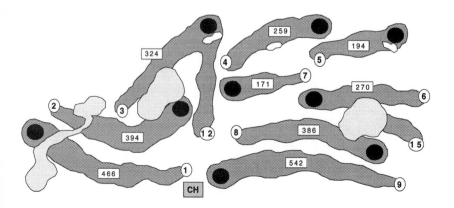

Orchard Hills Golf & Country Club (private, 18 hole course)
605 39th Street; Washougal, WA 98671
Phone: (360) 835-5444. Fax: (360) 835-0104. Internet: none.
Pro: Rick Edwards, PGA. Superintendent: Scott Coogan.
Rating/Slope: C 68.4/115; M 67.5/114; W 71.0/119. **Course record:** 62.
Green fees: private club members & guests only; reciprocates; M/C, VISA.
Power cart: private club. **Pull cart:** private club. **Trail fee:** private club.
Reservation policy: private club members & guests only. No outside play.
Winter condition: the golf course is open all year long. Dry conditions.
Terrain: relatively hilly. **Tees:** grass. **Spikes:** soft spikes preferred.
Services: lessons, snack bar, lounge, restaurant, beer, wine, liquor, pro shop,
lockers, showers, club memberships, driving range, putting & chipping greens.
Comments: the front nine is flat, easy to walk and sports narrow tree lined
fairways. The back nine is more wide open but plays much longer than the
yardage indicates. Greens are well bunkered with some being fronted by water.

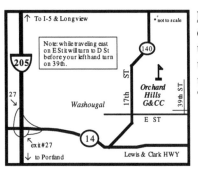

Directions: from I-5 southbound take
exit # 7 to I-205 southbound. Travel south
to exit # 27, Hwy 14E. Travel eastbound
to the Washougal exit. Follow the signs
to "E" St. and proceed 1.5 miles to 39th.
Turn left on 39th to the golf course.

Course Yardage & Par:

C-5896 yards, par 70.
M-5722yards, par 70.
W-5405 yards, par 73.

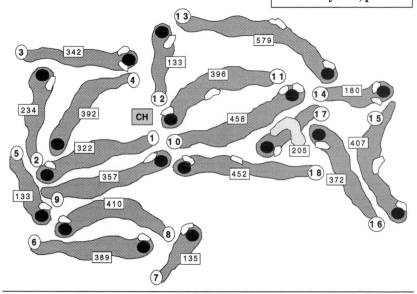

Oroville Golf Club (public, 9 hole course)
Off Nighthawk Road; Route 1, Box G-20; Oroville, WA 98844
Phone: (509) 476-2390. Fax: (509) 467-2390. Internet: none.
Pro: none. Manager: Dolly Sneve. Superintendent: Jerry Sneve.
Rating/Slope: M 67.8/113; W 74.0/126. **Course record:** 62.
Green fees: W/D $16/$12; W/E $19/$15; no special rates; VISA, M/C.
Power cart: $10 per 9 holes. **Pull cart:** $2. **Trail fee:** $7 for personal carts.
Reservation policy: yes, you may call ahead for a tee time. No restrictions.
Winter condition: the golf course is closed from November to February.
Terrain: relatively hilly. **Tees:** grass. **Spikes:** soft spikes preferred.
Services: club rentals, snack bar, beer, pro shop, putting & chipping greens.
Comments: the course is well-conditioned with dual tees for those wanting a different look for their second nine. Fairways are tree-lined but fairly open and there are a few sand traps which enter play on approach shots. Good 9 hole track. Be sure to call well in advance for your tee times as this course gets very busy.

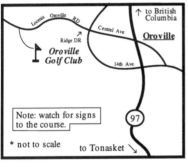

Directions: from Highway 2 westbound cut-off at Highway 97 northbound via Hwy 17 northbound. Travel north to Oroville and Nighthawk Road. Turn left and proceed 2 miles to the golf course. Look for signs marking your way to the golf course.

Course Yardage & Par:
M-2897 yards, par 36.
W-2897 yards, par 37.
<u>Dual tees for 18 holes:</u>
M-5938 yards, par 72.
W-5938 yards, par 74.

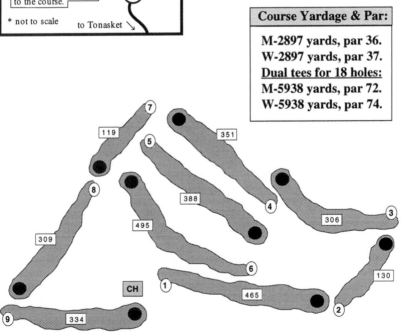

Othello Golf Club (public, 9 hole course)

West Bench Road; P.O. Box 185; Othello, WA 99344
Phone: (509) 488-2376. Fax: (509) 488-2376. Internet: none.
Pro & Owner: Doug Buck, PGA. Superintendent: none.
Rating/Slope: M 68.5/110; W 74.2/123. **Course record:** 61.
Green fees: W/D $15/$9; W/E $17/$11; no credit cards.
Power cart: $19/$10. **Pull cart:** $2. **Trail fee:** $5 for personal carts.
Reservation policy: you may call 2 days in advance for a tee time.
Winter condition: dry, course closed sometimes in December and January.
Terrain: flat, easy walking. **Tees:** grass. **Spikes:** no metal spikes permitted.
Services: club rentals, lessons, restaurant, lounge, beer, wine, liquor, pro shop,
lockers, showers, driving range. **Comments:** the course features many mature
trees lining the fairways. Bunkers front many of the greens that are medium to
large in size. Designed by the Trent Jones Corporation this golf course is kept
immaculate. For those traveling in an RV the course provides plenty of spaces.

Directions: from Hwy 17 take the exit for Bench Road. Travel west to the golf course. The golf course will be located on your left. The course is located 2 miles SW of Othello. Look for signs.

Course Yardage & Par:
M-3066 yards, par 35.
W-3066 yards, par 36.

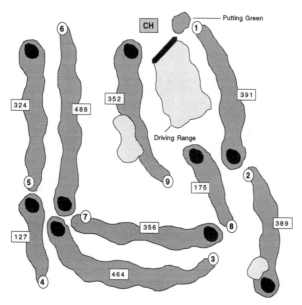

Overlake Golf & Country Club (private, 18 hole course)

8000 NE 16th; Bellevue, WA 98004
Phone: (425) 454-5031. Fax: (425) 451-3598. Internet: none.
Pro: Ron Hoetmer, PGA. Superintendent: Jeff Gullikson
Rating/Slope: C 71.2/127; M 69.6/123; M 67.8/117; W 65.8/113. **Record:** 61.
Green fees: private club members & their guests; reciprocates; M/C, VISA.
Power cart: private club. **Pull cart:** complimentary. **Trail fee:** not allowed.
Reservation policy: private club members only. No outside play allowed.
Winter condition: the golf course is open all year long. Damp conditions.
Terrain: flat, some hills. **Tees:** all grass. **Spikes:** soft spikes preferred.
Services: club rentals, lessons, snack bar, lounge, restaurant, beer, wine, liquor,
pro shop, club memberships, driving range, putting and chipping greens.
Comments: the course is relatively flat, well bunkered and fairly wide open.
Greens are fast and always in excellent condition. This track can play very tough
during the summer months. Past host to the Fred Couples Invitational.

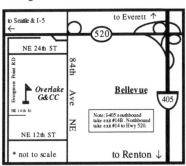

Directions: from I-5 N&S take exit
#168B to Hwy 520E. Travel east to the
84th Avenue NE exit. Take the exit and
go south for 1 mile to NE 12th. On 12th
travel west for .5 miles to Evergreen
Point Road. Turn north and travel to NE
16th. On 16th proceed east to the golf
course. Look for a small sign at the turn.

Course Yardage & Par:
C-6556 yards, par 71.
M-6150 yards, par 71.
M-5709 yards, par 71.
W-5709 yards, par 73.

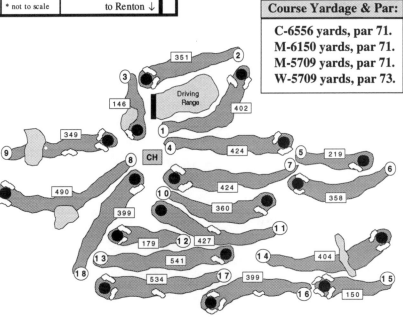

Overlook Golf Course (public, 9 hole course)
1753 State Highway 9; Mount Vernon, WA 98273
Phone: (360) 422-6444. **Fax:** none. **Internet:** none.
Manager/Owner/Superintendent: Neil Hansen.
Rating/Slope: C 61.2/101; M 60.4/97; W 60.6/96. **Course record:** 59.
Green fees: W/D $15/$9; W/E $18.50/$11; Sr rates (weekdays); no credit cards.
Power cart: $19/$10. **Pull cart:** $2. **Trail fee:** no charge for personal carts.
Reservation policy: yes, you may call 14 days in advance for tee times.
Winter condition: the golf course is open all year long. Fair conditions.
Terrain: flat, some hills. **Tees:** grass. **Spikes:** metal spikes permitted.
Services: club rentals, snack bar, lounge, beer, pro shop, putting green.
Comments: very friendly, family-owned facility that is fun for all. The golf course is fairly open with lovely views of Big Lake and the surrounding mountains. The course features elevated tees, small greens and fairly wide open fairways. This course is not a back-breaker so enjoy the peaceful area.

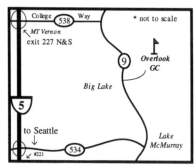

Directions: from I-5 N&S take exit #227 to Hwy 538 eastbound in Mount Vernon. Travel east to Hwy 9. Turn southbound and continue to Big Lake and the golf course. The golf course is located 7 miles from I-5. Look for signs marking your turn to the parking lot.

Course Yardage & Par:
C-2213 yards, par 33.
M-2026 yards, par 33.
W-1809 yards, par 33.

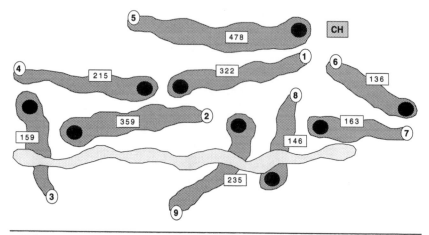

Painted Hills Golf Club (public, 9 hole course)

South 4403 Dishman-Mica; Spokane, WA 99206

Phone: (509) 928-4653. Fax: (509) 927-8825. Internet:www.spokanegolf.com

Teaching Pro: Patti Marquis. Superintedent: Ron Ridl.

Rating/Slope: M 70.2/123; W 69.0/110. Course record: 63.

Green fees: W/D $15/$11; W/E $17/$12; Jr. & Sr. rates Monday thru Thursday.

Power cart: $6 per 9 holes. Pull cart: $3. Trail fee: $4 for personal carts.

Reservation policy: yes, call ahead any time in advance for a tee time.

Winter condition: the golf course is open all year long. Dry conditions.

Terrain: flat (easy walking). Tees: all grass. Spikes: no metal spikes permitted.

Services: lessons, club rentals, restaurant, pro shop, putting green, range.

Comments: beautiful fairways, sand traps and water come into play. A well-conditioned golf course. Quality rental clubs for traveling executives. Great golf course that plays tough. This course is worth a trip if you are in the area.

Directions: from I-90 E&W take the Argonne/Dishman exit #287 and travel 5 miles south to the golf course. Argonne Road will become Dishman-Mica Hwy just south of Sprague Road.

Course Yardage & Par:
M-3288 yards, par 36.
W-2621 yards, par 36.
Dual tees for 18 holes:
M-6532 yards, par 72.
W-5417 yards, par 73.

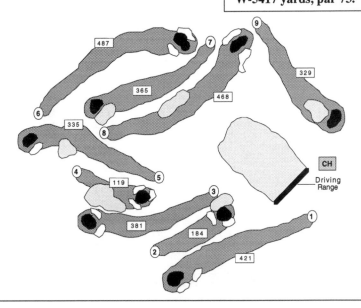

Pasco Golfland (public, 9 hole par 3 course)

2901 Road 40; Pasco, WA 99301
Phone: (509) 544-9291. Fax: (509) 544-0355. Internet: none.
Pro: Tony Beck, PGA. Superintendent: none.
Rating/Slope: the course is not rated. **Course record:** 47.
Green fees: $9 all week long, M/C, VISA.
Power cart: not available. **Pull cart:** $2. **Trail fee:** no charge.
Reservation policy: please call ahead for a tee time during the summer.
Winter condition: the course will be closed during inclement weather.
Terrain: flat. **Tees:** grass and mats. **Spikes:** soft spikes preferred.
Services: club rentals, lessons, club repair, pro shop, driving range.
Comments: the par 3 course is open and waiting for you to come bring the family! Dual tees are available for a full 18 hole round of golf. Be sure to heed the warnings of the out of bounds and do not retrieve your balls from the driving range area. Good practice center that will help improve your entire game.

Directions: from I-182 take the 20th Avenue exit. Proceed north to Argent. Left on Argent to Road 40. The range and course is located on your right hand side. Look for signs.

Course Yardage & Par:
M-1103 yards, par 27.
W-1103 yards, par 27.

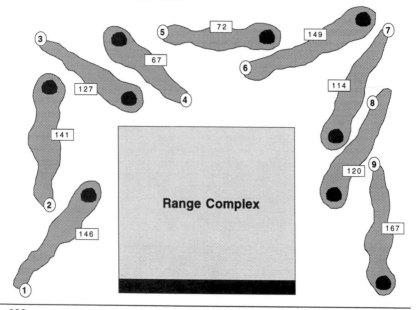

Peaceful Valley Golf Course (public, 9 hole course)

8225 Kendall Road; Maple Falls, WA 98226
Phone: (360) 599-2416. Fax: none. Internet: none.
Pro: none. Manager: Phil Cloward.
Rating/Slope: M 61/94; W 65.1/103. **Course record:** 64.
Green fees: W/D $11/$8; W/E $14/$11; Jr. & Sr. rates (M-F); VISA, M/C.
Power cart: $15/$10. **Pull cart:** $2. **Trail fee:** no charge for personal carts.
Reservation policy: yes, call up to 1 week in advance for your tee times.
Winter condition: dry, the course can become closed at certain times.
Terrain: flat, some hills. **Tees:** all grass. **Spikes:** metal spikes permitted.
Services: club rentals, snack bar, pro shop, club memberships, putting green.
Comments: bunkers come into play on five holes, however, the fairways are
quite open. The course is very flat and easy to walk. This track has excellent
views of the nearby mountains and surrounding countryside. A rustic golf
course that is excellent for beginners and families. Do not expect a posh resort.

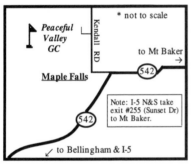

Directions: from I-5 take the exit for the
Mt. Baker Hwy. Travel northeast on the
highway past the 23 mile marker to the
Kendall-Sumas Road. Turn left and
proceed 2.5 miles to the housing development. Left, then right to the golf course.

Course Yardage & Par:
M-2467 yards, par 33.
W-2467 yards, par 34.

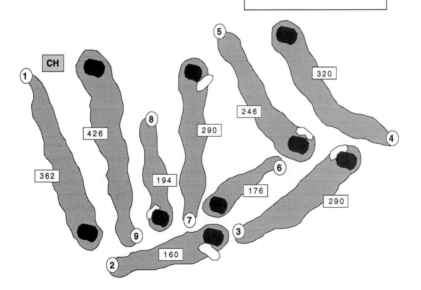

Pend Oreille Golf & Country Club (public)
off of Hwy 31; Box 97; Metaline Falls, WA 99153
Phone: no phone. Fax: none. Internet: none.
Pro: none. Manager: none.
Rating/Slope: the golf course is not rated. **Course record:** 27.
Green fees: $1; $1.50 weekends; students play for free; no credit cards.
Power cart: none. **Pull cart:** none. **Trail fee:** none.
Reservation policy: none needed. First come first served.
Winter condition: the golf course is closed from October to April.
Terrain: flat, some hills. **Tees:** grass. **Spikes:** metal spikes permitted.
Services: none. Bring your snacks, lunch, etc.
Comments: the course is on the honor system. Greens fees are placed in a honor box. The course features sand greens, rake before and after putting. The golf course has changed from 6 to 9 holes in the last few years. This course is on the rough side to say the least.

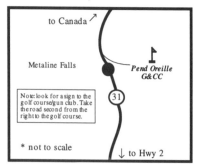

Directions: the golf course is located 4 miles north of Metaline Falls off of Hwy 31. Note the golf course/gun club sign for the turn off. Take the road second from the right to the golf course.

Course Yardage & Par:
M-2183 yards, par 31.
W-2183 yards, par 40.

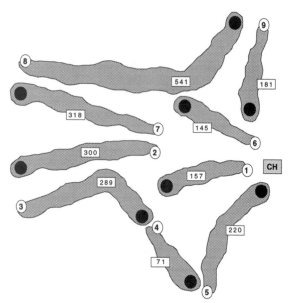

Peninsula Golf Club (private, 18 hole course)

824 South Lindberg Road; Port Angeles, WA 98362
Phone: (360) 457-6501. Fax: (360) 457-6501. Internet: none.
Pro: Chris Repass, PGA. Superintendent: Merle Pearce.
Rating/Slope: C 70.3/122; M 69.1/119; W 70.3/120. **Record:** 62.
Green fees: private club members and guests only; reciprocates. M/C, VISA.
Power cart: private club. **Pull cart:** private club. **Trail fee:** private club.
Reservation policy: yes, up to 1 week in advance for members. Private club
Winter condition: the golf course is open all year long. Damp conditions.
Terrain: very hilly. **Tees:** all grass. **Spikes:** soft spikes preferred.
Services: club rentals, lessons, snack bar, lounge, restaurant, beer, wine, liquor, pro shop, driving range. **Comments:** beautiful view of the mountains and the Strait of Juan de Fuca. This private course which used to be open to the public is near downtown Port Angeles and sports many unique features. Some of the holes are cut into a hillside offering a wide variety of lies in the fairway.

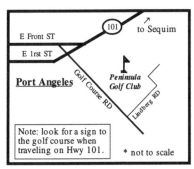

Directions: from Hwy 101. When you are first entering Port Angeles turn on Golf Course Road (south toward the mountains) and proceed .6 miles to Lindberg Road. Turn left on Lindberg Road and proceed to the golf course.

Course Yardage & Par:
C-6308 yards, par 72.
M-6235 yards, par 72.
M-5929 yards, par 72.
W-5480 yards, par 72.

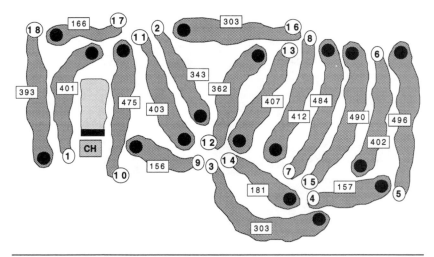

Peninsula Golf Course (public, 9 hole hole course)
9604 Pacific Highway; Box 536; Long Beach, WA 98631
Phone: (360) 642-2828. **Fax:** none. **Internet:** none.
Manager: Jerry Zorich. Superintendent: none.
Rating/Slope: M 59.9/90; W 64.2/100. **Course record:** 28.
Green fees: $15/$10 all week long; VISA, M/C, DISCOVER, AMEX.
Power cart: $15/$10. **Pull cart:** $2. **Trail fee:** $3 for personal carts.
Reservation policy: please call 7 days in advance for tee times.
Winter condition: the golf course is open weather permitting, damp.
Terrain: flat (easy walking). **Tees:** mats. **Spikes:** soft spikes preferred.
Services: club rentals, lessons, snack bar, small pro shop, putting green.
Comments: located in picturesque Long Beach on the Washington coast, this course is very flat and easy to walk. Fairways are narrow in scope but greens have generous landing areas. A great location for a relaxing round of golf.

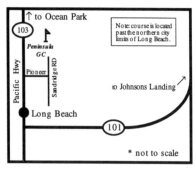

Directions: from I-5 N&S take exit #104 to Hwy 101 W. Follow 101 westbound to Long Beach. As you approach the peninsula turn right on Highway 103 northbound through Seaview. Proceed for 3 miles. The golf course is located just beyond the northern city limits.

Course Yardage & Par:
M-2057 yards, par 33.
W-2057 yards, par 33.
Dual tees for 18 holes:
M-4213 yards, par 65.
W-4213 yards, par 65.

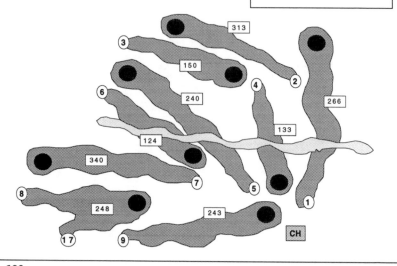

Pine Acres Par 3 Golf Course (public, 9 hole par 3 course)

11912 North Division; Spokane, WA 99218
Phone: (509) 466-9984. Fax: (509) 466-1143. Internet: none.
Owner/Pro: Jim Tucker Sr., PGA. Superintendent: none.
Rating/Slope: the golf course is not rated. **Course record:** 22.
Green fees: $9/$7 all week long; Jr. & Sr. rates (Monday thru Friday) $5.50.
Power cart: not available. **Pull cart:** $1. **Trail fee:** not allowed.
Reservation policy: advance reservations for tee times are not required.
Winter condition: damp, the golf course is open weather permitting.
Terrain: flat, slight some hills. **Tees:** mats. **Spikes:** metal spikes permitted.
Services: club rentals, lessons, pro shop, snack bar, driving range, putting green.
Comments: Good par 3 golf course that plays fairly short. Holes range from 62 to 115 yards in length. The facility has a great driving range which has been said to be the "best in the Spokane area".

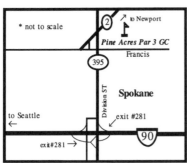

Directions: the golf course is located 7 miles north of Spokane city center off of Hwy 395N. From I-90 east & west exit on Hwy 395 northbound. Proceed on Hwy 395N to the golf course which will be located on your right hand side.

Course Yardage & Par:
M-760 yards, par 27.
W-760 yards, par 27.

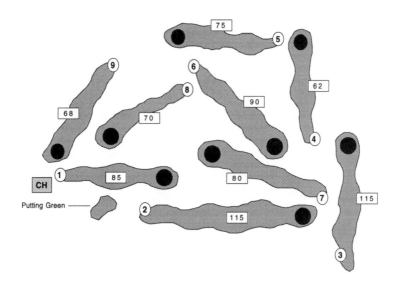

Pine Crest Golf Course (public, 9 hole par 3 course)

2415 NW 143rd Street; Vancouver, WA 98685
Phone: (360) 573-2051. **Fax:** none. **Internet:** none.
Pro: none. **Managers: Mark & Kathy Hart.**
Rating/Slope: the golf course is not rated. **Course record:** 25.
Green fees: W/D $6.50 W/E $7; Sr. rates (M-F) $5.50.
Power cart: not available. **Pull cart:** $1.75. **Trail fee:** not allowed.
Reservation policy: advance reservations for tee times are not required.
Winter condition: damp, the golf course is open all year, weather permitting.
Terrain: rolling hills (walkable). **Tees:** mats. **Spikes:** metal spikes permitted.
Services: club rentals, snack bar, beer, practice green, small pro shop.
Comments: great par 3 course that will challenge you at every turn. Several holes are bordered by a steep canyon that will catch any misguided tee shots. Greens are medium in size and can generally be found in good condition. Great course for the family golf outing.

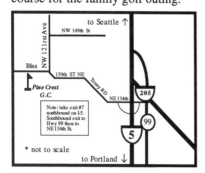

Directions: From I-5 take the 134th Street exit. Proceed westbound for about 2 miles to NW 143rd Street. Turn left on NW 143rd Street and proceed to the golf course. Look for signs marking your way to the course.

Course Yardage & Par:
M-1206 yards, par 27.
W-1206 yards, par 27.

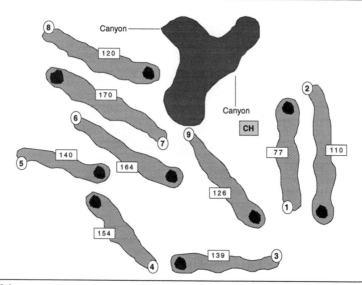

Plateau Golf & Country Club (private, 18 hole course)
25625 Plateau Drive.; Redmond, WA 98053
Phone: (425) 836-4653. Fax: none. Internet: www.plateaugc.com
Pro: Ken Wooten, PGA. Superintendent: Peter Colleran.
Rating/Slope: T 76.1/145; C 72.3/131; M 72.3/131; W 70.6/123. **Record:** N/A.
Green fees: private club, members and guest only.
Power cart: private club. **Pull cart:** private club. **Trail fee:** private club.
Reservation policy: you may call ahead for a tee time.
Winter condition: the course is considered dry and open all year long.
Terrain: some hills. **Tees:** all grass. **Spikes:** no metal spikes permitted.
Services: club rentals, lessons, lounge, restaurant, snack bar, beer, wine, liquor, showers, lockers, pro shop, driving range, putting, chipping greens, pool, tennis.
Comments: the course promises to be one of the premiere courses in the area. This track has been designed by the Taiyo Golf Development Company who has taken care to preserve the natural beauty of the area. This new track offers spectacular views from many vantage points.

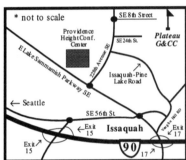

Directions: from I-90 E take exit #15. Turn left onto the Renton-Issaquah Road (it will become SE 56th Street). Proceed to E. Lake Samammish Parkway SE, turn left. Travel on E. Lake Samammish Parkway SE and turn right onto SE 43rd Way which will become 228th Avenue S.E. Proceed to S.E. 8th Street. Turn right. The course is located 1 mile ahead.

Course Yardage & Par:
C-7170 yards, par 72.
M-6335 yards, par 72.

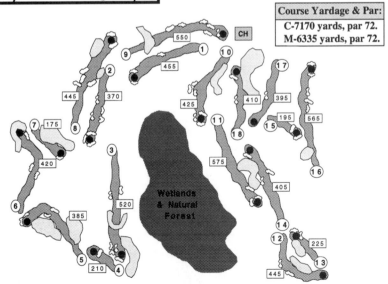

Pomeroy Golf Course (public, 9 hole course)
1610 Arlington Street; Box 400; Pomeroy, WA 99347
Phone: (509) 843-1197. **Fax:** none. **Internet:** none.
Pro: none. **Manager:** Ellis Johnson.
Rating/Slope: M 59.4/94; W 62.5/100. **Course record:** 29.
Green fees: W/D $10/$8; W/E $12/$10; Jr. & Sr. rates; no credit cards.
Power cart: $20/$10. **Pull cart:** $2. **Trail fee:** $3 for personal carts.
Reservation policy: none, some restrictions do apply during league play.
Winter condition: the golf course is closed from mid October through March.
Terrain: relatively hilly. **Tees:** grass & mats. **Spikes:** soft spikes preferred.
Services: club rentals, lessons, driving net, putting green, small, pro shop.
Comments: this course sports a number of rather hilly holes which increases its difficulty. Greens are very small in size and can be hard to hold. The course is very short in length but the course still can be hard to score on. This rustic course can get somewhat busy during the mid to late summer months

Directions: from Hwy 12 exit on Hwy 128 (15th Street). Proceed to Arlington Street and turn left. Proceed to the golf course. Look for signs marking your way to the golf course.

Course Yardage & Par:

M-2042 yards, par 31.
W-2042 yards, par 32.

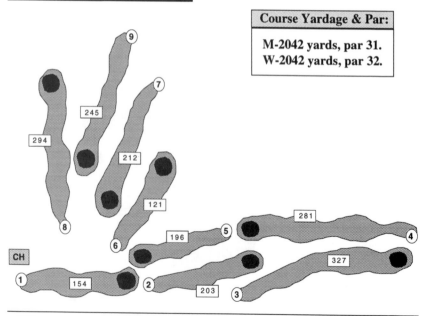

Port Ludlow Golf & Meeting Retreat (public, resort 27 holes)
751 Highland Drive; Port Ludlow, WA 98365
Phone: (360) 437-0272; 1-800-455-0272 WA. Fax: (360) 437-0637
Dir. of Golf: Mike Buss. Pro: Tony Manzanares, PGA. Supt.: Jerry Mathews.
Rating/Slope: Tide/Timber C 72.7/131; M 70.3/124; W 72.9/126.
Green fees: peak season $55/$29; off season, winter rates; AMEX, VISA, M/C.
Power cart: $14/$7.50 per person. **Pull cart:** $3/$1.50. **Trail fee:** not allowed.
Reservation policy: resort guests-upon room confirmation; public 5 days ahead.
Winter condition: the golf course is open all year long. Dry conditions.
Terrain: relatively hilly. **Tees:** all grass. **Spikes:** soft spikes preferred.
Services: club rentals, lessons, snack bar, beer, wine, pro shop, driving range.
Comments: Robert Muir Graves designed golf course. New "Trail" 9 has been totally redone and is tough. Facility regarded as one of the nation's best. The golf course meanders through fir trees and offers spectacular views of the nearby inlet. Greens are large with undulations and can get firm and quick. Worth a trip.

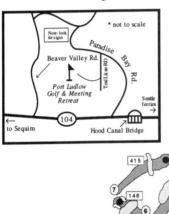

Directions: from Hwy 104 exit to Port Ludlow (immediately west of the Hood Canal Bridge). You will be on Paradise Bay Rd. Follow and turn left on Teal Rd. Stay on Teal Rd. Follow to Highland Dr. turn right. Follow to the clubhouse.

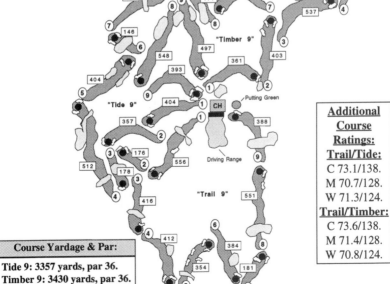

Additional Course Ratings:
Trail/Tide: C 73.1/138. M 70.7/128. W 71.3/124.
Trail/Timber: C 73.6/138. M 71.4/128. W 70.8/124.

Course Yardage & Par:
Tide 9: 3357 yards, par 36.
Timber 9: 3430 yards, par 36.
Trail 9: 3418 yards, par 36.

Port Townsend Golf Course (public, 9 hole course)
1948 Blaine; Port Townsend, WA 98368
Phone: (360) 385-4547. **Fax:** none. **Internet:** none.
Pro: Mike Early, PGA. **Superintendent:** Mike Early.
Rating/Slope: M 65.8/114; W 70.4/121. **Course record:** 61.
Green fees: $18/$12; Jr. rates (all week); Sr. rates (M-F); VISA, M/C.
Power cart: $17/$11 **Pull cart:** $4/$2. **Trail fee:** none (may change).
Reservation policy: yes, call up to 1 week in advance for tee times.
Winter condition: the course is open all year. The course drains very well.
Terrain: relatively hilly. **Tees:** all grass. **Spikes:** soft spikes preferred.
Services: club rentals, lessons, restaurant, beer, pro shop, club memberships, driving range (grass tees), putting green. **Comments:** the course sets atop a hill overlooking the town of Port Townsend and surrounding inlet. Rolling terrain, sand traps, small greens and water will challenge your shot making ability. Good public course that gets alot of play during the peak golfing season.

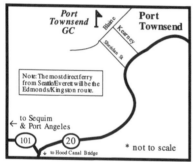

Directions: from Hwy 101 northbound exit to Hwy 20 eastbound toward Port Townsend. At Port Townsend turn left on Kearney Road. Go up the hill to Blaine Road. Turn right on Blaine road to the golf course which will be on your left. Look for signs marking your way.

Course Yardage & Par:
M-2763 yards, par 35.
W-2821 yards, par 35.
Dual tees for 18 holes:
M-5604 yards, par 70.
W-5604 yards, par 71.

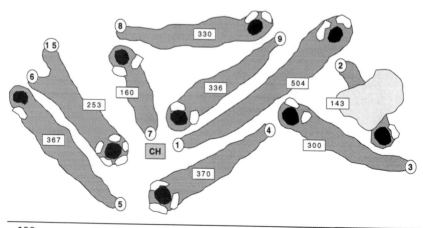

Potholes Golf Course (public, 9 hole course)
6897 O'Sullivan Dam Road; Othello, WA 99344
Phone: (509) 346-9491. Fax: none. Internet: none.
Manager: Randy DuFord. Superintendent: none.
Rating/Slope: C 60.2/090; M 59.5/088; W 62.4/093.
Green fees: $13/$9 (Monday-Thursday); $16/$11 (Friday-Sunday & Holidays).
Power cart: $17/$11. **Pull cart:** $2. **Trail fee:** $4 for personal carts.
Reservation policy: yes, call up to 1 week in advance for tee times.
Winter condition: the course is open all year long weather permitting. Dry.
Terrain: flat, easy walking. **Tees:** all grass. **Spikes:** soft spikes preferred.
Services: club rentals, lessons, restaurant (Italian menu), beer, wine, pro shop, driving range, RV spots, putting & chipping greens, club memberships.
Comments: narrow golf course that plays much longer than the yardage would indicate. RV hookups with full services and cable TV. The restaurants claim to fame is "We make the best garlic bread in North America". Good test of golf that can be demanding on your shot making ability. Fair public golf course.

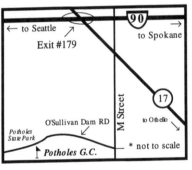

Directions: from Hwy 26 through Royal City to State Rd. 262. Turn left. Proceed 14 miles south to the course. From I-90 exit 179 turn left on Hwy 17 to "M" St. (2 1/2 miles) turn right. Proceed 7-8 miles to O'Sullivan Dam Road turn right (west) to the golf course. Look for signs.

Course Yardage & Par:
M-2269 yards, par 33.
W-2167 yards, par 33.
Dual tees for 18 holes:
M-4638 yards, par 66.
W-4334 yards, par 66.

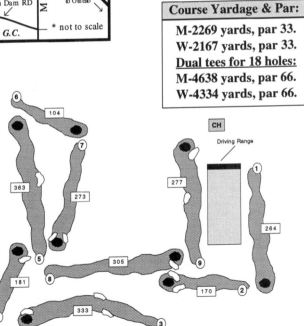

Quail Ridge Golf Course (public, 18 hole course)

3600 Swallow's Nest Drive; Clarkston, WA 99403

Phone: (509) 758-8501. **Fax:** (509) 758-4644. **Internet:** none.

Pro: unavailable. **Superintendent:** none.

Rating/Slope: C 68.1/114; M 68.1/113; W 66.2/107. **Course record:** 63.

Green fees: $17/$13 all week long; $19/$13 W/E in the summer; M/C, VISA.

Power cart: $20/$13. **Pull cart:** $3. **Trail fee:** $4 (annual fee available).

Reservation policy: please call 1 week in advance for your tee-times.

Winter condition: the golf course is open weather permitting. Dry conditions.

Terrain: flat, some hills. **Tees:** all grass. **Spikes:** soft spikes only.

Services: coffee shop, beer, beverages, pro shop, driving range, putting green.

Comments: formerly called Swallow's Nest the golf course has been expanded to 18 holes recently and is worth a trip. The new nine has spectacular views of the surrounding countryside and rolling terrain. Good public track.

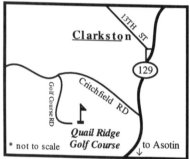

Directions: the golf course is located south of Clarkston WA. From Hwy 129 Turn westbound on Critchfield Road (across from the Snake River). Proceed on Critchfield Rd. for a 1/4 mile to Golf Course Rd. Turn left. Proceed to the golf course off of Swallow's Nest Loop.

Course Yardage & Par:
C-5861 yards, par 71.
M-5603 yards, par 71.
M-4720 yards, par 71.
W-4637 yards, par 71.

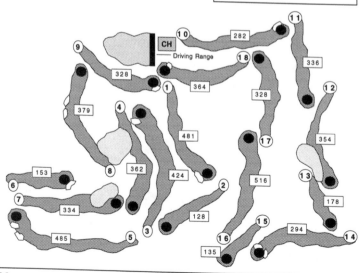

Quincy Valley Golf (public, 18 hole course)
1705 5th NW; Quincy, WA 98848
Phone: (509) 787-3244. Fax: (509) 787-6602. Internet: none.
Managers: Rob & Chuck Anabel. Pro: Bill Porter.
Rating/Slope: C 67.3/101; M 67.0/100; W 74.0/117. Course record: 32.
Green fees: W/D $15/$12; W/E $20/$14; Jr. & Sr. rates; M/C, VISA.
Power cart: $18/$10. **Pull cart:** $3/$2. **Trail fee:** $4 for personal carts.
Reservation policy: required for summer weekends. Call 4-5 days in advance.
Winter condition: the golf course is open all year long, when playable.
Terrain: flat, some hills. **Tees:** all grass. **Spikes:** soft spikes preferred.
Services: club rentals, snack bar, pro shop, driving net. **Comments:** the golf
course is well-conditioned with beautiful fairways and excellent greens.
RV sites are available for those overnighters who want to stay and play golf.
Very friendly golf course. The new 9 holes were opened in early 1997.

Directions: from Hwy 281 take 5 NW
(White Trail Road) to the golf course.
From I-90 E&W exit at Hwy 281 and
proceed toward Quincy. The golf course
will be off of the Hwy on your left hand
side. Look for sign marking your turn.

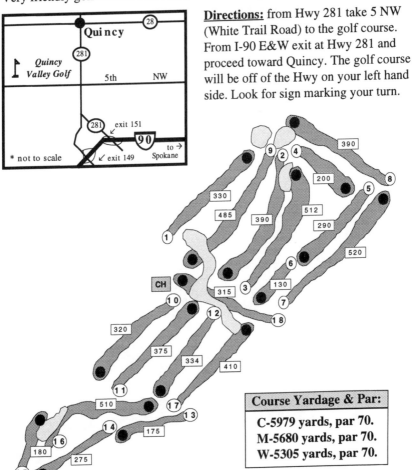

Course Yardage & Par:

C-5979 yards, par 70.
M-5680 yards, par 70.
W-5305 yards, par 70.

Rainier Golf & Country Club (private, 18 hole course)

1856 South 112th; Seattle, WA 98168
Phone: (206) 242-2800. **Fax:** (206) 242-4600. **Internet:** none.
Pro: Tony Wilkins, PGA. **Superintendent:** Ronald Proctor.
Rating/Slope: C 71.1/132; M 70.3/130; W 73.3/130. **Course record:** 63.
Green fees: private club, members and guests only; reciprocates.
Power cart: private club. **Pull cart:** private club. **Trail fee:** not allowed.
Reservation policy: private club, yes, up to 1 week in advance. No public play.
Winter condition: the golf course is open all year long. New drainage system.
Terrain: very hilly. **Tees:** all grass. **Spikes:** soft spikes June thru October.
Services: lessons, snack bar, beer, wine, pro shop, lockers, showers, driving range, putting & chipping green. **Comments:** beautiful views of Mount Rainier are seen from this course which sports tree-lined fairways, tricky greens, and many sand traps to contend with. Excellent private course that plays tough.

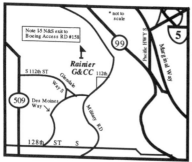

Directions: from I-5 N&S take exit # 158B to the South Boeing Access Road. Go west for .4 miles to Pacific Hwy S. Turn south on Pacific Hwy S. and follow for .5 miles to S 116th. Turn west on 116th up winding hill to 2nd light a Des Moines Memorial Drive, turn right going north to 112th turn left & proceed to the golf course.

Course Yardage & Par:
C-6352 yards, par 72.
M-6190 yards, par 72.
W-5756 yards, par 74.

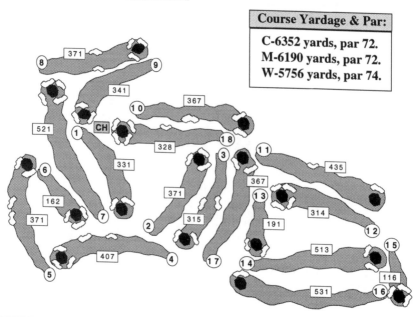

Raspberry Ridge Golf Community (public, 9 hole course)

6827 Hannegan Road; Everson, WA 98247
Phone: (360) 354-3029. Fax: none. Internet: none.
Pro/Owner: Bill Robins. Superintendent: John Olson.
Rating/Slope: C 65.1/106; M 63.9/104; W 67.3/110. **Course record:** 63.
Green fees: $16/$10; Jr & Sr rates, $14/$9; M/C, VISA, AMEX.
Power cart: $16/$10. **Pull cart:** $2. **Trail fee:** no charge for personal carts.
Reservation policy: yes, please call up to 7 days in advance for tee times.
Winter condition: the golf course is open all year long, dry (drains well).
Terrain: flat, some hills. **Tees:** all grass. **Spikes:** no spike restrictions.
Services: club rentals, snack bar, lounge, restaurant, beer, wine, pro shop, club
memberships, putting green. **Comments:** beautifully maintained golf course
with spectacular views of Mount Baker and the surrounding countryside.
Although relatively short, this course will challenge you at every turn. Water
and well bunkered greens are every where. Accuracy off the tee is a must for
scoring. Great out of the way course. Worth a special trip if you are in the area.

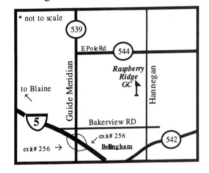

Directions: from I-5 N&S take exit
256A to Hwy 539 northbound and
continue 7.7 miles to Hwy 544
eastbound. Turn south on Hannegan
Road and proceed to the golf course.
Look for a sign marking your turn to
the golf course community.

Course Yardage & Par:
C-2825 yards, par 34.
M-2585 yards, par 34
W-2335 yards, par 34.

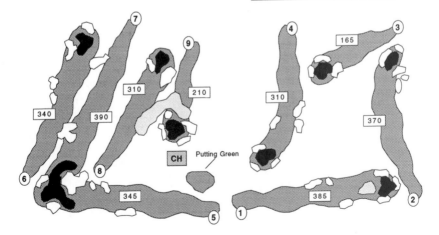

Ritzville Municipal Golf Course (public, 9 hole course)
104 East 10th Street; Ritzville, WA 99169
Phone: (509) 659-9868. **Fax:** (509) 659-1836. **Internet:** rabrgc@agritel.net.
Pro: Ron Barker, PGA. **Superintendent:** Ron Barker.
Rating/Slope: M 67.1/112; W 71.8/123. **Course record:** 62.
Green fees: $16/$11; Jr & Sr rates (weekdays only); no credit cards.
Power cart: $20/$10. **Pull cart:** $2. **Trail fee:** no charge for personal carts.
Reservation policy: advance tee times are not needed or required.
Winter condition: the course is closed from mid November to mid February.
Terrain: flat, some hills. **Tees:** grass. **Spikes:** soft spikes preferred.
Services: club rentals, lessons, restaurant, beer, pro shop, putting green.
Comments: a good walking course. Ritzville is fairly flat and in good condition. The track sports two sets of tees for a different look for 18 holes. Convenient RV park close by. Some greens are fronted by bunkers and sloping terrain. The golf course can play very tough if the wind picks up. Greens are in great shape.

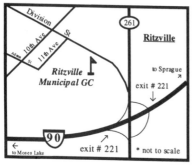

Directions: from I-90 take the Ritzville exit #221 and travel north 2 blocks to the golf course. The course has great freeway access. Look for signs marking your turn to the golf course.

Course Yardage & Par:
M-2812 yards, par 35.
W-2812 yards, par 36.
Dual tees for 18 holes:
M-5597 yards, par 70.
W-5597 yards, par 72.

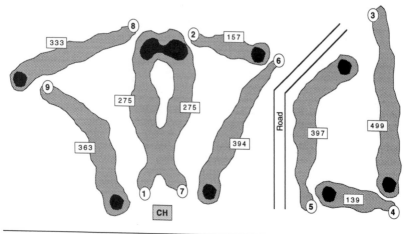

Riverbend Golf Complex (public, 18 hole, 9 hole par 3)

2019 West Meeker; Kent, WA 98032
Phone: (253) 854-3673 or (253) 859-4000. **Fax:** none. **Internet:** none.
Pro: Brett Wilkinson, PGA. **Superintendent:** Pete Petersen.
Rating/Slope: C 70.1/119; M 68.1/114; W 70.1/114. **Course record:** 64.
Green fees: W/D$22/$15; W/E $26/$18; Jr & Sr rates (M-F); M/C, VISA.
Green fees for the par 3 course: W/D $7 1st 9 holes; W/E $8 for 9 holes.
Power cart: $21/$11. **Pull cart:** $5/$3. **Trail fee:** personal carts not allowed.
Reservation policy: please call 1 week in advance for your tee times.
Winter condition: the golf course is open all year long. Drains fairly well.
Terrain: flat (easy walking). **Tees:** all grass. **Spikes:** soft spikes preferred.
Services: club rentals, lessons, snack bar, beer, chipping & putting green,
driving range, pro shop. **Comments:** championship caliber track. The course
is flat, well-bunkered and water comes in to play on 7 holes. The golf course is
excellent and worth a special trip. Be sure to call well ahead for your tee time.

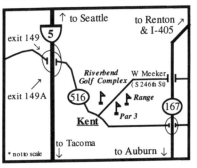

Directions: from I-5 N&S take exit
149 to Hwy 516 eastbound. Travel
east for 1.3 miles to West Meeker.
Turn east on Meeker to the golf course,
located on your left, the range and par 3
course will be on your right hand side.

Course Yardage & Par:
C-6633 yards, par 72.
M-6208yards, par 72.
W-5538 yards, par 72.

Par 3 Course Yardage & Par:
M/W-1260 yards, par 27.

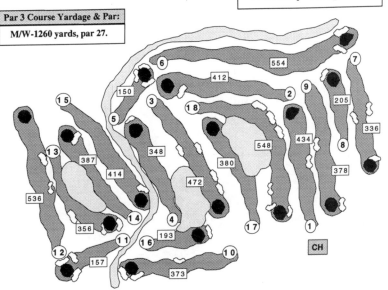

Riverside Country Club (public, 18 hole course)

1451 NW Airport Road; Chehalis, WA 98532
Phone: (360) 748-8182, 800-242-9486. Fax: (360) 748-4699.
Manager: Brent Klovdahl. Superintendent: Randy Scafturon.
Rating/Slope: C 69.3/118; M 67.6/112; W 71.2/116. **Record:** 63, 18 holes.
Green fees: W/D $17/$13; W/E's & Holidays. $23; M/C, VISA, DISCOVER.
Senior rates (Monday thru Friday); winter rates; winter specials.
Power cart: $20/$15 reserve the cart. **Pull cart:** $2. **Trail fee:** $10/$5.
Reservation policy: yes, please call up to 1 week in advance for tee times.
Winter condition: the golf course is open all year long. Fair conditions.
Terrain: flat, some slight hills. **Tees:** grass. **Spikes:** soft spikes preferred.
Services: lessons, snack bar, restaurant, beer, wine, pro shop, driving range,
putting and chipping greens, club memberships. **Comments:** this course winds
along the Chehalis River and is noted for its fast, undulating greens that are in
great shape all year long. Fairways are tree-lined with medium to large landing
areas. Great golf course to stop and play anytime of year. Easy freeway access.

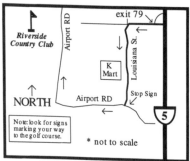

Directions: from I-5 N&S take exit # 79.
Head west. Turn left on Louisiana St.
Go to stop sign. Turn right on Airport Rd.
The golf course is 0.7 miles ahead on the
left. **Note:** Look for signs marking your
way to the golf course.

Course Yardage & Par:
C-6155 yards, par 71.
M-5771 yards, par 71.
W-5456 yards, par 72.

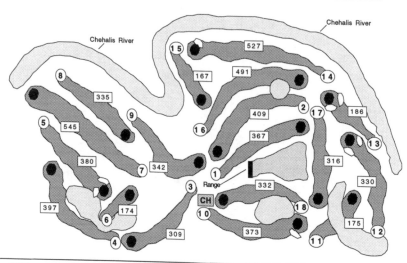

Riverside Golf Course (public, 9 hole course)

5799 Riverside Drive; Ferndale, WA 98248
Phone: (360) 384-4116. **Fax:** none. **Internet:** none.
Owner: Jeanne Olson Estie. **Superintendent:** none.
Rating/Slope: C 67.6/104; M 66.9/103; W 70.4/112. **Course record:** 66.
Green fees: W/D $12/$8; W/E & holidays $13/$9; Jr & Sr rates; M/C, VISA.
Power cart: $20/$10. **Pull cart:** $4/$2. **Trail fee:** no charge.
Reservation policy: advance reservations are not taken or required.
Winter condition: the golf course is open all year long. Damp conditions.
Terrain: flat, easy walking. **Tees:** all grass. **Spikes:** soft spikes preferred.
Services: club rentals, snack bar, restaurant, pro shop, putting green, club memberships. **Comments:** the course is well-kept, particularly the greens. Fairways are wide with generous landing areas. Greens are of medium size and have few hazards fronting them. A very friendly staff makes this facility a pleasure to visit and a treat to play. The golf course is generally flat and easy to walk. Easy freeway access for those traveling on I-5.

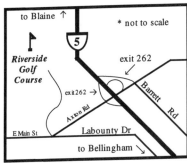

Directions: from I-5 N&S take exit # 262. Travel west for 1/10 of a mile to the golf course. Look for signs that are posted indicating your turn for the golf course.

Course Yardage & Par:
M-3000 yards, par 36.
W-2860 yards, par 37.

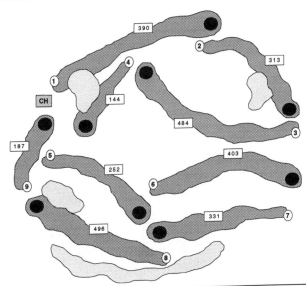

Riviera Golf & Country Club (private, 9 hole course)

11019 Country Club Drive; Anderson Island, WA 98303
Phone: (253) 884-9634. Fax: none. Internet: none.
Manager: N/A. Superintendent: Bill Ritchie.
Rating/Slope: M 55.3/99; W 56.3/95. **Course record: 26.**
Greens fee: private club, members & guests only; no credit cards.
Power cart: none. **Pull cart:** members & guests only. **Trail fee:** not allowed.
Reservation policy: yes, members may call for weekend tee times.
Winter condition: the golf course is open all year long. Wet conditions.
Terrain: relatively hilly. **Tees:** grass. **Spikes:** soft spikes preferred.
Services: restaurant, beer, wine, pro shop, putting green, club memberships.
Comments: friendly private course in set in a beautiful island community of
Washington State. This executive length golf course is a challenge at every turn.
Greens are small and the fronts are well bunkered. Fairways are very narrow.

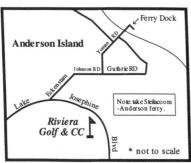

Directions: northbound from Olympia
take the Dupont/Steilacoom exit from I-5.
Go straight until you reach the ferry dock.
Am ferry leaves at 6am,7:40, 9 and 12pm.
From I-5 southbound take exit 129. Go
westbound to S Tacoma Way. Right to
Steilacoom Boulevard then left to the
ferry dock. Look for signs marking your
way to the golf course.

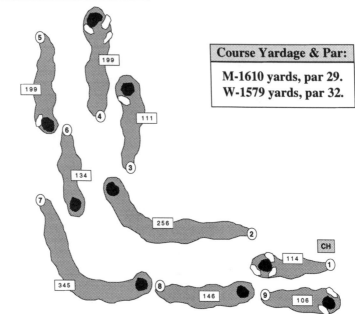

Course Yardage & Par:
M-1610 yards, par 29.
W-1579 yards, par 32.

Rock Island Golf Club (public, 9 hole course)
314 Saunders Road; Rock Island, WA 98850
Phone: (509) 884-2806. Fax: none. Internet: none.
Manager: Pam Orr. Superintendent: none.
Rating/Slope: M 70.1/112; W 73.4/120. **Course record:** 68 for 18 holes.
Green fees: W/D $16/$11; W/E $16/$11; Jr/Sr rates (Tues & Th); M/C, VISA.
Power cart: $19/$11. **Pull cart:** $2. **Trail fee:** no charge for personal carts.
Reservation policy: yes, you may call ahead for a tee time. No restrictions.
Winter condition: the course is open all year long, weather permitting.
Terrain: very flat. **Tees:** grass. **Spikes:** soft spikes preferred.
Services: club rentals, lessons, restaurant, lounge, beer, wine, pro shop, driving range, putting & chipping greens. **Comments:** this course sports large greens with some bunkers coming into play on approach shots. The course plays long from the back tees leaving many long irons for your second shots. Water comes into play on a number of holes. You can usually walk on during the summer.

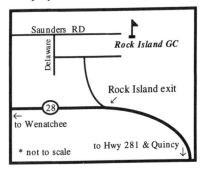

Directions: from Hwy 28 take the Rock Island exit. At the end of the street, turn left. Follow to Delaware and turn right. At the stop sign, turn right on Saunders Road and follow to the golf course. Look for signs marking your way to the golf course.

Course Yardage & Par:
M-3396 yards, par 36.
W-2884 yards, par 36.
Dual tees for 18 holes:
M-6467 yards, par 72.
W-5995 yards, par 72.

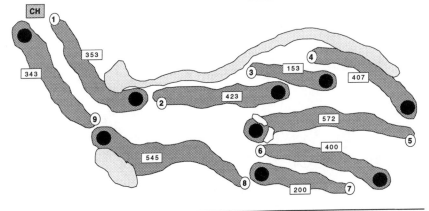

Rolling Hills Golf Course (public, 18 hole course)
2485 NE McWilliams Road; Bremerton, WA 98311
Phone: (360) 479-1212. Fax: (360) 479-2450. Internet: none.
Director of Golf: Tedd Hudanich, PGA. Pro: Roger O'Hara.
Rating/Slope: M 68.0/115; W 71.1/117. **Course record:** 63.
Green fees: Weekdays $22/$15; Weekends $24/$16; Jr. & Sr. and
military rates (Monday-Friday); M/C, VISA, AMEX, DISCOVER.
Power cart: $20/$14. **Pull cart:** $2. **Trail fee:** $3 for personal carts.
Reservation policy: yes, you may call 7 days in advance for tee-times.
Winter condition: the golf course is open all year long, damp conditions.
Terrain: relatively hilly. **Tees:** grass. **Spikes:** soft spikes preferred.
Services: club rentals, lessons, snack bar, beer, wine, beverages, pro shop,
excellent driving range, club memberships, putting green, practice bunker.
Comments: the course offers a beautiful view of the Olympic Mountains and
Mt. Rainier. Excellent public course with well bunkered greens and medium
wide fairways. The course has a well stocked pro shop for all your golfing needs.

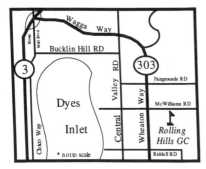

Directions: from the Bremerton ferry
terminal take Washington. Turn north
for .8 miles to Warren. Turn right on
Warren and proceed 3.6 miles to
McWilliams Rd. Turn right to the golf
course. Look for signs to the course.

Course Yardage & Par:
M-5910 yards, par 70.
W-5465 yards, par 70.

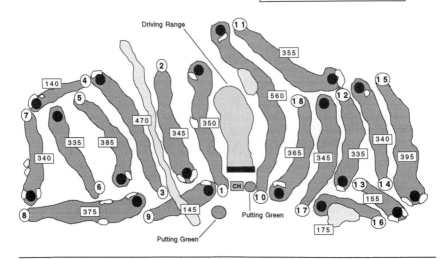

Royal City Golf Course (public, 9 hole course)

13702 Dodson Road South; Royal City, WA 99357
Phone: (509) 346-2052. Fax: none. Internet: none.
Manager: Wiley "Buck" Hurt. Superintendent: none.
Rating/Slope: M 68.6/113; W 71.9/114. Course record: 65.
Green fees: W/D $11/$8; W/E $13/$9; no credit cards.
Power cart: $15/$10. Pull cart: $3/$1.50. Trail fee: $4.
Reservation policy: please call 1 day in advance for tee-times.
Winter condition: call ahead for golf course conditions, course closed at times.
Terrain: flat, some hills. **Tees:** grass. **Spikes:** soft spikes only.
Services: snack bar, pro shop, driving range, putting green, RV parking.
Comments: newer golf course that varies in terrain. A canal runs through two holes and can present problems with your tee or approach shots. Fairways are wide and firm. RV park is next to the course with water and eletric hookups.

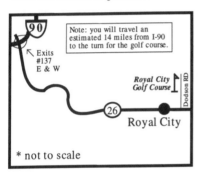

Note: you will travel an estimated 14 miles from I-90 to the turn for the golf course.

* not to scale

Directions: from I-90 E&W take the exit #137 for Hwy 26 to Royal City. Travel eastbound for approximately 14.2 miles to Dodson Road. Turn left. The clubhouse and golf course will be on your left hand side. Signs are posted indicating your turn on Dodson Road to the course.

Course Yardage & Par:
M-3106 yards, par 36.
W-2850 yards, par 36.

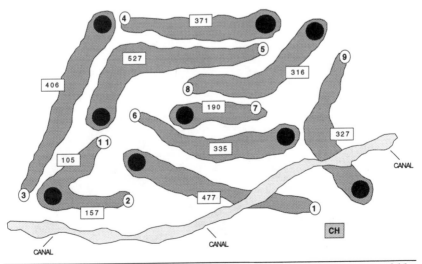

Royal Oaks Country Club (private, 18 hole course)

8917 NE Fourth Plain Road; Vancouver, WA 98662
Phone: (360) 256-1350. Fax: (360) 256-1253. Internet: none.
Pro: Steve Bowen, PGA. Superintendent: Alan Neilsen.
Rating/Slope: T 73.1/133; C 71.2/125; M 69.5/122; W 72.6/127. **Record:** 64.
Green fees: private club members & guests only; reciprocates; M/C, VISA.
Power cart: private club. **Pull cart:** private club. **Trail fee:** private club.
Reservation policy: no time limit for members, public is not allowed.
Winter condition: the golf course is open all year long. Dry conditions.
Terrain: flat, some hills. **Tees:** grass. **Spikes:** soft spikes April thru October.
Services: lessons, restaurant, lounge, beer, wine, liquor, pro shop, lockers,
showers, club memberships, driving range, putting & chipping greens.
Comments: regarded as one of the state's best, Royal Oaks fairway's are tight
and tree-lined. Greens are well bunkered and hard to hold. A very difficult
layout that is demanding from the tee and on the greens. Good private course.

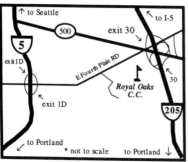

Directions: from I-5 N&S take exit #
1D (Fourth Plain Blvd E). Travel east
just beyond the 4 mile post to the golf
course which will be on your right hand
side. Look for a small sign at your turn.

Course Yardage & Par:

T-6900 yards, par 72.
C-6516 yards, par 72.
M-6138 yards, par 72.
F-5695 yards, par 72.
W-5208 yards, par 72.

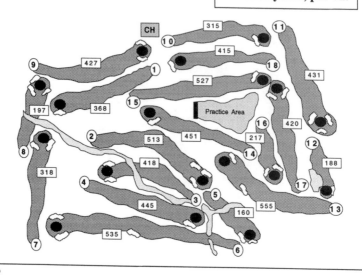

Sage Hills Golf Club (public, 18 hole course)

10400 Sage Hills Road SE; Warden, WA 98857
Phone: (509) 349-2603. Fax: (509) 349-0420. Internet: none.
Pro: Chad Disney. Superintendent: Martin Gallardo.
Rating/Slope: C 71.4/122; M 70.1/117; W 69.0/114. Course record: 64.
Green fees: W/D $17/$10; W/E $22/$12; Jr & Sr rates (M-F); M/C, VISA.
Power cart: $22/$12. Pull cart: $4/$2. Trail fee: $6/$3 for personal carts.
Reservation policy: yes, you may call 7 days in advance for tee-times.
Winter condition: the golf course is usually closed December to January.
Terrain: flat, some hills. Tees: grass. Spikes: soft spikes only.
Services: club rentals, lessons, restaurant, lounge, beer, wine, pro shop,
showers, driving range, putting and chipping greens, 42 RV hookups.
Comments: Good public course that can play very difficult if the wind picks up.
Greens are medium in size with some being fronted by bunkers. Water comes
into play on 5 holes and is a major factor off the tee and on your approach shots.
A full service RV park is adjacent to the parking lot for those spending the night.

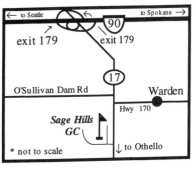

Directions: the golf course is located 2 miles south of the Warden cut-off on the west side of Hwy 17. From I-90 exit #179 to Hwy 17 and proceed southbound to the golf course. Make sure that you look for signs to the golf course from the Hwy.

Course Yardage & Par:

C-6591 yards, par 71.
M-6355 yards, par 71.
W-5128 yards, par 74.

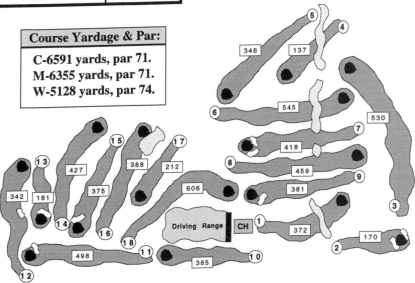

Sahalee Country Club (private, 27 hole course)

21200 Sahalee Country Club Drive; Redmond, WA 98053
Phone: (425) 453-0484. Fax: none. Internet: none.
Golf Professional: Jim Pike, PGA. Superintendent: Tom Wolff.
Rating/Slope: T 74.0/137; C 73.2/132; M 71.6/129; W 73.4/132. **Record:** 64.
Green fees: private club members & guests only; reciprocates (very limited).
Power cart: private club. **Pull cart:** private club. **Trail fee:** private club.
Reservation policy: private club members & guests only. No public play.
Winter condition: the golf course is open all year long. Dry conditions.
Terrain: relatively hilly. **Tees:** all grass. **Spikes:** soft spikes May-October.
Services: club rentals, lessons, lounge, restaurant, beer, wine, liquor, pro shop,
lockers, showers, club memberships, driving range, dress code, putting green.
Comments: course record was set by Nick Price and Greg Kraft during the
PGA Championship. Ranked in *Golf Digest's* top 100 courses in the nation
Sahalee is both demanding and spectacular. Fantastic private golf course.

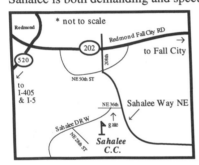

Directions: from I-5 N&S take exit
#168B to Hwy 520 eastbound. Go east
to Hwy 202E (Redmond-Fall City
Road). Travel east for 2 miles to 208th
Avenue NE-Sahalee Way NE. Turn
south for 1 mile to NE 36th. Veer left to
Sahalee Dr. W to NE 28th. Turn east to
the golf course.

Course Yardage & Par:
North: T-3467 yards, C-3377yards, M-3172 yards, W-2867 yards, par 36.
South: T-3488 yards, C-3377 yards, M-3159 yards, W-2845 yards, par 36.
East: T-3464 yards, C-3392 yards, M-3163 yards, W-2880 yards, par 36.

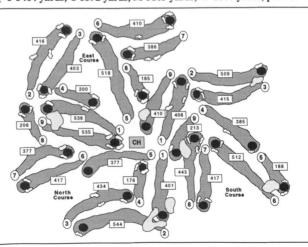

Saint John Golf & Country Club (semi-private, 9 hole course)
off Hwy 23; P.O. Box 232; Saint John, WA 99171
Phone: (509) 648-3259. **Fax:** none. **Internet:** none.
Pro: none. **Manager:** N/A. **Superintendent:** Curt White.
Rating/Slope: C 67.0/111; M 66.0/106; W 68.4/109. **Course record:** 32.
Green fees: $15 (all day); non-members welcome; no credit cards.
Power cart: none available. **Pull cart:** $2. **Trail fee:** $3.00 all day rate.
Reservation policy: advance tee times are not needed or required.
Winter condition: the golf course is closed from November thru February.
Terrain: very flat easy walking. **Tees:** grass. **Spikes:** soft spikes preferred.
Services: lessons, (occasionally), limited services. **Comments:** the course is
impeccably maintained with beautiful lush green fairways. A few sand traps and
one creek come into play. Easy walking golf course that is great for the senior.
The clubhouse is often closed so green fees are sometimes on the honor system.

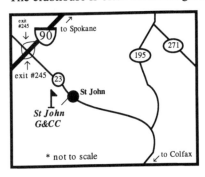

Directions: the golf course is located on
the northwest side of St. John off Hwy
23. Look for signs off of Hwy 23 in St.
John marking your way to the golf course.
The course is located right off Hwy 23.
Signs are posted at your turn.

Course Yardage & Par:

C-2876 yards, par 35.
M-2770 yards, par 35.
W-2564 yards, par 35.

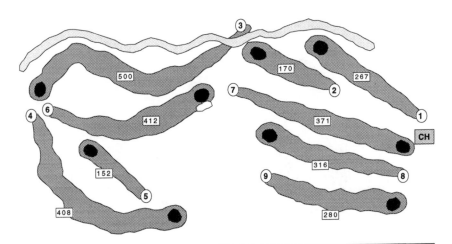

San Juan Golf & Country Club (public, 9 hole course)

2261 Golf Course Road; P.O. Box 246; Friday Harbor, WA 98250
Phone: (360) 378-2254. Fax: (360) 378-3107. Internet: none.
Pro: Steve Nightingale, PGA. Superintendent: Alan Dufur.
Rating/Slope: M 70.9/118; W 70.8/115. **Course record:** 66.
Green fees: $25/$17.50 all week long; twilight rates $10; M/C, VISA.
Power cart: $20/$12. **Pull cart:** $2.50. **Trail fee:** $5 (for pass unlimited use).
Reservation policy: yes, call 1 day ahead for tee-times June through August.
Winter condition: the golf course is open all year long. Dry conditions.
Terrain: flat, some hills. **Tees:** all grass. **Spikes:** soft spikes preferred.
Services: club rentals, lessons, snack bar, lockers, pro shop, driving range
putting green, RV parking. **Comments:** set in the scenic San Juan Islands, the
course is easy to walk but can be tough to score on. Tee shots play to medium
size landing areas. Two sets of tees available for those wanting to play a full 18
hole round. Excellent golf course that is well maintained during the peak season.

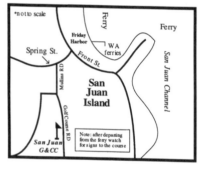

Directions: from the Anacortes ferry
travel to Friday Harbor. While in Friday
Harbor, take Spring Street. Proceed to
Mullins Road for 3.2 miles to Golf
Course Road. Turn left on Golf Course
Road and proceed to the golf course.

Course Yardage & Par:
M-3194 yards, par 35.
W-2663 yards, par 36.
Dual tees for 18 holes:
M-6508 yards, par 71.
W-5466 yards, par 72.

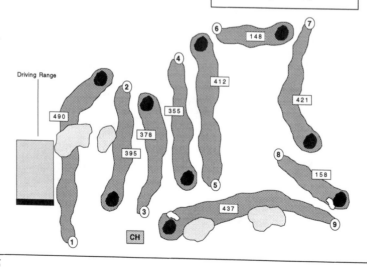

Sand Point Country Club (private, 18 hole course)
8333 55th NE; Seattle, WA 98115
Phone: (206) 523-4994. **Fax:** (206) 525-9867. **Internet: none.**
Pro: Ron Stull, PGA. Superintendent: Craig Sampson.
Rating/Slope: C 69.9/123; M 68.3/120; W 72.4/127; F 70.5/124. **Record:** 61.
Green fees: private club members and guests only; M/C, VISA.
Power cart: private club members and guests only. **Trail fee:** not allowed.
Reservation policy: private club members and guests only. No outside play.
Winter condition: the golf course is open all year long. Fair conditions.
Terrain: very hilly. **Tees:** all grass. **Spikes:** soft spikes only May to October.
Services: club rentals, lessons, snack bar, lounge, restaurant, beer, wine, liquor, pro shop, club memberships, putting & chipping greens, driving range, tennis.
Comments: the course offers a sweeping view of Lake Washington. Numerous sand traps, rolling terrain, and many trees provide a great test of golf.

Directions: from I-5 S take exit # 172 to NE 80th. Turn east to Banner Way NE. Turn south on Banner which will become NE 75th. Proceed 2.3 miles to the golf course. From I-5 N take exit # 171 to NE 73rd. Travel east for .1 mile to 12th NE. On 12th go north for .1 mile to NE 75th. Turn east for 1.8 miles to the golf course.

Course Yardage & Par:

C-6040 yards, par 71.
M-5690 yards, par 71.
M-5488 yards, par 71.
W-5127 yards, par 72.

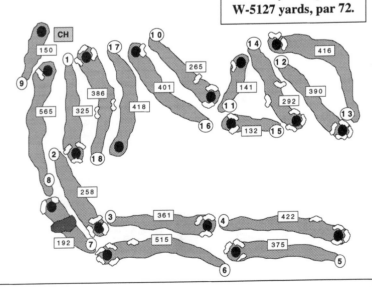

Sandy Point Golf Course (private, 9 hole course)
Box 1418; Ferndale, WA 98248
Phone: (360) 384-3921. **Fax:** none. **Internet:** none.
Manager: none. **Superintendent:** home owners.
Rating/Slope: the golf course is not rated. **Course record:** 24.
Greens fee: private club, members & guests only; no credit cards.
Power cart: none. **Pull cart:** members & guests only. **Trail fee:** private.
Reservation policy: yes, members may call for weekend tee times.
Winter condition: the golf course is open all year long. Wet conditions.
Terrain: flat gentle rolling. **Tees:** grass. **Spikes:** soft spikes preffered.
Services: limited services. Club members only.
Comments: postage stamp greens are this private courses trademark. These greens can be very hard to hold during the summer months when they are firm.

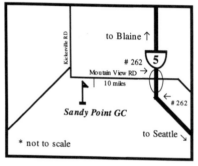

Directions: from I-5 N&S take exit #262 to Mountain View Road. Follow Mountain View Road westbound for 10 miles. The golf course and development is located on your left hand side.

Course Yardage & Par:
M-1000 yards, par 27.
W-1000 yards, par 27.

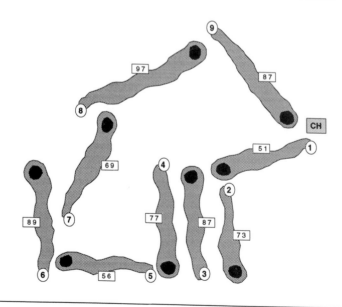

Scott Lake Golf Course (public, 9 hole course)

11746 Scott Creek Drive SW; Olympia, WA 98512
Phone: (360) 352-4838. Fax: none. Internet: none.
Owners: Joel and Karen Boede. Superintendent: none.
Rating/Slope: M 62.9/94; W 64.4/97. **Course record:** 62.
Green fees: W/D $12/$8; W/E $16/$9; Jr & Sr rates (W/D's); no credit cards.
Power cart: $16/$9. **Pull cart:** $2. **Trail fee:** $5/$3 for personal carts.
Reservation policy: yes, call up to 10 days the during summer and weekends.
Winter condition: the golf course is open all year long. Damp conditions.
Terrain: flat (easy walking). **Tees:** all grass. **Spikes:** metal spikes permitted.
Services: club rentals, coffee shop, beer, wine, pro shop, putting green, club
memberships. **Comments:** this friendly, family run 9 hole golf course sports
dual tees for a full 18 hole round. Greens are medium in size and sport few
undulations. Fairways are tree-lined and well kept. Two lakes come into play
throughout half of the nine hole track. Good golf course for family outing.

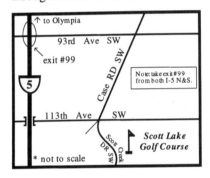

Directions: from I-5 N&S take exit #99. Travel east on 93rd Avenue SW to Case Avenue SW. Turn south. Proceed to Scott Creek Dr. SW and follow to the golf course. Look for signs to the course.

Course Yardage & Par:
M-2600 yards, par 35.
W-2189 yards, par 36.
<u>Dual tees for 18 holes:</u>
M-5045 yards, par 70.
W-4634 yards, par 72.

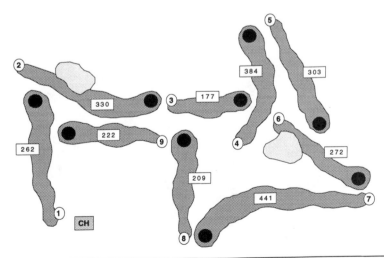

Sea Links   (public, 18 hole par 3 course)
7878 Birch Bay Drive; Blaine, WA 98230
Phone: (360) 371-7933. Fax: none. Internet: none.
Manger: Stuart Hill. Superintendent: none.
Rating/Slope: M 50.7/67; W 50.7/67. **Course record:** 47.
Green fees: W/D $11/$9; W/E $14; Jr./Sr. (M-F); M/C, VISA, DISCOVER.
Power cart: $15. **Pull cart:** $2. **Trail fee:** no charge for personal carts.
Reservation policy: yes, call up to 1 week in advance for tee times.
Winter condition: the golf course is open all year. Dry conditions.
Terrain: flat, some hills. **Tees:** grass. **Spikes:** soft spikes preferred.
Services: club rentals, lessons, restaurant, beer, wine, pro shop, liquor.
Comments: although short, this executive size layout has many hazards.
Ponds, sand traps, and postage stamp greens challenge golfers of any caliber.
Many of the holes have recently been lengthened from the championship tees.
If you are looking for a change of pace at an excellent facility try Sea Links.

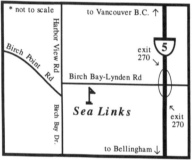

Directions: from I-5 N&S take exit # 270 to Lynden-Birch Bay Road. Travel westbound for 3.7 miles to Harborview. Turn south. Proceed .2 miles to the bay. Turn left and travel 1/2 mile to the golf course. Look for signs marking your turn to the facility.

Course Yardage & Par:
C-2701 yards, par 54. **M-2320 yards, par 54.** **W-2075 yards, par 54.**

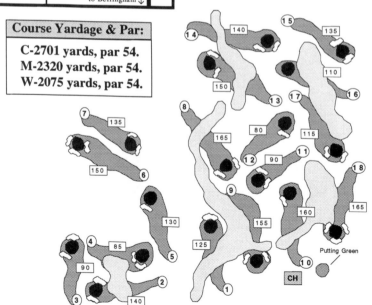

Seattle Golf Club (private, 18 hole course)

210 NW 145th; Seattle, WA 98177
Phone: (206) 363-8811. Fax: (206) 363-6658. Internet: none.
Pro: Doug Doxsie, PGA. Superintendent: Peter Wilson.
Rating/Slope: C 71.8/127; M 69.8/122; W 71.8/126. **Course record:** 63.
Green fees: private course, members only; no credit cards.
Power cart: private club. **Pull cart:** complimentary. **Trail fee:** not allowed.
Reservation policy: private club members only. No outside public is allowed.
Winter condition: the golf course is open year round. Dry conditions.
Terrain: very hilly. **Tees:** all grass. **Spikes:** soft spikes only April-October.
Services: lessons, snack bar, lounge, restaurant, beer, wine, liquor, pro shop, showers, putting green, driving range. **Comments:** a beautiful, stately old golf course. Mature trees line the fairways and are a major factor off the tee. Greens are large and well trapped. Water holes can play extremely difficult. From the back tees the golf course plays long, putting emphasis on accuracy.

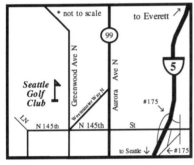

Directions: from I-5 N&S take exit # 175 to NE 145th. Turn west and travel 1.4 miles to the golf course entrance. The golf course is on your right hand side. Look for a small sign.

Course Yardage & Par:
C-6806yards, par 72.
M-6013 yards, par 72.
W-5418 yards, par 72.

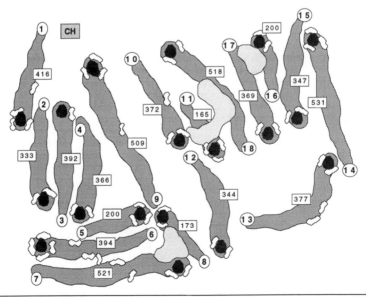

Semiahmoo Golf & Country Club (semi-private, 18 holes)

8720 Semiahmoo Parkway; Blaine, WA 98230 Internet: www.semiahmoo.com
Phone: (360) 371-7005, 800-231-4425. Fax: (360) 371-7012.
Pro: Michael Anderson, PGA. Superintendent: Vance Much.
Rating/Slope: T 73.6/130; C 70.9/125; M 69.9/120; W 70.7/121. **Record:** 65.
Green fees: peak golfing season rates: $65 all week long; twilite rates $49 after 4pm; winter rates $39 all week long; VISA, M/C, AMEX.
Power cart: $17 per seat. **Pull cart:** $5/$3. **Trail fee:** not allowed.
Reservation policy: Mon.-Friday 3 days in advance. Call Friday for weekend.
Winter condition: the golf course is open all year long. Dry conditions.
Terrain: flat, some hills. **Tees:** grass. **Spikes:** no metal spikes in summer.
Services: club rentals, lessons, snack bar, wine, beer, pro shop, driving range.
Comments: Arnold Palmer designed layout with numerous bunkers and ponds. Voted in 1992 as the 18th **Best Resort Course** in the nation by *Golf Digest.* It was also voted the #1 Resort Course in America by *Golf Digest* when it opened in 1987. This course is truely one of the finest facilities in the entire NW.

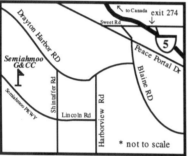

Directions: from I-5 N&S take exit # 274 to Bell Road. Turn left. The road becomes Blaine Road. Travel 1 mile to Drayton Harbor Road. Turn right and follow to the fork, stay left it becomes Harbor View Road. Proceed .5 miles to Lincoln Road. Follow the signs to the golf course.

Course Yardage & Par:

T-7005 yards, par 72.
C-6435 yards, par 72.
M-6003 yards, par 72.
W-5288 yards, par 72.

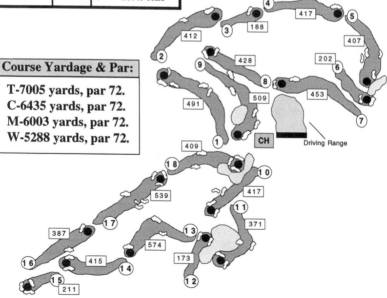

Serendipity Golf Course (public, 9 hole course)
North 31171 Le Clerc Road; Ione, WA 99139
Phone: (509) 442-3313. Fax: (509) 442-3621. Internet: none.
Owner: Karin Cox. Manager/Superintendent: David Cox.
Rating/Slope: the golf course is not rated. **Course record:** 32.
Green fees: $10 all week long; no special rates; no credit cards
Power cart: $10. **Pull cart:** $2.50. **Trail fee:** $2 for personal carts
Reservation policy: call ahead for tee-times on the weekend only.
Winter condition: the golf course is closed November 1st until thaw
Terrain: flat, easy walking. **Tees:** grass. **Spikes:** metal spikes permitted.
Services: club rentals. Private rental of golf course available for half day or all day special occasions. Large gazebo is for rent with BBQ, electricity, water and seating for about 50 persons. **Comments:** this 9 hole course is nestled along the banks of the Pend Oreille River. The surrounding beauty and friendly atmosphere provides the golfer with a enjoyable round. Fun for the whole family.

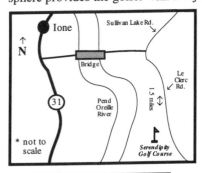

Directions: from the Spokane area, travel on Hwy 2 approx. 30 miles to Ione/Metaline Falls left turn-off onto Hwy 211. Travel 15 miles north to Hwy 31, turn left. Travel approx. 30 miles. Turn right approx. 2 miles south of the town of Ione for direction of Sullivan Lake (see GC sign). After crossing the orange bridge (Pend Oreille River) take immediate right (sign) and travel 1 1/2 miles. The course is on the right.

Course Yardage & Par:

M-2444 yards, par 34.
W-2444 yards, par 34.

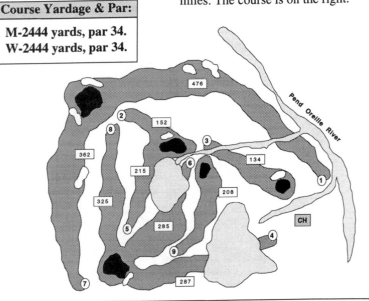

Shelton Bayshore Golf Club (public, 9 hole course)

3800 E Highway 3; Shelton, WA 98584
Phone: (360) 426-1271. **Fax:** (360) 427-6327. **Internet:** none.
Pro: Brian Davis, PGA. **Superintendent:** Mark Wigren.
Rating/Slope: M 69.2/116; W 72.5/121. **Course record:** 63.
Green fees: W/D $15/$10; W/E $18/$12; Sr. rates Mon. & Thur. $12/$8.
Power cart: $22/$13. **Pull cart:** $3. **Trail fee:** $5 for personal carts.
Reservation policy: yes, call 14 days in advance for weekends and holidays.
Winter condition: the golf course is open all year long. Dry (drains very well).
Terrain: flat, some hills. **Tees:** all grass. **Spikes:** soft spikes preferred.
Services: club rentals, lessons, pro shop, club memberships, snack bar, wine,
beer, putting & chipping greens. **Comments:** this golf course is very tight,
tricky, and well maintained. Greens are small and can be hard to hold. Two sets
of tees are available for a full 18 hole round. <u>Good test for any level of player</u>.

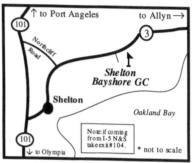

Directions: from I-5 N&S take exit #104
to Hwy 101 toward Shelton. Take the exit
for Hwy 3 (toward Allyn). The golf
course is located 4 miles out of Shelton.
Look for signs marking your way.

Course Yardage & Par:
M-2946 yards, par 36.   **W-2752 yards, par 36.**   <u>**Dual tees for 18 holes:**</u>   **M-6004 yards, par 72.**   **W-5698 yards, par 73.**

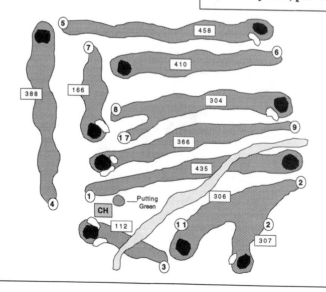

Sheridan Greens Golf Course (public, 9 hole course)

P.O. Box 454; 380 Sheridan Road; Republic, WA 99166
Phone: (509) 775-2767. Fax: none. Internet: none.
Pro: none. Superintendent: none.
Rating/Slope: the golf course is not rated. **Course record:** 68.
Green fees: $6; $8 all day rate; no credit cards.
Power cart: $8/$5. **Pull cart:** $1. **Trail fee:** not allowed.
Reservation policy: non advance reservations are required or needed.
Winter condition: the golf course is closed from October to mid-March.
Terrain: flat, some hills. **Tees:** grass. **Spikes:** soft spikes preferred.
Services: club rentals, snacks, pro shop, lounge. **Comments:** the course is often on the honor system. The golf course is very easy to walk. It now has expanded to 9 holes so you now can play a somewhat rustic but regulation golf course.

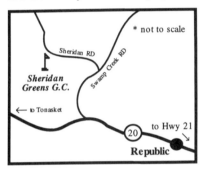

Directions: the golf course is located 2 miles west of Republic off Hwy 20. Turn right on Swamp Creek Road and proceed for 1.5 miles to the golf course. Note the sign for the golf course cut-off on Sheridan Road.

Course Yardage & Par:

M-2185 yards, par 32.
W-2185 yards, par 32.

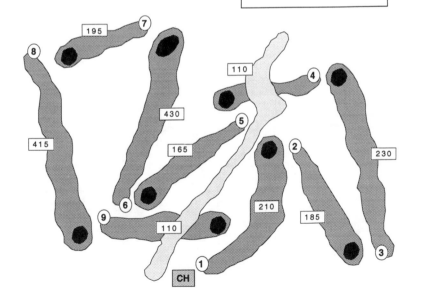

Shuksan Golf Club (public, 18 hole course)
1500 East Axton; Bellingham, WA 98226
Phone: (360) 398-8888. **Fax:** (360) 398-8272. **Internet:** www.cybergolf.com/shuks
Pro: Ben Harvey, PGA. **Superintendent:** Reg Riddle.
Rating/Slope: C 70.4/121; M 67.6/115; W 67.7/112. **Course record:** 72.
Green fees: Monday thru Thursday $27; Friday thru Sunday $37.
Power cart: $11+tax per person. **Pull cart:** N/A. **Trail fee:** not allowed.
Reservation policy: please call 7 days in advance for a tee time.
Winter condition: the golf course is open all year long. Weather permitting.
Terrain: flat, some steep hills. **Tees:** grass. **Spikes:** soft spikes May-October.
Services: club rentals, lessons, snack bar, restaurant, beer, wine, pro shop,
driving range, putting green, tournaments always welcome, banquet facilities.
Comments: excellent newer course that offers the golfer fantastic golf on every
hole. Magestic views of the mountains and surrounding countryside can be seen
from nearly every tee. The facility was recently ranked FOUR STAR by *Golf
Digest* Places to Play. This course is a must play for any northwest golfer.

Directions: from I-5 southbound take exit
#262 (Main St-City Center) eastbound.
Travel east on Main which will become
Axton Rd. The course is located approxi-
mately 7.8 miles ahead on the left. From
I-5 northbound take exit #256. Follow
Meridian to Axton Rd. and turn right.
The golf course will be on your left.
Look for signs to the golf course.

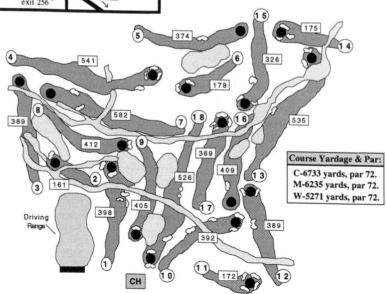

Course Yardage & Par:
C-6733 yards, par 72.
M-6235 yards, par 72.
W-5271 yards, par 72.

Similk Beach Golf Course (public, 18 hole course)

1250 Christianson Road; Anacortes, WA 98221
Phone: (360) 293-3444. Fax: (360) 293-2327. Internet: none.
Pro: Dick Freier, PGA. Superintendent: John Yandle.
Rating/Slope: M 67.1/107; W 71.1/111. Course record: 65.
Green fees: W/D $18/$12; W/E $20/$14; all day rates; M/C, VISA.
Power cart: $20/$10. **Pull cart:** $2.50. **Trail fee:** no charge for personal carts.
Reservation policy: call ahead for tee-times, no time limit on reservations.
Winter condition: the course is open all year. Damp conditions.
Terrain: flat, some hills. **Tees:** all grass. **Spikes:** soft spikes preferred.
Services: club rentals, lessons, snack bar, pop, driving range, putting green.
Comments: the layout of this course is fairly open with a few water hazards.
Greens are medium in size and are usually open in the front. The golf course has
a well stocked pro shop and excellent driving range to serve you. Good public
track that is very popular with the local golfer.

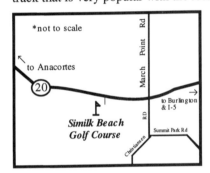

Directions: from I-5 northbound take
exit # 230 to Hwy 20 W (Burlington-
Anacortes). The golf course is located
5 miles east of Anacortes, just off of
Hwy 20. You will be able to see the golf
course from the highway.

Course Yardage & Par:
M-6232 yards, par 72. **W-5934 yards, par 76.**

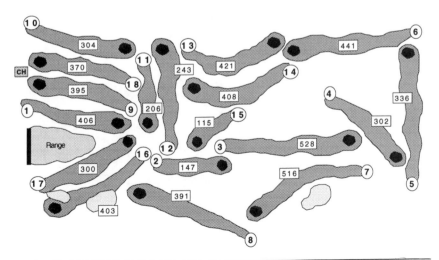

Skagit Golf & Country Club (private, 18 hole course)
1493 Country Club Drive; Burlington, WA 98233
Phone: (360) 757-0530. **Fax:** (360) 757-0154. **Internet: none.**
Pro: David Bobillot, PGA. Superintendent: Gregory Miller.
Rating/Slope: M 68.7/118; W 70.6/115. **Course record:** 65.
Green fees: private club members & guests only; reciprocates.
Power cart: private club. **Pull cart:** private club. **Trail fee:** not allowed.
Reservation policy: summer only 48 hours in advance. No outside play.
Winter condition: the golf course is open all year long. Damp conditions.
Terrain: flat . **Tees:** all grass. **Spikes:** no metal spikes in the summer.
Services: club rentals, lessons, snack bar, lounge, restaurant, beer, wine, liquor, pro shop, lockers, showers, club memberships, putting green, driving range.
Comments: the golf course is a combination of tree-lined and open fairways. Many bunkers front the large greens. Four ponds come into play off the tee and are a major factor on your approach shots. Excellent private golf course.

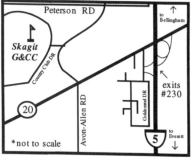

Direction: from I-5 N&S take exit # 230 to Hwy 20 W. Travel west for 2.1 miles to Avon-Allen Road (the flashing light). Turn right. Proceed .5 miles to the golf course. Look for a small sign.

Course Yardage & Par:
M-6019 yards, par 71.
W-5439 yards, par 73.

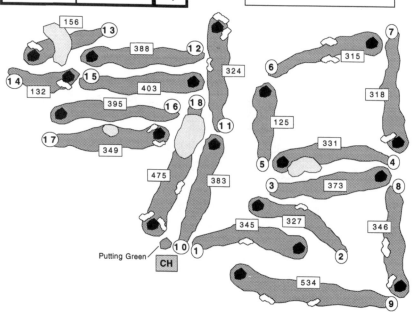

Skamania Lodge Golf Course (public, resort, 18 hole course)

P.O. Box 189; 1131 Skamania Lodge Way; Stevenson, WA 98648
Phone: 1-800-293-0418 or (509) 427-2541. Fax: (509) 427-2546.
Pro: Guy Puddefoot, PGA. Superintendent: James Medler.
Rating/Slope: C 68.9/127; M 66.7/122; W 65.2/115. **Course record:** 66.
Green fees: $40/$20 all week long; Jr. and twilight rates; winter rates.
Power cart: $26/$14. **Pull cart:** $5/$3. **Trail fee:** not allowed.
Reservation policy: yes, please call up to 2 weeks in advance for tee times.
Winter condition: the golf course is open all year. Weather permitting.
Terrain: flat, some hills. **Tees:** all grass. **Spikes:** soft spikes preferred.
Services: pro shop, restaurant, wine, liquor, driving range, lodge facilities.
Comments: This well kept golf course offers great views of the Columbia
River Gorge and surrounding countryside. If you plan on vacationing for a few
days stay at the Skamania Lodge. The course itself is narrow in spots and its
greens are well bunkered. Shot placement is a must from the tee if you want to
score well. This full service facility is worth a special trip if you are in the area.

Directions: From Portland take I-84
eastbound to the Bridge of the Gods.
Turn eastbound to Hwy 14 and proceed
1.1 miles eastbound to Stevenson. The
golf course is located on the north side
of Hwy 14. From I-205 exit at Hwy 14
and proceed eastbound to Stevenson and
to the golf course. Look for signs.

Course Yardage & Par:

C-5776 yards, par 70.
M-5351 yards, par 70.
W-4362 yards, par 69.

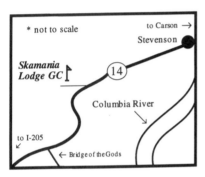

Skyline Golf Course (public, 9 hole course)
20 Randall Drive; Cathlamet, WA 98612
Phone: (360) 795-8785. **Fax:** none. **Internet:** none.
Manager: Wayne Cochran. **Superintendent:** Wayne Cochran.
Rating/Slope: M 62.7/106; W 66.7/111. **Course record:** 62.
Green fees: $15/$8 all week long; no credit cards.
Power cart: $16/$8. **Pull cart:** $1. **Trail fee:** $5.
Reservation policy: please call 1 day in advance for tee-times.
Winter condition: the golf course is open all year long, dry.
Terrain: very hilly. **Tees:** grass & mats. **Spikes:** metal spikes permitted.
Services: club rentals, snack bar (breakfast & lunch), club memberships.
Comments: the course is short and tight with a friendly atmosphere. Family
run and owned. The golf course can play much tougher than it appears.

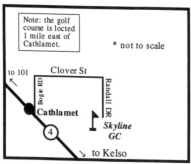

Directions: from I-5 N&S take the exit to
Hwy 4 westbound at Kelso to Cathlamet.
Turn right on Bogie Road. The road turns
right on Clover Street. Turn right at the
sign pointing to the golf course. The way
is well marked.

Course Yardage & Par:
M-2255 yards, par 35.
W-2012 yards, par 35.
Dual tees for 18 holes:
M-4774 yards, par 70.
W-4205 yards, par 70.

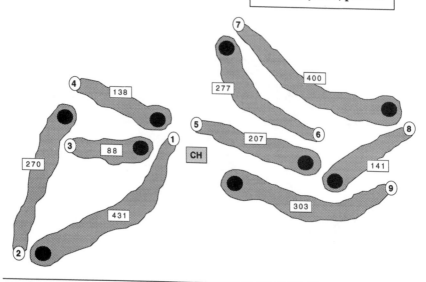

Snohomish Public Golf Course (public, 18 hole course)
7805 147th SE; P.O. Box 1188; Snohomish, WA 98290
Phone: (360) 568-2676 or 1- 800-560-2676. Fax: none. Internet: none.
Director of Golf: Fred Jacobson. Pro: John Brandvold, PGA.
Golf Course Superintendent: George Smith.
Rating/Slope: C 71.7/122; M 69.8/117; W 73.3/125. **Course record:** 63.
Green fees: W/D $20/$14*; W/E $25/$15*; Jr./Sr. rates (M-F); M/C, VISA.
Power cart: $21/$12.50*. **Pull cart:** $3/$2*. **Trail fee:** $9*. (*all add tax).
Reservation policy: yes, call up to 1 week in advance for your tee times.
Winter condition: the golf course is open all year long. Dry conditions.
Terrain: relatively hilly. **Tees:** grass & mats. **Spikes:** soft spikes preferred.
Services: club rentals, lessons, snack bar, restaurant, beer, wine, pro shop, club memberships, driving range, putting & chipping greens. **Comments:** beautiful rural course. Located on a hill the course is surrounded by trees. The greens are very large and well bunkered. Great public golf course that is a must play.

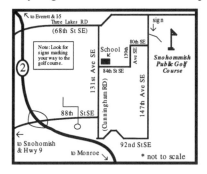

Directions: From I-5 N&S take exit #194 to Hwy 2 going eastbound. Follow Hwy 2 east to Snohomish. Take the Snohomish exit (look for a sign) to 88th St. SE. Go east on 88th to 131st Ave SE. Turn left on 131st. Proceed to 84th Ave. SE and turn right. 84th becomes 139th Ave. SE as you must turn left. At the T in the road turn right on 80th St. SE. Proceed on 80th to 147th Ave. SE. Turn left. The course will be on your right.

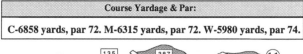

Course Yardage & Par:
C-6858 yards, par 72. M-6315 yards, par 72. W-5980 yards, par 74.

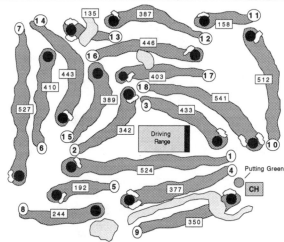

Snoqualmie Falls Golf Course (public, 18 hole course)
35109 SE Fish Hatchery Road; Box 790; Fall City, WA 98024
Phone: (425) 222-5244 or 392-1276. Fax: (425) 222-5666. Internet: none.
Pro: John Groshell, PGA. Superintendent: Lee Baldwin.
Rating/Slope: M 65.3/105; W 68.9/114. **Course record:** 60.
Green fees: W/D $24/$14; W/E $26/$16; Jr /Sr (M-F) $19/$11; VISA, M/C.
Power cart: $22/$12, single rider $15/$8. **Pull cart:** $3/$2. **Trail fee:** no.
Reservation policy: yes, call up to 6 days in advance for your tee times.
Winter condition: the golf course is open all year long. Drains well.
Terrain: very flat. **Tees:** grass & mats. **Spikes:** metal spikes permitted.
Services: club rentals, lessons, snack bar, restaurant, beer, pro shop, driving range. **Comments:** situated in the foothills of the Cascade Mountain Range, Snoqualmie Falls is easy to walk and fun to play. The golf course has a well stocked pro shop and great on course restaurant. Good public golf course.

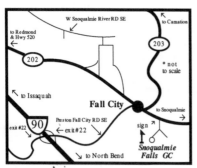

Directions: from I-90 eastbound take exit # 22 to Preston. Turn left over the freeway, then right to the Preston-Fall City Road for 6.2 miles to Hwy 202E. Turn right and proceed approximately .8 miles to SE Fish Hatchery Road (look for a sign at the turn). Turn right to the golf course.

Course Yardage & Par:
M-5413 yards, par 71.
W-5175 yards, par 71.

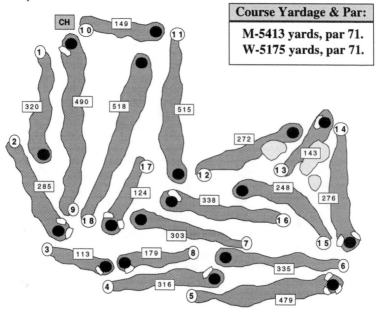

Snoqualmie Ridge TPC Golf Club (private, 18 hole course)
8008 356th Avenue SE; Snoqualmie, WA 98065
Director of Golf Operations: Arne Michaelsen. Supt.: Jack Clarberg.
Phone: (425) call information for phone number. Fax: N/A.
Rating/Slope: the golf course is not rated. **Course record:** N/A.
Green fees: private club members & guests only; reciprocates; no credit cards.
Power cart: private club. **Pull cart:** private club. **Trail fee:** private club.
Reservation policy: to be determined upon opening of the golf course.
Winter condition: the golf course is open year round, weather permitting.
Terrain: flat some big hills. **Tees:** all grass. **Spikes:** soft spikes only.
Services: upon opening the services of the golf course will be determined.
Comments: the target opening of this Jack Nicklaus designed layout is June or
July of 1999 depending on the spring weather. This course promises to
be nothing short of spectacular. Reaching nearly 7000 yards from the back tees
Snoqualmie Ridge features extensive mounding, generous landing areas from
the tees and large undualting greens. Great new course for NW golfers.

Directions: from I-90 east & west take
exit #25 (Hwy 18) turn northbound onto
Snoqualmie Ridge Parkway which is
about .4 miles ahead. From Hwy 202
turn southbound onto Snoqualmie Ridge
Parkway. Look for signs posted.

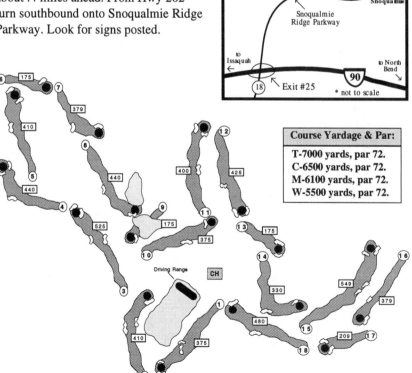

Course Yardage & Par:

T-7000 yards, par 72.
C-6500 yards, par 72.
M-6100 yards, par 72.
W-5500 yards, par 72.

Spokane Country Club (private, 18 hole course)

W 2010 Waikiki Road; P.O. Box 18750; Spokane, WA 99218;
Phone: (509) 466-9813. Fax: (509) 466-8044. Internet: none.
Pro: Les Blakley, PGA. Superintendent: Ron Kuhns
Rating/Slope: C 71.2/126; M 69.6/122; W 74.0/129. **Course record:** 61.
Green fees: private club members & guests only; reciprocates; no credit cards.
Power cart: private club. **Pull cart:** private club. **Trail fee:** private club.
Reservation policy: members only club, reciprocates call for policy.
Winter condition: the golf course is open all year, weather permitting.
Terrain: flat, some hills. **Tees:** all grass. **Spikes:** soft spikes only.
Services: club rentals, lessons, snack bar, restaurant, lounge, beer, wine, liquor, showers, driving range, putting green. **Comments:** this golf course was remodeled in 1988 by Robert Muir Graves. A very difficult layout that puts a premium on accuracy off the tee. Excellent private track that is very demanding.

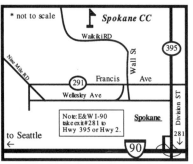

Directions: from I-90 take the exit at Division Street. Travel northbound on Division Street to Francis Avenue and turn left. Proceed on Francis Avenue to Wall Street and turn right. Then follow Wall Street to Waikiki Road which will lead to the golf course.

Course Yardage & Par:

C-6634 yards, par 72.
M-6301 yards, par 72.
W-5858 yards, par 73.
W-5549 yards, par 73.

Sudden Valley Golf & Country Club (semi-private, 18 holes)
2145 Lake Whatcom Boulevard; Bellingham, WA 98226
Phone: (360) 734-6435. Fax:(360) 734-1915. Internet: www.cybergolf.com/suddenvalley
Pro: Greg Paul, PGA. Superintendent: Bryan Newman.
Rating/Slope: C 71.8/126; M 70.0/123; W 72.8/124. **Course record: 64.**
Green fees: M-Thur. $27+tax; Fri-Sun. $37+tax; Jr. rates.; M/C, VISA, AMEX.
Power cart: $23/$13+tax. **Pull cart:** $3. **Trail fee:** personal carts not allowed.
Reservation policy: yes, call up to 1 week in advance for your tee times.
Winter condition: the golf course is open all year long. Good conditions.
Terrain: relatively hilly. **Tees:** all grass. **Spikes:** soft spikes preferred.
Services: club rentals, lessons, snack bar, lounge, restaurant, beer, wine, liquor,
pro shop, golf packages, range. **Comments:** Designed by Ted Robinson this
championship caliber course is considered a true masterpiece, stressing finesse
and accuracy with water hazards in play on 14 holes and some 47 sand bunkers
sprinkled throughout the layout. It's a golfing experience that you will not forget.

Directions: from I-5 south take exit #253
(Lakeway Dr.). Take a left at the stop light
onto Lakeway Dr. Proceed on Lakeway Dr.
(which turns into Lake Whatcom Blvd. for
10.2 miles then you will run right into
Sudden Valley. From I-5 north take exit #
240 (Alger). Turn right at the stop sign and
proceed for 1 mile to the next stop sign
(Alger Tavern on left). Go straight through
this intersection onto Cain Lake Rd.
Proceed for 8 miles. Turn left onto Lake
Whatcom Blvd. Proceed for 3.5 miles
to the entrance on the right hand side.

Course Yardage & Par:
C-6553 yards, par 72.
M-6143 yards, par 72.
W-5627 yards, par 72.

Sumner Meadows Golf Links　(public, 18 hole course)

14802 8th Street E; Sumner, WA 98390. Internet: www.cybergolf.com/sumnermeadows
Phone: (253) 863-8198; T-Times: 1-888-258-3348. Fax: (253) 863-8341
Dir. of Golf: Ron Hagen, PGA. Pro: Julian Slane, PGA. Supt.: Lee Anderson.
Rating/Slope: T 72.2/128; C 72.2/128; M 69.0/116; W 71.3/125. **Record:** 66.
Green fees: Monday-Thursday $22/$17; Friday-Sunday & Holidays $28/$23;
early bird specials, Jr. & Sr. and twilight rates; punch cards VISA, M/C, AMEX.
Power cart: $20/$15 (+tax). **Pull cart:** $3/$2. **Trail fee:** not allowed.
Reservation policy: please call 30 days in advance for tee times (can get busy).
Winter condition: the golf course is open all year long. Good conditions.
Terrain: flat, some hills. **Tees:** all grass. **Spikes:** soft spikes preferred.
Services: club rentals, pro shop, lessons, deli, driving range, putting green.
Comments: This excellent newer facility is one of the finest courses in the
Northwest. This links style track has many challenging holes with approach
shots that carry over the water. Greens are large and bunkered. Golf groups are
welcome. This is a City of Sumner facility managed by Golf Resources NW.

Directions: from Hwy 167 north and south
bound exit in Sumner on the 8th Street E
exit. Proceed eastbound on 8th Street E for
1 mile to the golf course on your right hand
side. Look for signs from the highway
marking your turn to the golf course.

Course Yardage & Par:
T-6753 yards, par 72/73.
C-6582 yards, par 72/73.
M-6170 yards, par 72/73.
M-5682 yards, par 72/73.
W-5364 yards, par 72/73.

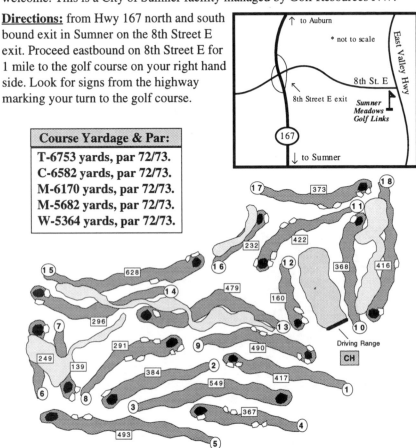

Sun Country Golf Resort (public, 9 hole course)

Golf Course Road; P.O. Box 364; Cle Elum, WA 98922
Phone: (509) 674-2226. Fax: none. Internet: none.
Manager: Ken Riach. Superintendent: none.
Rating/Slope: M 68.8/119; W 70.9/124. **Course record:** 33 for 9 holes.
Green fees: W/D $15/$10; W/E $20/$10; no credit cards.
Power cart: $18/$10. **Pull cart:** $1. **Trail fee:** $2 for each 9 holes.
Reservation policy: yes, call ahead 7 days for your tee times.
Winter condition: the golf course is closed from mid October to mid April.
Terrain: very hilly. **Tees:** grass. **Spikes:** soft spikes only please.
Services: club rentals, snack bar, RV park.
Comments: beautiful setting in the eastern Cascade Mountain foothills. RV park adjacent to the clubhouse for those traveling. Two sets of tees for a full 18 holes of golf. Good course with medium to large greens with few hazards.

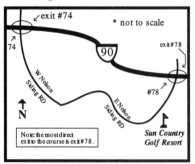

Directions: from I-90 E&W take exit #78 Golf Course Road. Follow signs to the RV park. The golf course is located on the south side of I-90 in the Sun Country Resort signs are posted.

Course Yardage & Par:
M-2861 yards, par 36.
W-2742 yards, par 37.
Dual tees for 18 holes:
M-5715 yards, par 72.
W-5466 yards, par 74.

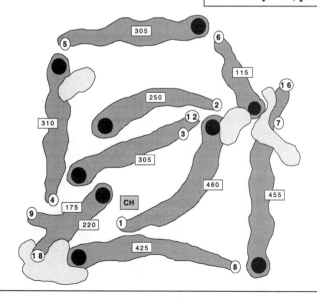

Sun Dance Golf Course (public, 18 hole course)

9725 Nine Mile Road; Nine Mile Falls, WA 99026
Phone: (509) 466-4040. Fax: (509) 465-0361. Internet: www.sundancegc.com
Director: Ken Johnston, PGA. Pro: Denny Johnston.
Rating/Slope: M 67.9/112; W 72.6/ 119. **Course record:** 63.
Green fees: W/D $16/$12; W/E $17; Sr. rates $12 (M-F) Jr. rates $9.
Power cart: Mon.-Th. $16/$12; Fri.-Sun. $22/$11. **Pull cart:** $3. **Trail fee:** $6.
Reservation policy: please call ahead 1 week for your tee times .
Winter condition: the golf course is closed from November to March.
Terrain: flat, some hills. **Tees:** grass. **Spikes:** no metal spikes permitted.
Services: club rentals, lessons, snack bar, restaurant, lounge, beer, wine, pro
shop, driving range, putting green & chipping green, club memberships.
Comments: this public course sports tree-lined fairways and small greens. The
golf course can get very busy during the summer so call ahead. Well conditioned
track that plays much longer than the yardage may indicate. Good golf course.

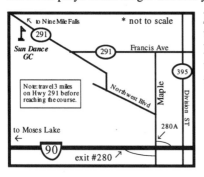

Directions: from I-90 take exit # 280A
to Walnut St. Turn north for 1.5 miles to
Northwest Blvd. Turn left. Travel 5 miles
to Hwy 291. Turn left and proceed 3 miles
to the golf course. Look for a sign.

Course Yardage & Par:
M-6004 yards, par 70.
W-5905 yards, par 70.
F-5658 yards, par 72.

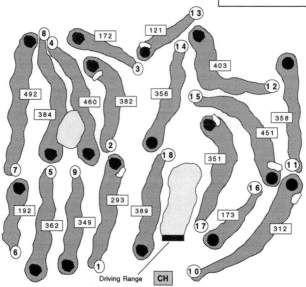

Sun Willows (public, 18 hole course)

2035 20th Avenue; Pasco, WA 99301
Phone: (509) 545-3440. Fax: (509) 545-6758. Internet: none.
Pro: Joe Dubsky, PGA. Superintendent: Pete Tice.
Rating/Slope: C 72.0/120; M 69.8116; W 71.6/119. Course record: 63.
Green fees: $18/$13 all week long; Jr. rates (Monday-Friday); VISA, M/C.
Power cart: $24/$12. Pull cart: $3. Trail fee: $8 for personal carts.
Reservation policy: yes, call up to 1 week in advance for tee times.
Winter condition: usually open all year long depending on the weather, dry.
Terrain: flat, walking course. Tees: grass. Spikes: metal spikes permitted.
Services: club rentals, lessons, restaurant, lounge, beer, wine, pro shop, driving range, putting & chipping greens. Comments: this excellent public facility has well-trapped greens and gentle rolling terrain. The tree-lined fairways are very wide with large landing areas. Water comes into play on several holes.

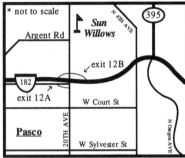

Directions: from I-182/Hwy12 take the 20th St. exit #128 and travel northbound to the course. The golf course is located across from the Red Lion Inn in Pasco. Look for signs indicating your turn.

Course Yardage & Par:
C-6715 yards, par 72.
M-6325 yards, par 72.
W-5665 yards, par 72.

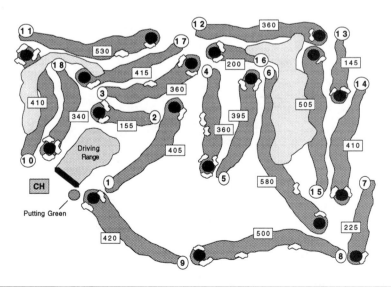

SunLand Golf & Country Club (private, 18 hole course)
109 Hilltop Drive; Sequim, WA 98382
Phone: (360) 683-6800. Fax: (360) 683-4989. Internet: none.
Pro: Kelly O'Meara, PGA. Superintendent: Daniel Ratcliff.
Rating/Slope: C 70.2/121; M 69.0/119; W 71.3/119. **Course record:** 64.
Green fees: members club, weekend tournaments, reciprocals encouraged.
Power cart: private. **Pull cart:** private. **Trail fee:** personal carts not allowed.
Reservation policy: call the pro shop as outside play is restricted.
Winter condition: the golf course is open all year long. Dry conditions.
Terrain: flat, some hills. **Tees:** all grass. **Spikes:** soft spikes only in summer.
Services: club rentals, lessons, snack bar, pro shop, driving range, putting green.
Comments: the course winds through a variety of forest and homesites. Greens
are well-trapped and water comes into play on 3 holes. Great golf course located
in the banana belt of Washington State. Very limited outside play available.

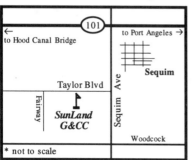

Directions: from Hwy 101 as you enter
Sequim turn right on Sequim Avenue
proceed 2.1 miles to Taylor Blvd. Turn
right and follow to Fairway Dr. Turn left
on Fairway Dr. to the clubhouse. Look for
signs marking your turn to the complex.

Course Yardage & Par:
C-6313 yards, par 72.
M-6051 yards, par 72.
W-5554 yards, par 73.

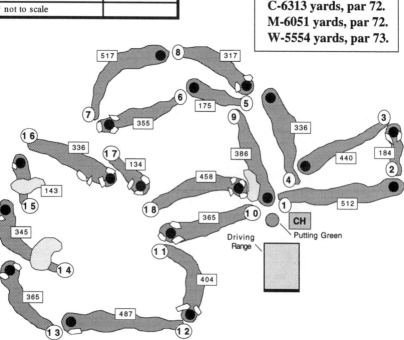

Sunny Meadows Golf & Four Seasons Resort (semi-private, 9 holes)
280 West Chewuck Road; Winthrop, WA 98862
Phone: (509) 996-3103, 1-800-433-3121. Fax: none.
Owner: Bob Odenthal. Superintendent: none.
Rating/Slope: the golf course is not rated. **Course record:** 31.
Green fees: private golf course, members & guests only. Some outside play.
Power cart: not available. **Pull cart:** $2. **Trail fee:** personal carts not allowed.
Reservation policy: yes, please call ahead for all tee time & B&B reservations.
Winter condition: the golf course is closed during the winter months.
Terrain: relatively hilly. **Tees:** all grass. **Spikes:** metal spikes permitted.
Services: the golf course is tied to a bed & breakfast arrangement with two self-sufficent apartments, limited golf course services. Rental clubs available.
Comments: this fairly new par 3 course has 3 water hazards, 3 blind holes, and tough, small elevated greens. This short par 3 course will challenge you at every turn. Tied to a great bed & breakfast. Plan on staying the whole weekend.

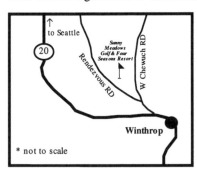

Directions: the golf course is located 2.7 miles north of Winthrop. From Hwy 20 turn on West Chewuck Road to the Bed & Breakfast and golf course. Look for signs.

Course Yardage & Par:
M-1439 yards, par 27.
W-1134 yards, par 27.

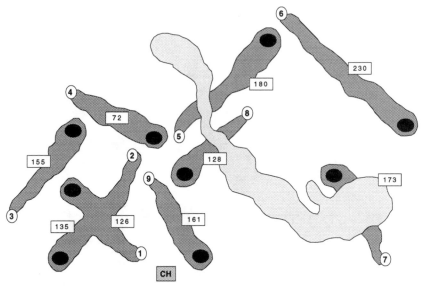

Suntides Golf Course (public, 18 hole course)

231 Pence Road; Yakima, WA 98908
Phone: (509) 966-9065. Fax: (509) 966-2742. Internet: none.
Pro: Paul Cobleigh, PGA. Superintendent: Jim Rogers.
Rating/Slope: C 67.8/112; M 66.4/110; W 69.2/112. Course record: 62.
Green fees: $20/$12 all week long; winter rates; Jr. rates; VISA, M/C.
Power cart: $20/$10. Pull cart: $2/$1. Trail fee: $5 for personal carts.
Reservation policy: call Tuesday for Friday, Wednesday for the weekend
and Monday to book your Tuesday through Thursday tee-times.
Winter condition: the golf course is open all year long. Weather permitting.
Terrain: flat easy walking. **Tees:** grass. **Spikes:** soft spikes required.
Services: club rentals, lessons, snack bar, restaurant, lounge, beer, wine, liquor,
pro shop, driving range, putting course, RV park. **Comments:** a small creek
winds through the course which comes into play on numerous holes. A very
pleasant course to walk. New putting course opened in June of 1998.

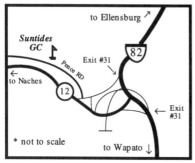

Directions: the golf course is located 3
miles west of Yakima off of Hwy 12.
You will find the golf course on the north
side of the highway with the exit .5 miles
west of the Naches River. At traffic light
turn right, then quick right on Pence Rd.

Course Yardage & Par:
C-6232 yards, par 70.
M-5941 yards, par 70.
W-5509 yards, par 71.

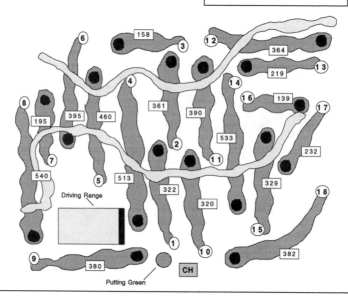

Surfside Golf Course (public, 9 hole course)
31508 "J" Place; Ocean Park, WA 98640
Phone: (360) 665-4148. **Fax:** none. **Internet:** none.
Pros: Louis Runge, PGA, Scott Basse, PGA. **Superintendent:** none.
Rating/Slope: M 68.6/119; W 72.5/124. **Course record:** 66.
Green fees: $20/$12 all week long; Jr & Sr, winter rates (M-F); VISA, M/C.
Power cart: $20/$12. **Pull cart:** $2.50/$1.50. **Trail fee:** $10/$5.
Reservation policy: yes, recommended. Call 7 days in advance for tee times.
Winter condition: dry, the golf course is open all year long weather permitting.
Terrain: flat (easy walking). **Tees:** all grass. **Spikes:** metal spikes permitted.
Services: club rentals, snack bar, pro shop, club memberships, lessons, driving range, putting & chipping greens. **Comments:** the course is very easy to walk. Water comes into play on four holes of the nine holes. The wind plays a major factor from the tee and on your approach shots. Greens are on the small size and can be hard to hold. Good place to play when visiting the Washington coast.

Directions: from I-5 N&S take exit # 104 to Hwy 101 south to Long Beach to Hwy 103. Go north to Ocean Park, following signs to Surfside. The course is located 2 miles north of Ocean Park. Look for signs marking your turn to the golf course. The way is well marked.

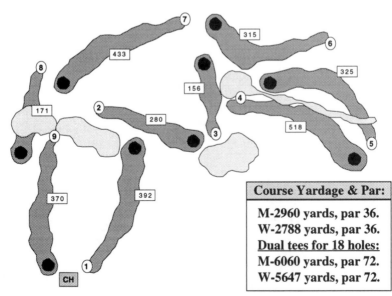

Course Yardage & Par:
M-2960 yards, par 36.
W-2788 yards, par 36.
Dual tees for 18 holes:
M-6060 yards, par 72.
W-5647 yards, par 72.

Tacoma Country & Golf Club (private, 18 hole course)

Gravelly Lake Drive SW; Tacoma, WA 98498
Phone: (253) 588-0404. **Fax:** none. **Internet:** none.
Pro: Rich Friend, PGA. **Superintendent:** Paul Colleran.
Rating/Slope: C 71.6/124; M 70.1/121; W 72.7/124. **Course record:** 62.
Green fees: members only & guests only; very limited reciprocation.
Power cart: private club. **Pull cart:** private club. **Trail fee:** not allowed.
Reservation policy: private club members & guests of members only.
Winter condition: the golf course is open all year long. Dry conditions.
Terrain: flat, some slight hills. **Tees:** grass. **Spikes:** soft spikes required.
Services: club rentals, lessons, snack bar, lounge, beer, wine, liquor, pro shop,
lockers, showers, club memberships, driving range, putting & chipping greens.
Comments: the course was built in 1894, the oldest private golf club, west of
the Mississippi. Greens are large with bunkers coming into play on nearly every
hole. Fairways are tree-lined and play tight in certain area's of the course.

Directions: from I-5 N&S take exit # 124
to Gravelly Lake Dr. Travel west for .5
miles to Country Club Dr. SW. Turn south
to the course.

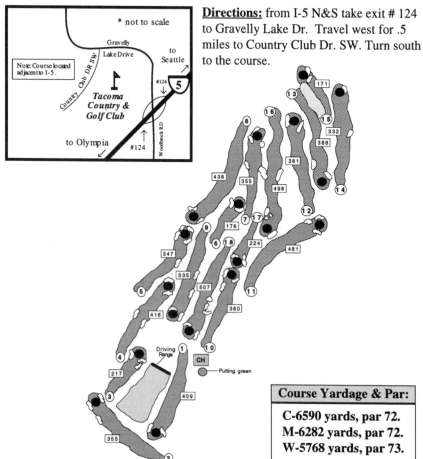

Course Yardage & Par:

C-6590 yards, par 72.
M-6282 yards, par 72.
W-5768 yards, par 73.

Tall Chief Golf Course (public, 18 hole course)
1313 West Snoqualmie River Road SE; Fall City, WA 98024
Phone: (425) 222-5911. Fax: (425) 222-5054. Internet: www.tallchiefgolf.com
Pro: Rick Larson, PGA. Superintendent: Craig Labelle.
Rating/Slope: C 64.4/102; M 63.4/101; W 65.8/105. **Course record:** 63.
Green fees: W/D $20/$14; W/E $23/$15; Jr. & Sr. rates are available
(Monday thru Friday only); outside tournaments are welcome. VISA, M/C.
Power cart: $22/$13. **Pull cart:** $3. **Trail fee:** not available.
Reservation policy: call up to 6 days in advance by phone, 7 days in person.
Winter condition: damp conditions. The golf course is open all year long.
Terrain: flat, some hills. **Tees:** all grass. **Spikes:** metal spikes permitted.
Services: club rentals, lessons, cafe, beer, wine, practice area, driving net.
Comments: this golf course is set in the foothills of the scenic Cascade Mountain Range. An excellent facility for tournaments and private functions. There is a Campground adjacent to the golf course. Friendly course that is worth the trip if you want a fun casual day of golfing with the whole family. Good golf course.

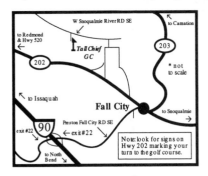

Directions: from I-5 N&S take exit # 168B to Hwy 520 eastbound. Travel east to Hwy 202 E (Redmond-Fall City Road). Turn right and travel 10.5 miles to 308th SE. Turn left and proceed .8 miles, follow the arterial to West Snoqualmie River Road. Go left and proceed .9 miles to the golf course. There are signs on Hwy 202 marking your turn to the golf course.

Course Yardage & Par:

C-5422 yards, par 70.
M-5218 yards, par 70.
W-4945 yards, par 71.

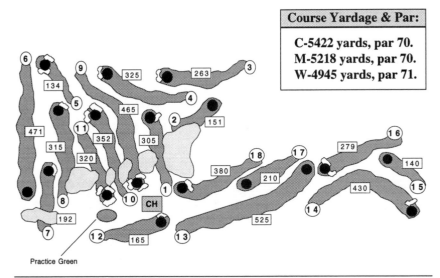

Practice Green

Tam O' Shanter Golf & Country Club (private, 18 hole course)

1313 183rd Avenue NE; Bellevue, WA 98008;
Phone: (425) 746-3502. Fax: (425) 746-4667. Internet: none.
Pro: John Thorsnes, PGA. Superintendent: Tom Corlett.
Rating/Slope: C 70.1/123; M 68.7/121; W 73.8/127. **Course record:** 60.
Green fees: private, members & guests of members only, limited reciprocation.
Power cart: private club members only. **Pull cart:** private. **Trail fee:** private.
Reservation policy: private club members only. No outside play allowed.
Winter condition: the golf course is open all year long. Wet conditions.
Terrain: relatively hilly. **Tees:** grass.• **Spikes:** soft spikes preferred.
Services: club rentals, lessons, snack bar and grill, lounge, restaurant, beer, wine, liquor, large pro shop, putting/chipping green, driving range (irons only).
Comments: must be a homeowner to gain membership in the golf club. Dual tees and dual flags are provided for a full 18 hole round. The greens are large, well bunkered and fast. Well kept private facility that was opened in 1964.

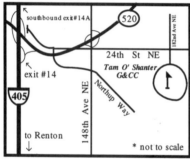

Directions: from I-5 N&S take exit #168B to Hwy 520 eastbound. Exit at 148th SE. Turn south (right) and make the first available left which is NE 24th. Travel east on NE 24th for 2.1 miles to 182nd Ave. NE. Turn south for .7 miles to the golf course.

Course Yardage & Par:

C-3072 yards, par 36.
M-2984 yards, par 36.
W-2704 yards, par 36.
Dual tees for 18 holes:
C-6168 yards, par 71.
M-5854 yards, par 71.
W-5383 yards, par 72.

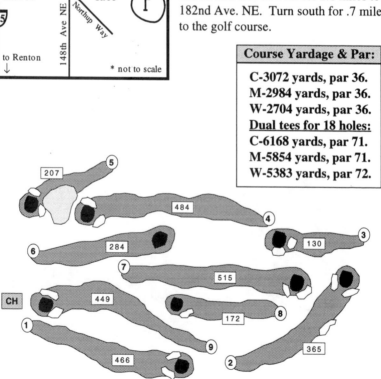

Tanwax Greens (public, 9 hole course)

36510 Mountain Hwy East; Eatonville, WA 98328
Phone: (360) 832-8400. **Fax:** none. **Internet:** none.
Manager: Ray Hendricksen. **Superintendent:** Mark Hendricksen.
Rating/Slope: the golf course has yet to be rated. **Course record:** 62.
Green fees: $22/$12 all week long; Jr & Sr rates ($20/$12); M/C, VISA.
Power cart: $22/$12. **Pull cart:** $5. **Trail fee:** $5 for personal carts.
Reservation policy: yes, call up to 1 week in advance for reservations.
Winter condition: the golf course is open all year long. Dry conditions.
Terrain: flat, some hills. **Tees:** all grass.' **Spikes:** soft spikes preferred.
Services: club rentals, pro shop, putting green, driving range.
Comments: this new layout set in Pierce County is fianlly ready for public play. The new course has water coming into play on four holes. Greens are huge with bumps, swales and tricky ridges. Not overly long Tanwax does challenge any level of golfer. The track sports dual tees for 18 hole play.

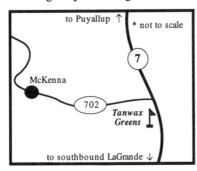

Directions: from Hwy 512 E&W exit southbound to Hwy 7. Follow Hwy 7 southbound through Spanaway and beyond for approximately 16 miles. The golf course is located on Hwy 7 just south of the junction of Hwy 702. The course is on the west side of the Hwy.

Course Yardage & Par:
C-3056 yards, par 36.
M-2908 yards, par 36.
W-2686 yards, par 36.
Dual tees for 18 holes:
C-5970 yards, par 72.
M-5697 yards, par 72.
W-5277 yards, par 72.

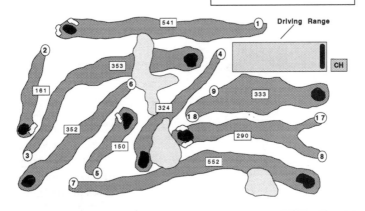

Tapps Island Golf Course (public, 9 hole course)

20818 Island Parkway East; Sumner, WA 98390
Phone: (253) 862-7011. Fax: (253) 862-3310. Internet: none.
Pro: Bob Gelinas. Superintendent: Mark Seman.
Rating/Slope: M 66.5/117; W 68.1/120. **Course record:** 62.
Green fees: W/D $20/$13; W/E $22/$15; Jr & Sr rates (M-Thur.); M/C, VISA.
Power cart: $20/$15. **Pull cart:** $3. **Trail fee:** $8 for personal carts.
Reservation policy: yes, call up to 1 week in advance for tee time reservations.
Winter condition: the golf course is open all year long. Dry conditions.
Terrain: flat, some hills. **Tees:** all grass. **Spikes:** soft spikes preferred.
Services: club rentals, coffee shop, beer, wine, pro shop, putting green.
Comments: water comes into play on five holes. Well bunkered greens and narrow tree-lined make this golf course a real challenge. Do not let the lack of distance fool you this course is very demanding. Rated as the #1 nine hole course in Washington Tapp Island offers good food and challenging golf. Some of the greatest greens around make Tapps Island G. C. worth a special trip.

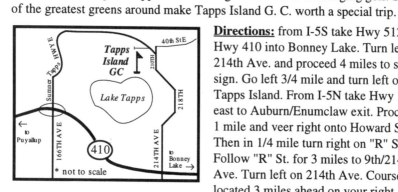

Directions: from I-5S take Hwy 512 to Hwy 410 into Bonney Lake. Turn left at 214th Ave. and proceed 4 miles to stop sign. Go left 3/4 mile and turn left on to Tapps Island. From I-5N take Hwy 18 east to Auburn/Enumclaw exit. Proceed 1 mile and veer right onto Howard St. Then in 1/4 mile turn right on "R" St. Follow "R" St. for 3 miles to 9th/214th Ave. Turn left on 214th Ave. Course located 3 miles ahead on your right.

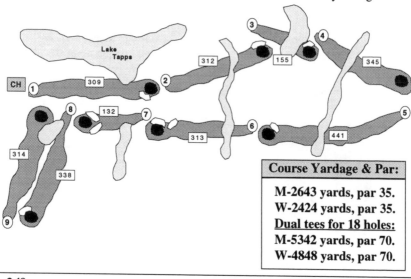

Course Yardage & Par:

M-2643 yards, par 35.
W-2424 yards, par 35.
Dual tees for 18 holes:
M-5342 yards, par 70.
W-4848 yards, par 70.

Tekoa Golf Club (public, 9 hole course)
off of Hwy 27; P. O. Box 809; Tekoa, WA 99033
Phone: (509) 284-5607. **Fax:** none. **Internet:** none.
Pro: none available. **Manager:** none available.
Rating/Slope: M 64.2/105; W 68.2/113. **Course record:** 30.
Green fees: W/D $10; W/E & holidays $12; no credit cards.
Power cart: $12. **Pull cart:** none available. **Trail fee:** $3.
Reservation policy: none required play is on a first come first serve basis.
Winter condition: depending on the weather, but the course is generally closed.
Terrain: flat, some rolling hills. **Tees:** grass. **Spikes:** metal spikes permitted.
Services: the golf course has very limited services, putting green, league play.
Comments: this course features wide open rolling terrain and a few trees. The golf course plays very short with no hole over 500 yards. Great walking course for the first time or senior golfer. This course is rustic in design and grooming.

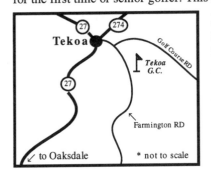

Directions: the golf course is located 1/2 mile south of Tekoa off of Hwy 27. Look for Farmington Road for your turn to the golf course. When you get to Golf Course Road you will turn left. Proceed on Golf Course Road to the clubhouse. Look for signs marking your turn to the clubhouse.

Course Yardage & Par:
M-2550 yards, par 35.
W-2550 yards, par 35.

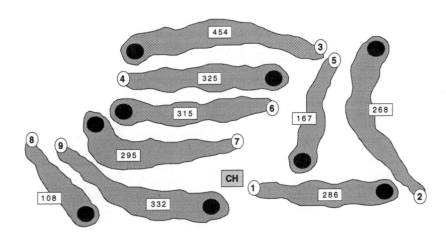

The Golf Club @ Newcastle (public, 36 hole course)

15401 SE Newcastle-Coal Creek Pkwy; Newcastle, WA 98059
Phone: (425) 455-0606. Fax: not available. Internet: none.
General Manager: Matthew Guzik. Superintendent: to be determined.
Rating/Slope: the golf course is not yet rated. **Course record:** N/A.
Green fees: to be determined; call for information on credit card usage.
Power cart: to be determined. **Pull cart:** to be determined. **Trail fee:** N/A.
Reservation policy: you may call ahead for a tee time.
Winter condition: the golf course is open all year long. Weather permitting.
Terrain: some hills. **Tees:** all grass. **Spikes:** soft spikes required.
Services: club rentals, lessons, snack bar, pro shop, driving range, putting &
chipping greens, club memberships available, state of the art practice facility.
Comments: this is a unique new course built atop the old Newcastle landfill.
The course is already gaining notariety. The course has received the "Excellence
in Environmental Health" award from the National Assocaition of County and
City Health Officials. The basic design is by the renowned architect Robert E.
Cupp of Atlanta with Fred Couples of PGA Tour fame acting as design consult-
ant. Spectacular views of the surrounding countryside and the Bellevue area
abound from nearly every tee. Championship caliber golf awaits you when you
step up to the first tee. This whole facility promises to be one of the best in the
state of Washington. The first 18 holes is set to open in the spring of 1999
with another 18 soon to follow. Be sure to put Newcastle on your must play list.

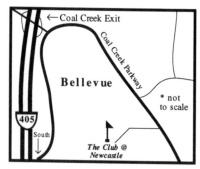

Directions: from I-405 take the Coal
Creek exit. Proceed east on Coal Creek
Parkway to your turn up to the golf
course. Signs will be posted to the course.

Course Yardage & Par:
Coal Creek North Course **Gold: 7065 yards, par 72.** **Blue: 6635 yards, par 72.** **White: 6100 yards, par 72.** **Red: 5135 yards, par 72.**

Course Yardage & Par:
China Creek South Course **Gold: 6940 yards, par 72.** **Blue: 6440 yards, par 72.** **White: 6030 yards, par 72.** **Red: 5120 yards, par 72.**

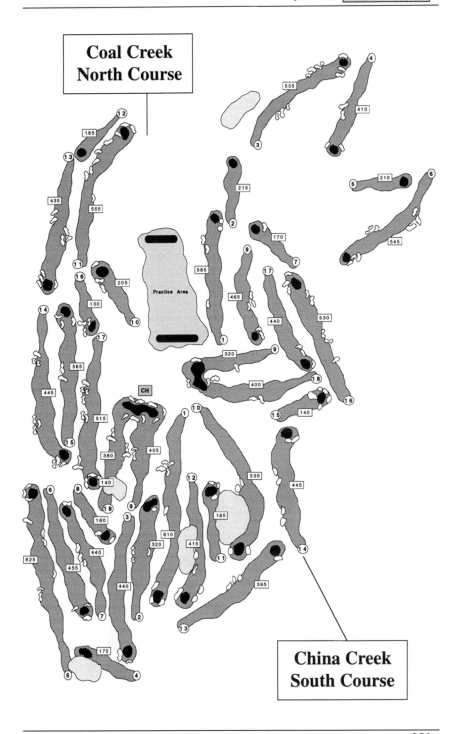

**Coal Creek
North Course**

**China Creek
South Course**

Three Lakes Golf Course (public, 18 hole course)
2695 Golf Drive; Malaga, WA 98828
Phone: (509) 663-5448. **Fax:** (509) 662-5355. **Internet:** none.
Pro: John Christensen, PGA. **Superintendent:** Casey Creighton.
Rating/Slope: M 65.2/104; W 70.1/121. **Course record:** 61.
Green fees: Mon.-Thur. $20/$12; Friday-Sunday $25/$15; Jr. rates available.
Power cart: $22/$13. **Pull cart:** $3/$2. **Trail fee:** $10 (annual pass available).
Reservation policy: yes, please call 7 days in advance for a tee time.
Winter condition: closed December to February depending on the weather.
Terrain: relatively hilly. **Tees:** grass. **Spikes:** soft spikes required.
Services: club rentals, lessons, restaurant, beer, wine, pro shop, driving range, putting green. **Comments:** narrow tree-lined fairways make this course a real challenge. The golf course is well-kept and offers scenic views of the Columbia River and the surrounding countryside of the Wenatchee Valley.

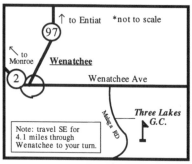

Directions: from Hwy 97 take the Wenatchee exit. Go through the city center (on Wenatchee Ave). Travel 4 miles to the golf course turnoff which is southeast of the city. Turn right at West Malaga Road. The golf course will be on your left hand side. Look for signs.

Course Yardage & Par:
M-5327 yards, par 69.
W-5233 yards, par 72.

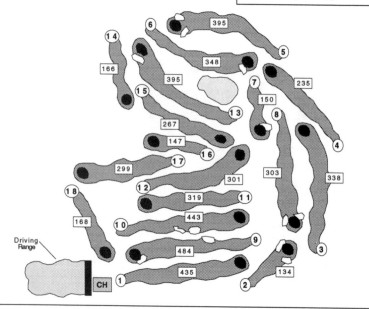

Three Rivers Golf Course (public, 18 hole course)

2222 South River Road; Kelso, WA 98626
Phone: (360) 423-4653. Fax: (360) 423-4653. Internet: none.
Pro: Chris Smith, PGA. Superintendent: Walt Stender.
Rating/Slope: C 70.8/117; M 68.3/112; W 67.2/110. **Course record:** 64.
Green fees: W/D $18/$13; W/E $20/$16; Jr & Sr rates (M-F); no credit cards.
Power cart: $22/$12. **Pull cart:** $2. **Trail fee:**$10 (annual pass available).
Reservation policy: yes, call up to 1 week in advance for tee time reservations.
Winter condition: the golf course is open all year long, dry (drains very well).
Terrain: flat, some slight hills. **Tees:** grass. **Spikes:** metal spikes permitted.
Services: club rentals, lessons, snack bar, lounge, restaurant, beer, wine, lockers,
pro shop, club memberships, covered driving range, putting & chipping greens.
Comments: the course is built upon the Mt. St. Helens ash that filled the area, it
therefore has excellent drainage. The course is wide open and has large greens.

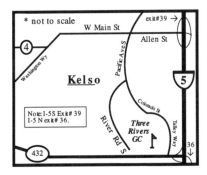

Directions: from I-5 take exit #36 and go
west on Hwy 432, turn north on Talley
Way which becomes Colorado Street and
then S. Pacific Avnue, Turn left on to
South River Road and follow signs to the
golf course.

Course Yardage & Par:
C-6846 yards, par 72.
M-6161 yards, par 72.
W-5455 yards, par 72.

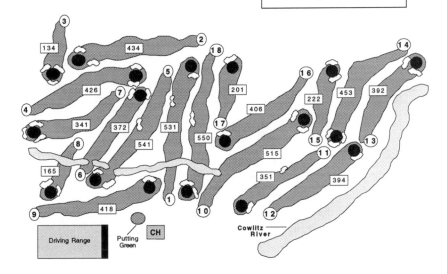

Touchet Valley Golf Course (public, 9 hole course)
North Pine Street; P.O. Box 54; Dayton, WA 99328
Phone: (509) 382-4851. Fax: none. Internet: none.
Manager: unavailable. Pro: unavailable.
Rating/Slope: C 67.8/114; M 66.8/115; W 72/122. **Course record:** 30.
Green fees: W/D $14/$10; W/E $16/$12; no special rates.
Power cart: $18/$10. **Pull cart:** $2.50. **Trail fee:** $5 for personal carts.
Reservation policy: please call ahead for weekend tee times. 1 day in advance.
Winter condition: the golf course is closed from October 16th to March 15th.
Terrain: flat (easy walking). **Tees:** all grass. **Spikes:** soft spikes only.
Services: club rentals, snack bar, restaurant. **Comments:** a unique setting within
the grounds of a horse racing track (Columbia Co. Fairgrounds Racing Track).
The golf course is flat and is very easy to walk. Greens are large and very flat.

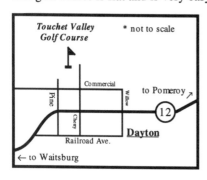

Directions: the golf course is located
in Dayton on the north side of Hwy 12.
You will turn westbound on Main Street.
Then turn right at the Dayton Mercantile
store. Follow street north for 2 blocks.

Course Yardage & Par:
C-2931 yards, par 36.
M-2841 yards, par 36.
W-2745 yards, par 36.
Dual tees for 18 holes:
C-5862 yards, par 72.
M-5682 yards, par 72.
W-5490 yards, par 72.

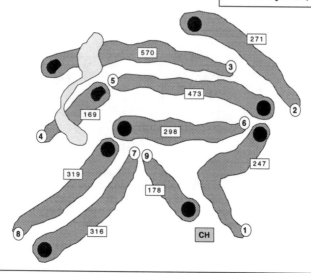

Tri City Country Club (semi-private, 18 hole course)
314 North Underwood Street; Kennewick, WA 99336
Phone: (509) 783-6014. **Fax:** (509) 783-1773. **Internet:** none.
Pro: Chris Isaacson, PGA. **Superintendent:** LeAnn Brosseau.
Rating/Slope: C 64.2/114; M 62.5/112; W 65.2/115. **Course record:** 57.
Green fees: Monday-Thursday $22; Friday-Sunday $30; no credit cards.
Power cart: $24/$12. **Pull cart:** $2.50. **Trail fee:** $15 for personal carts.
Reservation policy: yes, you may call 2 days ahead for your tee time.
Winter condition: the golf course is open all year long, weather permitting.
Terrain: relatively hilly. **Tees:** all grass. **Spikes:** soft spikes only.
Services: club rentals, lessons, pro shop, restaurant and lounge (members only).
Comments: the course sports tree-lined fairways and many well-trapped greens.
Water comes into play on three holes. In order to score well you must be able to
place your tee shot in the proper position. Excellent course that can play tough.

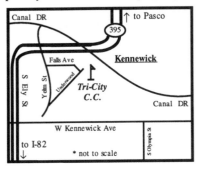

Directions: from Hwy 12 take the exit
Hwy 14 and continue to Yelm St. Turn
left. Travel to Clearwater. Left on
Clearwater and proceed to Underwood
where you turn into the golf course.

Course Yardage & Par:
C-5010 yards, par 65.
M-4693 yards, par 65.
W-4400 yards, par 65.

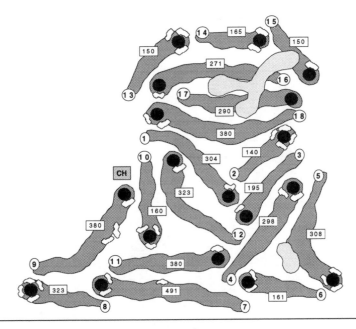

Tri-Mountain Golf Course (public, 18 hole course)

1701 NW 299th Street; Ridgefield, WA 98642
Phone: (888) TRI-MNTN. **Fax:** (360) 887-3004. **Internet:** www.cybergolf.com/tri-mtn
Pro: Chuck DaSilva, PGA. **Superintendent:** Dan Bierscheid.
Rating/Slope: C 71.1/120; M 68.6/117; W 69.8/117. **Course record:** 67.
Green fees: W/D $25/$16; W/E & Hol. $31/$20; call for winter, twilight rates.
Power cart: $24/$14. **Pull cart:** $3/$2. **Trail fee:** no private carts allowed.
Reservation policy: please call 7 days in advance for a tee time reservation.
Winter condition: the golf course is open all year long. Good conditions.
Terrain: flat, w/ rolling hills. **Tees:** all grass. **Spikes:** metal spikes permitted.
Services: club rentals, lessons, coffee shop, liquor, pro shop, aquatic driving range, putting green, putting course, banquet room, on course beverage cart.
Comments: the course offers a number of challenges such as 74 sand traps, 11 lakes and award winning greens. This links-stlye golf course offers a new clubhouse, restaurant and new drainage for 1999. Golf Groups are welcome. This is a Clark County facility professionally managed by Golf Resources NW.

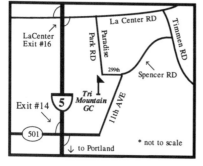

Directions: from I-5 northbound and southbound take exit #14. Travel eastbound on Hwy 501 to 11th Ave. Turn left on 11th. Proceed to 299th. Turn left on 299th to the golf course. Look for signs to the golf course.

Course Yardage & Par:
C-6850 yards, par 72.
M-6091 yards, par 72.
W-5284 yards, par 72.

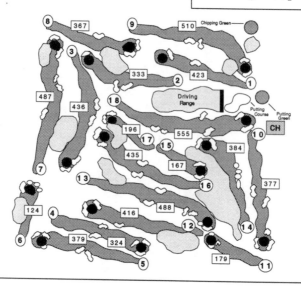

Trophy Lake Golf & Casting Club (public, 18 hole course)
3900 SW Lake Flora Road; Port Orchard, WA 98366
Phone: (360) 876-8337. Fax: (360) 876-6197. Internet: none.
Pro: Brady Hatfield, PGA. Superintendent: unavailable.
Rating/Slope: the golf course has not been rated. **Course record:** N/A.
Green fees: to be determined upon opening of the golf course.
Power cart: to be determined. **Pull cart:** to be determined. **Trail fee:** N/A.
Reservation policy: please call 30 days in advance for a tee time reservation.
Winter condition: the golf course is open all year long. Good conditions.
Terrain: flat, some hills. **Tees:** all grass. **Spikes:** metal spikes permitted.
Services: club rentals, lessons, restuarant, snack bar, pro shop, beer, wine,
liquor, driving range. **Comments:** opening May 15th 1999 this champion
ship layout will offer something for both the golfing and fishing enthusiast.
Gently rolling terrian provides spectacular views of Mt. Rainier and the Olympic
Mountains. The tournament pavilion and clubhouse oversee action on the 18th
green. Fishing reservations will be available in fall of 1999. Worth a special trip.

Directions: from Hwy 16 exit at the Sedwick Road exit. Head westbound on Sedwick Road (which will become Lake Flora Road) for 3.8 miles. The golf course entrance will be on your left.

Course Yardage & Par:
T-7206 yards, par 72.
C-6756 yards, par 72.
M-6162 yards, par 72.
W-5342 yards, par 72.

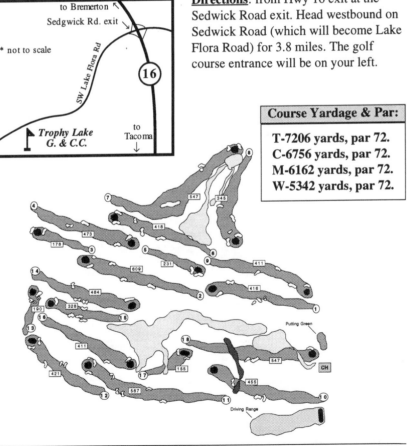

Tumwater Valley Golf Club (public, 18 hole course)

4611 Tumwater Valley Drive; Tumwater, WA 98501
Phone: (360) 943-9500. **Fax:** (360) 943-4378. **Internet: none.**
Pro: Chris Mitchell, PGA. Superintendent: Skip Wirtz.
Rating/Slope: T 73.1/120; C 70.7/115; M 68.8/111; W 70.4/114. **Record:** 60.
Green fees: $24/$17 all week long (no 9 hole rate on weekend play).
Power cart: $22/$11. **Pull cart:** $2. **Trail fee:** $10 for personal carts.
Reservation policy: yes, please call up to 7 days in advance for reservations.
Winter condition: dry, excellent drainage. Course is open all year long.
Terrain: flat, some slight hills. **Tees:** grass. **Spikes:** soft spikes only.
Services: club rentals, lessons, snack bar, beer, beverages, pro shop, driving range, putting & chipping green, golf schools available, club memberships.
Comments: the course sports quick, undulating greens, and numerous sand or water hazards on seemingly every hole. Fairways are wide giving you room to work the ball off the tee. An excellent facility that has a great learning program.

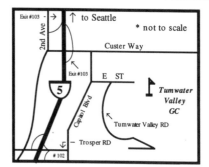

Directions: from I-5 N&S take exit #103. Proceed southbound for .3 miles to Custer Way. Turn left and proceed for .2 miles to Capitol Blvd. Turn right for .4 miles to "E" Street. Turn left and proceed for .4 miles to the golf course. Look for signs marking your way.

Course Yardage & Par:
T-7154 yards, par 72.
C-6523 yards, par 72.
M-6108 yards, par 72.
W-5428 yards, par 72.

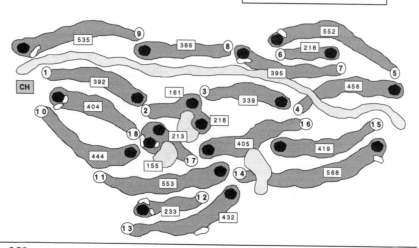

Twin Lakes Golf & Country Club (private, 18 hole course)
3538 SW 320th; Federal Way, WA 98023
Phone: (253) 838-0345. Fax: none. Internet: none.
Pro: Joe Trembly, PGA. Superintendent: Dennis Campbell.
Rating/Slope: C 70.6/122; M 68.7/119 W 69.7/118. **Course record:** 62.
Green fees: private club member and guests only; reciprocates (very limited).
Power cart: private club members only. **Pull cart:** private. **Trail fee:** private.
Reservation policy: private club members only & guests of members only.
Winter condition: the golf course is open all year long. Dry conditions.
Terrain: flat, some hills. **Tees:** all grass. **Spikes:** soft spikes only.
Services: club rentals, lessons, lounge, restaurant, snack bar, beer, wine, liquor, lockers, showers, pro shop, putting & chipping greens, club memberships.
Comments: sweeping views of Puget Sound are seen from some fairways. A very tight, tree-lined track. Greens are large, fast and firm. Bunkers come into play throughout the golf course and are a major factor. Excellent private course.

Directions: from I-5 N&S take exit #143 to SW 320th. Travel west for 2.8 miles to the golf course which will be on your left hand side. The golf course can be seen from SW 320th Street which is a main road in Federal Way. Look for a small sign indicating your turn into the parking lot.

Course Yardage & Par:
C-6221 yards, par 72.
M-5852 yards, par 72.
W-5123 yards, par 72.

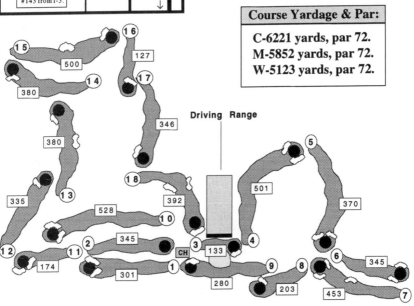

Twin Rivers Golf Course (public, 18 hole course)

4446 Preston-Fall City Road SE; Fall City, WA 98024
Phone: (425) 222-7575. Fax: (425) 222-6924. Internet: none.
Pro: Jeff Tachell, PGA. Manager: Richard Rutledge. Supt.: Doug Rutledge.
Rating/Slope: C 65.0/100; M 61.3/92; W 65.4/100. **Course record:** 63.
Green fees: $25/$16 everyday; Jr. & Sr. rates (Monday thru Friday).
Power cart: $22/$12. **Pull cart:** $4. **Trail fee:** no charge.
Reservation policy: you may call 7 days in advance for your tee-times.
Winter condition: the golf course open all year long. Good conditions.
Terrain: flat, easy to walk. **Tees:** all grass. **Spikes:** metal spikes permitted.
Services: club rentals, snack bar, beer, wine, driving range, putting green.
Comments: this newer 9 hole track has been expanded to 18 holes. The layout is fairly wide open featuring medium to small greens that are in excellent condition. Twin Rivers is a very friendly course that is a pleasure to play.

Directions: from I-90 take exit #22. Follow the Preston-Fall City Road approximately 4.5 miles to the course which will be on your right. From Redmond travel east on Hwy 202 to Fall City. Turn right (south) on the Preston-Fall City Rd. approximately .5 miles to the course on your left. Look for sign.

Course Yardage & Par:
M-5760 yards, par 70.
W-4862 yards, par 70.

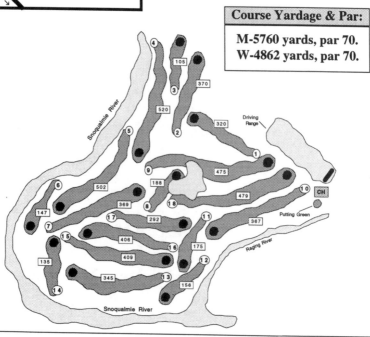

Tyee Valley Golf Course (public, 18 hole course)

2401 South 192nd; Seattle, WA 98188
Phone: (206) 878-3540. **Fax:** none. **Internet:** none.
Pro: Mark Olson. **Superintendent:** Jeremy Islam.
Rating/Slope: C 64.3/106; M 63.1/104; W 69.2/114. **Course record:** 60.
Green fees: W/D $19/$13.50; W/E $20/$14; Sr./Jr. rates (M-F); M/C, VISA.
Power cart: $18/$10. **Pull cart:** $3.50/$2.50. **Trail fee:** $7.
Reservation policy: yes, call up to 1 week in advance for tee time reservations.
Winter condition: the golf course is open all year long, dry (drains well).
Terrain: relatively hilly. **Tees:** grass. **Spikes:** metal spikes permitted.
Services: club rentals lessons, restaurant, beer, wine, pop, putting green.
Comments: fairly easy walking course. Greens are guarded by green side bunkers. The course is fairly wide open giving the golfer room off the tee. Water comes into play on a few holes and can be a factor. Fair conditioned golf course.

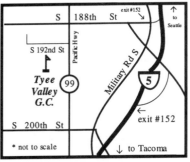

Directions: from I-5 N&S take exit #152 to S 188th. Proceed west for 1.1 miles to Pacific Hwy S. (Hwy 99S). Turn south for 2 miles to S 192nd. Turn west for .3 miles to the golf course. Look for signs marking your way to the golf course.

Course Yardage & Par:

C-5845 yards, par 71.
M-5812 yards, par 71.
W-5414 yards, par 73.

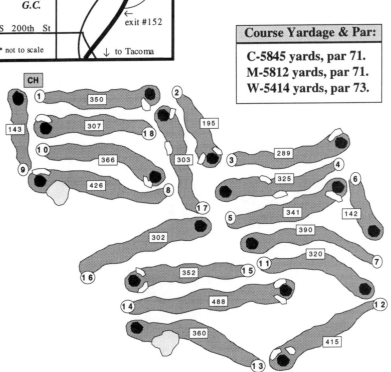

University Golf Club (public, 9 hole course)
754 124th South; Tacoma, WA 98444
Phone: (253) 535-7393. **Fax:** none. **Internet:** none.
Pro: Gary L. Cinotto. **Superintendent:** Benjamin Cinotto.
Rating/Slope: M 64.7/101; W 69.7/108. **Course record:** 62.
Green fees: $14/$9; Jr & Sr rates (weekdays only) $ 11/$7; M/C, VISA.
Power cart: $14/$7. **Pull cart:** $2. **Trail fee:** $3/$2 for personal carts.
Reservation policy: strictly open play, times are on a first come first play basis.
Winter condition: dry, drains well. The course is open all year long.
Terrain: very flat. **Tees:** all grass. **Spikes:** soft spikes preferred.
Services: club rentals, lessons, snack bar, pro shop, club memberships, putting
& chipping greens. **Comments:** the course is easy to walk and has excellent
greens. The track stays very dry during the winter months due to its excellent
drainage. Greens are medium in size with some guarded by bunkers.

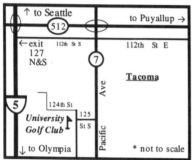

Directions: from I-5 N&S take exit
127 to Hwy 512 E. Travel east for 2.1
miles to Highway 7 south. Proceed
southbound on Highway 7 for 1 mile to
125th Street S. Turn west and proceed to
Yakima Avenue, then turn right to the
golf course. Look for signs.

Course Yardage & Par:
M-2732 yards, par 35.
W-2732 yards, par 36.
Dual tees for 18 holes:
M-5391 yards, par 70.
W-5391 yards, par 71.

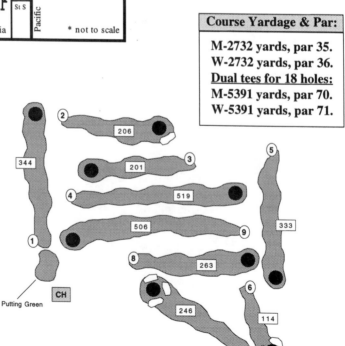

Useless Bay Golf & Country Club (private, 18 hole course)

5725 South Country Club Drive; Langley, WA 98260
Phone: (360) 321-5958. **Fax:** none. **Internet:** none.
Pro: Bill Davis, PGA. **Superintendent:** Fred Vanbenschoten.
Rating/Slope: C 70.1/119; M 69.0/116; W 70.9/121. **Course record:** 65.
Green fees: private club members & guests only; reciprocates.
Power cart: private club members only. **Pull cart:** private. **Trail fee:** private.
Reservation policy: private club members & guests of members only.
Winter condition: damp conditions. The golf course is open all year long.
Terrain: flat, some hills. **Tees:** all grass. **Spikes:** soft spikes only.
Services: club rentals, lessons, snack bar, lounge, restaurant, beer, wine, liquor, pro shop, putting green, club memberships. **Comments:** there are many water hazards to contend with, along with a number of holes defined by out-of-bounds. Greens are large in size and have some undulations. Great private golf course that is set in a beautiful area of Washington State. No outside play allowed.

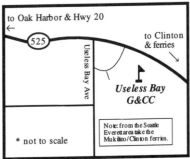

Directions: from the Mukilteo-Clinton ferry take Hwy 525 for approximately 7 miles to Useless Bay Road. Turn left to the golf course. Look for signs.

Course Yardage & Par:
C-6389 yards, par 72.
M-6134/6040 yards, par 72.
W-5493 yards, par 74.

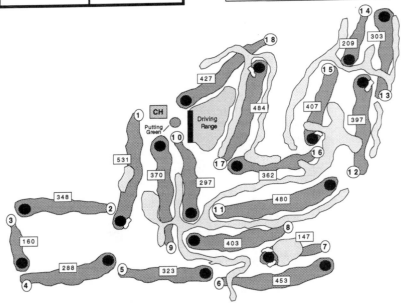

Valley View Golf Course (public, 9 hole course)

Liberty Lake Road; P. O. Box 326; Liberty Lake, WA 99019
Phone: (509) 928-3484. Fax: none. Internet: none
Pro: Dennis Reger, PGA. Superintendent: Dennis Reger.
Rating/Slope: M 58/no slope; W 62/no slope. **Course record:** 28.
Green fees: W/D $12.50/$8.50 W/E $13/$9; Jr/Sr rates (M-F); no credit cards.
Power cart: $12/$7. **Pull cart:** $2.50. **Trail fee:** no charge.
Reservation policy: not required. Times are on a first come first served basis.
Winter condition: the golf course is closed from December to March.
Terrain: flat (easy walking). **Tees:** all grass. **Spikes:** soft spikes only.
Services: club rentals, lessons, restaurant, lounge, beer, wine, driving range.
Comments: Spokane's only executive course. The course is well maintained and easy to walk. Water comes into play on two holes. Two sets of tees.

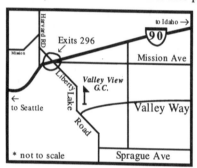

Directions: from I-90 eastbound and westbound take exit # 296 (Liberty Lake). The golf course is located two blocks to the south on Liberty Lake Road. Look for signs marking your way to the course.

Course Yardage & Par:
M-2072 yards, par 32.
W-2072 yards, par 32.
Dual tees for 18 holes:
M-4095 yards, par 62.
W-4095 yards, par 62.

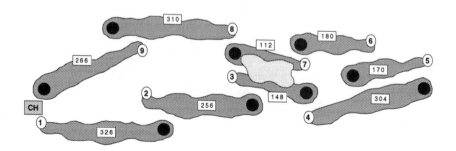

Vashon Island Golf & Country Club (private, 9 hole course)

24615 75th Avenue SW; Vashon, WA 98070
Phone: (206) 463-2006. **Fax:** (206) 463-6489. **Internet: none.**
Pro: Steve Englund, PGA. **Superintendent:** Ron Krieger.
Rating/Slope: M 68.0/117; W 70.3/120. **Course record:** 63.
Green fees: private club members only; reciprocates.
Power cart: private club. **Pull cart:** private. **Trail fee:** private.
Reservation policy: private club with limited outside play. Call pro shop.
Winter condition: the golf course is open all year long. Dry conditions.
Terrain: very hilly. **Tees:** all grass. **Spikes:** no metal spikes in summer.
Services: lessons, lounge, restaurant, beer, wine, liquor, pro shop, putting green, club memberships. **Comments:** dual tees available for a full 18 hole round. Few hazards to contend with. The course is tree lined with bunkers guarding the greens. Excellent track that plays much longer than the yardage.

Directions: from the West Seattle ferry follow Vashon Island Hwy for 6.1 miles to SW 204th. To east for 1 mile to George Edwards Road. Turn south for 12 miles to SW 228th. Turn east for .1 mile to Portage-Dockton Road. Turn south and proceed 1 mile to the course.

Course Yardage & Par:
M-3006 yards, par 35.
W-2618 yards, par 36.
Dual tees for 18 holes:
M-5890 yards, par 70.
W-5195 yards, par 72.

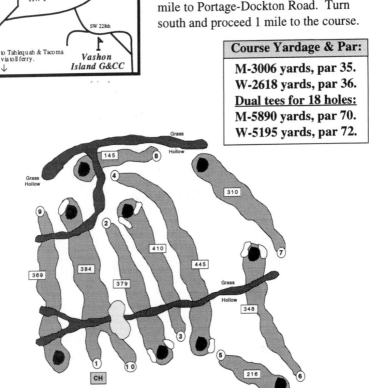

Veterans Memorial Golf Course (public, 18 hole course)
201 East Rees; P.O. Box 70; Walla Walla, WA 99362
Phone: (509) 527-4507. Fax: (509) 529-7586. Internet: weman@wwwcs.com.
Pro: Pat Welch, PGA, Nick Manolopoulos, PGA. 18 hole course, range.
Rating/Slope: C 70.7/115; M 69.2/111; W 70.0/114. **Course record:** 63.
Green fees: $18/$13 all week long; Jr. & Sr. rates; M/C, VISA (merchandise only).
Power cart: $24/$13. **Pull cart:** $3. **Trail fee:** $6 for personal carts.
Reservation policy: yes, please call Tuesday for the following weekend.
Winter condition: the golf course is open all year long weather permitting, dry.
Terrain: flat, some hills. **Tees:** all grass. **Spikes:** metal spikes permitted.
Services: club rentals, lessons, snack bar, resturant, lounge, beer, wine, liquor,
pro shop, lockers, putting green, driving range. **Comments:** Veterans Memorial
is well-kept with tree-lined fairways and good greens. If you are looking for a
course in eastern Washington try Veterans you will not be disappointed.

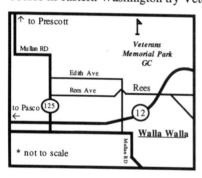

Directions: the golf course is located east
of the city of Walla Walla off of Hwy 12.
Take the Rees Rd. exit to the golf course.
Go westbound for 1 block and turn right
on Rees Rd. Proceed and turn left to the
golf course. Look for signs at your turn.

Course Yardage & Par:
C-6646 yards, par 72.
M-6304 yards, par 72.
W-5403 yards, par 72.

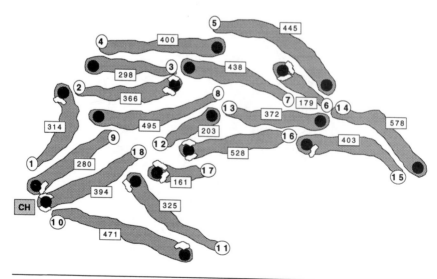

Vic Meyer's Golf Course (public, 9 hole course)

34228 Park Lake Road NE; Box 141; Coulee City, WA 99115
Phone: (509) 632-5738. **Fax:** none. **Internet:** none.
Pro: none. **Superintendent:** John Johanson.
Rating/Slope: C 70.9/105; M 67.9/102; W 70.8/108. **Course record:** 69.
Green fees: W/D $14/$10; W/E $16/$11; no special rates; VISA, M/C.
Power cart: $20/$12. **Pull cart:** $2. **Trail fee:** none for personal carts.
Reservation policy: yes, call ahead for a tee time. (especially in summer).
Winter condition: the golf course is closed from mid-October to mid-March.
Terrain: relatively hilly. **Tees:** grass. **Spikes:** soft spikes preferred.
Services: club rentals, snack bar, pro shop, showers, putting green, RV parking.
Comments: the course is a part the the Sun Lakes recreation area. The golf course is set atop the cliffs over looking Sun Lakes. Fairways are bordered by desert and is a major factor off the tee. This is a fair conditioned golf course.

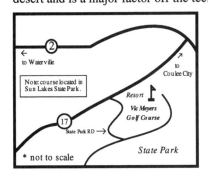

Directions: the golf course is located off Hwy 17 north of Ephrata and Soap Lake at the Sun Lakes State Park Resort. From Hwy 17 turn at the park entrance and follow signs to the golf course.

Course Yardage & Par:
C-3123 yards, par 35.
M-2897 yards, par 35.
W-2702 yards, par 35.

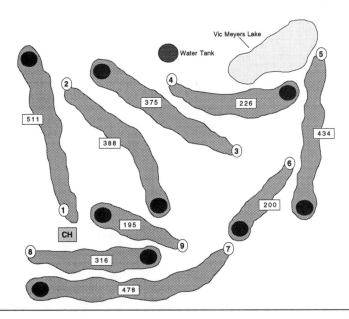

Vicwood Links Golf Course (public, 18 hole course)
8383 Vicwood Lane; Lacey, WA 98516
Phone: (360) 455-8383 or 1-800-55-TEE-IT. **Internet:** www.cybergolf.com/vicwood
Dir. of Golf: Ron Coleman. **Pro:** Mike Philippart, PGA. **Supt. Kirk Anderson.**
Rating/Slope: Unavailable. **Course record:** to be determined.
Green fees: to be determined; M/C, VISA, AMEX.
Power cart: to be determined. **Pull cart:** N/A. **Trail fee:** not allowed.
Reservation policy: please call up to 7 days in advance for tee times.
Winter condition: course open all year long. Drains very well.
Terrain: relatively flat, walkable. **Tees:** grass. **Spikes:** soft spikes April-Sept.
Services: full service clubhouse featuring Two-Woods Eatery, beverage cart services, club rentals, lessons, pro shop, driving range, putting green & course.
Comments: opening March 1999 this links-style course features commanding views of Mount Rainier and Puget Sound. Large greens and wide fairways make this course very playable for every level of golfer. Golf groups are welcome any time of year. Professionally managed by Golf Resources Northwest.

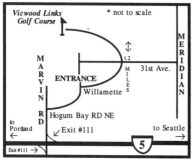

Directions: from the north take exit #111 from I-5. Turn right at the light. Go approximately 125 yards and turn right on Hogum Bay Rd. Go .3 miles to Meridian Campus Entrance at Willamette Dr., go 2.2 miles to the golf course. From the south take exit #111 from I-5. Turn left at the light and go over the freeway. Proceed through stop light and follow the above directions.

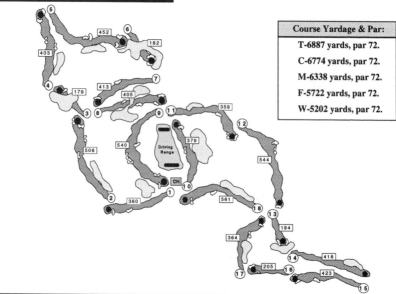

Course Yardage & Par:
T-6887 yards, par 72.
C-6774 yards, par 72.
M-6338 yards, par 72.
F-5722 yards, par 72.
W-5202 yards, par 72.

Village Greens Golf Course (public, 18 hole course)

2298 Fircrest Drive SE; Port Orchard, WA 98366
Phone: (360) 871-1222. Fax: none. Internet: none.
Pro: Doug Hathaway, PGA. Superintendent: Doug Hathaway.
Rating/Slope: M 55.7/87; W 58.4/90. **Course record:** 51.
Green fees: $14/$12 all week long; Jr & Sr rates and military rates.
Power cart: $15/$10. **Pull cart:** $2. **Trail fee:** no trail fee.
Reservation policy: yes, please call ahead for a tee time.
Winter condition: the golf course is open all year long. Dry conditions.
Terrain: flat, some hills. **Tees:** all grass. **Spikes:** metal spikes permitted.
Services: club rentals, lessons, snack bar, pro shop, club memberships,
putting & chipping greens, driving range. **Comments:** narrow tree-lined
fairways and small greens make this short golf course very difficult. Varied
terrain gives the golfer a wide variety of lies from the fairway. Worth a trip if
you want a change of pace from the back breaker 6500 yard course. The new
course record at Village Greens was just posted by 12 year old Brady Sharp.

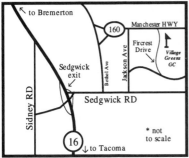

Directions: from I-5 N&S take the exit
for Hwy 16 W. Exit Hwy 16 at the 2nd
Port Ochard exit, (sign will read Tremont
and old Clifton Rd.). Stay on Tremont
through four stop lights and continue
until you reach a stop sign. Turn right and
proceed for 1 1/2 blocks and then turn left
on Fircrest. The course should be ahead.

Course Yardage & Par:
M-3255 yards, par 58.
W-3255 yards, par 62.

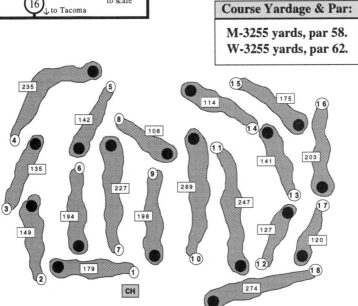

Walla Walla Country Club (private, 18 hole course)

1390 Country Club Road; Box 2246; Walla Walla, WA 99362
Phone: (509) 525-1562. Fax: (509) 525-1257. Internet: none.
Pro: Steve Stull, PGA. Superintendent: Jeff Blanc.
Rating/Slope: M 70.8/125; W 71.9/125. **Course record:** 63.
Green fees: private club members only; reciprocates; no credit cards.
Power cart: private club. **Pull cart:** private club. **Trail fee:** private club.
Reservation policy: private club members only & guests only.
Winter condition: varies on the weather. Generally open during the winter.
Terrain: relatively hilly. **Tees:** all grass. **Spikes:** metal spikes not permitted.
Services: club rentals, lessons, restaurant, lounge, beer, wine, liquor, pro shop,
lockers, showers, driving range, putting & chipping greens, club memberships.
Comments: The course features sand and grass bunkers, narrow tree-lined
fairways, and water. The fairways are plush during the summer and the views
from this course are great. This well kept facility is one of the state's finest.

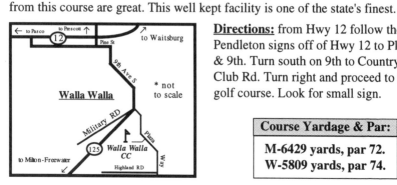

Directions: from Hwy 12 follow the
Pendleton signs off of Hwy 12 to Plaza
& 9th. Turn south on 9th to Country
Club Rd. Turn right and proceed to the
golf course. Look for small sign.

Course Yardage & Par:
M-6429 yards, par 72.
W-5809 yards, par 74.

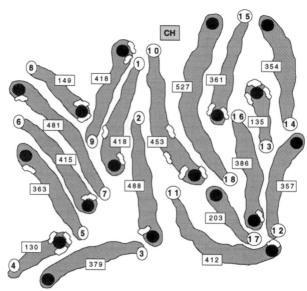

Walter E. Hall Memorial Golf Course (public, 18 hole course)

1226 West Casino Road; Everett, WA 98204

Phone: (425) 353-4653. **Fax:** (425) 423-9134. **Internet:** www.cybergolf.com/walterhall
Dir. of Golf: Mike Coury. **Pro:** Tyrone Hardy, PGA. **Supt.:** Barry Galde.
Rating/Slope: C 69.6/117; M 68.6/115; W 71.6/118. **Course record:** 63.
Green fees: Everett resident $16/$12; non-resident $21/$16; Jr. & Sr. rates.
Power cart: $20/$10. **Pull cart:** $3. **Trail fee:** no private carts allowed.
Reservation policy: please call up to 1 week in advance for weekday tee times.
Please call on Monday 9am for your weekend and holiday tee times.
Winter condition: the golf course is open all year long. Drains fairly well.
Terrain: flat, some hills. **Tees:** all grass. **Spikes:** metal spikes permitted.
Services: club rentals, lessons, restaurant, beer, wine, pro shop, club member-
ships, putting green, practice area. **Comments:** the course is very busy during
the summer. An easy walking golf course that only has a few elevation changes.
Walter E. Hall hosts a creek which winds through most of the back nine. This is
a City of Everett Parks facility, professionally managed by Golf Resources NW.

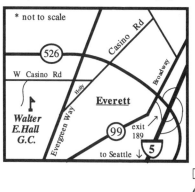

Directions: from I-5 N&S take exit # 189 to Hwy 526 W. Turn west and travel .6 miles to Evergreen Way. Turn south. Proceed 1/10 of a mile to West Casino Road. On W Casino Road turn west and travel 1 mile to the golf course.

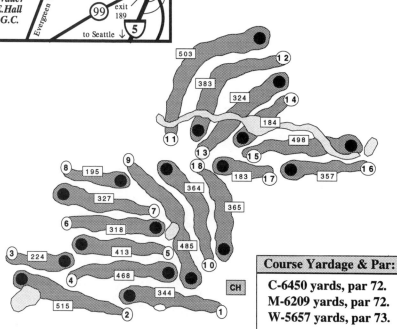

Course Yardage & Par:

C-6450 yards, par 72.
M-6209 yards, par 72.
W-5657 yards, par 73.

Wandermere Golf Course (public, 18 hole course)
North 13700 Division Street; Spokane, WA 99208
Phone: (509) 466-8023. Fax: (509) 468-0718. Internet: none.
Pros: Bob Ross, PGA, Bill Ross, PGA. Superintendent: Herb Brown.
Rating/Slope: C N/A; M 68.9/109; W 70.7/111. **Course record:** 62.
Green fees: W/D $18/$14; W/E $20; Jr. & Sr. rates (M-F); VISA, M/C.
Power cart: $22/$11. **Pull cart:** $5/$3. **Trail fee:** $6 for personal carts.
Reservation policy: please call 7 days in advance for weekend and holiday
tee times. You may call 1 day in advance for weekday tee times.
Winter condition: the course is closed from December 23rd to late February.
Terrain: flat, some hills. **Tees:** all grass. **Spikes:** soft spikes preferred.
Services: club rentals, lessons, restaurant, lounge, beer, wine, pro shop, driving
range, putting green, club memberships. **Comments:** the course features rolling
fairways in which a creek comes into play on two holes. The fairways have
generous landing area's giving you room off the tee. Greens are small, firm and
hard to hold. This public play course can get very busy so be sure call ahead.

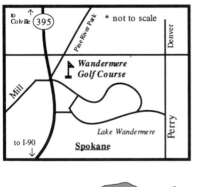

Directions: the golf course is located 10
miles north of Spokane off of Hwy 395.
Take the Division St exit off of I-90
eastbound and westbound. This will
turn into Hwy 395. Proceed on Hwy 395
northbound. Turn right on Wandermere
Road, the course will on your right.

Course Yardage & Par:
C-6115 yards, par 70.
M-5795 yards, par 72.
W-5420 yards, par 71.

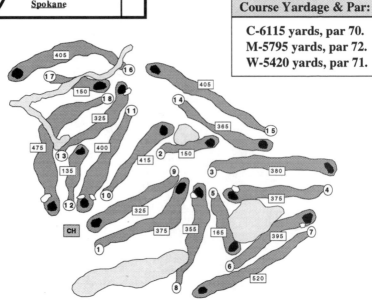

Wayne Golf Course (public, 18 hole course)
16721 96th NE; Bothell, WA 98011
Phone: (425) 486-4714 or 485-6237. Fax: (425) 487-2462.
Pro: Steve Richards. Superintendent: Richard Gettle.
Rating/Slope: M 60.6/97; W 64.5/105. **Course record: 57. 18 hole course.**
Green fees: W/D $16/$13; W/E $18/$14; Jr & Sr rates (Monday thru Friday).
Power cart: $19/$13. **Pull cart:** $3. **Trail fee:** no charge (summer only).
Reservation policy: yes, call up to 1 week in advance for tee time reservations.
Winter condition: the golf course is open all year long. Wet conditions.
Terrain: relatively hilly. **Tees:** grass & mats. **Spikes:** metal spikes permitted.
Services: club rentals, lessons, snack bar, beer, pro shop, club memberships, putting green, practice net. **Comments:** the course is split by the Lake Washington-Sammimish Slough which winds through the golf course. A unique layout that sports eight par three holes including one of the shortest par fours on record. The 172 yard 12th hole. Greens are very small and can be hard to hold. The metropolitan location of this course makes it very popular with the local crowd.

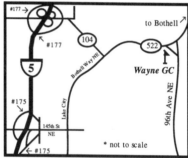

Directions: from I-5 southbound take exit # 177 to Hwy 104E. Travel east for 2.5 miles to Hwy 522E. Travel east for 3.1 miles to 96th NE. Turn south to the course entrance on your right. From I-5 northbound take exit # 175 to NE 145th. Proceed east on NE 145th to for 1.5 miles to Bothell Way NE. Turn north and proceed 4.8 miles to 96th NE and to the course entrance on your right.

Course Yardage & Par:
M-4326 yards, par 65. **W-4237 yards, par 66.**

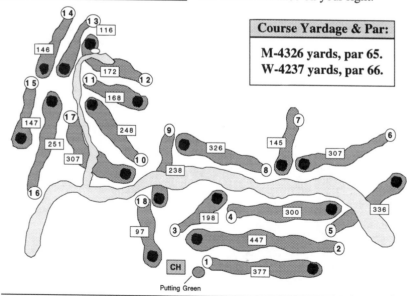

273

Wellington Hills Golf Course (public, 9 hole course)

7026 240th Street SE; Woodinville, WA 98072
Phone: (425) 485-5589. Fax: none. Internet.
Managers: Mimi Racicot, Jan Japar. Superintendent: Bob Japar.
Rating/Slope: M 63.2/102; W 67.8/107. **Course record:** 30 for 9 holes.
Green fees: W/D \$14/\$9; W/E \$15/\$10; Jr/Sr rates (weekdays); M/C, VISA.
Power cart: \$20/\$10. **Pull cart:** \$2. **Trail fee:** \$1 for personal carts.
Reservation policy: yes, weekends only, call up to 1 week in advance.
Winter condition: the golf course is open all year long, with damp conditions.
Terrain: relatively hilly. **Tees:** mats. **Spikes:** metal spikes permitted.
Services: club rentals, snack bar, restaurant, beer, wine, pro shop, putting green.
Comments: course is under new management. While the long-term range is
uncertain, the "Golf Options Company" has made many improvements over the
last three years, including a new irrigation system for putting greens and five
new grass tees. The pro shop has been expanded, featuring top of the line golf
merchandise and apparel. At present time the course plans to operate indefi-
nitely. This track has rolling terrain, one pond and tree-lined fairways.

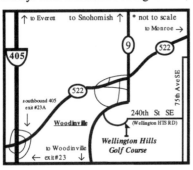

Directions: from I-405 N&S take exit
23 to Hwy 522 eastbound. Travel east
to Hwy 9S. Turn south. At 240th Street
SE turn east to the course. Look for signs
to the course from the exit from Hwy 522.

Course Yardage & Par:
M-2567 yards, par 34.
W-2557 yards, par 34.
Dual tees for 18 holes:
M-5175 yards, par 68.
W-5055 yards, par 68.

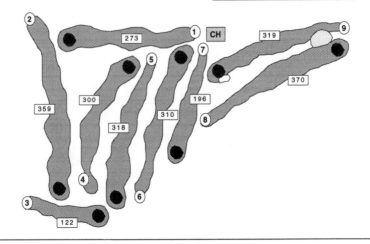

Wenatchee Golf & Country Club (private, 18 hole course)
1600 Country Club Drive; East Wenatchee, WA 98802
Phone: (509) 884-7050. Fax: none. Internet: none.
Pro: Patrick Welch, PGA. Superintendent: Larry Farwell.
Rating/Slope: C 71.0/126; M 69.6/124; W 71.8/123. **Course record:** 62.
Green fees: private club members only; reciprocates; no credit cards.
Power cart: private club members only. **Pull cart:** private. **Trail fee:** private.
Reservation policy: private club members & guests of members only.
Winter condition: the golf course is open all year long weather permitting.
Terrain: relatively hilly. **Tees:** all grass. **Spikes:** soft spikes only.
Services: club rentals, lessons, lounge, restaurant, beer, wine, showers, grass driving range, locker room, putting & chipping greens, club memberships.
Comments: narrow fairways and quick greens characterize this course. Greens are well fronted by bunkers. Great private golf course that is a challenge to all.

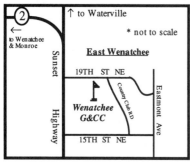

Directions: from Hwy 2, after crossing the Columbia River traveling toward East Wenatchee, turn right at the Sunset Hwy to 19th Street. Turn left. Follow to Country Club Drive and the golf course.

Course Yardage & Par:
C-6405 yards, par 72.
M-6119 yards, par 72.
W-5519 yards, par 73.

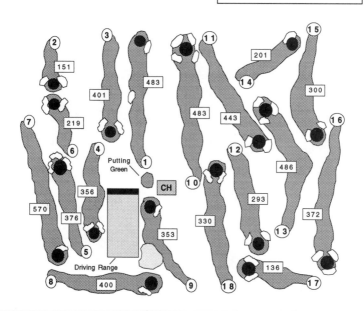

West Richland Municipal Golf Course (public, 18 holes)
4000 Fallon Drive (P.O. Box 41); West Richland, WA 99352
Phone: (509) 967-2165. Fax: (509) 967-5353. Internet: none
Pro: Rod Marcum, PGA. Superintendent: Dan Miksch.
Rating/Slope: M 67.7/114; W 70.3/114. **Course record:** 61.
Green fees: $14 all week long; Jr & Sr rates (all week long); VISA, M/C.
Power cart: $20/$10. **Pull cart:** $2. **Trail fee:** $5 for personal carts.
Reservation policy: please call in 7 days advance for a tee time.
Winter condition: the golf course is open all year long. Dry conditions.
Terrain: very flat. **Tees:** grass & mats. **Spikes:** metal spikes permitted.
Services: club rentals, lessons, restaurant, pro shop, putting green, driving range, club memberships. **Comments:** this is a good course to walk due to its flat terrain and few elevation changes. The Yakima River borders the golf course and comes into play on numerous holes. Greens are large in size and have few hazards fronting them. Fairways are wide given you lots of room.

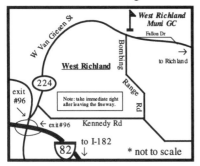

Directions: from I-82 take the West Richland exit #96 and enter town. Turn left on Fallon Road (by the Yakima River) to the golf course. From the Hwy 240 Bypass take the Van Gliesen exit, turn right onto 38th Street and follow this to the golf course. Look for signs.

Course Yardage & Par:
M-6103 yards, par 70.
W-5516 yards, par 71.

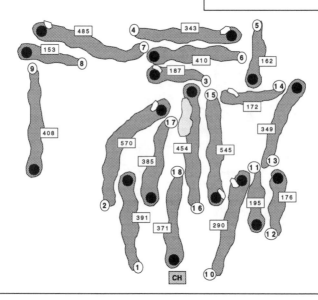

West Seattle Golf Club (public, 18 hole course)

4470 35th SW; Seattle, WA 98126
Phone: (206) 935-5187; Tee-Times 301-0472. Fax: (206) 937-7946.
Pro: Matt Amundsen, PGA. Superintendent: Vern Rollin.
Rating/Slope: C 70.8/118; M 68.8/116; W 71.6/120. **Records:** M 63; W 69.
Green fees: $18.50 all week long; M/C, VISA; Jr. & Sr. rates.
Power cart: $20/$13. **Pull cart:** $3.50. **Trail fee:** $10 for personal carts.
Reservation policy: up to 7 days ahead in person. Up to 6 days ahead by phone.
Winter condition: the golf course is open all year long. Damp conditions.
Terrain: relatively hilly. **Tees:** all grass. **Spikes:** soft spikes preferred.
Services: club rentals, lessons, snack bar, lounge, restaurant, beer, wine, liquor, beverages, pro shop, lockers, putting & chipping green, club memberships.
Comments: the course sports a terrific view of the Seattle skyline. Fairways are tree-lined with a creek meandering throughout. Greens are large with bunkers guarding the front. Good track that plays much longer than the yardage indicates.

Directions: from I-5 N&S take exit # 163 to the West Seattle Freeway. Travel west for 2.5 miles to Fauntleroy Way. At 35th SW (the first light), turn left to the golf course. The golf course is next to the West Seattle Stadium. Look for a sign marking your turn to the golf course.

Course Yardage & Par:
C-6623 yards, par 72.
M-6175 yards, par 72.
W-5611 yards, par 72.

CH — Putting Green

564
354
1
10
18
17
368
9
541
382
8
403
375
15
16
2
346
413
320
11
378
186
12
14
7
193
6
195
5
435
3
4
127
540
515
13

Westwood West Golf Course (public, 9 hole course)

6408 Tieton Drive; Yakima, WA 98908
Phone: (509) 966-0890. **Fax:** none. **Internet:** none.
Pro/Manager: N/A. **Superintendent:** Bob Cyr.
Rating/Slope: M 64.3/104; W 69.1/110. **Course record:** 29.
Green fees: $19/$12; monthly Senior rates; no credit cards.
Power cart: $20/$10 (+ tax). **Pull cart:** $2. **Trail fee:** no charge.
Reservation policy: call 7 days in advance for a tee time reservations.
Winter condition: the course is closed from mid-November to mid-February.
Terrain: flat, some slight hills. **Tees:** grass. **Spikes:** metal spikes permitted.
Services: club rentals, lessons, pro shop, putting green, covered driving range.
Comments: course is built in a unique setting, within an old apple orchard. The course offers rolling terrain and small greens to challenge your play. For those wanting to practice the course features a covered driving range with grass tees. Be sure to visit the fruit stand at the course when its apple picking time.

Directions: from I-82 take the exit at Nob Hill Road #34. Travel west to S 64th Avenue. Turn right and follow to Tieton Drive and the golf course. From Hwy 12 exit onto 40th Avenue S for 2.3 miles. Proceed to Tieton Drive and turn right to the golf course. Look for signs.

Course Yardage & Par:
M-2691 yards, par 35.
W-2607yards, par 36.
Dual tees for 18 holes:
M-5378 yards, par 70.
W-5252 yards, par 72.

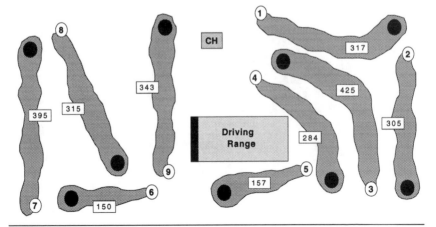

Whidbey Golf & Country Club (private, some outside play)

2430 West Fairway Lane; Oak Harbor, WA 98277   (18 hole Course)
Phone: (360) 675-4546. **Fax:** (360) 679-9395. **Internet:** none.
Pro: Chuck West, PGA. **Superintendent:** Kurt Buckly-Noonan.
Rating/Slope: C 71.2/120; M 69.6/117; W 70.6/120. **Course record:** 61.
Green fees: private club members and guests only; reciprocates. The course
does allow outside play in the afternoon. Mon. to Thur. $30, Fri. to Sun. $35.
Power cart: $22/$13. **Pull cart:** $2.50. **Trail fee:** $5 for personal carts.
Reservation policy: yes, call up to 7 days in advance for tee time reservations.
Winter condition: the golf course is open all year long. Drains very well.
Terrain: flat, some hills. **Tees:** grass. **Spikes:** metal spikes permitted.
Services: lessons, snack bar, restaurant, driving range, putting & chipping
greens, club memberships. **Comments:** the course has excellent greens all year
long. A very demanding layout with numerous sand traps and ponds to contend
with. Good private golf course that will challenge you at every turn.

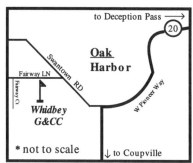

Directions: from I-5 N&S take exit 230
to Highway 20 West. Travel through
Oak Harbor. Turn right at Swan Town
Road to the golf course. Look for a sign
at the turn.

Course Yardage & Par:
C-6392 yards, par 72.
M-6059 yards, par 72.
W-5342 yards, par 72.

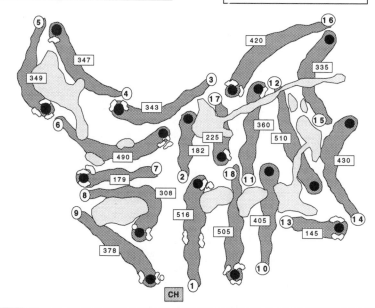

Whispering Firs Golf Club (private, 18 hole course)

NAFFMB Box 4369; McChord AFB 98438
Phone: (253) 984-2053 w/pin #; (253) 984-4927 w/out pin #.
Manager: James Tompkins. **Superintendent:** Terry Beck.
Rating/Slope: C 71.8/122; M 70.5/119; W 73.3/120. **Course record:** 63.
Green fees: private military club; All military ID holders, call for rates.
Power cart: private club. **Pull cart:** military only. **Trail fee:** not allowed.
Reservation policy: please call 7 days in advance for your tee times.
Winter condition: the golf course is open all year long. Dry conditions.
Terrain: flat, some hills. **Tees:** grass. **Spikes:** no metal spikes permitted.
Services: club rentals, lessons, snack bar, pop, beer, wine, pro shop, lockers,
showers, club memberships, covered driving range, putting & chipping greens.
Comments: the course is well-kept all year long. Narrow tree-lined fairways
and numerous sand traps make this a very difficult course. Water comes into
play on several holes and is a major factor off the tee. Great military golf course.

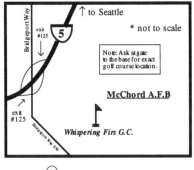

Directions: from I-5 southbound take
the exit at Lakewood/McChord. Turn
left at Bridgeport and travel straight to
the AFB where the golf course is
located. You will take exit #125 and
head toward the main gate. Ask at the
Main gate for exact directions to the golf
course once you are inside the base.

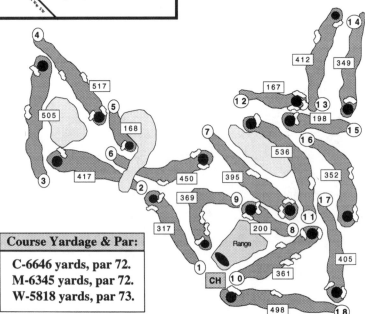

Course Yardage & Par:
C-6646 yards, par 72.
M-6345 yards, par 72.
W-5818 yards, par 73.

Willapa Harbor Golf Club (public, 9 hole course)

Route 3, Box 441; 2424; Fowler Street; Raymond, WA 98577
Phone: (360) 942-2392. Fax: (360) 942-5715. Internet: www.willapaharborgolf&rv.com
Pro: Louis Runge, PGA. Superintendent: none.
Rating/Slope: M 68.8/119; W 72.7/123. Course record: 64.
Green fees: $18/$12 (7 days a week); M/C, VISA.
Power cart: $20/$12. Pull cart: $2.50/$1.50. Trail fee: $10/$7.
Reservation policy: call 7 days in advance for tee times during the summer.
Winter condition: the course is open all year long. Good playing conditions.
Terrain: flat, some hills. **Tees:** all grass. **Spikes:** metal spikes permitted.
Services: club rentals, lessons, snack bar, coffee shop, beer, beverages,
club memberships, pro shop, driving range, putting green, chipping area.
Comments: this golf course plays rather difficult with tree-lined, narrow
fairways. There are also pot bunkers in which to contend with. RV hook-ups on
site for those wanting to play golf and spend the night. Good walking course.

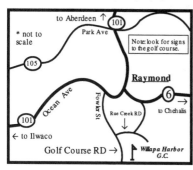

Directions: from I-5 N&S take exit #104
to Hwy 101. Follow 101 to Raymond.
Turn west on Fowler Road and travel
1 mile to the golf course. Look for signs
indicating your turn to the golf course.

Course Yardage & Par:
M-3004 yards, par 36.
W-2878 yards, par 36.

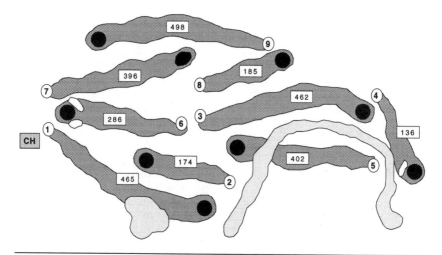

Willows Run Golf Club (public, 36 hole regulation course, 9 hole par 3)
10442 Willows Road NE; Redmond, WA 98052
Western Washington 1-800 833-4787 or call (425) 883-1200
Fax: (425) 869-7607. Internet: www.willowsrun.com
Director Golf: Travis Cox, PGA
Head Golf Professional: Evan Davis. Superintendent: Ben Nelson.
Rating/Slope: C 72.3/120; M 69.1/118; W 71.6/117. **Course record:** 66.
Green fees: Monday to Thursday $40; Friday to Sunday $50 (add tax).
Green fees Family Course: $15 all week long; Jr. & Sr. rates.
Power cart: $24/$12. **Pull cart:** N/A. **Trail fee:** not allowed.
Reservation policy: up to 1 week in advance all year long. A must in summer.
Winter condition: the golf course is open all year long. Dry conditions.
Terrain: flat, some hills. **Tees:** all grass. **Spikes:** soft spike preferred.
Services: club rentals, pro shop, covered/heated practice range, practice putting and chipping greens, practice bunker, lessons, instuctional program and clinics, restaurant, bar, beer, wine, spirits, club memberships, 18 hole putting course.
Comments: This excellent newer facility has a metropolitan location and is fast becoming one of the finest newer courses in the entire Northwest. This links style track has few trees, rolling terrain, and numerous bunkers. The new 18 championship holes are now under construction and expected to open in summer of 1999. The Family Course an executive par 3 along with the 18 hole putting course will open shortly thereafter. This eastside golf complex is a must play.

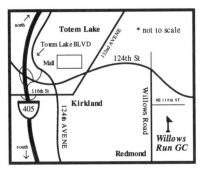

Directions: from I-405 N&S take the 124th St. exit (Totem Lake). Travel eastbound on 124th Street for 1.4 miles to Willows Road NE. Turn right on Willows Road NE. Proceed on Willows Road NE for 1 mile to the golf course which will be on your left hand side.

Players Course

Course Yardage & Par:
C-6337 yards, par 72.
M-5836 yards, par 72.
W-5194 yards, par 72.

Family Course

Course Yardage & Par:
M-1122 yards, par 27.
W-1122 yards, par 27.

Tour Course

Course Yardage & Par:
C-6876 yards, par 72.
M-6340 yards, par 72.
W-5545 yards, par 72.

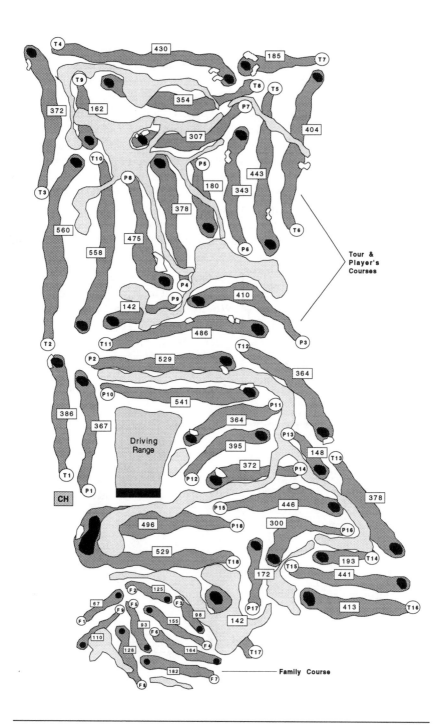

Tour &
Player's
Courses

Family Course

Wing Point Golf & Country Club (private, 18 hole course)

811 Cherry Avenue; P.O. Box 10460; Bainbridge Island, WA 98110
Phone: (206) 842-7933. Fax: (206) 842-5088. Internet: none.
Pro: David Tunkkari. Supt.: Bill Schilling. Manager: Tom Zahaba.
Rating/Slope: C 69.2/127; M 67.6/123; W 71.8/124. **Course record: 63.**
Green fees: private club, members & guests of members only; reciprocates.
Power cart: private club members only. **Pull cart:** private. **Trail fee:** private.
Reservation policy: private club, members & guests of members only.
Winter condition: the golf course is open all year weather permitting, damp.
Terrain: flat, some hills. **Tees:** grass. **Spikes:** soft spikes May 1st to October.
Services: club rentals, lessons, lounge restaurant, beer, wine, liquor, pro shop,
lockers, putting & chipping greens, practice area, club memberships available.
Comments: the front nine is fairly open with numerous traps coming into play.
The back nine winds through tree lined fairways and plays short. In order to
score well you must place the ball in the right position off the tee. The layout
is designed to be a challenging target style golf course. Good private track.

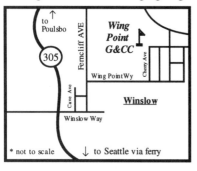

Directions: from the Seattle-Winslow
ferry terminal travel north for .2 miles to
Winslow Way. Turn right and proceed .5
miles to Ferncliff. Turn left. Continue .3
miles to Wing Point Way. Turn right and
travel another .5 miles to Cherry NE.
Turn left on Cherry NE to the golf course
clubhouse which will be on your left.

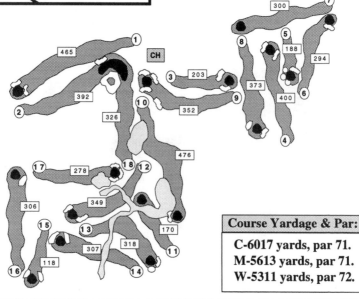

Course Yardage & Par:

C-6017 yards, par 71.
M-5613 yards, par 71.
W-5311 yards, par 72.

WSU Golf Course (public, 9 holes)

North Fairway Drive; CUB 337; Pullman, WA 99163
Phone: (509) 335-4342. **Fax:** none. **Internet:** none.
Manager: Les Davies. **Superintendent:** none.
Rating/Slope: M 65.4/110; W 69.8/119. **Course record:** 29.
Green fees: $13/$10 (public) $11/$8.50 (student) all week long; VISA, M/C.
Power cart: $20/$12. **Pull cart:** $3. **Trail fee:** $3 for personal carts.
Reservation policy: yes, you may call 14 days in advance for a tee time.
Winter condition: the golf course is closed from November to mid-March.
Terrain: relatively hilly. **Tees:** all grass. **Spikes:** metal spikes permitted.
Services: club rentals, lessons, pro shop, driving range, putting & chipping
greens. **Comments:** this is a well-conditioned, scenic course located in the
heart of the Palouse on the campus of Washington State University. The
terrian varies from being flat on the first few holes then becoming very steep
on the inward holes. Greens are medium in size and fronted by sand bunkers.

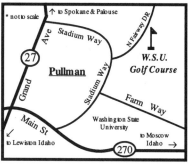

Directions: from Hwy 270, turn into
the main WSU campus entrance. Follow
Stadium Way to Fairway Drive. Turn
right on Fairway Drive to the course.
The golf course is located on the
Washington State University campus.
Look for signs marking your way.

Course Yardage & Par:
M-2880 yards, par 36.
W-2623 yards, par 36.
Dual tees for 18 holes:
M-5764 yards, par 72.
W-5259 yards, par 72.

Yakima Country Club (private, 18 hole course)
500 Country Club Drive; Yakima, WA 98901
Phone: (509) 452-2266. Fax: (509) 575-8527. Internet: none.
Pro: Jim Gilbert, PGA. Supt.: Rob Robillard. Manager: John Thomas.
Rating/Slope: C 70.7/123; M 69.4/120; W 72.6/126. **Course record: 67.**
Green fees: private club members & guests only; reciprocates; no credit cards.
Power cart: available. **Pull cart:** available. **Trail fee:** $25 for personal carts.
Reservation policy: private club, members & guests only. The golf club does
reciprocate with other Northwest private clubs with established accounts.
Winter condition: the golf course is open all year long, weather permitting.
Terrain: flat, some hills. **Tees:** all grass. **Spikes:** no metal spikes permitted.
Services: lessons, restaurant, lounge, beer, wine, liquor, showers, driving range.
Comments: nicely treed well kept private course. Back nine plays very tight in
places making it tough to score on. Good course that is very demanding from
tee to green. Greens are large with bunkers and water coming into play.

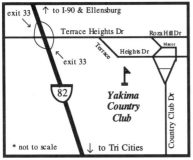

Directions: from I-82 take exit #33 and
travel eastbound. Turn north on Terrace
Heights Drive to Country Club Drive.
Turn right on Country Club Drive.
Proceed on Country Club Drive to the
golf course which will be located on
your right hand side.

Course Yardage & Par:

C-6494 yards, par 71.
M-6181 yards, par 71.
W-5654 yards, par 72.

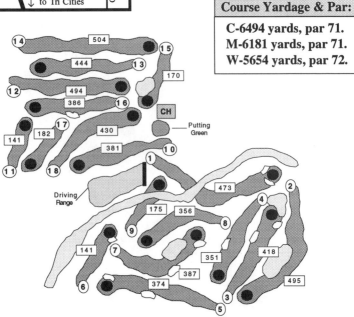

Yakima Elks Golf & Country Club (private, 18 hole course)
Golf Course Road; Selah, WA 98942
Phone: (509) 697-7177. Fax: (509) 697-3662. Internet: none.
Pro: Stuart Kitzmiller, PGA. Superintendent: N/A.
Rating/Slope: C 71.0/120; M 69.8/118; M 67.2/113; W 72.7/117. **Record:** 64.
Green fees: private club, members & guests only; reciprocates.
Power cart: private club. **Pull cart:** private club. **Trail fee:** private club.
Reservation policy: private club members & guests of members only.
Winter condition: the golf course is open all year, weather permitting.
Terrain: flat (easy walking). **Tees:** all grass. **Spikes:** no metal spikes permitted.
Services: club rentals, lessons, restaurant, lounge, beer, wine, liquor, lockers, showers, driving range, putting green, club memberships. **Comments:** this is a well conditioned, easy walking course with tree lined fairways and a number of water hazards to contend with. All the bunkers have been reconditioned and four bunkers have been added to improve play of the golf course.

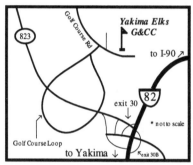

Directions: from I-82 take the Selah exit (#30A) proceed eastbound to Golf Course Loop (the first right). Turn right and follow this to the golf course.

Course Yardage & Par:
C-6640 yards, par 71.
M-6360 yards, par 71.
M-5796 yards, par 71.
W-5844 yards, par 74.

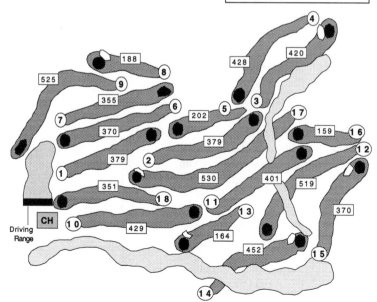

Batstone Hill Driving Range
321 Mason Lake Road; Shelton, WA 98584
(360) 426-4276. Pro: none.
Hours: 8 am to dusk. **Lights:** no. **Covered:** yes.
Putting & chipping: putting & chipping.
Services: lessons, vending machines.
Directions: 5 miles north of Shelton on Hwy 3
to Mason Lake Road. The range is located .25
miles up Mason Lake Road on the left.
<u>Map 1; Grid D4</u>

Beacon Hill Golf Center
4848 Valley Spring Road; Spokane, WA 99207
(509) 482-0622. Pro: unavailable.
Hours: 8am-dark. **Lights:** no. **Covered:** yes.
Putting & chipping: 18 hole course, chipping area.
Services: club repair, lessons, small pro shop.
Directions: from I-90 E&W take the Freya/Thor
exit. Go north for 3 miles to Euclid Avenue. Go
right for 3 blocks to Freya. Turn left to the range.
<u>Map 4; Grid C4</u>

Columbia Super Range
511 128th SE; Everett, WA 98208
1-800-478-4887, (425) 742-5790, (425) 338-2424
Pros: Kevin Mackay, PGA, Steve Rehul, PGA.
Hours: 7 am-11 pm; extended summer hours.
Lights: yes. **Covered:** 50 stalls (heated).
Putting/chipping: 18 hole par 2 scramble course.
Services: club repair, lessons, Nevada Bobs Golf
Store, snack bar. **Directions:** I-5 N&S take exit 186.
Go east for 1/2 mile to the range. **<u>Map 2; Grid C2</u>**

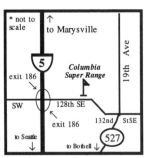

Desert Lakes Driving Range
610 Yakima Ave.; Moses Lake, WA 98837
(509) 766-1553. Pro: 2 pros to serve you.
Hours: to be determined. **Lights:** yes.
Covered: yes.
Putting & chipping: yes.
Services: lessons, pro shop, club repair.
Directions: range is located right off of Wapato
Drive in Moses Lake Washington.
<u>Map 3; Grid D3</u>

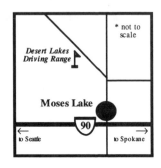

Emerald Links Driving Range
22719 Highway 410; Bonney Lake, WA 98390
(253) 891-8300. Pro: PGA lessons
Hours: W/D 11am-7pm; W/E 9am-7pm (winter);
(summer) 9am-8pm daily. **Lights:** yes.
Covered: yes. **Putting/chipping:** no.
Services: lessons, club repair, custom clubs, club
fitting, discount pro shop. **Directions:** the range is
located on the north side of State Hwy 410.
Map 2; Grid D1

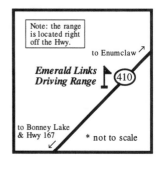

Evergreen Golf Center
16703 SE 1st; Vancouver, WA 98684
(360) 253-3184.
Hours: 9am-9pm (winter), 9am-10pm (summer).
Lights: yes. **Covered:** yes. **Putting/chipping:** yes.
Services: lessons, club repair, custom clubs, pro
shop, heated tees. **Directions:** From I-205 take the
Mill Plain E exit to 164th. Turn north on 164th
proceed to the stoplight which is 1st. Turn right on
1st to range. **Map 1; Grid G4**

Family Golf Center @ Kent
9116 212th Street; Kent, WA 98032
(253) 850-8300. Pros: 2 PGA pros on staff.
Hours: 7:30am to 10pm (summer). **Lights:** yes.
Covered: most. **Putting & Chipping:** putting.
Services: full service pro shop, PGA golf instruction,
video teaching, deli, beverages, heated tee line.
Directions: range is located at the intersections of
Highway 167 & 212th St. Take the exit for 212th off
Hwy 167 proceed east the range. **Map 2; Grid D1**

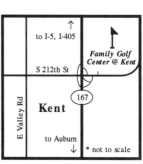

Family Golf Center @ Lacey
8000 72nd Lane SE; Olympia, WA 98513
(360) 493-1000. Pro: Mike Fosnick, PGA.
Hours: 9am to dark. **Lights:** no. **Covered:** yes.
Putting/chipping: yes, 3 hole course, grass tees.
Services: golf camps, lessons, pro shop.
Directions: from I-5 N&S exit at Martin Way.
Proceed 3.4 miles east on College St. to Yelm Hwy.
Turn left. Proceed to Spurgeon Creek Rd. turn right.
Map 1; Grid E4

Family Golf Center @ Tacoma
708 122th Street E; Tacoma, WA 98445
(253) 537-3037. Pro: Keith Sanden, PGA.
Hours: 8am-10pm (April-September);
9am-9pm (October-February). **Lights:** yes.
Covered: yes, heated, raised target greens.
Services: club repair, lessons, video lessons, pro
shop. **Directions:** from Hwy 512 take Pacific Ave.
exit.Turn left on 112th St. The range is located 1/2
mile on the right. **Map 2; Grid D1**

Gateway Golf Center
725 Port Way; Clarkston, WA 99403
(509) 758-4366. Pro: Steve Servick.
Hours: 7am to 10pm (daily).
Lights: yes. **Covered:** yes.
Putting & Chipping: 18 hole putting course.
Services: lessons, club repair, pro shop.
Directions: the range is located next to the
Quality Inn on Port Drive, just off Hwy 12.
Look for signs. **Map 4; Grid F4**

Gold Creek Tennis & Sports Club
15327 140th PL NE; Woodinville, WA 98072
(425) 487-1090.
Pros: Juanita Reinhardt, Steve Stoia, PGA.
Hours: M-F 6 am - 10 pm, Sat-Sun 8am - 9pm.
Lights: yes. **Covered:** yes.
Putting & chipping: yes. **Services:** lessons.
Directions: the range is located off of Hwy 202
in Woodinville. Look for the signs to the tennis &
sports club. **Map 2; Grid C2**

Golf Club, The
6311 W Clearwater Ave.; Kennewick, WA 99336
(509) 735-6072. Pros: Jim Vance.
Hours: 10am-9pm Mon. to Sat; 10am-8pm Sun.;
extended summer hours.
Lights: yes. **Covered:** yes and heated.
Services: lessons, pro shop,
miniature golf, bank shot basketball.
Directions: from Hwy 395 turn right on Clearwater
Avenue. The range is located up Clearwater Ave. 2.5
miles on the left. **Map 3; Grid F3**

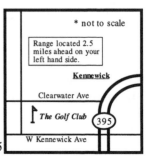

Grand Mound Driving Range
20525 Old Highway 9; Centralia, WA 98531
(360) 273-9335. Pro: no.
Hours: 10am to dusk, 7 days a week (summer).
Lights: no. **Covered:** yes. **Putting/chipping:** yes.
Services: custom clubs, used clubs, practice bunker.
Directions: from I-5 N&S take exit #88 (Hwy 12).
Procced west for 1 block to Old Hwy 99 and turn
south. Procced to Old Hwy 9 and turn left to range.
Map 1; Grid E4

H&H Driving Range
11405 NE 72nd Avenue; Vancouver, WA 98661
(360) 573-3315. Pro: none.
Hours: vary depending on season. **Lights:** yes.
Covered: yes. **Putting & chipping:** no.
Services: lessons, custom clubs, club repair,
pro shop. **Directions:** from I-5 take exit #4 and
proceed east on NE 78th to NE Andresen Rd.
Turn left on Andresen and proceed to the range.
Map 1; Grid G4

Harvest Valley Golf Center
530 Cherry Hills Road; Granger, WA 98932
(509) 854-1800. Pro: none.
Hours: vary depending on season. **Lights:** no.
Covered: yes. **Putting & chipping:** yes.
Services: lessons, club repair, pro shop.
Directions: the range is located in Granger, WA
just off of Cherry Hills Road. Look for signs
posted at the turn.
Map 1; Grid G4

Iron Eagle Sports Center
16651 Currie Road; Monroe, WA 98272
(360) 794-0933. Pro: Ray Bloom, PGA.
Hours: 10am-8:30pm M/Sat.; 10am-7:30pm Sun;
range has extended summer hours. **Lights:** yes.
Covered: yes. **Putting/chipping:** putting only.
Services: pro shop, lessons, heated stalls.
Directions: From Hwy 522 take 164th St. exit. Left
off exit (under highway). Take first right on Curry
Rd. to the range. **Map 2; Grid C2**

Kaddyshack Golf Center
4003 204th SW; Lynnwood, WA 98036
(425) 775-8911. Pros: Pete Dixon PGA,
Doug Lee, KPGA, app. **John Spencer.**
Hours: Sun.-Thur. 8am-11pm; Fri.-Sat. 8am-midnight.
Lights: yes. **Covered:** yes & heated. **Putting:** yes.
Services: club repair, lessons, discount pro shop.
Directions: I-5 N take 44th St. (Lynnwood) exit
#181A. Straight through light at the bottom of hill
and follow to range. **Map 2; Grid C2**

Ken's Golf
1899 S Burlington Blvd.; Burlington, WA 98233
Phone: (360) 757-4653.
Pros: Ken Harrsch, PGA, Mark Flitton, PGA.
Hours: 9am to dusk; extended summer hrs.
Lights: no. **Covered:** yes. **Putting &chipping:** no.
Services: pro shop, basic club repair, lessons.
Directions: I-5S take exit 229 to stop sign.
Turn right, the range is located100 yards ahead.
Map 2; Grid B1

Longshots Driving Range
1215 80th Street SW; Everett, WA 98203
(425) 355-2133. Pro: Bob Osgood, PGA.
Hours: summer 9am-9pm; winter hours vary.
Lights: yes. **Covered:** yes. **Putting:** yes.
Services: putters, lessons, wedges.
Directions: From Hwy 99 go west on Casino Road
to 5th Ave. North on 5th. Take first left on 80th.
The range is 4 blocks up on the right hand side.
Map 2; Grid C2

Mulligan's Driving Range
7431 64th Drive NE; Marysville, WA 98270
(360) 653-2000. Pro: Mike O'Keefe, PGA.
Hours: hours vary depending on day of the week.
Lights: yes. **Covered:** yes. **Putting/chipping:** soon.
Services: club repair, lessons, pro shop.
Directions: From I-5 N&S take exit #199, go east
on 4th St .3 miles to State Ave. Left on State for .8
miles to Grove St. Right. Follow 1.9 mi to 64th Ave.
SE. Right to range. **Map 2; Grid C2**

North West Golf Range
368 NE Bucklin Hill Rd; Bremerton, WA 98311
(360) 692-6828. Pro: Devin Loudon.
Hours: Monday-Sunday 9 am-10 pm. **Lights:** yes.
Covered: yes. **Putting & chipping:** no.
Services: lessons, club repair, club fitting,
pro shop. **Directions:** range is located between
Bremerton and Silverdale just off Wagga Way.
Take the Schold Road exit.
Map 1; Grid C4

Par IV Golf Learning Center
500 Robinson Road; Woodland, WA 98674
(360) 225-8869. Pro: Jim Howard.
Hours: hours vary depending on the season.
Longer hours in the summer months.
Lights: no. **Covered:** yes.
Putting/chipping: yes.
Services: club repair, lessons.
Directions: the range is located in Woodland just
off Robinson Road. **Map 2; Grid G4**

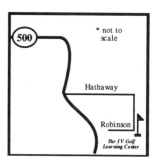

ParFect Driving Range *New Driving Range*
91 S. Boyce Road; Sequim, WA 98382
Phone: (360) 681-5228.
Owner: Randy Simmons.
Hours: 9 am-10pm daily.
Lights: yes. **Covered:** yes. **Putting/chipping:** yes.
Services: club repair, lessons, pro shop.
Directions: The range is located at the intersections
of Boyce Rd. and State Hwy 101 west of the the city
of Sequim. **Map 1; Grid B3**

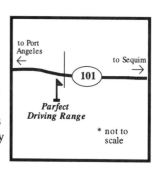

Performance Golf Center
2416 14th Ave. NW; Gig Harbor, WA 99335
(253) 853-4653. Pro: Jeff Mehlert.
Hours: 7am to 11pm (summer) 8am-9pn (winter).
Lights: yes. **Covered:** yes.
Putting/chipping: yes.
Services: pro shop, lessons, club repair, 74 covered,
20 heated tees, food service, grass tees, mini golf.
Directions: the range is located right off of Hwy 16
in Gig Harbor, Washington. **Map 2; Grid D1**

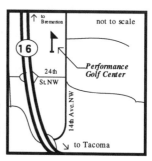

Puetz Golf Range
11762 Aurora North; Seattle, WA 98133
(206) 362-2272. Pro: Rand Veal, PGA.
Hours: Mon.-Sat. 9-10; Sun. 9-8; summer hours.
Lights: yes. **Covered:** yes. **Putting/chipping:** yes.
Services: club repair, lessons, video lessons,
large discount pro shop, heated tee line.
Directions: From I-5 N&S take exit #173 to NE
Northgate Way W. West for .7 mi to Aurora Ave.
Right on Aurora. **Map 2; Grid C1**

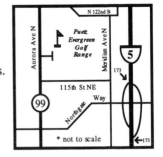

Rainbow Golf Driving Range
2723 Harrison Avenue; Centralia, WA 98531
(360) 330-0585. Pro: N/A.
Hours: Monday thru Sunday 12pm-8pm.
Lights: yes. **Covered:** yes. **Putting/chipping:** yes.
Services: pro shop, lessons, espresso.
Directions: from I-5 N&S take exit #82 to Harrison
Avenue. Proceed westbound on Harrison for 2.3
miles. The range is located on your left.
Map 1; Grid E4

Red Wood Golf Center
13029 Red-Wdnl Road NE; Redmond, WA 98052
(425) 869-8814. Pro: Paul Johanson, PGA.
Hours: 9:30am-9pm all week long.
Lights: yes. **Covered:** yes & heated.
Putting/chipping: yes. **Services:** full service pro
shop, private, group, video & Jr. lessons, custom
clubs, and repair. **Directions:** from I-405 N&S take
exit 20B (NE 124th St). Follow 124th east 3 miles to
Hwy 202, turn left. **Map 2; Grid C2**

Rodarco Golf Range
8020 Kickerville Road; Blaine, WA 98230
(360) 332-2665. Pro: Roger D. Cook, PGA.
Hours: summer 7-9 daily. **Lights:** no.
Covered: 3 stalls with mats, 20 grass tees.
Putting/Chipping: yes, practice bunker.
Services: club repair, lessons, pro shop, snack bar.
Directions: I-5 N&S take exit #270 to Birch Bay-
Lynden RD. West for 2 miles to Kickerville RD,
Turn south to range. **Map 2; Grid A1**

Southcenter Golf
18791 Southcenter Pkwy; Tukwila, WA 98188
(206) 575-7797. Pro: Jim Bennett, PGA.
Hours: Mon.-Fri. 9 am-9 pm; W/E's 9am-9pm.
Lights: yes. **Covered:** yes. **Putting/chipping:** yes.
Services: club repair, lessons, pro shop, video
studio, custom clubs. **Directions:** proceed straight
on Southcenter Pkwy beyond the Pavillion thru the
intersection to the range located 2 blocks ahead.
<u>**Map 2; Grid D1**</u>

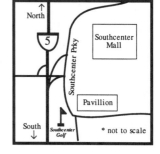

Steamboat Golf
3605 Steamboat Is. Road; Olympia, WA 98502
(360) 867-0562. Pros: Scott Geroux.
Hours: 7am to 10pm, 7 days a week (summer).
Lights: yes. **Covered:** yes, grass tees.
Putting/chipping: yes.
Services: lessons, ladies night.
Directions: from Hwy 101 exit for Steamboat
Island Road. Range located 1/4 mile east on the left.
<u>**Map 1; Grid E4**</u>

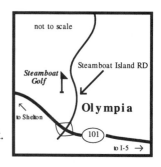

Straight Arrow Driving Range
61 East Allen Road; Sunnyside, WA 98944
no phone listed.
Pro: none. Manager: N/A.
Hours: hours vary depending on time of year.
Lights: yes. **Covered:** no.
Putting/chipping: yes. **Services:** lessons.
Directions: the range in located in Sunnyside WA
just off Allen Road.
<u>**Map 2; Grid C2**</u>

Tour Fairways Golf Center
1150 Abadie, Walla Walla, WA 99362
(509) 529-5810.
Pros: Jim Henderson, Mike Rostollan, PGA.
Hours: 8am-10pm daily. **Covered:** 12 covered, 75
grass tees. **Putting & chipping:** yes. **Lights:** yes.
Services: excellent pro shop, lessons, custom clubs,
club repair, batting cages for baseball & softball.
Directions: Hwy 12 exit at 2nd Ave. South to Rose
St. Turn right on Rose. Go to 13th. Right on 13th.
Left on Abadie. <u>**Map 4; Grid F1**</u>

University of Washington Driving Range
1/2 mi north of stadium; Seattle, WA 98195
(206) 543-8759. Pro: Doug McDonald.
Hours: 10am-7pm (winter) 9am-10pm (summer).
Lights: yes. **Covered:** yes.
Putting & chipping: yes. **Services:** lessons.
Directions: I-5 N&S take exit 169 to NE 45th.
Go east for 1.8 miles to Union Bay Pl NE. E for
.1 mile to Clark Road. West to range. The range is
located right off Montlake Blvd on the UW campus.
__Map 2; Grid D2__

Vanco Golf Range
703 N Devine; Vancouver, WA 98661
(360) 693-8811; FAX: (360) 735-1966.
Pros: Scott Blake, PGA. Chuck Milne, PGA.
Hours: 9am-10pm (summer). 9am-9pm(winter).
Lights: yes. **Covered:** yes. **Putting/chipping:** yes.
Services: club repair, lessons, pro shop, miniature
golf. **Directions:** From I-5 N&S take exit 1C to
Mill Plain Road E for 4.1 miles to Devine Road.
Range is on left. __Map 1; Grid G4__

Westside Golf Range
106 NW 139th Street; Vancouver, WA 98685
(360) 573-2565
Manager: Kent Schmidt.
Hours: hours vary depending on the season.
Lights: yes. **Covered:** yes. **Putting/chipping:** yes.
Services: club repair, lessons, pro shop.
Directions: take 134th street exit off of I-5. Turn
west bound on 134th street it will become Tenny
Road. Range on the right. __Map 1; Grid G4__

Woodalls World Driving Range
8400 NE W Kingston RD; Kingston, WA 98436
(360) 297-4653. Pro: Ted Wurtz, PGA.
Hours: 9am-8pm summer; 9am-6pm winter.
Lights: yes. **Covered:** yes. **Services:** lessons,
custom clubs, retail pro shop. **Directions:** from
Kingston turn left at Country Corners (Millers Bay
Suquamish RD). Proceed for 1 mile to the first left
(West Kingston RD) turn left. Range 1/4 mile on
your left. __Map 2; Grid C1__

Bogey's Golf
2019 Hewitt Avenue; Everett, Wa. (425) 258-5300
Services: club repair, club refinishing.

Caddy Shack Golf Shop
2614 A West Nob Hill Boulevard; Yakima, Wa. (509) 575-6461
Services: club repair, indoor driving range, sport tech swing analyzer, lessons.

Cascade Athletic Academy
9805 NE 116th; Kirkland, Wa. (425) 821-8372
Services: golf instruction.

Clarke-Stephens Golf
E. 116 Nora; Spokane, Wa. (509) 325-5905
Services: club repair, custom clubs, club refinishing, lessons.

Doug McDonald's Golf in the 80's
7531 Lake City Way NE; Seattle, Wa. (206) 522-8940
Services: lessons, video lessons.

Fairway Golf Club Repair
27239 132nd SE; Kent, Wa. (253) 639-0740
Services: club repair, custom clubs, club refinishing.

Fairways and Greens Golf Center
1301 5th Avenue; Seattle, Wa. (206) 341-9193
Services: golf merchandise.

Farwest Golf Cars of Washington, INC
7916 Pacific Highway East; Tacoma, Wa. 1-800-924-9424
Services: golf carts, golf cart repair.

Gals Golf Gear
Highway 512 & Pacific Avenue South; Tacoma, Wa. (253) 531-2773
Services: womens golf apparel and golf merchandise.

Golf USA
1300 N. Miller Wenatchee, Wa. (509) 662-7714
Services: club regripping, retail store, apparel, indoor range.

Golf Zone Training Studio
6804 188th Stree NE; Arlington, Wa. (360) 403-9660
Services: lessons, swing analysis.

Golf Zone Training Studio
713 110th NE; Bellevue, Wa. (425) 646-9445
Services: lessons, swing analysis.

Golf Zone Training Studio
240 NW Gilman Blvd.; Issaquah, Wa. (425) 392-2210
Services: lessons, swing analysis.

Golf Zone Training Studio
2264 15th Avenue W; Seattle, Wa. (206) 298-0205
Services: lessons, swing analysis.

Golfsmith Golf Center
240 Andover Park West; Tukwila, Wa. (206) 444-9586
Services: discount golf merchandise, snack bar, putting area, swing analysis.

Jorgensen Golf *Julius Jorgensen, Owner/Pro, PGA*   **1-800-218-2373**
11700 Mukilteo Spdwy; STE 407; Mukilteo, Wa. (425) 349-1347, 787-9186
Services: indoor video lessons, club repair, upscale pro shop, USGA GHIN G.C.

Moe's Custom Golf
9616 Roosevelt Way NE; Seattle, Wa. (206) 523-7533
Services: club repair, custom clubs, club refinishing, club regrips.

National Golf
5114 Dartmouth Road; Spokane,Wa. (509) 927-GOLF
Services: discount golf merchandise, club repair.

National Golf
8701 N Division; Spokane, Wa. (509) 468-0660
Services: discount golf merchandise, club repair.

Nevada Bob's Discount Golf
14603 NE 20th; Bellevue Wa. (425) 641-6399
Services: large discount pro shop, club regripping and repairs.

Nevada Bob's Discount Golf
2020 W. Meeker (Riverbend Golf Complex); Kent, Wa. (253) 859--4000
Services: large discount pro shop, club regripping and repairs

Nevada Bob's Discount Golf
4926A 196th SW; Lynnwood, Wa. (425) 774-1892
Services: large discount pro shop, club regripping and repairs.

Nevada Bob's Discount Golf
6409 Tacoma Mall Boulevard; Tacoma, Wa. (253) 474-8288
Services: club repair, club refinishing.

O'briens Golf Shop/Studio Fore Golf
13434 NE 16th; STE #110; Bellevue, Wa. (425) 957-9810; (425) 454-6766
Services: indoor practice facility, 9 hitting stations, retail golf shop, lessons.

Olsen's Golf Shop
7612 Beverly Boulevard; Everett, Wa. (425) 355-9241
Services: club repair, club refinishing..

Pacific Discount Golf
31830 Pacific Highway S; Federal Way, Wa. (253) 839-6488
Services: club repair, club refinishing, lessons.

Pro Golf Discount
14121 NE 20th; Bellevue, Wa. (425) 641-6766
Services: club repair, club refinishing, discount pro shop.

Pro Golf Discount
1680 NW Mall Street; Issaquah, Wa. (425) 392-2333
Services: club repair, club refinishing, discount pro shop

Pro Golf Discount
301 Tukwila Parkway (Southcenter); Tukwila, Wa. (206) 431-0100
Services: club repair, club refinishing, discount pro shop.

Pro Golf Discount
10409 Aurora Avenue North; Seattle, Wa. (206) 527-7770
Services: club repair, club refinishing, discount pro shop.

Pro Golf Discount
18905 33rd Avenue West; Lynnwood, Wa. (206) 525-5518 or (425) 771-2131
Services: club repair, club refinishing, discount pro shop.

Pro Golf Discount
5015 Tacoma Mall Boulevard, Suite C; Tacoma, Wa. (253) 473-4290
Services: club repair, club refinishing, discount pro shop.

Pro Golf Discount
4225 Meridian Street; Bellingham, Wa. (360) 738-7101
Services: club repair, club refinishing, discount pro shop.

Pro Golf Discount
905 S 1rst Street; Yakima, Wa. (509) 248-0800
Services: club repair, club refinishing, discount pro shop.

Puetz Golf Superstore
402 Strander Blvd.; Tukwila, Wa. (206) 439-1740
Services: club repair, club refinishing, discount pro shop, brand name clubs.

Puetz Golf Superstore
1645 140th Avenue NE; Bellevue, Wa. (425) 747-0664
Services: club repair, club refinishing, discount pro shop, brand name clubs.

Puetz Golf Superstore
11762 Aurora Avenue N.; Seattle, Wa. (206) 362-2272
Services: club repair, refinishing, discount pro shop, lessons, video lessons.

Puget Sound Golf Shop
2708 Locust Avenue West; Tacoma, Wa. (253) 566-1934
Services: club repair, regrip, custom clubs, limited instruction..

Studio Fore
12003 NE 12th, Suite 56; Bellevue, Wa. (425) 454-6766
Services: lessons.

The Golf Club Co.
2423 Harrison Avenue NW; Olympia, Wa. (360) 352-1331
Services: custom-fitted clubs, full service repairs, accessories.

The Golfing Gallery
1969 SW Hillcrest; Seattle, Wa. (206) 242-PUTT
Services: collectable golf art, prints, limited editions.

Tom Wells Golf Company
7806 Aurora Avenue N.; Seattle, Wa. (206) 523-7124
Services: club repair, club refinishing, custom clubs, lessons

Von's Golf Plus *Jim Von Lossow owner*
7419 48th Avenue NE; Seattle, Wa. (206) 524-6716
Services: custom clubs, club repair, used clubs, putter collector & sales.

Wide World of Golf
N. 4921 Division; Spokane, Wa. (509) 489-4653
Services: club repair, custom clubs.

Our newest section in *Golfing in Washington* is called **Weekend Getaways.**
We have received calls from people using the book for suggestions on weekend
trips and my family and I personally enjoy going golfing in the morning and
seeing other attractions in the afternoon. We have designed this section, therefore, to give you some ideas of short weekend trips you could take in the area
and you can tailor them to your taste! Any further information you would like
on specific lodging availability the Chamber of Commerce in the destination
city would be eager to provide. Some of our suggestions may be seasonal so it
is always best to call ahead.

Burlington: Avalon Golf Course is situated a short distance from I-5 and offers
a lovely restaurant for your "after golf" meal. Burlington itself has one of the
first and largest outlet malls and is the gateway to the North Cascades Hwy.
This is a very popular and scenic drive highlighting many beautiful sights in the
Cascades. Make sure the Highway is open, however, because it is closed during
the winter. Another very beautiful trip is State Route 11 from Burlington called
Chuckanut Drive. This trip provides panoramic views of the San Juans as you
wind your way to Bellingham following the Washington coastline. The Skagit
Valley would be another destination to travel to from Burlington and, if you
timed it right, you could see the Tulip Festival. The waterfront town of
LaConner also offers shopping and dining. It is located south of the Burlington
Highway on Skagit Bay.

Lake Chelan/Orondo: This vacation location offers two golf courses, Lake
Chelan Golf Course and Desert Canyon in Orondo. Desert Canyon is located at
a resort which has full amenities. This is a desert course similar to those of
Palm Springs. South of Orondo is the Rocky Reach Dam which is open for the
public to tour. Lake Chelan has the full gamut of activities available as any
resort town. There is boating, lodging right on the lake, shopping in town, and
other water activities. If your time allows you might like to take the Lady of the
Lake trip from Chelan to the remote village of Stehekin, 55 miles northwest.
This breathtaking trip will take you through steep cliffs, waterfalls, and beautiful
mountain scenery. Stehekin and the Lake Chelan National Recreation area are
not accessible by road.

Leavenworth: The Bavarian village of Leavenworth is located east of Stevens
Pass and Lake Wenatchee. There are two golf courses in the area, Leavenworth
and Kahler Glen. Leavenworth offers lodging, extensive gift shopping, and
restaurants in a scenic unique mountain setting. All of the storefronts are
Bavarian style. The town often has special events happening including art
exhibits, folk dancing, and the Octoberfest. If you prefer, Lake Wenatchee
offers a large campground with swimming and kayaking on the Wenatchee
River. There are guided river trips available.

Ocean Shores: A trip to Ocean Shores is always a treat. There is plenty of lodging and dining available. The golf course is located right in the heart of Ocean Shores. Other activities include horseback riding, kite flying, mopeds, bike riding and beachcombing. During limited seasons clam digging and other fishing activities are within a stones throw of Ocean Shores. A day could easily be spent driving the coastline and visting such communities as Klaloch, Copalis, Forks and even Lake Crescent.

Port Orchard/Bremerton/Gig Harbor: This is a widespread area has many golf courses available for play. McCormick Woods, Horseshoe Lake, Gig Harbor, Madrona Links, Rolling Hills, Clover Valley, and Gold Mountain. There are dining and lodging facilities in any of the towns. There is art gallery shopping in Gig Harbor, the Bremerton Naval Museum, or drive up to Poulsbo "Little Norway" for a waterfront Scandinavian adventure in shopping. *Or* take the ferry from Seattle to Bremerton, play golf and enjoy the afternoon in Kitsap Co., return to Seattle that evening and stay downtown. The following day could include a trip to the Pike Place Market and visiting the other beautiful Seattle sights.

Port Townsend: The Port Townsend area has three golf courses, the Port Townsend Golf Course, Chevy Chase, and The Port Ludlow Golf & Meeting Retreat. Port Ludlow offers full resort accommodations, a restaurant, lounge, tennis courts and marina. Golf packages are available. Chevy Chase is the oldest resort golf course in the state of Washington having been built and continually operated since 1925. The accommodations reside on a bluff over-looking Discovery Bay. The amenities available with cabin rental are: swimming pool, tennis court and a clam rich private beach. Port Townsend is famous for its many bed and breakfast inns housed in old Victorian mansions built in the historical town. The downtown waterfront has many galleries and small shops as well as waterfront dining. There are numerous sites at Fort Wordon State Park including a Marine Science Center, The Rothschild House (a 1868 home owned by a Port Townsend merchant with mostly original furnishings) and a Commanding Officer's House which has been restored to reflect actual officers quarters of the Victorian period. There is also a museum of yesteryear located in Port Townsend.

San Juan Islands: The San Juans are home to three golf courses, Orcas Island, San Juan and Lopez Island. A trip to the San Juans is breathtakingly beautiful, peaceful, and a real break from the hustle and bustle of city life.
Orcas Island: Rosario Resort offers fine cuisine and lodging. Moran State Park features a stone tower, fishing, and beachcombing. The Orcas Island Historical Museum focuses on early pioneer and indian life on the island.
San Juan: Whale watching is available at Lime Kiln State Park (west of Friday

Harbor, daytime only), and the Whale Museum featuring art exhibits and the natural habitat and history of whales and dolphins. **Lopez Island:** Bring your bicycles and ride the Lopez Loop covering 13 miles around the island (this route sees the minimum of traffic). The Washington State Ferry System provides service to the San Juans, call them for further detail and schedules.

Semiahmoo/Blaine/Bellingham: The Washington-Canadian border is rich with golf courses and historical sites. The Semiahmoo Resort is a wonderful getaway just for the Arnold Palmer designed golf course and the peaceful surroundings of the resort. Bellingham also offers lodging and dining. There is a myriad of things to do. Vancouver British Columbia is a beautiful city and is only an hour from Blaine. There is the famous Stanley Park, the former Expo site, Gastown and exquisite dining. Attractions in the Bellingham area you might enjoy for the afternoon include the Lake Whatcom Railway which provides views of everything from the San Juan Islands to Mt. Baker. Hovander Homestead (Ferndale) is a restored 1903 homestead furnished with antiques and antique farm equipment. Pioneer park (Ferndale) has a number of restored log cabins on site. The Whatcom Museum of History and Art (Bellingham) focuses on Northwest, maritime, and indian artifacts

Sequim: Sequim offers two golf courses, Dungeness and SunLand (semi-private). You can check with the Dungeness Golf Course for the packages they offer with local motels. Located nearby is the Olympic Game Farm, and the Dungeness Spit (a beautiful, peaceful, beach trail on the Straits of Juan de Fuca). The 3 Crabs Restaurant is also located right on the beach and serves excellent fresh seafood. A nice addition to this trip would be a drive to Port Angeles and up to Hurricane Ridge which is located in the heart of the Olympic Mountains. There is a visitor center with spectacular views of the Olympics. If you have an extended weekend you can take the ferry from Port Angeles to Victoria and all the sites of this lovely city which could include the Butchart Gardens, downtown shopping, the British Columbia Museum of Natural History, the Empress Hotel and Capitol Building.Don't forget to bring your golf clubs as Vancouver Island is host to many fine golf courses.

Snoqualmie: The Salish Lodge located at Snoqualmie Falls is a beautiful and peaceful hide-a-way only 30 minutes from Bellevue. There are many golf courses located in all directions from the Salish. Mt Si Golf Course, Twin Rivers Golf Course, Snoqualmie Falls Golf Course, Tall Chief Golf Course and Carnation Golf Course. There are trails at the lodge leading to scenic views of the falls. Some of the other activities in the area include the most popular hike in Washington up Mt Si, North Bend has an outlet mall, Remlinger Farm located in Carnation is a family operated farm offering a restaurant, nursery, gift shop, fresh produce and farm products, a working steam train, as well as seasonal events. Boehm's Candies in Issaquah offers a tour of the home, chapel, candy making and an art gallery. The Puget Sound & Snoqualmie Railroad provides a very scenic train ride covering approximately a 10 mile route. Snoqualmie also has the Snoqualmie Winery open for wine tasting and tours.

Spokane: The Spokane area has many fine golf courses, check the geographical index for the listing. This major city offers superb lodging and dining. Other attractions include: Finch Arboretum (includes nature trail), Manito Park featuring formal and Japanese gardens, Crosby Library on Gonzaga University's campus (Bing Crosby memorabilia), the Cathedral of St. John the Evangelist (constructed over a 50 year time period), Fort Spokane (a previously active army post) with a walking trail and four original buildings, the Museum of Native American Cultures, the Walk in the Wild (a walk through wooded acreage includes wide variety of wildlife), and the Riverfront Park, the site of the Spokane world's fair which includes a science center, kiddie rides and more.

Stevenson: The Skamania Lodge offers full amenities and is home to the Bridge of the Gods Golf Course which opened in 1993. The Columbia River Gorge is nearby as well as the Skamania Co Historical Museum. If you don't mind the drive this would be a great time to see the new visitor center at Mt. St. Helens and hike the trails there.

Yakima: Dubbed the "Palm Springs of Washington" this town has a wonderful climate. Apple Tree Golf Course (with the famous 17th island green shaped as a Washington apple), Westwood West, and Suntides are the local public regulation golf courses. The city is thriving in the midst of many apple orchards and has all amenities. After your round of golf you might enjoy taking the "Wine Country Road" which is approximately a 50 mile trip from Yakima to Prosser. There are 8 wineries along the way which all offer vineyard or winery tours and wine tasting. Yakima also has a large arboretum with Japanese gardens. The Yakima Valley Museum features a restored Victorian farmhouse, or take a ride on the Yakima Trolleys which travel over an old trestle and steep rock cliffs.

We hope you have found this new section useful. Above all else enjoy yourself, the peace and quiet that a round of golf provides, and the majestic beauty of the State of Washington.

Aberdeen: Grays Harbor C.C., Highland G.C., Oaksridge G.C.
Allyn: Lakeland Village G. & C.C.
Anacortes: Similk Beach G.C.
Anderson Island: Riviera G. & C.C.
Arlington: Gleneagle G.C.
Auburn: Auburn G.C., Jade Greens Golf Course & Driving Range
Bainbridge Island: Meadowmeer G. & C.C., Wing Point G. & C.C.
Bellevue: Bellevue Municipal Golf Course, Brae Burn G. & C.C.,
Crossroads Park G.C., Glendale G. & C.C., Overlake G. & C.C.,
Tam O' Shanter G. & C.C., The Club @ Newcastle
Bellingham: Bellingham G. & C.C., Dakota Creek G. & C.C.,
Evergreen G.C., Grandview G.C., Lake Padden G.C., Peaceful Valley G.C.,
New World Pro Golf Center, North Bellingham Public G.C., Raspberry Ridge
G.C., Riverside G.C., Shuksan G.C., Sudden Valley G. & C.C.
Bingen: Husum Hills Golf Course
Blaine: Birch Bay Village G.C., Loomis Trail G.C., Rodarco Driving Range,
Sea Links, Semiahmoo G. & C.C.
Bonney Lake: Emerald Links Driving Range
Bothell-Kenmore: Inglewood Golf Club, Mill Creek G. & C.C.,
Wayne Golf Course, Wellington Hills Golf Course
Bremerton-Port Orchard: Clover Valley G.C., Gold Mountain Golf Course
(Cascade Course, Olympic Course), Horseshoe Lake G.C., Kitsap G. & C.C.,
Lakeland Village G. & C.C., McCormick Woods, North West Driving Range,
Rolling Hills Golf Course, Trophy Lake G & CC, Village Greens Golf Course
Bridgeport: Lake Woods Golf Course
Brush Prairie: Cedars Golf Club, Hartwood Golf Course
Burlington: Avalon Golf Club, Ken's Golf, Gateway G.C., Overlook G.C.,
Skagit G. & C.C.
Camano Island: Camaloch Golf Club
Carnation: Carnation Golf Course, Tall Chief Golf Course
Carson: Hot Springs Golf Course
Cashmere: Homeplace Golf
Cathlamet: Skyline Golf Course
Centralia-Chehalis: Centralia Public G.C., Newaukum Valley G.C.,
Rainbow Driving Range, Riverside Country Club
Chelan: Alta Lake Golf Course, Desert Canyon Golf Resort, Lake Chelan
Golf Course, M A 8 Golf
Cheney: The Fairways at West Terrace
Chewelah: Chewelah G. & C.C.
Clarkston: Clarkston G. & C.C., Quail Ridge Golf Course
Cle Elum: Sun Country Golf Resort
Clinton: Island Greens
Colfax: Colfax Golf Club
Colville: Colville Elks Golf Course

Cosmopolis: Highland Golf Course
Coulee City: Vic Meyer's Golf Course
Custer: Dakota Creek G. & C.C., Grandview Golf Course
Davenport: Deer Meadows Golf Course
Dayton: Touchet Valley Golf Course
Deer Park: Deer Park G. & C.C.
Desert Aire: Desert Aire Golf Course
Eatonville: Tanwax Greens
Ellensburg: Carey Lakes Golf Course, Ellensburg Golf Club
Elma: Oaksridge Golf Course
Enumclaw: Enumclaw Golf Course
Ephrata: Oasis Park Par 3
Everett: Columbia Super Range, Everett G. & C.C., Harbour Pointe G.C.,
Hat Island G.C., Legion Memorial G.C., Longshots, Walter E. Hall G.C.
Everson: Evergreen G.C. Peaceful Valley G.C., Raspberry Ridge G.C.
Fall City: Carnation G.C., Snoqualmie Falls G.C., Tall Chief G.C.,
Twin Rivers G.C.
Federal Way: Christy's Range & Par 3, Twin Lakes G. & C.C.
Ferndale: Riverside Golf Course
Fort Lewis: Fort Lewis Golf Course
Freeland: Holmes Harbor Golf Club
Gig Harbor: Canterwood G. & C.C., Gig Harbor G. & C.C.,
Madrona Links Golf Course, Performance Golf Center.
Glenoma: Ironwood Green Public Golf Course
Goldendale: Goldendale Country Club
Gorst: Gold Mountain Golf Course
Grand Coulee: Banks Lake Golf Club, Big Bend G. & C.C., Vic Meyer's G.C.
Grand Mound: Grand Mound Driving Range
Granger: Harvest Valley Center
Harrington: Harrington Golf & Country Club, Odessa Golf Club
Hood Canal: Alderbrook Golf & Yacht Club, Batstone Hill Driving Range,
Gold Mountain Golf Course (Cascade Course, Olympic Course),
Lake Cushman Golf Course, Lake Limerick Country Club,
Lakeland Village G. & C.C., Shelton Bayshore Golf Club
Ione: Serendipity Golf Course
Kelso: Three Rivers Golf Course
Kennewick: Buckskin Golf Club, Canyon Lakes Golf Course,
The Golf Club, Tri-City Country Club
Kent-Renton: Family Golf @ Kent, Druids Glen Golf Club, Course @ Taylor
Creek, Fairwood G. & C.C., Lake Wilderness Golf Course
Kingston: Woodall's World Driving Range
Lacey: Family Golf @ Lacey, Meriwood G.C., Vicwood Golf Links
Lakewood: Meadow Park Golf Course
Leavenworth: Kahler Glen Golf Course, Leavenworth Golf Club

Liberty Lake: Liberty Lake Golf Course, MeadowWood Golf Course, Valley View Golf Course (see Spokane for additional listings)
Long Beach: Peninsula Golf Course, Surfside Golf Course
Longview: Golfgreen Golf Center, Longview Country Club, Mint Valley Golf Course (see Kelso for additional listings)
Lopez Island: Lopez Island Golf Course
Lynden: Homestead G. & C.C., Raspberry Ridge Golf Community
Lynnwood: Lynnwood Municipal, Kaddyshack Golf Center
Manson: MA 8 Golf
Maple Falls: Evergreen Golf Course, Peaceful Valley Golf Course
Maple Valley: Elk Run Golf Course, Lake Wilderness Golf Course, The Course @ Taylor Creek (see Kent for additional listings)
Marysville: Battle Creek Golf Course, Cedarcrest Municipal Golf Course, Kayak Point Golf Course, Mulligan's Driving Range
McChord A.F.B: Whispering Firs Golf Club
Metaline Falls: Pend Oreille Golf & Country Club
Monroe: Blue Boy West, Iron Eagle Sports Center, Monroe Golf Course
Moses Lake: Desert Lakes Driving Range, Hylander Greens, Moses Pointe Golf Resort, Moses Lake Golf & Country Club, Sage Hills Golf Club,
Mount Vernon: Eaglemont, Gateway Golf Course, Ken's Golf, Overlook Golf Course, Skagit Golf & Country Club
Mountlake Terrace: Ballinger Park Golf Course, Nile Golf & Country Club
Newcastle: The Golf Club at Newcastle
Nine Mile Falls: Sun Dance Golf Course
North Bend: Cascade Golf Course, Mount Si Golf Course, Snoqualmie Falls Golf Course, Tall Chief Golf Course, Twin Rivers Golf Course
North Bonneville: Beacon Rock Golf Course
Oak Harbor: Gallery Golf Course, Lams Golf Links, Useless Bay Golf & Country Club, Whidbey Golf & Country Club
Ocean Park: Peninsula Golf Course, Surfside Golf Course
Ocean Shores: Ocean Shores Golf Course
Odessa: Odessa Golf Club
Othello: Othello Golf Club, Potholes Golf Course
Olympia: Capitol City G.C., Delphi G.C., Family Golf @ Lacey, Family Golf @ Tumwater, Indian Summer G.& C.C., Meriwood G.C., Olympia Country & Golf Club, , Scott Lake G.C., Steamboat Golf, Tumwater Valley G.C.
Omak: Okanogan Valley Golf Club
Orondo: Desert Canyon Golf Resort
Oroville: Oroville Golf Club
Orting: High Cedars Golf Club, Maplewood Golf Course, Meridian Valley G. & C.C., Riverbend Golf Complex, Southcenter Golf
Packwood: High Valley Country Club
Pasco: Pasco Golfland, Sun Willows, (see Tri-Cities for additional listings)
Pateros: Alta Lake Golf Course, Lake Chelan Golf Course

Pomeroy: Pomeroy Golf Course
Port Angeles: Peninsula Golf Club
Port Ludlow: Port Ludlow Golf & Meeting Retreat
Port Orchard: Clover Valley Golf Course, Horseshoe Lake Golf Course, McCormick Woods, Trophy Lake G & CC, Village Greens Golf Course
Port Townsend: Chevy Chase Golf Club, Port Townsend Golf Course
Pullman: Washington State University Golf Course
Puyallup: Linden G. & C.C., Lipoma Firs G.C., Meridian Greens G.C. & D.R.
Quincy: Crescent Bar Resort, Quincy Valley Golf
Randle: Maple Grove Golf
Raymond: Willapa Harbor Golf Club
Redmond: Bear Creek Country Club, Plateau Golf & Country Club, Redwood Golf Center, Sahalee Country Club, Willows Run Golf Club
Renton: Eaglequest @ Golf Park, Maplewood Golf Course, Fairwood G.& C.C., The Course @ Taylor Creek (see Kent for additional listings)
Republic: Sheridan Greens Golf Course
Richland: Buckskin Golf Club, Columbia Park G.C., Columbia Point Golf Course, Horn Rapids Golf & Country Club, Meadow Springs Country Club, West Richland Golf Course (see Tri-Cities for additional listings)
Ridgefield: Tri-Mountain Golf Course
Ritzville: Ritzville Municipal Golf Course
Rock Island: Rock Island Golf Club, Three Lakes G.C., Wenatchee G.&C.C.
Royal City: Royal City Golf Course
Saint John: St. John Golf & Country Club
San Juan Islands: Orcas Island G.C., Lopez Island G.C., San Juan G. & C.C.
Seattle: Ballinger Park G.C., Broadmoor G.C., Foster Golf Links, Glen Acres G. & C.C., Green Lake G.C., Interbay Family Golf Center, Jackson G.C., Jefferson G.C., Nile G. & C.C., Puetz Evergreen Golf Range, Rainier G.& C.C., Sand Point Country Club, Seattle Golf Club, Tyee Valley G.C., U of W Driving Range, West Seattle Golf Club.
Sedro-Wooley: Gateway Golf Course
Selah: Suntides Golf Course,Yakima Elks Golf & Country Club
Sequim: Dungeness Golf & Country Club, ParFect Driving Range, SunLand Golf & Country Club
Shelton: Batstone Hill Driving Range, Lake Cushman Golf Course, Lake Limerick Country Club, Shelton Bayshore Golf Club
Snohomish: Flowing Lake G.C., Kenwanda G.C., Lobo Country Club, Snohomish Golf Course
Snoqualmie: Mount Si Golf Course, Snoqualmie Ridge TPC Course
Soap Lake: Lakeview Golf & Country Club
Spanaway: Brookdale Golf Course, Classic Country Club, Lake Spanaway Golf Course, University Golf Club
Spokane: Beacon Hill Golf Center, Creek @ Qualchan, Downriver G.C., Esmerelda G.C., Fairways @ West Terrace, Hangman Valley G.C., Indian

Canyon G.C., Latah S.C., Liberty Lake G.C., Manito G. & C.C., MeadowWood G.C., Painted Hills G.C., Pine Acres
Par G.C., Spokane C.C., Sun Dance G.C., Valley View G.C., Wandermere G.C.
Stanwood: Camaloch Golf Club, Kayak Point Golf Course
Stevenson: Skamania Lodge Golf Course
Sumner: High Cedars Golf Club, Sumner Meadows G.L., Tapps Island G.C.
Sunnyside: Lower Valley G.C., Mount Adams C.C., Straight Arrow D.R.
Tacoma: Allenmore G.C., Brookdale G.C., Family Golf @ Tacoma, Fircrest Golf Club, Ft. Lewis G.C., Ft. Steilacoom G.C., Highlands Golf Course, Lake Spanaway G.C., Meadow Park G.C., North Shore G.C., Oakbrook G. & C.C., Tacoma C. & G.C., University G.C., Whispering Firs G.C.
Tekoa: Tekoa Golf Club
Toppenish: Lower Valley G.C., Mount Adams Country Club
Tri Cities: Buckskin Golf Club, Columbia Park G.C., Canyon Lakes G.C., Horn Rapids G. & C.C., Longest Drive, Meadow Springs Country Club, Pasco Golfland, Sham Na Pum G.C., Tri City Country Club, West Richland G.C.
Tumwater: Family Golf @ Tumwater, Meriwood G.C., Olympia Country & G.C., Scott Lake G.C., Steamboat Golf, Tumwater Valley G.C.
Union: Alderbrook Golf &Yacht Club
Vancouver: Bowyer's Par 3 Golf, Cedars G.C., Club Green Meadows, Evergreen G.C., Fairway Village G.C., H&H D.R., Hartwood Golf Course, Green Mountain G.C., Lakeview G.C., Orchard Hills G.&C.C., Pine Crest G.C., Royal Oaks C.C., Vanco Driving Range, Westside Driving Range
Vashon Island: Vashon Golf & Country Club
Walla Walla: Tour Fairways D.R., Veterans Memorial G.C., Walla Walla C.C.
Warden: Hylander Greens, Moses Lake G. & C.C., Sage Hills G.C.
Washougal: Orchard Hills Golf & Country Club
West Richland: West Richland Golf Course
Wenatchee: Desert Canyon Golf Resort, Rock Island G.C., Three Lakes Golf Course, Wenatchee Golf & Country Club
Whidbey Island: Gallery Golf Course, Island Greens Golf Course, Lams Golf Links, Useless Bay Golf & Country Club, Whidbey G.&C.C.
Whidbey Island Naval Air Station: Gallery Golf Course
Wilbur: Banks Lake G.C., Big Bend G.C.
Winthrop: Bear Creek Golf Course, Sunny Meadows 4 Seasons Golf Resort
Woodinville: Bear Creek Country Club, Echo Falls Country Club, Gold Creek Tennis & Sport, Red Wood Golf Center, Wellington Hills G.C.
Woodland: Lewis River Golf Course, Par IV Golf Learning Center
Yakima: Apple Tree G.C., Fisher Park G.C., Suntides G.C., Westwood West, Yakima Country Club, Yakima Elks Golf & Country Club
Yelm: Nisqually Valley Golf Course

I have been writing golf books since 1986 and watched how the golf industry has changed over these years. Titanium. Who had heard of it in 1986? Well...you know the story.

The internet is growing at an incredible rate. It is quickly becoming the medium of choice for purchasing everything from cars, toys, airline tickets, even groceries. In only the first four years it reached over 50 million users, something that took radio 38 years to achieve and 13 years for television. With this tremendous growth, access to information and many other services is growing daily. The technology is revolutionizing the way we live, and play. I am pleased to say that this new medium is bringing golf reservations into the 21st century. MAC Productions is dedicated to providing the most accurate, up to date information available for each and every book. When we go to press we go to great lengths to make sure that the information is the best available at the time. I take pride in my product and in the service I provide to my customers. In all my years of business **LinksTime.com** is the first service that has been presented to me that complimented my books. Like myself, **LinksTime.com** is also, truly dedicated to customer service to golfers and the golf industry alike. I am pleased to be a part of this emerging network.

Internet based golf reservations are here. At the time that this edition of *Golfing in Washington* went to press, **LinksTime.com** was in the process of launching a national network of golf courses to join this service, with the Pacific Northwest as the initial market. Willows Run in Redmond Washington will be the very first course to use the service in this area. In future publications I will note this service as an additional feature on the participating course pages. Since the network is just forming I suggest that you visit the Web site frequently to see who has been added as it is sure to grow at a rapid pace.

The advantages to this technology are many. You can go to the golf course's web page to get instant information on the course, pro shop specials at the time, tournaments, rates, driving directions, just to name a few features. The most compelling feature, however, is the ability to make reservations without calling the course. This service will be available 7 days a week, 24 hours a day. Making a tee time couldn't be easier. In fact, you can even inquire about tee time availability at multiple courses at the same time. You can book mark your favorite courses, request a time and day that you want to play, and the service will tell you which of your courses of choice have that tee time available for the number of players you want.

Imagine....you are sitting in your office, it is Monday...lunchtime. Stale sandwich in hand, followed by a lukewarm soda, you are dreaming of Saturday afternoon at your favorite course. You know that getting a tee time can be tough if you don't call right away the first available day that the reservations are taken for the weekend times. You can't take 20 minutes to call course after course to find one that has the slot you want, nor can you make long distance calls from work.

Solution! LinksTime.com

The golf course now stores it's tee times on a computerized tee sheet. This tee sheet is connected to the internet. When you put in your request you are actually communicating with the Tee Sheet, real time! A response will come back telling you if the time is available as well as the nearest time before and after. If you want to play, select the time, fill out your profile and reserve it. **LinksTime.com** will charge you a small convenience fee at the time of booking. No more busy signals, no more endless phone calls, no more wasted long distance charges...it couldn't be easier or more convenient. Now all you have to worry about is improving that golf swing...

So you want to play GOLF....